Diminishing the Bill of Rights

Studies in American Constitutional Heritage
Justin Wert and Kyle Harper, Series Editors

Diminishing the Bill of Rights

Barron v. Baltimore and the Foundations of American Liberty

William Davenport Mercer

University of Oklahoma Press : Norman

Library of Congress Cataloging-in-Publication Data

Names: Mercer, William Davenport, 1972– author.
Title: Diminishing the Bill of Rights : Barron v. Baltimore and the foundations of American liberty / William Davenport Mercer.
Description: Norman : University of Oklahoma Press, [2017] | Series: Studies in American Constitutional Heritage series ; volume 3 | includes bibliographical references and index.
Identifiers: LCCN 2016033874 | ISBN 978-0-8061-5602-6 (hardcover : alk paper)
Subjects: LCSH: Federal government—United States—History. | States' rights (American politics)—History. | Constitutional history—United States | United States. Constitution. 1st–10th Amendments. | United States. Constitution. 5th Amendment. | United States. Constitution. 14th Amendment. | Legal positivism.
Classification: LCC KF4600 .M47 2017 | DDC 342.7308/5—dc23
LC record available at https://lccn.loc.gov/2016033874

Diminishing the Bill of Rights: Barron v. Baltimore *and the Foundations of American Liberty* is Volume 3 in the Studies in American Constitutional Heritage series.

The paper in this book meets the guidelines for permanence and durability of the Committee on Production Guidelines for Book Longevity of the Council on Library Resources, Inc. ∞

1 2 3 4 5 6 7 8 9 10

For Sally

Contents

Illustrations

Acknowledgments

I would foremost like to thank Elizabeth Dale, not only for her guidance and advice on this project over the years, but also for encouraging me to look more closely at *Barron* in the first place. I also want to thank my many other mentors at the University of Florida, as well as my former colleagues at UF Student Legal Services. In addition, I must recognize for their invaluable assistance all my friends and colleagues at the University of Tennessee, Knoxville, in the History Department and the College of Law.

I would like to thank Tom Krause and Chuck Rankin at the University of Oklahoma Press. Tom has been an incredible advocate for this project, and I am grateful for his support. I am also very appreciative of the outside reviewers who provided helpful comments on the manuscript. Thanks are also in order to the staff members at the Baltimore City Archives, the Maryland State Archives, the Maryland Historical Society, the National Archives, and the Library of Congress, all of whom were gracious with their time and assistance. I also acknowledge the organizers and fellow participants of two workshops that were particularly influential: "Westward Expansion and Constitutionalism in the Early American Republic," sponsored by the National Endowment for the Humanities and the University of Oklahoma's Institute for the American Constitutional Heritage; and "Assessing the U.S. Constitution," sponsored by the Institute for Constitutional Studies and held at Stanford Law School. Thanks are also in order for the organizers and attendees of the various academic forums—the Law and Society Association Annual Meeting; the San Francisco State Rights Conference; and the Association for the Study of Law, Culture and the Humanities Annual Conference—that allowed me to work out many of my ideas.

I must thank all of my friends and colleagues for their support—Joel Black, Scott Catey, David Wolitz, Monica Black, Matthew Gillis, Ernie Freeberg, Doug Blaze, Charles Sanft, Jordan Kinley, Steve Fugate, Jovana Babovic, Eric Garcia McKinley, Matt Dean, Cory Chase, Bret Manner, Bob Leonard, and Lynn Sacco. I am grateful for the many ways that you have all helped me finish this project, whether by reading chapters, commenting on the manuscript, sitting through stories about Baltimore, or just helping keep my spirits up. I would also like to recognize my students, who have humored me in my belief that the *Barron* story was worthy of mention in pretty much every one of my classes. I am fortunate to work with a great group of young scholars at UTK.

Most important, I must recognize and thank my parents and my sister, Jennifer. I am so very grateful for them, as I am for my aunts, uncles, nephews, and cousins. I am eternally thankful for the many incredible sacrifices my parents made for me and my sister. Finally, I would like to thank my wife, Sally Morris, for everything. This book would quite simply not have been possible without her. I treasure our life of terrible decision making together. I dedicate this most of all to her.

And now, before the music plays me off, I thank you for reading this book. I hope you enjoy it.

Knoxville, Tennessee
February 2016

Diminishing the Bill of Rights

Introduction

On February 16, 1833, Chief Justice John Marshall prepared for another day presiding over the United States Supreme Court, in much the same way he had done for the previous three decades. On this cold Saturday morning, Marshall entered the courtroom to issue the Court's decision in the case of *Barron v. Baltimore,* a matter brought by two wharf owners who contended that the city of Baltimore owed them damages for taking their property without compensation in violation of the Fifth Amendment to the U.S. Constitution. The issue before the Court was the extent to which the state of Maryland, and thus any state, was bound by liberties set forth in the Bill of Rights. In this term of the Supreme Court, though, the circumstances seemed different for Marshall. Since Congress had convened its second session two months earlier, it had been consumed by events in South Carolina.[1] Enraged by federal tariffs, the voters of the state had elected a convention that nullified the tariffs and declared that South Carolina would withdraw from the Union if any attempts were made by the federal government to enforce its revenue laws.[2] Throughout that winter, Congress debated ways to confront and diffuse the tension that caused many congressmen to openly fear civil war and the disintegration of the republic.[3]

In 1833 the Supreme Court still sat on the ground floor of the U.S. Capitol, directly under the old Senate chamber.[4] Thus at the same time that Marshall prepared to deliver his opinion in *Barron v. Baltimore,* directly upstairs from the courtroom South Carolina senator John C. Calhoun was in the middle of a lengthy speech in the

Senate justifying nullification. For two days, Calhoun thundered against measures undertaken by President Andrew Jackson to force South Carolina into compliance.[5] That afternoon, Massachusetts senator Daniel Webster rose to challenge Calhoun, arguing well into the night.[6] As the Senate debated the fate of the Union upstairs, downstairs Marshall prepared to deliver his *Barron* opinion.

Unlike decades past when Marshall had skillfully and forcefully navigated the Court through the shifting political currents of the early republic, on this particular February morning he was facing the end of his career, was in poor health, and was fundamentally disillusioned and concerned with the direction of the United States. He was seventy-eight years old, and not the same person who thirty years earlier, in 1803, had told President Thomas Jefferson and the Republican-led Congress that his Court had the right to review federal legislation.[7] Nor was it 1810, when the Marshall court invoked the contract clause of the Constitution in striking down the Georgia legislature's rescindment of an earlier sale of its western lands.[8] Nor was it 1819, when the Court turned back Maryland's efforts to impose a tax on the Bank of the United States.[9] Instead, it was 1833, and the last few years had not gone well. In addition to the troubling news out of South Carolina, just the year before, the Marshall court had sided against the state of Georgia for violating federal treaties by extending its laws over Cherokee territory. Not only did President Jackson fail to enforce the Court's decision, but his administration attacked Marshall's opinion in the press. By January 1833, Jackson's private dealings with Georgia allowed the matter to quietly resolve itself and moved the state closer to its ultimate goal: the removal of the Cherokee Nation.[10] One month later, in the middle of a constitutional crisis that raged upstairs, Marshall prepared to announce his decision regarding whether the Court could force the states to observe the Bill of Rights.[11]

Close to two decades earlier, Baltimore had breathed a collective sigh of relief as the War of 1812 drew to a close. Early in the new year of 1815, word of the rout of the British in New Orleans was joyously received by the residents of Baltimore, as only a few months before, the city had repelled the British military juggernaut that had just torched the nation's capital. Baltimore now looked forward to a bright future after years of commercial disruption. Before the war, Baltimore had grown seemingly overnight from a small village to the third largest city in the nation, primarily on the strength of its maritime industry. Everyone expected that peace would allow this spectacular growth to resume. Two of the most hopeful were merchants John Barron, Jr., and John Craig. In 1815, they purchased a wharf in the new Fell's Point district. Located one mile east of downtown, Fell's Point was attractive as it protruded farther into the Patapsco River than the shallow inner harbor, allowing the city's merchants to build, repair, load, and unload the largest ships of the day. Of the many wharves jutting into the river, Barron and Craig's was noted by many to have the deepest water.[12]

The merchants' seeming good fortune in buying one of the best wharves in the city was short-lived, however, as the harbor floor surrounding the piers silently filled with sand. This did not occur because of happenstance or environmental bad luck; rather, the city openly admitted it caused the problem. Because of serious drainage issues in Fell's Point, the city diverted the water pouring throughout the district and redirected it, including the accompanying sediment, to empty at a single location in the eastern harbor just north of Barron and Craig's wharf. When the debris ultimately rendered the wharf unsuitable for unloading large ships, Barron and Craig lost everything. They sued the city for the damage to the wharf, relying on well-worn common law remedies that allowed recovery for damages incurred as a consequence of a wrongful act.[13] Although the trial court agreed with the wharf owners, they lost on appeal. By the time the case reached the Supreme Court, the issue had morphed into whether the city's actions constituted a taking of property without just compensation, a violation of the Fifth Amendment. On February 16, 1833, Barron and Craig lost.

Barron v. Baltimore was John Marshall's final constitutional opinion. During his thirty-four-year tenure, he penned decisions that helped set the new federal government on a solid foundation independent of the states, which often sought to limit its power and potential. His thoughts on the role of the federal courts and the supreme power of the U.S. Congress over those of the states—contained in *Marbury v. Madison, McCulloch v. Maryland,* and *Fletcher v. Peck*—are today an indispensable and routine part of the history both of constitutional law and of the development of the United States itself. There are scores of works that tell the story of Marshall's vision of a strong federal union. The titles themselves hint at this triumphant narrative: *John Marshall: Defender of the Constitution*; *M'Culloch v. Maryland: Securing a Nation*; or *Aggressive Nationalism: McCulloch v. Maryland and the Foundation of Federal Authority in the Young Republic.*[14]

Barron and Craig's wharf dispute found its way to Marshall's chambers at the twilight of his career. Instead of ruling that the states were obligated to apply the Bill of Rights, Marshall held that the Fifth Amendment, on which Barron and Craig based their claim, did not apply to actions by the city, a municipality of the state of Maryland. However, Marshall went further. He decreed that the entire Bill of Rights applied only to the federal government and not the states, a decision seemingly contrary to Marshall's own pro-federal jurisprudence. His opinion is even more puzzling given that Marshall could have reached the same result and sidestepped the larger Fifth Amendment question by ruling that the wharf was not physically appropriated; alternatively, he might have decided the case on non-constitutional common law grounds, as prior state courts had done. As the vast majority of interaction between the citizenry and government took place at the state level during this era, *Barron* ensured that the Bill of Rights had little practical application for much of American history.

Barron has always been an anomaly. W. Allan Wilbur noted that "in light of Marshall's expansionist views of national power, [*Barron*] has been a difficult decision for Marshall's admirers to explain."[15] Peter Irons likewise found that since Marshall spent his career broadly interpreting the constitutional text to expand the powers of the federal government, "it would have been more in character for him to force the states into compliance with federal standards."[16] H. Jefferson Powell argued that the decisions of the Supreme Court under Marshall's tenure exhibited a strongly textualist tendency, but he conceded that *Barron* represented the "one striking deviation" from this pattern.[17] According to Scott Douglas Gerber, the framers of the Constitution believed that courts would decide rights cases in the light of natural law principles. The early history of U.S. courts, both state and federal, evidences they did just that.[18] Gerber found that the Supreme Court in particular routinely used natural law arguments, but only in cases where individual rights were concerned. But Gerber admits an outlier to his thesis: *Barron v. Baltimore.*[19]

Generally remembered only for its succinct ruling that limited the Bill of Rights to the federal government, *Barron* has proven useful in teaching the standard story of the genesis of the Fourteenth Amendment. Its usefulness in the story, however, is typically only as a case symbolic of the pre–Civil War constitutional order. From that starting point the story usually then moves to the post-War ratification and evolution of the Fourteenth Amendment, detailing the betrayal of its promise in the late nineteenth century and its ultimate triumph as the vehicle through which the Bill of Rights were incorporated against the intransigent state governments of the twentieth century. *Barron* is made to appear as a logical starting point to the story of the incorporation of the Bill of Rights against the states, as the ruling is uncomplicated only from a modern vantage point.

Modern legal practice understands that rights matter only if they are contained in written documents like constitutions, a thoroughly routine and accepted fact that helps explain the near worship of documents like the U.S. Constitution. It is precisely because *Barron* echoes this positive-law view of rights that it is not often questioned or meaningfully examined. Consider the ways that many contemporary debates about our current constitutional order are framed: a bumper sticker promotes rights for gun owners by explaining that the Second Amendment has protected the First Amendment since 1791; a sign on a doctor's office encourages familiarity with privacy rights by posing the question, "Have you read your constitution lately?"; and Catholic nun and social justice activist Sister Simone Campbell expresses this understanding of guaranteed rights by stating, "We've tried to lift up in a pluralistic culture what Jesus' story is about . . . you know where it ends up coming together? It's the Constitution."[20] Finally, think of the movement to formally amend the Constitution to overturn the 2010 Supreme Court ruling in *Citizens United* and to limit the rights of corporate personhood.[21] From the popular to the formal, all of these views of the Constitution's role as protector of rights have a commonality: for rights to matter, they must be recognized as constitutional.

Diminishing the Bill of Rights will not tell this story. Instead, it explains *Barron* on its own terms and in its own era, without the distorting prism of the Fourteenth Amendment. The inevitability often ascribed to the *Barron* decision obscures its deep contingencies. The span of the entire case evidences a contest regarding how to understand where rights obtained their authority, a confusion that was not limited to the parties in *Barron*. Since colonial days, Americans perceived their liberties as secured by a blend of multiple sources: the common law, the Magna Carta, natural law or right, positivist legal guarantees, Greek and Roman precedents, colonial charters, or divine blessing.[22] By the early republic era, these ideas seem more or less to have narrowed down into four general categories: rights as protected by the common law; rights as extragovernmental natural or fundamental liberties; rights as guaranteed by written constitutions; and, finally, rights as emanating from an inchoate blend of many of these sources.

First, those who framed rights as liberties unique to Englishmen celebrated the Magna Carta as the baseline. They invoked the English constitutional tradition and viewed the common law as the mechanism that protected their rights. They echoed the writings of Blackstone for support and attached themselves to the mythology of the English people as the particular protectors and inheritors of the freedoms enjoyed by their Germanic forefathers. Second, those who espoused rights as recognized, but not granted, by constitutions saw their liberties as innate possessions provided by nature or by providence. This view invoked Greco-Roman precedents and found further support in Enlightenment-era thinkers like Grotius and Pufendorf, as well as in the colonial favorite, John Locke. Third, the idea that rights found their moorings in written constitutions was of much newer invention. Many felt this understanding derived from the idea that constitutions represented written evidence of the Lockean social contract, but supporters of the view drew also on more concrete examples from their own colonial heritage, such as rights as emanating from positive-law type sources like colonial charters. Finally, there were those who viewed rights as a blend of many of these different foundations all at once. The argumentation that went into *Barron* displayed all of these interpretations as part of the constitutional imagination of the early republic.

Despite this rich tradition, the Court's opinion located the source of Barron and Craig's property rights as emanating from a written constitution alone. According to the opinion, Barron and Craig could not assert the right of payment for a taking of their property because the Fifth Amendment did not apply to Maryland, and moreover the state did not have a similar provision in its constitution. This property right existed in some written form as far back as the Magna Carta in 1215 and was maintained as a part of the evolving common law. In addition, courts regularly viewed this right as a fundamental or natural principle that must be respected by all free governments. By denying remedy to Barron and Craig because the Fifth Amendment did not apply to the states, Marshall's court had to view this right as granted—and not simply recognized—by the Fifth Amendment. In this light, Marshall was not enunciating an unobjectionable rule of law, as it appears from a modern interpretation of rights, but was instead taking sides on a very unsettled point.

In an immediate sense, Marshall latched onto a view of rights as existing exclusively in written documents, a view that would allow him to exempt John C. Calhoun's South Carolina from compliance, for example. In this way, *Barron* represents an instance when popular agitation regarding the proper balance of power between the states and the federal government ultimately translated into formal constitutional jurisprudence. In the larger context of the events pushing the Union to the brink of dissolution, however, the decision of Marshall's court was a shrewd political maneuver that helped hasten the reconceptualization of rights from a multisourced concept toward our modern view of rights as granted by written documents. *Barron*'s legacy shows up in the many ways that modern Americans have turned away from a traditional view that understands rights as emerging from a variety of sources and toward a view of written documents like the Constitution as the exclusive repository of rights. *Barron*'s legacy also helps explain the rise of methods of constitutional interpretation that prioritize the intent of its drafters or the text alone. If the Constitution itself contains all of our rights, more intense scrutiny of the document becomes the paramount concern.

Diminishing the Bill of Rights examines this evolution of the understanding of rights, beginning in chapter 1 with a look at early Baltimore and the city's environmental challenges that led to the famous case. It also introduces merchants John Barron and John Craig and traces their early successes that allowed them to purchase the wharf. It describes the combination of bad luck, terrible timing, and being on the losing side of a citywide debate over municipal improvements that resulted in the collapse of their business only a few years later.

Chapter 2 reveals that the problems experienced by Barron and Craig were not unique. At the same time Baltimore officials were fixing the drainage problem in Fell's Point, they began a number of other municipal improvement projects, like the taming of Jones Falls and the completion of Pratt Street on the border of the inner harbor. When officials addressed these pressing issues, despite very vocal opposition by many residents, doing so ignited a dissent that consumed the city for years. Aggrieved residents used mostly political methods reminiscent of the Revolutionary era to contest the city. In contrast, the city asserted that its authority to ensure the welfare of the community, or its police power, allowed it to take these actions.

Before moving to the trial, chapter 3 explores the options of Barron and Craig's attorneys in taking on the city. This chapter examines the many ways that Americans in this era imagined where their rights existed. When their attorneys planned their strategy against the city, no consensus existed on this issue of rights or the applicability of the federal constitution in providing them. The property rights claimed by Barron and Craig were perceived as deriving their authority from a number of different, often overlapping sources. Whereas a modern attorney seeking redress under the same facts as Barron and Craig would have a clearer procedural avenue to relief, an attorney in early nineteenth-century Baltimore would not see the case with the same clarity. Instead, he would be presented with a varied, complicated, and in many ways richer ideological landscape regarding the conceptual location of rights. Chapter 3 expands the focus from Baltimore to look at the ways that judges, lawyers, and litigants across the country were framing their rights claims in this era.

Chapter 4 returns to Baltimore in 1822 with the filing of the case against the city and concludes six years later with the trial in Maryland state court. The unsettled location of rights was especially evident in the ways that Barron and Craig and the city sparred over the property rights in question. Although Justice Marshall's court famously dismissed the matter as not protected by the Fifth Amendment, the parties at the initial trial viewed the issue as determined by the common law. The lower court agreed and ruled that the city's actions damaged the property in a way that comported with a more traditional view of the common law as well as, to a lesser extent, fundamental or natural law principles.

Chapter 5 picks up in 1830 before the appeals court in Annapolis. Here, the parties continued their dispute regarding the correct interpretation of the ways the common law should be interpreted in the expanding republic. Barron and Craig maintained a vision of an older, more protective version, whereas the city sought to play a more dynamic role that would largely free municipalities like Baltimore from endless lawsuits. Barron and Craig also expanded the view of rights made by the trial court and began to discuss them as fundamental, extragovernmental liberties, and all sides now began to debate the role of the Maryland and U.S. Constitutions in the litigation.

Chapter 6 takes us to the Supreme Court in February of 1833, where Marshall's court made the decision that freed the states from observing the Bill of Rights. Instead of engaging the rich debate over the location of rights that was taking place across the early republic, Marshall's court reframed the issue as one where rights hinged solely on the explicit language of written constitutions. This chapter analyzes Marshall's motives in the Court's seemingly uncharacteristic ruling and looks narrowly at Marshall's worldview in 1833. Still reeling from his bitter loss to the Jackson administration and the state of Georgia in the Cherokee Cases and witnessing at seventy-eight years old what many contemporaries felt was the possible collapse of the Union in the midst of the South Carolina nullification crisis, Marshall may have considered unthinkable an opposite decision requiring the states to apply the Bill of Rights.

Chapter 7 considers the larger effects of *Barron* by tracing the influence of the Court's logic after the decision was issued. In courtrooms across the country, Americans continued to express claims of rights as secured by a variety of sources. Whereas many found rights as emanating from written constitutions, *Barron* did not make this interpretation exclusive. Many still envisioned rights as secured by other sources, such as natural or fundamental law, or as arising from the common law. Some courts found *Barron* as binding on their decisions, some did not, and some ignored the case completely.

Finally, the epilogue tells the story of what became of the players in this drama after Marshall's court ruled against Barron and Craig. Although the city was freed from the threat of nonstop lawsuits, the ending for Barron, Craig, and their families was not as happy. The epilogue also locates the larger implications of the decision in the evolution toward our modern view of rights. Our current constitutional order recognizes rights largely as creations of positive law, that is, of constitutions and statutes. Although *Barron* was an essential step toward this model, it was nonetheless very much a product of a specific set of circumstances that existed in the early republic. We now turn to those conditions.

1 American Amsterdam

> From the small quantity of ground originally taken for the town, and from the difficulty of extending the town in any direction, as it was surrounded by hills, water-courses or marshes, it is evident that the commissioners did not anticipate either its present commerce or population. The expense of extending streets, of building bridges, and of leveling hills and filling marshes, to which their successors have been subjected, and which unfortunately increases that of preserving the harbor as improvements increase and soil is loosened, have been obstacles scarcely felt in other American cities.
>
> *Col. Thomas Scharf (1874)*

Court cases arise out of particular needs, desires, and conflicts between actual people seeking some resolution. Countless files in courthouse basements hold records of the hopes, fears, aspirations, and anxieties of people who ended up before some tribunal to hear their dispute. Whereas a few cases achieve a degree of significance from the beginning, the vast majority of litigants do not expect their names to end up as shorthand for legal principles. William Marbury wanted his commission delivered, Dred Scott wanted his freedom, and Clarence Earl Gideon wanted an attorney; however, these names became enshrined in the American constitutional imagination as representing something monumentally larger than the story of a single person seeking their day in court.

John Barron was not much different. However, now only his surname is invoked to succinctly stand for the principle that the Bill of Rights did not originally apply to the states. This obscures the essential narrative much in the same way that simply equating *Marbury v. Madison* as standing for the principle of judicial review fails to recognize the deep conflict between Republicans and the Federalists who lost in the "Revolution" of 1800. Similarly, if we reopen John Barron's court file, we see that this dispute was much more than a dispassionate conflict over the balance of federalism, the role of the federal courts, the basis and nature of individual rights, or even the location of sovereignty in the early republic. While all of these themes ultimately emerged at one point or another, Barron's story can give us a window on early Baltimore if we care to look past the case opinion docketed in the Supreme Court reporter. What we discover are two merchants trying to succeed in a rapidly expanding port city of the early American republic. The story of their early success and ultimate failure is not just one of individuals who did not make it. Instead, their journey illuminates the changes that all Baltimoreans were navigating in this era. Because its port gave it the ability to tap into international trade, Baltimore rapidly became one of the country's largest cities. People like Barron hoped to take advantage of the countless opportunities offered by Baltimore's position.

However, this expansion came at a price. As the city grew, it could no longer act as if it were still the communal hamlet of the early 1700s. Muddy streets needed paving and straightening, the harbor required constant deepening and maintenance, and, most important for our purposes, the water pouring through the city demanded attention. Besides John Barron, we also see in this drama many other players who were reacting to these changes: his business partner, John Craig; their dubious benefactor Luke Tiernan; their families; the attorneys; the judges; neighboring wharf owners; the other residents of Fell's Point; and the mayor, city council, and city commissioners, to name just a few. We will assess all of their roles. In addition, we will see that water, sand, and silt are at a fundamental level also principal actors in this story. Long before John Barron battled the city for his wharf, the inhabitants of Baltimore struggled to solve the problem of living on a stretch of land that lies between steep hills and a marshy river. The story of their struggle is the foundation on which Barron's story stands, and it is where to begin.

The location of Baltimore makes sense from the perspective of a political map, where elevations and drainage are not taken into account. The most famous depiction of early Baltimore—the 1822 Poppleton Map, after its namesake Englishman Thomas Poppleton—is a classic example of this approach and its deficiencies. The city hired Poppleton to design the map over several other qualified local candidates, primarily because of his ability to create highly artistic work, and his finished product is a testament to those wishes. Poppleton's creation attractively detailed the streets and neighborhoods that constituted early Baltimore, and he ringed the border of his map with illustrations of its handsome buildings and landmarks. Revised and updated with a color version in 1852, it endured as the authoritative map of Baltimore until 1896.[1] However, like all political maps, Poppleton's work was in many ways an idealized projection of society's mastery over its natural surroundings. For all its detail and artistry, Poppleton failed to include any sense of topography, giving the impression that Baltimore was at peace with its surroundings.[2] If, however, one were to consider early Baltimore on a physical map, the resulting picture would not be as serene. Baltimore County drops dramatically toward the Chesapeake Bay, with the elevation in some places reaching five hundred feet only ten miles north of downtown. For comparison, farther south along the Potomac River, a similar drop in elevation takes more than one hundred miles.[3]

These types of environmental challenges are the backstory to *Barron v. Baltimore* and to the creation and evolution of the city itself.[4] The level, fertile land and accessible waterways that attracted thousands of European immigrants to Virginia and Maryland beginning in the seventeenth century stopped at the Patapsco River, the southernmost boundary of Baltimore County.[5] North of the Patapsco, the desirable plain gave way to more rugged, mountainous terrain unsuitable for traditional farming, causing most early English settlers to cede the piedmont to fur traders and hunters. As a result, for much of its early history the county of Baltimore was the least populated in Maryland.[6] Baltimore was laid out along the low-lying tidewater abutting the Patapsco River, which rises sharply to the piedmont. It is ringed by a line of higher ground approximately thirty miles away, beginning at the Susquehanna River in the north and ending at the Potomac River in the south, which allows for natural drainage to the Patapsco and Chesapeake Bay, often through the city itself.[7] Baltimore was originally divided by several falls, rivers, and streams that ran through the city, turning much of the shoreline into an ill-defined marsh that provided a perfect breeding ground for mosquitoes.[8]

For much of its early existence, Baltimore was faced with the task of trying to mitigate these difficulties inherent in its founders' choice of location.

In 1729, the colonial governor, Benedict Leonard Calvert, authorized the laying out of a town on a designated sixty-acre parcel north of the Patapsco, to be called Baltimore Town after his family's peerage title.[9] Soon thereafter, in 1732, the colonial governor authorized the surveying and parceling of lots east of Baltimore Town. These later became Jones Town, or Old Town, which was incorporated as a part of Baltimore in 1745.[10] Again, geography and water presented problems. Particularly troublesome was Jones Falls, which carried water south to the Patapsco and separated the east side of Baltimore Town from Jones Town. The falls required residents to construct bridges in order to carry on trade with Jones Town, effectively bisecting the city. Not only was this inconvenient, but the falls also had a tendency to overflow its banks.[11] Periodic floods violently carried away bridges, carts, livestock, and any other items in the way, vexing the city government as to the best way to tame the falls.[12] Even more troubling for the city, every day the falls silently dumped sediment into Baltimore basin, now known as the inner harbor, making it much too shallow for larger ships.[13]

One solution that seemed viable was to expand east of Jones Town to access the Patapsco farther upriver in deeper water. Fell's Point, jutting into the river well before it dead-ends into Baltimore's ever shrinking inner harbor, proved a perfect choice.[14] Named after Edward and William Fell, English Quaker immigrants and brothers who gradually obtained and consolidated land beginning in 1726 on the Patapsco east of Baltimore, Fell's Point was formally incorporated into Baltimore in 1781.[15] It was an ideal destination for dockyards and for arriving and departing ships. While Baltimore continued its herculean task of keeping the shallower inner harbor from choking with sediment and debris, Fell's Point faced fewer of these disadvantages. The Fell's peninsula could naturally reach farther into deeper water and provided an attractive alternative to Baltimore, which had to contend with Jones Falls and the marshes it produced at its intersection with the inner harbor, not to mention its often-clouded land titles that discouraged capital investment.[16]

Despite Baltimore's marshy shorelines, the habitually overflowing rivers, and the constant battle to keep the harbor free of sediment, at a macro level the city was nonetheless strategically placed to eventually take advantage of its position as a deep-water port, though it started slowly. After its first twenty-two years of existence, Baltimore Town had twenty-five houses, one church, and two taverns.[17] By the mid-eighteenth century, this began to change. In the 1750s, the population began to increase exponentially, beginning with the disruptions resulting from the French and Indian War, which temporarily halted westward expansion and forced further growth within Baltimore.[18] As Baltimore was situated between the fertile growing regions of southern and central Maryland and Pennsylvania, the expansion of the interior wheat market provided the spark for its early growth. German immigrants, wanting to plant a familiar crop, introduced wheat after settling in southeastern Pennsylvania in the early eighteenth century. For the rest of the century, these German immigrants spread primarily southward into central Maryland and transformed Frederick County into the agricultural center of the state. Because of poor sales and soil damage due to overproduction, planters from Maryland's eastern shore of the Chesapeake also began switching their farms from tobacco to wheat.[19] Unlike tobacco, which was grown primarily on plantations closer to the water, wheat flourished in the Maryland and Pennsylvania interior. While tobacco planters with their waterfront locations could easily sell their crop without the need for transportation or middlemen, upstate wheat farmers could not realistically engage the market without the services of merchants in a deep-water port, and this gave Baltimore its opening.[20] Thus, although Baltimore was initially stymied by its poor geographic qualities, its location later made it the perfect candidate to capitalize on its position between the wheat-growing interior and the larger Atlantic market.

Baltimore's success helped it attract the new residents essential to its continued growth. Supplementing the contributions made by German immigrants, several other immigrant groups arrived and benefited Baltimore, including French Acadians from Nova Scotia in 1756 and the Scots-Irish in the 1760s.[21] Baltimore also acted as a regional magnet for domestic migration. Many of the children of rural white farmers streamed into Baltimore as the southern tobacco-growing regions dried up. Likewise, free African Americans flocked to the city from across the Chesapeake Bay region while many of their enslaved brethren were purchased by Baltimore slaveholders.[22] This infusion of labor helped Baltimore maintain its connection to markets in southern Europe, the other Atlantic seaboard colonies, and Great Britain. Baltimore was able to capitalize on this success and became an essential port for the European colonies in the Caribbean. The city found particular success in exporting wheat, lumber, and iron goods to the West Indies, which required a nearby trading partner since Caribbean planters had long since decided to funnel most agricultural production into maximizing the output of their main cash crop, sugar.[23]

Though it started slowly, Baltimore had seemingly awakened overnight and emerged as a major port city and a prime engine of economic development for the new republic. While international trade fueled this success, it also tied the city's economic health to world events outside its control and led to boom-and-bust cycles that characterized much of its early history. Baltimore generally thrived during periods of European instability; for example, it successfully exploited the wars between Britain and France in the aftermath of the French Revolution, supplying Spanish and French colonies in the West Indies in defiance of the British and later the French.[24] Despite risking capture by both nations, Baltimore's merchants found the financial incentives too lucrative to pass up. The value of exports from Baltimore rose from approximately $1.7 million in 1792 to over $10 million by 1800.[25] European conflicts like these allowed Baltimore's merchants to step into the vacuum temporarily created by preoccupied European powers and led it, less than one century from its founding, to claim the title of third-largest city in the United States.[26]

Of course, Baltimore paid a price for tying its economic health so closely to international trade. As the new century progressed, the young nation was forced to navigate European power struggles that played out in the upheaval of the various Napoleonic Wars. For much of his administration, President Thomas Jefferson attempted to chart a course of neutrality, a plan that became increasingly difficult to maintain. While Napoleon prohibited any trade between the French-controlled Continent and Britain, Britain dictated in 1807 that all neutral countries were prohibited from trading with France or any of its colonies. In response, Jefferson proposed the first in a series of embargo acts designed to punish the British economically by outlawing the U.S. shipping trade with all foreign nations.[27] Since Baltimore profited handsomely from foreign trade, the withdrawal of the United States from international markets devastated the city.[28]

While the resulting War of 1812 proved a defining moment for Baltimore, it was the subsequent peace that its residents most anticipated. Following the end of the war in 1815, Baltimore attracted record numbers of new residents seeking to take part in the anticipated postwar prosperity.[29] Peace with Britain would finally allow for a full resumption of commerce. John Barron and John Craig were among the many who expected that Baltimore's boom times would return. In December 1815, Barron and Craig purchased the three lots on the east side of the Fell's Point peninsula that comprised the wharf.[30] While the succinct rule of *Barron*—that the Bill of Rights does not apply to the states—is known to students of U.S. constitutional law, little is known of the circumstances that gave rise to the claim, and less still about Barron or Craig themselves.

Both lived in Fell's Point, the newer and grittier section of Baltimore where most inhabitants identified as workers somehow connected to the maritime business: sea captains, riggers, mariners, sail makers, and ship carpenters. In addition, Fell's Point was home to others—laborers, carters, grocers, innkeepers, and cordwainers—who supplied the maritime workers with essentials.[31] One of these men was John Barron. On June 2, 1807, John Barron, Jr., an Irish immigrant, was naturalized as a U.S. citizen in Baltimore.[32] Before purchasing the wharf with Craig eleven years later, Barron's life was one of constant motion and continuous hustling to get ahead. After 1807, Barron listed his occupation alternately as "lumber merchant" or "merchant," though after losing the wharf, he described himself as a rope maker.[33] As with his shifts in occupation, Barron's residence changed at least six times between 1807 and 1824, with him moving toward and away from the profitable docks of the shoreline as his fortunes rose and then sank.[34] One month after naturalization, Barron was able to piece together the profits from his various business endeavors and began investing in real estate in Fell's Point. Barron was able to do so even with his modest profits thanks to the initial efforts of the Fells to attract residents.

Edward Fell, Jr., began the process of developing Fell's Point in 1761 by consolidating the four tracts he inherited into one 343-acre parcel, arranging streets, and selling lots. However, much of the credit for the success of Fell's Point lies with Ann Fell, Edward's wife, who continued to successfully market and sell lots after her husband's death in 1766. Ann Fell offered attractive financing that lured laborers, shop owners, and artisans—people like John Barron—by offering lots with no down payment and the balance payable in ground rents.[35] This form of financing was especially attractive to persons who could not afford the full or even partial purchase price, especially during this time when both specie and credit were not readily available.

Fell's financing differed from a traditional landlord–tenant arrangement in that the leases were usually for ninety-nine-year terms that were renewable, essentially forever, at a fixed annual sum. Fell's Point grew quickly as the generous financing terms allowed many Baltimoreans not only to buy property but also to act as speculators who could then subdivide the land and build row houses for further sublease. Ann Fell made sure that the land she sold attracted actual residents; she increased the land's value by including in the leases a stipulation that the purchaser would erect a home or business on the property within two years; otherwise it would revert back to her control.[36]

On July 18, 1807, Barron purchased property under this arrangement three blocks north of the water, at the corner of Ann and Fleet Streets, for a term of ninety-nine years, renewable forever for $275.00 plus $5.00 per year rent.[37] Barron was prospering, and one year later, on June 18, 1808, he was able to purchase a second property in Fell's Point, located on the southeast corner of Wilkes and Washington Streets, three blocks north of his future wharf. This time, Barron did not have to rely on ground rent financing but instead purchased the property outright for $835.00.[38] The next year, in 1809, Barron sold his first property on the corner of Ann and Fleet Streets to John Craig, which evidences the first record of their interaction. Still adhering to the ground rent financing system installed by Ann Fell, Barron sold the property to Craig for $600.00 plus a yearly ground rent of $5.00 for ninety-nine years.[39]

John Craig made his first appearance in the historical record with his marriage to Peggy (Margaret) Smith on June 23, 1801, at the St. Paul's Protestant Episcopal Church in Baltimore.[40] Like his future partner Barron, Craig had achieved some degree of success before purchasing the wharf and had invested in real property in Fell's Point, again aided by the ground rent lease finance plan.[41] Craig obtained two contiguous parcels at the corner of Ann and George Streets, a prime location approximately two blocks west of his future wharf, one block north of the harbor, and one block east of the main thoroughfare of Market Street. Craig acquired the northernmost parcel in 1805 and property immediately to the south in 1808.[42] There, Craig established himself as a grocer and apparently also resided at the same address, presumably upstairs.[43] Like Barron, Craig managed to prosper economically and achieved a corresponding degree of social status. Craig was active in the defense of Baltimore during the

War of 1812, serving as a second corporal in the Fifth Regiment of the Maryland Cavalry Militia. In addition to his military service, Craig had the financial resources to supply material for the war effort, including a vessel he was part owner of that was sunk at the mouth of the harbor to thwart the expected British naval advance.[44] By the end of the decade, Craig purchased one enslaved female, and two other free women of color also resided under his roof.[45]

Although Barron's and Craig's fortunes were on the rise, purchasing the wharf was still a very expensive proposition. Buying lots in Fell's Point was one thing; acquiring a wharf was a whole different matter. Property in Fell's Point was going for a few hundred dollars; a wharf cost upward of $25,000, not including improvements or maintenance. This price tag would seem to place wharf ownership out of reach for a small merchant and a grocer. In Baltimore, however, there were other unique ways to make money. Craig would have had access to capital not only from the ownership of his grocery but also from his participation in the privateering trade—or legal piracy—that emerged during the war and was especially common in Baltimore. To compete with the mighty British Navy in the War of 1812, the United States licensed scores of private vessels as de facto U.S. warships. Baltimore ship owners, merchants, and craftsmen quickly received privateering commissions and outfitted their ships for raids. Whether for profit, from a sense of republican patriotism, or as an opportunity to recover the losses they suffered from British raids on American shipping, the Baltimore maritime community quickly delivered a flotilla of ships for the fight.[46] Many of the ships were owned by the Baltimore elite; for example, Barron and Craig's soon-to-be benefactor Luke Tiernan financed a ship.[47] However, many vessels were outfitted by groups of men of more modest means, including John Craig.[48]

Craig invested in several privateering vessels during the war, including the *Sarah Ann*, the *Saranac*, and the *Chasseur*.[49] Like many other privateers during the war, Craig financed these endeavors with numerous other partners. It is estimated that it cost $40,000 on average to fully outfit a privateering vessel during the War of 1812.[50] This would price privateering out of reach for most lower- and working-class Baltimoreans, except to the extent that they served on such a vessel. Rather, such an endeavor was necessarily restricted to the upper class or to merchants and others of the middling classes who could pool resources. This places Craig in the middle class, as his most successful venture, the *Chasseur*, had upward of eighteen owners at any one time.[51] Craig's first ship, the *Sarah Ann*, received her commission on July 27, 1812, but was captured by the British less than two months later.[52] Undeterred, and whether from financial necessity or acumen, Craig then invested in the *Chasseur* with at least seventeen other partners, receiving the commission on December 24, 1813.[53] The decision to reinvest in the privateering business was a gamble, but Craig's investment most certainly paid off. The *Chasseur* was one of the most successful and storied privateering vessels of the war. Captained by Thomas Boyle, the *Chasseur* valiantly battled the British and brought in an estimated total haul of $221,000 for her many owners.[54] Craig reinvested some of his profits in the less successful *Saranac*, commissioned on January 3, 1815.[55] In addition to these three vessels, Craig also purchased an ownership interest with three others in the privateering vessel the *Swallow*, the ship later scuttled to protect Baltimore Harbor from the Royal Navy.[56] Clearly, Craig had enough financial resources, as he was able to purchase shares of at least four vessels between 1812 and 1815. While not all his ventures were successful, his investment in the *Chasseur* alone would have been sufficient to purchase the wharf.

Baltimore's reputation as a haven for privateers did not cease with the end of hostilities between the British and the Americans in 1815. Craig, and now Barron, continued investing in privateers even after the war. While most believed that the end of the war would bring a return of prosperity, in reality it would be years before Baltimore recovered. British goods resumed their flow into the American market, and the Maryland industry that had begun out of necessity from the Jeffersonian embargo found itself struggling with unwelcome competition.[57] To compound these problems, the end of the Napoleonic Wars after 1815 also meant that Maryland farmers had to reckon with falling prices due to European competitors. The Baltimore maritime economy was also hurt by the full resumption of French and British trade in the Caribbean.[58]

While peace in Europe caused economic problems for the United States, it also presented opportunities for many aggressive Baltimoreans like Barron and Craig. After driving Napoleonic forces from Spain, the crown sought to reassert control over those of its South American possessions that had used the turmoil to grasp for independence. Seeking to supplement their navies much in the same way the United States had during the War of 1812, these former colonies turned to privateering. Along with New Orleans, Baltimore proved well equipped to meet the need. Although privateering against a country with which the United States was at peace was against U.S. neutrality laws, the chance for wealth proved too great for many Baltimoreans to resist, especially in such precarious economic times.[59] Barron and Craig were two who could not resist, investing in the privateer *Paz*, also known as the *Patriota*, along with a third investor who listed his occupation as "biscuit baker."[60]

After years of saving and investing—from the grocery, investing in real estate, and financing privateers—Barron and Craig were finally in a position to purchase the wharf. In December 1815, they purchased three lots on the east side of the Fell's Point peninsula, a prime location between George Street (now Thames Street) and Lancaster Alley (now Lancaster Street). They purchased the wharf property from Frederick Mackubin and his wife, Mary, both of Ann Arundel County, the home of the state capitol, Annapolis. Barron and Craig purchased the lots as tenants in common. This is significant, as tenants in common, as opposed to joint tenants, do not necessarily possess equal interests in the property.[61] As becomes evident, Craig was considered by most the senior partner in this venture. Regardless of Craig's status, he was still not able to purchase the wharf outright. Barron and Craig agreed to purchase the wharf for $25,000 but paid only $10,000 as a down payment, financing the remaining $15,000.[62] They agreed to pay this remainder in three installments of $5,000, the first due in nine months, the second in twelve months, and the third in eighteen months, perhaps helping to explain why Barron and Craig continued to try to cash in on the privateering trade even after the end of the war.[63] To secure the future payments, they gave Mackubin a mortgage on the property.[64]

Barron and Craig hit the ground running. The 484-ton schooner the *Fox* docked at the wharf in November 1815, as did the *Maria* in April 1816 and the *Erie* and the *Rachel* in November of the same year.[65] The lots they purchased were physically underwater for most of the existence of Fell's Point, as maps as late as 1801 showed these three lots as an inlet of the Patapsco.[66] In April 1816, in an attempt to further improve their rudimentary wharf, Barron and Craig received permission from the city to build two piers from the wharf into the Patapsco so as to increase capacity.[67] At 120 feet each, these piers gave them the ability to dock eight ships at once.[68]

Although Barron and Craig made their first $5,000 payment due in September 1816, their fortunes quickly faded. Frederick Mackubin died on January 30, 1816, only two months after selling the wharf. While there was no guarantee that Mackubin would have been more flexible in granting extensions for late payments had he lived, gaining these types of concessions from an impersonal executor of an estate was likely more difficult. Barron and Craig quickly found themselves unable to make the second payment, due in December 1816, and looked to prominent Baltimore merchant Luke Tiernan for help.[69] For better or worse, Tiernan came to the rescue. However, this money came with a price; the loan cost much more than a high interest rate. By accepting Tiernan's financial help, Barron and Craig ultimately lost control of everything: the wharf, the case, and their homes.

Consider that the actual name of the case is not *Barron v. Baltimore*, but instead *John Barron, Survivor of John Craig, for the use of Luke Tiernan, Executor of John Craig v. The Mayor and City Council of Baltimore.*[70] However, Luke Tiernan was not just the executor of Craig's estate; he was the driving force behind the case. Born in Ireland in 1757, Tiernan immigrated to the United States in a fashion similar to that of many other elite Baltimore families. He started out in western Maryland in 1783 before moving to Baltimore in 1795. Once there, Tiernan distinguished himself as a successful merchant and one of the city's elites, credited as the first person to connect trade between Baltimore and Liverpool. Tiernan was a well-respected and powerful member of the business and civic community, a key supporter of the Catholic Church, and a man of significant political influence.[71] He supported his many religious and charitable endeavors through his merchant firm, Luke Tiernan and Company, which was located downtown north of the inner harbor on Baltimore Street, close to the courthouse and most of the city's banks and insurance companies. Meanwhile, his house was located just west of downtown at the corner of Sharp and German Streets, far from the muddy alleys of Fell's Point.[72] Unlike Barron and Craig, Tiernan had the luxury of splitting commerce from leisure. In both, Tiernan's location was befitting a Baltimorean of his status.

Tiernan's financial successes allowed him access to political power and influence. He served as a member of the first branch of the Baltimore city council in 1803, 1812, and 1813 and unsuccessfully sought a seat in the Maryland State House of Delegates in 1828.[73] Politically, his affiliations evolved along with the early American political system. During the first party system, Tiernan identified as a Republican.[74] After the dissolution of their Federalist opponents following the conclusion of the War of 1812, the party of Jefferson was left largely unchallenged. As such, the "era of good feelings" that began with James Monroe's presidency in 1817 quickly started to fray during his second term. With no Federalist foil, the party divided along ideological lines, with each claiming the true Jeffersonian mantle.[75] With the realignment of the political system into the second party system, Tiernan became instrumental in the genesis of the Whig Party in the state to oppose the Democrats. Tiernan was considered a "warm personal friend" of perennial Whig presidential candidate Henry Clay, who stayed at his home whenever Clay visited Baltimore. In turn, Clay reportedly referred to Tiernan as the "patriarch of the Whig Party in Maryland."[76] Tiernan, along with a group of six other prominent Baltimoreans, including his attorney David Hoffman, had enough political clout to convince President John Quincy Adams to accept an invitation to Baltimore. They were even able to persuade Adams to remain an extra day for the intervening funeral of Revolutionary War veteran John Eager Howard.[77]

While Tiernan failed in his quest for an elective office higher than that of the city council, he was named to countless corporate and charitable boards by virtue of his membership in the Baltimore political and business elite.[78] Tiernan served as a director of the Union Bank of Maryland since its creation in 1804, an institution notable as it served as one of the "pet banks" of the Jacksonian Bank War.[79] Tiernan served on the board of the Athenian Society, incorporated in 1811 to help promote the manufacture of American textile products, as well as the Chesapeake Insurance Company.[80] He was also a manager of the Baltimore and Frederick-Town Turnpike Company and treasurer of the Maryland Auxiliary Society for the Colonization of Free Peoples of Color of the U.S.[81] Tiernan was a primary contributor for building the first Catholic cathedral in the United States, the Cathedral of the Assumption, dedicated in 1821.[82] Tiernan quickly rose to elite status in Baltimore and took advantage of the many responsibilities and benefits afforded to a man of his standing.

Tiernan was thus able to throw Barron and Craig a lifeline. Given that in a little over one year Barron and Craig had sunk a considerable fortune into the wharf—$10,000 for the down payment, $5,000 for the first payment, and $6,000 for the construction of the piers—they were certainly drowning. In January 1817, Barron and Craig borrowed $15,000 from Tiernan, agreeing to repay the loan with interest within twelve months. As security, they gave Tiernan a second mortgage on the wharf property, with Mackubin's estate still holding the first position.[83] Two months after this initial loan from Tiernan, in March 1817, estate administrator James Mackubin agreed to extend the time for the second payment from December 1816 to September 1817. Barron and Craig signed a new note promising to pay the missed second installment of $5,000, plus $225 and interest to be paid in six months.[84]

The year of 1817 was a critical one for Barron and Craig, and they went all in to save the wharf. Barron and Craig had until September to make the second payment to Mackubin, not to mention the enormous lump sum payment due Tiernan in January 1818. However, their problems—some of their own making, some caused by the city, and some due to terrible timing—continued to mount. Their first full year of business was 1816; however, the winter of 1816–1817 proved to be one of the coldest on record. By February 1817, plummeting temperatures caused the inner harbor to freeze, stalling the economy at a time when Barron and Craig were desperately trying to pay off their obligations to Mackubin.[85] Second, on May 24, 1817, only two months after Mackubin granted the extension, Craig faced another lawsuit. This time it was from a shipbuilder who claimed that Craig failed to pay for a brig he ordered built. The builder claimed that Craig agreed to a certain design and price, but that Craig's later inclusion of so many modifications had doubled the original price. The builder still expected payment.[86]

Most important, while Barron and Craig were scrambling to cover these ever-mounting debts amid a dreadful winter, the city finally began to address the serious water and drainage issues that had plagued Baltimore since its founding. Fell's Point had to continually contend with water and the accompanying sediment and debris that flowed to the harbor from its neighboring hills, often running right through the center of the district. With no sewer system, much of this water either drained through streams that ran directly into the harbor or was diverted through man-made canals, albeit with limited capacity. The biggest problem with this drainage plan was that many of the streams did not extend cleanly to the harbor, thus dumping water and sediment into the streets. Further, those streams that did connect with the harbor were little better as they ran haphazardly through private lots and down public streets. The city had taken piecemeal measures to address the Fell's Point drainage situation as far back as 1809, but their efforts amounted to little more than burdening one part of Fell's Point over another.[87] In 1817, the city became serious about addressing the problem. In April, the city council passed two ordinances that together would effectively redirect all of the water flowing though Fell's Point. The city ordered streets paved and embankments built. This channeled all the waters that had flowed southwesterly across Fell's Point and redirected them east to empty at one spot in the eastern harbor of the peninsula, directly north of Barron and Craig's wharf.[88]

When September 1817 arrived and it was time to finally make the overdue payment to the Mackubin estate, Barron and Craig knew they were in trouble. Instead of seeking a second extension, they tried to sell the property. On September 18, 1817, their wharf was advertised for sale by auction, to take place on September 30. The property did not sell, and Barron and Craig continued to advertise the ships arriving at their wharf.[89] Adding to their sediment problem, Mackubin had finally refused to forbear any longer; the estate filed suit in Baltimore County Court on September 16, 1818.[90] The filing of the Mackubin lawsuit meant they had to reckon with their largest debt. Barron began selling off his property. Two days after the Mackubin estate filed suit, he deeded his property at the corner of Wilkes and Washington Streets to the firm of Schley and Schroeder to satisfy existing debt of $880.[91] To defend against the Mackubin suit, attorney David Hoffman appeared on behalf of Barron and Craig.

A well-recognized legal figure not only in Baltimore but also nationally, Hoffman was faced with a decision regarding how to respond. His first response gives us a good window into his legal strategy. Hoffman chose initially to evade, or more likely delay, the suit by filing a demurrer on July 15, 1819—some ten months after the case was filed. A demurrer is generally a denial that a complaint has legal merit, as opposed to the filing of an answer that requires a defendant to address the facts of a complaint and to present any defenses to its allegations. The critical difference is that a trial is generally possible only after the filing of an answer.[92] While likely a delaying tactic, Hoffman's ploy still required him to allege a legal basis for his denial that Barron and Craig were indebted to Mackubin. Hoffman did so by reminding the court that Frederick Mackubin's passing had left several underage heirs with potential claims to the property. Accordingly, argued Hoffman, the suit was defective as these heirs were not made parties to the lawsuit.[93] On December 16, 1819, finding this defense "insufficient," the court overruled the demurrer, ordered Hoffman to file an answer, and ordered Barron and Craig to pay court costs.[94] Nonetheless, this maneuver accomplished its goal, as by the time Hoffman filed the answer to the complaint on February 7, 1820, nearly a year and a half had passed since Mackubin first filed suit.

In his answer to the lawsuit, Hoffman did not raise defenses that could somehow overcome the claim. Rather, Hoffman admitted that Barron and Craig owed the last two payments and court costs. Hoffman also admitted that Barron and Craig signed the mortgage that the estate was seeking to foreclose. Hoffman chose to highlight the economic problems facing Baltimore and, indeed, much of the United States at the time, writing that "owing to the extraordinary and unprecedented difficulties and pecuniary embarrassments of the commercial world the performance of which is particularly oppressive in the City of Baltimore, these respondents would find it very difficult to procure so large a sum as is due by them."[95] Hoffman did not object to the court ordering a sale of the wharf but simply asked for as much time as possible before such a sale, perhaps to allow Barron and Craig to redeem the property or simply to allow time for the market to recover so that it would draw a higher price.[96]

Writing in February 1820, Hoffman's description of the "pecuniary embarrassments" facing Baltimore referred to the postwar economic collapse known better as the Panic of 1819. Western expansion made possible by the end of hostilities with the British and through concessions wrought from American Indian nations following the war cleared the way for settlement. Planting cotton in the southern territories and wheat in the north, settlers fueled a feverishly paced expansion as they transformed the lands west of the Appalachians into farms and plantations. Europe finally began to recover from the upheavals of the Napoleonic Wars and, in 1818, began to enjoy productive harvests once again. At the same time, scores of new farms in the old southwest churned out cotton, causing a glut on the market. As the price of cotton cratered, English banks cut back on their extension of credit to American farms. In response, the Bank of the United States put the brakes on further credit as well, hoping to protect its hard currency reserves and causing the state banks to call in their loans to comply with this new policy.[97]

The collapse was accelerated in Baltimore by fraud committed by a number of local bankers and merchants. The most notorious was the embezzlement of funds from the Baltimore branch of the Second Bank of the United States by its president, James Buchanan, a partner in one of the nation's largest mercantile companies, Smith and Buchanan. Buchanan, along with the bank cashier, James McCulloh, and numerous associates including bankers at the Baltimore City Bank and the Union Bank of Maryland, all drained the bank's reserves by making numerous unsecured loans for themselves and their friends. Most commonly, they used this money to buy stock in the Bank of the United States in their own names. Word of these activities spread, and by early 1819 many Baltimoreans had begun demanding payment of their accounts in specie. However, it was too late for most as the banks began to collapse in March.[98] By July 1819, close to one hundred of Baltimore's merchants were out of business and approximately 6,000 workers had lost steady employment.[99] While the Panic of 1819 was a nationwide phenomenon, the malfeasance in the local banking community ensured that it hit Baltimore earlier.[100]

This economic collapse staggered Baltimore, but news out of Fell's Point in August 1819 delivered the knockout blow. As if economic catastrophe and massive unemployment were not enough, yellow fever broke out in Fell's Point. While the city scrambled to deal with this crisis, including the formation of a board of health invested with investigatory and enforcement power, 350 died over the next two months. Wealthier Baltimoreans relocated to the Maryland countryside, leaving the rest of the population behind to suffer through the epidemic.[101] The mayor pleaded with the city council for more funding for the city health department to try to halt the spread of the disease. The fever had been contained to the very tip of Fell's Point at the convergence of Wolf and Pitt Streets, one block south of Barron and Craig's wharf, but the containment did not hold.[102] In the midst of these twin crises ravaging the city, Mackubin's suit managed to continue, albeit slowly. On February 23, 1820, two weeks after Hoffman formally responded to the bill of complaint by filing his written answer, the court finally knocked down all of the legal hurdles he erected and ordered Barron and Craig to pay $11,730.45, the entire amount they still owed on the wharf, plus interest and court costs. If these payments were not made in two months, by April 25, 1820, the estate's attorney George Mackubin would be appointed trustee for purposes of selling the wharf.[103]

This certainly seemed like the end of the line. Two months was not enough time to cobble together this type of money. However, a recent change to the state law on mortgage foreclosure gave them the extra space they needed. Likely motivated by the economic crisis wrought by the Panic of 1819, the state legislature passed what amounted to mortgage moratorium law. Passed in late 1819, this law prohibited the sale of any mortgaged property before November 30, 1821, as long as the owners posted a bond equal to eighteen months of interest.[104] Waiting until the last day of the court's deadline, on April 25, 1820, Craig, Barron, and Tiernan posted a bond that prohibited any sale of the wharf before the following December.[105]

While the mortgage moratorium law gave Barron and Craig breathing room to regroup, their finances did not improve in the interim. In fact, the two-year moratorium saw Craig go even further in debt to Tiernan, who began to regularly advance him money. Throughout the ordeal, Tiernan displayed a certain legal and financial shrewdness: the initial mortgage given by Barron and Craig to Tiernan on the wharf not only secured Tiernan's initial loan of $15,000 but also secured any future advances that he might give.[106] In 1820, two years after receiving Tiernan's loan, Craig still owed Tiernan $4,780.01. However, Tiernan continued to loan Craig money—$250 in April 1820, $300 two months later in June, $250 in July. He also paid to cover unpaid checks Craig had written—$402 in May 1821, $1,024 in November 1821.[107] As Craig's debt mounted, Tiernan demanded further security in addition to the mortgage he already had on the wharf. On December 4, 1820, in consideration of a $3,000 advance, Craig gave Tiernan a mortgage on his home and grocery at the corner of Ann and George Streets.[108] In the meantime, Barron and Craig tried to mitigate their damages by renting out the wharf.[109]

Eventually the inevitable occurred. Twelve days after the moratorium expired by its own terms at the end of November 1821, the estate's attorney posted the requisite bond for purposes of selling the wharf.[110] Tiernan was also ready to call in his loans from Barron and Craig. Not only had Tiernan periodically loaned Craig money to keep him afloat, there was also the matter of the $15,000 loan that had been due since January 1818. Accordingly, Tiernan began to position himself to foreclose on Craig's assets, beginning with the wharf. On January 3, 1822, Tiernan wrote directly to estate administrator James Mackubin. Tiernan began by reminding Mackubin that Craig, along with Barron, paid $25,000 for the wharf, but that improvements pushed the total investment to over $30,000. Pivoting from this point, Tiernan then wrote, "Nevertheless, owing to the state of times and the fever at the point the last two years" it was doubtful whether the wharf was worth anywhere near that amount. Tiernan further excused Craig's failure to pay, explaining that "he has experienced heavy losses the last three years by Mercantile Insolvency and other transactions to a much greater amount than would pay all that was due on the wharf," and he also acknowledged that Craig and Barron were indebted to him as well. With respect to Barron, Tiernan quickly dismissed him and offered his own solution, stating, "as the person interested with him (Mr. Barron) is of no use and has no property, I have suggested to Mr. Craig that if you make a sale of the wharf under the decree, that I would become the purchaser." Tiernan stated also that Craig not only had claims he hoped to receive in the spring against the government for boats sunk during the war, but that "he also has claims in suit and others," perhaps forecasting the *Barron v. Baltimore* litigation against the city.[111] Finally, Tiernan asked for the sale to be postponed until March or April.[112]

On the same day that Tiernan wrote to James Mackubin, Craig's attorney David Hoffman wrote to James Mackubin's attorney, George Mackubin, in an apparent coordinated effort. Hoffman advised that Tiernan would purchase the wharf for the benefit of Craig and would pay off Mackubin in six months. Hoffman echoed Tiernan, writing that "the fact is that the property is worth much more than your debt and vastly more than it will bring. Mr. Tiernan has always been a great friend of Craig, and Barron is worth not a cent, and considerably indebted to Tiernan."[113] Mackubin refused to delay the sale any further. On January 17, 1822, the wharf property was sold at auction to the highest bidder—Luke Tiernan at $16,000.[114] While Tiernan bought the property at auction for $16,000, the total amount owed to the Mackubin estate was only $13,520.66. Accordingly, with George Mackubin, the estate's attorney, now representing Tiernan in his petition to the court, Tiernan sought and received the difference of $2,479.34.[115] While Tiernan now owned the wharf, he apparently let Barron and Craig still run operations, transforming them from proud owners into employees.

Barron and Craig expected they could get in on the ground floor of the anticipated prosperity that peace with Britain would bring. Their wharf would serve as the vehicle that would propel them into upper-class merchant respectability and validate their years of struggling. However, every hit that Baltimore took in the postwar years landed squarely on Barron and Craig. Through the freezing of the port, the yellow fever epidemic that began on their doorstep, and the Panic of 1819, Barron and Craig kept working. Even if that meant borrowing more money, renting parts of the wharf, or seeing if they could sell the wharf at auction to pay off their debts, they kept going. Of course all of these efforts failed to prevent the loss of the wharf and the crushing debt that came with it. They could curse their bad luck, but this would take them only so far as there was no one to blame for the weather, disease, or global economic collapse. They could and did, however, blame the city. Had the city not followed through with its plan to divert all of the Fell's Point runoff water into the harbor directly north of the wharf, Barron and Craig could have withstood these other blows. Instead, the wharf—the end result of their years of scraping, gambling, and grinding—had been sacrificed because of haphazard and ill-advised planning by the city. They had lost their wharf so that Fell's Point would stay dry. To deal with this insult, they were going to recover through the courts. However, as the following chapter shows, Baltimore in the 1810s contained scores of residents struggling with the new order created by the city's emergence as the third largest in the United States. This distinction came with a price: namely, how would the city resolve the practical problems posed by such explosive growth? This is the tension that forms the backdrop of Barron and Craig's dispute. Indeed, a closer examination reveals that Barron and Craig were not the only Baltimoreans who were damaged by the actions of the city. As a rapidly expanding community, Baltimore had to address public safety and health concerns. The reality of actually paving streets, for example, was fraught with much more difficulty and, in many cases, outright angst from many of the persons over whose property the new roads were to run.

2 A Spirit of Improvement

> I have no objection to that spirit of improvement which appears to have seized the members of the City Council . . . save that I think it is too violent; too much is attempted to be done at once, and that to raise the necessary funds to effect their purposes will be oppressive to the people. A spirit of improvement when restrained within due bounds is laudable; carried to excess it is excessive and injurious.
>
> "Aristides," *Baltimore Patriot*

Barron's and Craig's problems with Baltimore were not unique to them. The city battled with a number of residents in its attempts to create a safer and more efficient community. Many Baltimoreans struggled with the practical questions that accompanied the transformation of their town into the third-largest city in the United States by the turn of the nineteenth century.[1] Unlike the growth of New York and Philadelphia, Baltimore's development was not spread out over generations. The city seemed to blink itself into existence overnight, and it was officially incorporated as a city only in 1796. City officials had to address the numerous public safety and health concerns that came with such explosive growth. In addition, officials found themselves managing growth on a topography ill-suited for a major city. While these seem unobjectionable duties required by all city officials, the process of carrying out these plans was fraught with difficulty, and in many cases it met with outright anger from many Baltimoreans.

Although Barron and Craig's dispute may be the most famous, the resistance facing the city over its other plans proved even more acrimonious. When Baltimore began several pressing municipal improvement projects, dissent ignited, consuming the city for years.

Barron is remembered for the ruling that the Bill of Rights did not apply to the states, an essential part of the evolution of American constitutional history. However, the legal language used for most of the litigation differed from the constitutional language by which we now remember the case. Likewise, the other Baltimoreans who were upset with the city's plans did not use constitutional law as their vernacular. Instead, the disputes over all of these postwar projects evidenced a clash over the proper scope of Baltimore's power to spend city funds, take property, or otherwise infringe on the rights of individual residents in the name of civic improvement. By examining these disputes, we discover that they were not limited to the courtrooms of the early republic. Many Baltimoreans used methods of resistance that recalled older political traditions, such as authoring pamphlets, petitions, and anonymous newspaper editorials. Historians have noted that in looking for the ways that people used the language of rights, we too often take state-level pronouncements as conclusive.[2] Although this evidence is important and is examined in the following chapter, we must first begin by looking at the ways that people in Baltimore envisioned the proper limits of the city's power when measured against the rights of individual citizens. Indeed, this is the tension we will see throughout the course of the *Barron* litigation.

In the trial court, Barron and Craig used the common law to justify their claim, whereas their argument on appeal grounded their right more generally as a requirement of fundamental law or natural right. To the extent that the common law was present in the appeal, it served as the vehicle that applied timeless principles attributable to natural law or the social compact. By the time the case went before the Supreme Court, Barron and Craig's rights claims had been transformed into existing by virtue of the Fifth Amendment itself. In contrast, the city continuously maintained that its inherent right to provide for the health, safety, and welfare of the Baltimore community—in other words, its police power—allowed it to take the actions it took. This chapter examines two of the city's largest municipal improvement projects—the opening of the inner harbor district by extending Pratt Street, and the Fell's Point drainage plan—to understand how Baltimoreans envisioned the ways they could oppose the city. We use these disputes also to examine the power of the city that Barron and Craig tried unsuccessfully to contest over the course of nearly two decades. By locating Barron and Craig's case within these larger Baltimore conflicts, we can better appreciate why they were indignant at the complete, uncompensated loss of their wharf.

BALTIMORE POLITICS

All of these conflicts began in response to the city's plan to bring municipal services in line with a rapidly expanding population. Paving streets and sidewalks, opening new roads, and addressing Baltimore's acute water and drainage issues were responsibilities not dissimilar to other cities of its size. While Baltimore's officials were taking steps to ensure that these services were keeping pace with the population and to help mitigate the natural impediments to the city's continued growth, their methods of governance did not keep pace. To understand the crises that racked postwar Baltimore, we must appreciate the city's political situation. Gritty and bustling, Baltimore was unquestionably the biggest city in the state. Nevertheless, it was still controlled by the General Assembly of Maryland, which was located on the coast in picturesque Annapolis. Baltimore thus found itself largely constrained by an entity that represented very different economic and political interests. As the center of power in the state, Annapolis used its lawmaking authority to maintain its dominance; indeed, this subordination was a hallmark of Baltimore governance from its founding in 1729. While much had changed in the century that followed, Baltimore still operated under a structure of government more fitting for a rural hamlet than an emerging center of international commerce.[3] For the most part, commissioners appointed in Annapolis ran Baltimore for its first seven decades.[4] In addition to being politically frustrating, this arrangement crippled the local government's ability to effectively manage the sanitation, transportation, and security concerns of the ever-growing community.[5] Despite its inefficiency, this arrangement persisted until the Maryland legislature finally incorporated Baltimore as a city in 1796. Even then, Annapolis was determined to retain its control over the burgeoning metropolis. The city's original charter divided the power of the city government between a mayor and a bicameral city council. This replicated the division of power found in the newly ratified federal constitution, complete with an upper house and mayor appointed by electors.[6] In addition to this woefully inadequate representation at the state level, the city did not have its own court system until Baltimore City was made its own county in the 1851 Maryland constitution. Before that time, the city had to use the county courts established by the state.[7]

After the end of the War of 1812, Baltimore was ready to resume its growth. The following year, in 1816, the city elected George Stiles as its new mayor. A former captain of a naval artillery company and the kind of force that proved so crucial in the Battle of Baltimore, Stiles charged ahead on several of the city's most pressing problems.[8] Stiles focused on the many improvements Baltimore had put off for too long: streets needed paving, the city markets needed repair, a House of Industry was needed to better address the plight of the poor, and the city needed to purchase springs to help ensure the continued supply of fresh water.[9] The following year, the mayor's wish list grew more ambitious. A number of factors likely contributed to this bolder vision: not only was Stiles eager to fully focus his efforts on city affairs after being in ill health for the previous eight months, but the ferociousness of the natural environment that plagued Baltimore since its creation forced his hand. On August 9, 1817, Jones Falls overflowed its banks during a severe storm, killing several people, washing away carts, carriages, and horses, and destroying bridges.[10] In February 1818, Stiles announced to the city council his priorities for the coming year: he wanted them to seriously consider the engineers' recommendations to stop the overflows from Jones Falls; the city should continue its efforts to support the lottery to fund the House of Industry; the paving of streets in Fell's Point that had helped lessen the drainage issues should continue; and, finally, as the General Assembly of Maryland ordered, the city needed to demolish several wharves on the inner harbor and extend Pratt Street.[11]

Despite Mayor Stiles' vision, the city did not have the financial or legal independence necessary to undertake these massive projects. This began to change in 1816 following the general assembly's forced merger of two sections of Baltimore County with the city. While both the city and the annexed areas were overwhelmingly opposed, the state persisted. The pro-Federalist general assembly wanted these two pockets of Republican votes in the county merged into the already distinctly Republican city of Baltimore. Although

Baltimore gained upwards of 16,000 or more new residents, it still sent only two delegates to the state legislature.[12] The city exploded with anger.[13] One city commissioner tendered his resignation so that he would not be responsible for carrying out the new law.[14] In 1817, the city council unsuccessfully petitioned the general assembly to amend the constitution to allow for more representatives after a bill to double the delegates from Baltimore was significantly defeated.[15] Even a personal plea from Mayor Stiles that same year noting that the city had far outgrown the two delegates it was allotted in the 1776 state constitution was not persuasive.[16] Likely figuring that proximity would offer the city better access to state power, the city council even offered to furnish all accommodations at its own expense if the assembly would relocate to Baltimore.[17]

The general assembly decided in its 1817–1818 session to give the city more autonomy over local affairs. Some historians have chalked this up to a "quid pro quo" for the forced annexation, but it may be just as likely that the state recognized it would continue to be burdened by the practical problems stemming from its micromanagement of the city.[18] The general assembly may have also passed these measures as a result of Baltimore's dire financial situation going into the winter of 1817. On November 24, 1817, Mayor Stiles informed the city council that Baltimore's income was "far from equal" to its expenditures. Stiles planned to cover this shortfall by proposing a law to the general assembly that would allow Baltimore to revalue property in the city, presumably to tax it at a higher rate. Stiles advised the city council that Baltimore needed the additional revenue because of its spiraling debt and the difficulty in collecting the assessments actually due. The mayor also noted the difficulty the next several months would bring to other Baltimore public services, such as the House of Industry, whose capacity was severely tested every winter.[19]

The December 1817 session of the general assembly somewhat loosened the reins on Baltimore, finally granting it the ability to impose direct taxes on personal and real property to fund improvements, pay down debt, or other purpose for the benefit of the city.[20] On February 9, 1818, the general assembly passed a comprehensive law that addressed many of the city's outstanding problems. First, Baltimore was given the power to impose direct taxes on property in any amount deemed necessary to accomplish public purposes.[21] While the city already possessed a limited power to tax, including an 1815 ordinance allowing a tax of two dollars on every one hundred dollars of personal property, this new power did not contain a cap.[22] The city could also now issue stock certificates or borrow up to one million dollars for municipal improvement projects.[23] In addition to granting the city the power to tackle the long problematic Jones Falls, the general assembly standardized the methods for opening, paving, or widening streets in the city.[24] Notably, while the state gave Baltimore the power to mark out and name new streets, the city still needed the assent of the contiguous property owners. Two-thirds of the adjacent owners needed to agree to an opening, extending, widening, or straightening of any street, while a majority had to agree before the city could pave a street.[25] Finally, to properly undertake these massive projects, the city was specifically granted the power of eminent domain to take any property necessary. If the city and the subject property owner could not agree on a price, or if the owner was simply unwilling to sell, the city could appeal to a board of three persons appointed by the court.[26] In addition, during the same session, the general assembly also passed a law that directed the city to remove all the wharves and other obstructions directly north of the inner harbor and to finally extend Pratt Street.[27]

Armed with its new powers, the city pressed ahead and chose to address several outstanding items: redirecting the water pouring through Fell's Point, taming Jones Falls, and opening the cramped inner harbor by extending Pratt Street. These seemingly routine actions kindled an opposition that burned for years. At the base of all of these disputes was a contest between the power of the city to make these improvements and the rights of many Baltimoreans to hit the brakes. The popular language of resistance in many ways is one of the American revolutionary era, of using petitions, anonymous newspaper editorials, and political meetings to express the idea that the other side was driven by corrupt motives.

The city countered this resistance by advancing a view that its inherent right to provide for the health, safety, and welfare of the community, also known as the police power, allowed it to take these actions. The term "police power" does not refer simply to "the police" as we would understand the term today. Rather, the police power represents the conceptual right of a sovereign to pass all laws necessary to ensure the common well-being of the citizenry.[28] This notion of the police power predates the American federal union. As noted by Marcus Dirk Dubber, states in the Western tradition are governed through two mechanisms: law and police. While law perceives individuals as equal participants, police harkens back to an older form where the state is the head of the political household. Replacing the king but replicating his necessary functions, the state uses its inherent police power to ensure the welfare of the polity.[29] As an essential attribute of sovereignty, the police power allows the sovereign to enact regulations to ensure the common welfare, such as the ability to prohibit horses and carriages from clogging public roads, to regulate the cost of bread, and, as was the case in Baltimore, to pave streets and build dams to provide for the orderly drainage of water in Fell's Point.

Historians have traced the origin of the term "police power" to eighteenth-century English legal philosopher William Blackstone, who classified certain offenses as being against the "public police and economy."[30] Blackstone likewise likened the individuals that made up a polity as members of a family who were "bound to conform their general behaviour to the rules of propriety, good neighbourhood, and good manners."[31] As a result of the "very miscellaneous" nature of this category, the police power provided for responses to a broad range of concerns, including most notably the power to abate common or public nuisances, as opposed to private nuisances.[32] Blackstone cited a long list of what constituted a public nuisance, which, to name only a few, included "annoyances" in common highways like public rivers, roads, or bridges; ale houses, gambling dens, unlicensed theaters, and inns that promoted disorderly conduct; lotteries; fireworks; the presence of idlers, "gypsies," or vagrants; and poaching.[33] Early Baltimore exercised its police power to regulate a whole range of subjects in ways very similar to that described by Blackstone. For example, the city imposed mandatory inspection to ensure the quality of ginseng,[34] regulated the speed of horses and carriages,[35] detailed the correct way to measure grain and flour in the market,[36] mandated that candles be sold only by weight,[37] built bridges,[38] licensed brokers,[39] inspected and regulated the purity of bread,[40] and even sought to reduce the dog population.[41]

It is important to consider the actions leading to the *Barron* litigation in the context of these changes during the postwar years. All of these improvement projects had laudable goals. However, they also required the resolution of a number of highly contested questions. Did the city have the power to undertake projects that infringed on the rights of many residents? What about the rights of property owners in the way of the city's plans? Would they be reimbursed for any damage? If so, who should pay for these damages? Should it be the residents benefiting from the extension, or the community at large? The answers to these questions were far from settled in Baltimore. What is absent from all of these debates, however, is any notion that the answers were somehow to be found exclusively in the Constitution. Rather, many Baltimoreans framed the terms of the debate as a mostly political one that concerned the limits of the power of the city.

PRATT STREET

The Pratt Street extension is a good example of this tension. Pratt Street is more famously known as the site of the first intentional bloodshed in the U.S. Civil War.[42] Pratt Street runs east and west directly north of the inner harbor and today is home to many of the city's main downtown tourist attractions. It was not always this way. In early Baltimore, Pratt Street dead-ended into the many wharves that jutted into the inner harbor. If you wanted to travel the length of Pratt Street in the 1810s, you were forced upon reaching the wharves to detour north through a maze of smaller streets before returning to Pratt Street once clear of the inner harbor, where the street resumed. As a matter of city planning, the extension of Pratt Street made sense. However, just as the Poppleton Map discussed in the previous chapter failed to reflect the topographical challenges presented by Baltimore's geography, so too the idea that extending Pratt Street was a simple matter of imposing logical order and efficiency failed to acknowledge the animosity and resentment expressed by many residents over the plan.[43]

The 1818 state law that authorized the opening of Pratt Street addressed a number of practical concerns. First, the general assembly appointed a number of prominent Baltimoreans to a board of electors tasked with selecting seven commissioners.[44] By appointing selected residents to handpick commissioners to carry out the project, the assembly bypassed the existing city commissioners appointed by the city council, despite this project fitting perfectly with their job duties.[45] Once selected, the Pratt Street commissioners would survey the route and determine whether any damages were owed to property owners by virtue of the extension. Notably, the law authorizing the plan specifically stated that no one would be compensated for damages unless their property was actually taken in some form, thereby implicitly rejecting claims for damages suffered as a consequence of the repairs. The commissioners were also required to identify the property owners who would benefit from the project. After calculating all the damages and adding the associated costs, including the salaries of the surveyors and their own expenses, the commissioners were to submit the entire report to the Baltimore County Court. From there two processes occurred. First, any property owner that disputed the amount of the damages assigned by the commissioners could petition the court for a hearing to review the award. Second, the city would pay its required one-third of the cost and then collect the remaining amounts from those property owners the commissioners deemed to have benefitted from the improvements. The law made it clear that the Pratt Street project was designed not only to make transporting goods through downtown easier, but it was intended also to unclutter the inner harbor. It allowed the city to remove not only the obstructions in the way, but also any structures south of the street, which included a number of wharves.[46]

To appreciate why the Pratt Street extension was met with such hostility almost from the start, we must consider the scheme for paving streets in Baltimore. Funding for the paving reflected a limited appreciation of who would benefit from the improvement, as the property owners who would benefit were assessed a paving tax, while those owners whose property was injured had a claim for damages.[47] This concern over who was liable was largely responsible for the failure of the original act to extend Pratt Street.[48] For example, on December 5, 1815, an anonymous petition to the Maryland legislature argued that the Pratt Street plan suffered from so many difficulties that it would likely fail.[49] For the authors, the prevailing legal mechanism for paying for road projects was not sustainable for a project of this nature. For example, Pratt Street property owners would lose their property entirely while many of their neighbors would be responsible to them for these damages. More importantly, many others in the community would benefit tremendously from this project but not have to contribute any payment at all. As a major thoroughfare, the Pratt Street opening would benefit commerce throughout the city. These objections regarding who would benefit versus who would actually pay for the improvement drove the debate for years.

When the Pratt Street law was successfully reintroduced in early 1818, these same concerns came roaring back. The timing of the repairs could not have been worse for Baltimore. As noted, the finances of the city headed into the winter of 1817–1818 were especially bleak. The spring did not bring much relief. On March 6, 1818, the city collector reported to the mayor that of approximately $74,000 in taxes assessed in the prior year, roughly one-third of the debt was still unpaid. Roughly two weeks later, the Ways and Means Committee of the city council painted an even worse picture of the city's finances. Their report gives us a good window into the challenges that faced the city when tasked with undertaking the Platt Street extension. First, the committee lamented that while the city was given the authority to collect the direct taxes, it failed to collect an adequate amount and would have to return to this task in the future. Second, the city had to deal with a $20,000 court tax imposed on it by the legislature. Most importantly, however, the committee's forecast for 1818 predicted a budget shortfall of $50,000. This annual deficit did not include the preexisting city debt of over $212,000. Notwithstanding this, the committee nonetheless recommended pushing forward with the municipal projects already in the works. For the city, improving Baltimore was a non-negotiable task. Prosperity and continued growth could not be sacrificed for short-term austerity.[50]

Over the course of 1818, the residents of Baltimore prepared pamphlets, held ward meetings, and waged a war of letters in the city's newspapers, the *American* and the *Baltimore Patriot*, over this project. From one viewpoint, these debates concerned the propriety of these public improvements, especially in the light of the budget shortfall and the recent tax increase. At a more basic level, though, Baltimoreans argued over the fundamental question of who should be responsible for these large-scale projects. Was Baltimore a community that would tax all of its residents for the long-term common good? Was it a collection of neighborhoods that should each be responsible for its own street paving and nuisance abatement? Were these projects really designed to promote the welfare of Baltimore as a whole, or was it an attempt to have the entire city enrich wealthy property owners?

If we examine letters to the local newspapers, we see these cleavages appearing over the proper direction of the city. The methods by which these residents chose to debate this issue are very much of an older vintage. They did not limit themselves to formal political debates in ward meetings, and an explosive conflict erupted in the newspapers with all sides writing anonymous letters to the editors under assumed names. Some chose classical pseudonyms like "Civitas," "Pericles," or "Demetrius," thereby harkening back to revolutionary- or founding-era models, such as John Adams writing in 1774 as "Novangelus" or Alexander Hamilton, James Madison, and John Jay writing collectively as "Publius" during the constitutional ratification debates.[51] Others chose more democratic monikers like "Fair Play," "a State Democrat," or "Equal Rights." Finally, some were more comical or meant to insult, like "No Whiner," "No Meddler in other Men's Matters," or "No Hypocrite."

The debates that took place in the Baltimore papers were not simply objective analyses of the role of the city government in promoting the common prosperity through municipal improvements. Rather, the papers exploded with accusations that conflated these projects with designs by those in power to benefit under the guise of public improvement. At one point, the editors pled for more time to print all the letters that seemed to never stop arriving.[52] Although begun as a way of debating the merits of the municipal works projects, the letters gradually transformed into a referendum on the city council and, more directly, the character of Mayor Stiles. One side in the debate took an expansive view of its role, stating that the methods of financing city improvements under a scheme that for the most part sought to tax those persons deemed to directly benefit was no longer feasible. They maintained that the city had become too large to consider itself a collection of small neighborhoods, each responsible for its own maintenance and well-being. In contrast, their opponents believed that the cost of improvements should fall to those property owners directly benefitted and viewed the actions of the city in highly conspiratorial terms.

The letter on August 1, 1818, to the *American* from "No Whiner" is a good example of the pro-improvement point of view. "No Whiner" was incredulous that the city council was being publicly accused of self-dealing, as it had been in office for only eighteen months, whereas many of the city's debts pre-existed their tenure. More fundamentally, though, "No Whiner" argued that all these projects were designed to benefit the city as a whole. Pratt Street was overwhelmingly approved, and the related South Street project would help connect the city with the York turnpike into Pennsylvania. The Jones Falls situation had to be addressed not because of its danger to those living nearby, but because of its role in decimating the depth in the inner harbor. He noted that as the city was paying roughly $20,000 per year to dig out the inner harbor, addressing the Jones Falls issue was of interest to the entire city. Whether certain councilmen would also benefit was immaterial. Finally, "No Whiner" addressed the method of assessing who should pay for these improvements, truly the central complaint of those opposing these improvements. He pointed out that the arguments that those who lived near Jones Falls should pay more for the project than those residents who lived farther away would lead to absurd and unjust results. Wharf owners would have to pay more to deepen the harbor, or those who lived near a spring would contribute more to its upkeep, despite the fact that the entire city benefitted from these resources. "No Whiner" did however note that the Jones Falls project, which should require the contribution of the entire citizenry, was unlike the opening or paving of a street, which would presumably be more appropriate for contiguous property owners to fund.[53]

On August 8, 1818, "Civitas" argued that these improvements were helping make marshy Baltimore one of the healthiest cities in the nation, a grand feat considering that the original proprietors kept the high ground to themselves. These types of improvements had turned the unhealthy, leftover coastline into a prosperous city. "Franklin" felt that dividing up the costs among different neighborhoods made no sense given the nature of the projects. For example, the improvements to Jones Falls would benefit all of Baltimore because it would help preserve the depth of the harbor and prevent a replay of the disastrous flood of August 1817. He was thus opposed to a plan to tax only those who live near Jones Falls for the costs of the project. As "Franklin" noted, there was a large difference between a project designed to benefit contiguous owners of property and actions taken to do away with a nuisance.[54] "Truth" sought to parry some of the objections to the Pratt Street extension by observing that the state law directing the project would give Baltimore a public wharf on the inner harbor that could generate for the city up to $6,000 per year in wharfage fees.[55] Echoing the first printer in England from the fifteenth century, "William Caxton" began his letter to the citizens of Baltimore with the reminder that "Salus populi suprema lex," or "the welfare of the people is the supreme law," a fundamental maxim of the common law that supported the vigorous use of the city's police power.[56] While many "thoughtless" or "ignorant" people had "raised an unwarranted bustle" against these improvements, the reality was that these projects were helping make Baltimore a complete city instead of one composed of neighborhoods competing against each other.[57] "William Caxton" continued this argument in his next letter, where he argued that all future improvements of this nature should be paid for entirely by the city. Caxton countered the characterization by many that the city government was acting in secret or obtaining individual benefits; rather, the city was performing one of its essential duties in preserving the navigation of the harbor and ensuring the health and safety of its residents.[58]

"Demetrius" likewise took issue with those who opposed these improvements; he saw virtue in the city council's decision to address fundamental problems like Jones Falls.[59] Writing as a renter of a commercial stall, "A Renter" supported opening Pratt and South Street because doing so would provide more locations to transact business. Titling his letter "No Monopoly," he argued that these streets would help break up the current state of monopolized trade in Baltimore, where Howard, Baltimore, and Bridge Streets were claimed for the country produce trade, Market Street was staked out for retail, and the docks at the Basin were the domain of the millers. He argued that if the city did not open up these spaces for new commerce, this monopoly would continue. Contrary to the overheated rhetoric of those who mischaracterized these projects as conspiratorially foisting the burden of private property upgrades on the whole city, "A Renter" argued that opening these streets did not take away anyone's rights but instead extended "the privileges of the poor but industrious renter."[60]

All of these anonymous writers emphasized a common theme: the city had the right, and indeed the duty, to take these actions that would provide for the common welfare of the community. As "William Caxton" noted, the welfare of the people was the supreme law. William Novak has most convincingly taken on the myth of laissez-faire government in the early American republic. As opposed to those who wish to read the American past as a golden age of unfettered free market capitalism, Novak has argued that robust governmental regulation at the state and local level, such as that occurring in Baltimore at this time, was instead the norm.[61] On issues ranging from public safety to fair play in the marketplace, these Baltimore letter writers echo Novak's view that local governments vigorously regulated the cities of the early republic to provide for the common good. The idea that only those Baltimoreans who lived near Jones Falls, for example, needed to pay to keep it from overflowing its banks was wholly incompatible with this view. This study agrees with Novak; it is true that municipalities were able to use their police power to construct public works, improve transportation and sanitation, and generally provide a safer and more efficient standard of living. This does not mean, however, that all residents shared this view of what was best for the public welfare or conceded this forceful right to their state and local governments.

Rather, many other Baltimoreans viewed the city's actions as corrupt attempts to force all residents to pay for the self-interested transactions of the ruling elite. "A Whiner" lampooned "No Whiner's" promotion of the South Street project as one that would help connect the city to Pennsylvania. For "A Whiner," this project was "flattering nonsense" designed to induce Baltimoreans into thinking that there was a "vast region of wealth hid in Pennsylvania" only waiting for a road to allow it to flow into the city.[62] Echoing this sentiment a day later, "H" also answered "No Whiner." Unlike "A Whiner," "H" did not portray "No Whiner's" vision that the opening of the streets would lead to an abundance of commerce from Pennsylvania simply as unrealistic. Rather, "H" charged that men like "No Whiner" were seeking to put the poor of Baltimore out of work, or at least out of the way. If commerce from Pennsylvania could flow to and from Baltimore rapidly, what would happen to the thousands of poor families that survived only by acting as carters delivering goods from the Baltimore wharves to the outskirts of the city and back again? For "H," this was the end of "No Whiner's" corrupt scheme: two-thirds of the city would be forced to flee to the backwoods to try to support their families, while "No Whiner" would find bargains in the real estate market.[63]

Whereas "No Meddler in other Men's Matters" wrote on August 10, 1818, to argue for the good character of the mayor, "P" and "O" penned letters the following day and asserted that the new ward limits were drawn to help re-elect the mayor.[64] "No Meddler" wrote back to defend the mayor and talk about the ways that the city was a better place because of improvements like those made to the markets. According to "No Meddler," if women could vote, they would overwhelmingly "unite in huzzaing for Stiles" because of his role in making the markets safe and acceptable for women and their families. This characterization betrays a certain emerging middle-class sensibility on the part of "No Meddler," who lumps all women into the category of those who would "huzzah" for Stiles, except for the "industrious, weather-beaten class of women yelept hucksters."[65]

It is this class sensibility of "No Meddler" that "Fair Play" exploited in the same edition of the *American*. "Fair Play" posited a fictional plan on the part of the residents of Howard Street to improve their thoroughfare in order to raise the value of their property. Given the other projects to pave Pratt and South Streets, the residents of Baltimore would naturally pay the cost. Howard Street would become the grandest in the city and would draw commerce from as far as Kentucky. It would be paved with stone of white marble of the exact same size, resembling billiard balls. All the current houses would be knocked down and replaced with identical rows of five-story homes. Of course, as this plan will cost more than what the current owners could afford, they would apply to the city for the funds. Given their liberality in their other projects, such as Jones Falls or the many street-paving jobs, they cannot refuse the request if they hope to be consistent. If anyone residing on these other streets that have already been improved objected, the Howard Street owners will simply remind them of the Howard Street contribution to their well-being. If they continued to object, "No Whiner" should be unleashed to silence them in the press. Finally, in a postscript, "Fair Play" advised the members of the city council that should they or their friends wish to purchase lots on Howard, they should do so before they approve the appropriation for the project; this way their "public spirit and disinterestedness will not be liable to suspicion."[66]

The charges of self-interested dealings versus the promotion of the common good continued. "I Know" propounded a series of seventeen questions intended to show that the members of the city council who were promoting the Jones Falls project under the guise of improving navigation in the harbor were actually owners of property known as the Meadows, located on the west side of the falls. By having the city pay to improve the falls, they were actually benefitting their own property.[67] "Frugality" mostly concurred in this sentiment but felt that the mayor and city council were not necessarily enriching themselves so much as they were promoting the interests of favored constituents. For "Frugality," it was the Pratt and South Street projects that evidenced this favoritism, as the city was unjustly and excessively taxed in order to purchase the property needed for the road extension from favored friends of those in power. As further evidence of this scheme that was more befitting a European monarch,

"Frugality" noted that the city first determined what the owners of the property to be demolished would take before seeking and receiving a $100,000 loan to help pay for this property. "Frugality" repeated the common refrain that if the residents of South Street, for example, wanted improvements to the road, they should pay for it.[68] "Equal Rights" echoed this sentiment, questioning why the residents of Fell's Point should help pay one-third of the costs to open Pratt Street downtown.[69] While "A Lover of Peace" lamented the violence of party spirit that was raging daily in the city's papers and called on the editors to refuse to publish any anonymous letters, the debate continued.[70]

In the same edition of the *American*, "An Observer" repeated the charge that members of the city council were essentially acting as land speculators when they approved the Jones Falls project. "An Observer" did not stop with Jones Falls, however. Instead, the South Street project would provide a proper thoroughfare through the Meadows and would increase the councilmen's personal land values, while the Pratt Street project would aid those councilmen who owned property closer to the inner harbor.[71] "Hortensius" agreed with this assertion and named the men who owned property in the Meadows that would benefit, including elite Baltimoreans like merchant Robert Oliver and Maryland soldier and statesman John Eager Howard. Although the citizens of Old Town on the other side of the falls would be ruined, they were still obligated to pay one-third of the costs to benefit the property owned by Oliver and Howard.[72] "Aristides" was not opposed to the "spirit of improvement" that had seized the city council, but he felt this spirit had gone too far, comparing it to the farmer that would recklessly mortgage his estate to make a decade's worth of improvements in a single year. After making the common point about the fiscal irresponsibility of the city, he then moved to the second general complaint, namely, that the entirety of the city's residents should not have to pay for one-third of the cost of the projects, as set forth in the enabling legislation. For example, what benefit did Old Town derive from the South Street project that was underway on the other side of the falls? Further, projects to abate nuisances like the overflowing Jones Falls likewise did not escape the disapproval of "Aristides." If Jones Falls was a nuisance that the city had to address rather than an elective public-improvement project, the project should be paid for like any other nuisance, by taxing the persons who owned the property where the overflows occurred.[73]

The war of public opinion that occurred in the local newspapers was the tip of the iceberg. The debate over the role of the city in these public projects naturally led to the use of more formal political mechanisms to either oust or retain the city government. Ward meetings were held where the city began to line up either behind or against the mayor and city council. For example, in August 1818, the First Ward published the results of its inspection of the city's actions over the course of the last two years. Located on the western edge of the city and thus well away from any of these projects, the First Ward lambasted the city for squandering the treasury and seeking to grab power.[74] The fundamental concern was over the city's support for projects like the extension of Pratt Street. For example, the First Ward committee noted that the mayor himself had complained in the fall of 1817 that the city was in a dire financial situation. However, instead of lining up behind those who sought to have the state legislature reconsider the Pratt Street bill, he consented to the January 1818 ordinance that not only supported the opening but obligated the city to pay one-third of the damages to injured property owners.

The First Ward committee, however, did not simply criticize the mayor and city council for reckless spending. Rather, they indicted them on charges of conspiracy to secretly gain more power for themselves. For example, the committee charged that the city delegation sent to Annapolis for the avowed purposes of seeking additional representatives for Baltimore in the state legislature, a law to improve Jones Falls, and additional powers for the city corporation, was really a charade masking a secret purpose. The true goal of that delegation was to obtain more power for the city government. The evidence of the secret design rested in the February 1818 Maryland law that gave Baltimore increased power over its own affairs, including most notably the power of direct taxation. The committee charged that with these powers, the city now had the ability to accomplish its true goal of taxing Baltimoreans up to one million dollars. For the committee, this plan had already been put in place. Considering the preexisting debt of $212,614.66 on the date the law was passed (February 9, 1818), plus the $250,000 in combined loans to complete the Pratt and South Street projects, as well as the $25,000 of preliminary work on Jones Falls, one can see that the city was already close to a half-million dollars in debt. While the city leaders continued to argue that such a debt was in line with the other great cities of New York and Philadelphia, the committee argued that those cities were much larger and able to sustain the debt. Indeed, the committee maintained that the leaders of Baltimore, who would financially gain from these self-interested transactions, were leading the city into a public bankruptcy. The committee resolved that all the wards should hold meetings for the purpose of electing new members of the council and new electors for the mayor, as their presumptuous and arrogant conduct was "unparallelled [*sic*] in the history of the world."[75] Other wards were split. For example, in the same edition of the *American* in which the Second Ward published its resolutions approving of the actions of the city council and strongly supporting the reelection of that "tried patriot and excellent chief magistrate" Mayor Stiles, there appeared a notice for a Second Ward meeting of voters opposed to the mayor and city council to nominate a slate of opposition candidates.[76] This pattern was replicated in many other wards as well. A similar split was evident in the Third Ward.[77]

Ultimately, though, Pratt Street was extended despite the protest from many corners. In the face of these vociferous and sustained objections, the city nonetheless was able to finish the project. Mayor Stiles did not live to see the results of the project for which he was so vilified. Battling illness for several years, Stiles relented and resigned his office on February 15, 1819, passing away four months later.[78] Stiles's predecessor Edward Johnson was reelected to fill out the remainder of his term.[79] At the same time that the city was trying to impose order on its downtown harbor, one mile east the flooded and muddy streets of Fell's Point also needed attention.

FELL'S POINT

As opposed to the outrage sparked by the Pratt Street project, the Fell's Point drainage plan provoked much less public scorn. Unlike these other projects that spread the burden among a much larger number of Baltimoreans, the Fell's Point plan ultimately fell on the shoulders of Barron, Craig, and a handful of other neighboring wharf owners. In addition, the residents of Fell's Point were likewise divided over the best way to attend to the drainage issue. While wharf owners like Barron and Craig were devastated by the city's plans, other residents had been demanding action for years.

In Fell's Point the buildings, wharves, and homes sprung up before the infrastructure of paved roads, sidewalks, and drainage canals, exacerbating the drainage situation there and leading to a swampy, muddy mess with every rain. As early as 1801, the city commissioners were hatching plans to pave streets in lower Fell's Point to alleviate the drainage issues, while at the same time trying to make these changes without damaging the many structures that were already built.[80] Fell's Point residents routinely petitioned the city to register their complaints about the drainage. Some complained about the water that pooled near a brickyard and that maintained standing water of several feet, even in the driest conditions.[81] Others wanted the city to pave the roads or footways.[82] The city's responses to these petitions were by no means comprehensive. Rather, the city proceeded by fits and starts and regularly changed its plans.

The water that had always bedeviled Fell's Point originated northeast of the neighborhood and ran southwesterly until reaching the harbor.[83] For illustration, a map of Fell's Point noting the drainage patterns that tracked the trial court testimony appears in chapter 4. The city's first attempt to address the problem came in 1809, when it built a dam at Market and Pratt Street to divert one of the largest streams into a small pond already in the district. Descriptively known by residents as the "Brick Pond," it was soon overflowing. In 1813, the city decided to prevent the stream from filling up the Brick Pond. To do so, they paved the east–west Pratt/German Street, which caused the stream that crossed the district from the northeast to the southwest to redirect southward into the water.[84] The problem was that the water now partly entered the Patapsco by way of Market Street, the largest and busiest thoroughfare in Fell's Point. In 1815, with the war over, the city was able to return to its Fell's Point drainage plan. This time, the city believed it should grade two main east/west Fell's Point thoroughfares, Dulaney and Wilkes, that would send water westward into Harford Run, a waterway that served as the western border for Fell's Point. However, by that summer the commissioners advised the city council to abandon this plan. Instead, they now recommended regrading Ann Street, another large north–south roadway parallel to Market Street. This would take the water that crossed Fell's Point in a generally southwest direction or down Market Street and redirect it southward into the harbor along Ann Street.[85] The commissioners also struck an agreement with the owner of property north of Barron and Craig's wharf to allow the runoff to enter the eastern harbor at the intersection where Washington Street met the water. The city specifically agreed that it would maintain the depth of the water at the point of entry at its own expense.[86] This was critical, as the decision to redirect the Fell's Point drainage into the harbor now meant that the wharf owners in eastern Fell's Point would now bear the brunt of the improvements.

Barron and Craig were not the only wharf owners affected by the Washington Street drainage plan. Seven men owning wharfs that jutted into the harbor on the eastern side of Fell's Point directly south of Washington Street would suffer because of these improvements. The northernmost wharf was owned by William Dawson, who owned one lot and shared a second with his neighbor James Curtis directly to the south.[87] In addition to the lot shared with Dawson, Curtis owned two lots of his own.[88] To the south of Dawson lied Barron and Craig's three lots that boasted two piers.[89] William and John Price owned a wharf to the south of Barron and Craig, while Hezekiah Waters's wharf was the southernmost on the eastern side of Fell's Point.[90]

On February 26, 1817, Barron and Craig, Dawson, Curtis, the Prices, Waters, and fourteen others petitioned Mayor Stiles and the city council to register their complaints.[91] These men knew that the depth of the harbor was critical to their businesses. They complained that the sediment carried by the water that washed into the harbor had already lowered its depth. As the city was debating the passage of the ordinance to pave the four streets directly north of the eastern harbor, these wharf owners were desperate to prevent the new law from passing. They were incredulous that the city was diverting the water that for the last forty years ran generally westward into Harford Run and then into the Patapsco. From their perspective, the city had made a herculean effort since 1809 to gradually turn all of this water in the opposite direction. If the city truly wanted to redirect the drainage to the east, there was a much better option. Indeed, before the war, the city passed an ordinance appointing three port wardens responsible for maintaining the depth of the harbor.[92] As part of their duties, the wardens were directed to survey the east side of Fell's Point to determine the feasibility of turning all the water then flowing to the southwest toward Harris's Creek, a waterway to the east of Fell's Point.[93] Although they apparently did not actually survey the land until 1816, the wardens nonetheless determined that the Harris's Creek proposal was possible and presented to the city an estimated cost of between $6,000 and $10,000.[94] However, the city never acted on these estimates.

In response to the petition, on March 17, 1817, a joint committee of both branches of the city council formed to study the concerns of the wharf owners regarding the Washington Street plan. A week and a half later, both branches agreed that the committee should meet with the port wardens in Fell's Point to inspect the problems personally.[95] Perhaps hoping to build on the attention their plight was getting from the city, the wharf owners sent a second petition on April 2, 1817, less than a week after the city's inspection. They reminded the city that its plan to divert the water to the eastern harbor at Washington Street was ruining their wharves. They stated that in the last year, the accompanying sediment had raised the sea floor around their wharves from four to six feet. If the city continued its course of building dams and digging ditches to send all the water into the eastern harbor, their wharves would be useless. The wharf owners not only sought to dissuade the city from continuing its plans, but also demanded that it pay to clear out the sediment from between their wharves, presumably by use of the city's mud machine.[96] Their hopes were quickly dashed; just over one week later, the city passed the ordinance paving the four streets just north of the eastern harbor.[97]

Recognizing that their actions were damaging the wharf owners, the city directed the port wardens a few days before the contested paving ordinance to build abutments at the end of the streets that emptied into the harbor to catch the mud, sand, and other debris.[98] However, the city never seemed to fully commit to the plan and continued to convene committees to again determine if some water could be brought westward to take the pressure off of the Washington Street plan.[99] Similarly, the city continued the work of the joint committee to monitor the progress of the drainage plan. The committee appointed by the city to investigate whether these ordinances were in need of any modification reported in June 1817 that the ordinances were fine as written. Indeed the preservation of the depth of the harbor required it. The committee reported that not only were the ordinances appropriate, but that the city, to protect the navigation of the harbor from "total ruin," should pave all of the streets south of Dulaney.[100]

The wharf owners did not idly wait on the work of yet another committee. On May 14, 1818, Barron and Craig, Dawson, Curtis, the Prices, Waters, and two others petitioned the city about the water pouring into the harbor. They lambasted the city commissioners, and Commissioner Henry Stouffer specifically, for building a dam at Ann and Dulaney, which they began referring to as "Stouffer's dam." Since the dam altered the path of an "ancient" watercourse, they had suffered and would continue to incur damage. They were pleased with the city's law that directed the building of abutments at the ends of the affected streets to catch the sediment. However, they complained that the commissioners had continued to design against their interests; Stouffer's dam was damaged by the recent rains but was fixed before the abutments were completed. Finally, as they complained that the water near their wharves once had the "deepest water in the harbor" but could now not float a "loaded scow," they demanded the city pay to clean out the water near their wharves, returning it to a depth similar to what existed before Stouffer's dam.[101]

The pattern continued as the city assigned another committee to respond to the petition. On June 8, 1818, the committee delivered its report. They reported that they inspected both Stouffer's dam as well as the intersection at Aliceanna and Washington where the Fell's Point water was being funneled into the harbor. At first, the committee appeared to support the complaints of the wharf owners. The committee reported that water in the eastern harbor of Fell's Point had been significantly injured. Further, unless measures were taken to stop the debris that was washing into the harbor from the surrounding hills, the navigation would continue to worsen. However, the committee then hedged and kept its recommendations in line with the city's preexisting plans. Noting that it was unnecessary to "offer any arguments in favor of an exertion on the part of the city council" since they were "well convinced that every member of the corporation is ready and willing to adopt and cheerfully concur in any measure which can improve or preserve the navigation of our fair city," the committee's recommendations were limited as expected. They recommended, first, that the abutments approved on April 4, 1817, should be built where County and Washington Streets met the water. Second, they recommended trying to turn some of the water that was funneling into the eastern harbor westward to empty into the western cove of Fell's Point.[102]

By February 1819, the tide seemed to start turning against the city. The city appointed another commission to study the problem of the water pouring down its main Fell's Point thoroughfares of Washington, Wolf, Ann, and Market Streets.[103] Unlike the many past committees, this one was much less charitable. The committee reported that the harbor in the eastern cove of Fell's Point was materially injured. The intersection of Aliceanna and Washington, where the city funneled the water to enter the harbor, would completely flood during heavy rains. In addition, at that spot, the harbor was drying up. Many of the wharves in this area, which seven years before enjoyed water between twelve and fourteen feet deep, were now dry. Unless the city took immediate steps to remedy this "evil," it would ruin the harbor, Baltimore's source of prosperity.[104]

However, the calamitous outbreak of yellow fever in Fell's Point later that fall hindered any real chance Barron and Craig had to convince the city to change its plans.[105] After the outbreak had been contained and the quarantine lifted, Barron and Craig, the Prices, Waters, Dawson, Curtis, and several others in January 1821 pleaded with Mayor Montgomery for relief, hoping still to divert some of the water westward into Harford Run.[106] The petition was referred to the city commissioners, who replied that it was simply no longer possible to turn the water to the west given the new grades of the streets. Instead, the commissioners restated the idea that it would be feasible to run the water eastward toward Harris's Creek.[107] While this most certainly gave the wharf owners hope, the city council did not act on the recommendations of its commissioners. Indeed, not only did the city council fail to entertain their advice on the Harris's Creek proposal, but by March 1821 they passed a resolution that two of the commissioners had been appointed illegally, that is, without their consent. Accordingly, those commissioners, including Henry Stouffer, would not receive pay.[108] Instead, by December, the city passed an ordinance providing for the paving of portions of four more streets north of the eastern harbor: Ann Street (from Dulaney to Gough); Gough Street (from Ann to County); and County Street and Castle Alley (from Gough to the harbor).[109] This ordinance sought not only to preserve the depth of the harbor but to maintain the health of the city, and it signaled the end of any chance that Barron and Craig or the other owners had to convince the city to redirect the water. One month later, Barron and Craig's wharf was auctioned to satisfy the debt they still owed to the seller.[110] The ordinance was reaffirmed in March 1822, and the city commissioners and port wardens were required to get to work on not only ensuring that the streets were paved, but that all contiguous property owners paid their required share for the construction.[111] By this time, however, Barron and Craig had already determined to file suit against the city. A month earlier, Barron and Craig's attorney had the sheriff issue the summons for the mayor and city council to appear in court. One week later, the Baltimore County Court entertained the first appearance of the attorneys in *Barron v. Baltimore.*[112]

In all of these projects, the power of the city to provide for the common welfare of the larger community was pitted against the rights of those citizens who felt they were shouldering too much of the burden. Barron and Craig looked at their dispute with the city in much the same way. As residents they too were pleased that Fell's Point was no longer a collection of muddy streets and ad hoc drainage lakes. However, they felt that they and their neighboring wharf owners alone had been asked to pay the entire price tag for these benefits. Moreover, if the Fell's Point drainage project operated like the construction in the rest of the city, they should have been reimbursed since they suffered damage. If street paving operated in that manner, why should a wharf be treated differently? Throughout the Pratt Street, Jones Falls, and Fell's Point projects, the city was able to withstand the objections of many of its residents regarding its vigorous use of its powers. From a political standpoint, the process was difficult, but it had been overcome. Many had petitioned, held ward meetings, and used anonymous editorials to try to curb the city's growing use of its police power. Some Baltimoreans, however, would take the next step of legally contesting these actions. In fact, not only Barron and Craig sued the city in March 1822; Dawson and Curtis also filed suit at the same time. The following chapter examines the options available in this era to bring individual rights claims before the courts to contest the power of the city.

3 Rights before *Barron*

> One very much in liquor, while shaking my hand, said, "Mr. President, I hope the Constitution may never be broken." I answered, "I concur heartily with you in that wish, and hope also that *your* constitution may never be broken."
>
> John Quincy Adams, *Memoirs*

By 1822, Barron and Craig had had enough. Multiple petitions had not stopped the city from rerouting all of the water in Fell's Point to empty into the eastern harbor. Nor had the petitioning convinced the city to reimburse the wharf owners for the damages to their business. Indeed, in January their wharf was auctioned to satisfy the debt they still owed to the seller. Their neighbors, William Dawson and James Curtis, were likewise fed up. Barron and Craig, Dawson, and Curtis filed three simultaneous lawsuits against the city seeking identical damages of $20,000. They hired the same attorneys—David Hoffman and Charles Mayer—well-regarded practitioners in a town known for its excellent bar association.[1] In the previous chapter, we saw how many Baltimoreans used political methods to challenge the power of the city to undertake these massive improvement projects. As those were unsuccessful, what were the legal options available to their attorneys to contest the city's actions? In a Maryland state court in 1822, how could they characterize their claims for damages? If the city relied on its police power, Barron and Craig could try to show that it overstepped its authority by infringing on their property rights.

But were claims of right sufficient to overcome the city's authority? Furthermore, where did these rights exist? To answer these questions, we must first think more fundamentally about the concept of rights.

What are rights? Generally speaking, a right is a claim that a person or group can invoke to legitimately contest some action. In a modern sense, we generally appreciate rights as effective by virtue of their inclusion in written documents, such as constitutions. Indeed, the expression "right" is now almost synonymous with the concept of constitutionality. Both terms have become the very basic, elemental core of most debates. Once these concepts are invoked, very little thought of further examining either of them usually occurs. Questions about where an invoked right comes from remain unasked. If a right appears in a written constitutional document that applies to the court and party in question, it exists. For example, the European Convention on Human Rights affirms scores of liberties; however, a party in the United States seeking to claim its protections based on those affirmed rights would be unsuccessful. Since the United States is not a signatory to the convention and is thus outside the applicable jurisdictions, those rights do not apply to persons within it, despite the convention's claim to have set forth "human rights." In this way, rights are subject to many of the same rules of jurisdiction and construction as other laws passed by legislatures as part of their normal duties. However, we must recognize that the concept of conflating rights with written constitutions was not always the prevailing sentiment. When Barron and Craig's attorney planned the strategy against the city, there was no consensus on the question of where rights existed or on the role of the state and federal constitutions in providing them.

Any attorney seeking to win a case has to consider how to transform a litany of client complaints, offenses, and outrages into a neat and legally recognized cause of action that would provide the desired remedy for the client. Barron and Craig's attorneys had to address a number of critical questions: What rights were violated? What legal authorities supported this claim? What was the proper cause of action? Consider how a contemporary attorney would handle a case with similar facts. We have a claim that certain ordinances enacted by a governmental entity—here the city of Baltimore—resulted in actions that led to the diminishment in the value of private property, namely, a wharf. Today, Barron and Craig could bring suit against the city for an inverse condemnation of the property, an action essentially the reverse of a suit for eminent domain, its better-known cousin. An eminent-domain suit is filed by the government when it seeks a judicial determination that it can take property and have the court establish a reasonable value to compensate the owner.[2] A common example would be when the government builds an expressway and needs to "take" farmland in order to construct the route. In contrast, an inverse-condemnation action is filed by a property owner against a governmental entity that has taken actions that, without physically appropriating any property, nevertheless renders that private property worthless. This occurs most commonly where a regulatory taking occurs, arising when governmental regulations significantly impair the use of the property, such as with zoning laws. In *Pennsylvania Coal Co. v. Mahon* (1922), Justice Oliver Wendell Holmes most famously summed up the concept behind a regulatory taking, as opposed to a physical taking. The court recognized that some governmental acts could operate as takings without actual physical appropriation, stating that "while property may be regulated to a certain extent, if regulation goes too far it will be recognized as a taking."[3]

The legal basis underlying both inverse condemnation and eminent domain is that some governmental entity infringed a property right. But where does this right exist? Today, Barron and Craig could allege a violation of their property rights as guaranteed by the U.S. and Maryland constitutions. The Fifth Amendment to the U.S. Constitution prohibits the taking of private property for public use without just compensation and has been interpreted since 1897 to apply to the states.[4] The current Maryland state constitution contains two provisions: one that specifically premises the ability of Baltimore to acquire land within city limits for development on payment of just compensation, and another that more generally prohibits in its Declaration of Rights "that no man ought to be taken or imprisoned or disseized of his freehold, liberties or privileges, or outlawed, or exiled, or, in any manner, destroyed, or deprived of his life, liberty or property, but by the judgment of his peers, or by the Law of the land."[5]

Filing this case against Baltimore in the early nineteenth century, though, presented a different set of challenges. There was a live controversy regarding whether the Fifth Amendment applied to the states or only limited the federal government. There were many lawyers and jurists who believed the Bill of Rights applied to the states, whereas others thought it irrelevant to rights claims. Of course, not only had *Barron* not yet been decided, but the Civil War and the resulting changes to the constitutional order had not yet occurred. The gradual process of applying the Bill of Rights against the states by reading them into various provisions of the Fourteenth Amendment would not take place by and large until the twentieth century. However, these challenges were not fatal to their case, as this simply meant that there was no established *constitutional* prohibition against uncompensated takings of property. In this era, the right to receive compensation for a taking of private property, or at least the requirement that it be done in accord with legal process, was not tethered exclusively to any constitution. Because rights in this era were multi-sourced concepts, Barron and Craig's attorneys had a much richer pallet from which to choose. For example, while the prohibition in the Maryland constitution that one shall not be "taken or imprisoned or disseized of his freehold . . . but by the judgment of his peers, or by the Law of the land" can be considered a constitutional right by virtue of its inclusion in the state constitution, it had a much longer life as a fundamental maxim of the common law.[6] William Blackstone also recognized property as an absolute right of Englishmen, a right that had been declared by numerous fundamental documents going back to the Magna Carta.[7] Likewise, John Locke recognized the sanctity of property, which drives the belief that it cannot be infringed except under legal process and sometimes accompanied by compensation. Along with life and liberty, property retains its character as an absolute right even after man left the mythical state of nature and entered into civil society.

Thus, the property rights implicated in this case were perceived as deriving their authority from a number of different and often overlapping sources. While a modern attorney seeking redress under the same facts as Barron and Craig would have a clearer procedural avenue to relief—an inverse condemnation action for a regulatory taking of property—he or she would also have no question about where the right to receive compensation existed: in the U.S. and state constitutions. For this reason, *Barron* is often unquestioned because its holding is so thoroughly modern. An attorney in Baltimore in 1822 would not see the case with the same clarity. Instead, he would be presented with a varied, complicated, and in many ways richer ideological landscape regarding the conceptual location of rights. If we consider rights in this way, the ultimate textual approach of Marshall's court becomes less commonsense. Reading the opinion today complements our modern sensibilities regarding written laws or constitutions as the sources of rights. Reading the case from the view of the attorneys and judges in the early nineteenth century betrays no such familiarity. In earlier generations, Americans thought of their rights as provided by multiple sources. In the colonial era, some identified natural-law principles as the basis, some predicated rights on the unique characteristics of the English Anglo-Saxon heritage, and some espoused the ideas of an original compact and consent of the governed. Their theories evidenced a blend of rights as confirmed and secured by the common law, the Magna Carta, natural law, positivist legal guarantees, Greek and Roman precedents, or divine blessing.

Following independence, Americans begin to reassess the basis for their rights. Since their political situation had fundamentally changed, their concepts of the limits on government had to evolve as well. The breadth of the *Barron* litigation—from its antecedents in the attempts by the city to correct a drainage nuisance in the aftermath of the War of 1812 to its ultimate conclusion in John Marshall's courtroom in 1833—helps track these evolutions. Immediately upon independence, many states began writing their own constitutions to address the new political order. Both in these constitutions as well as in the federal constitution framed a decade later, certain rights were textually included. While certain rights from the colonial era were no longer salient, such as those existing by virtue of colonial charters, there remained a general appreciation that certain rights were fundamental and extraconstitutional. Into the early nineteenth century, many Americans continued to express a view that the American constitutions recognized the existence of these rights, but did not provide their basis. By the first decades of the nineteenth century, these views fell generally into three categories: rights as protected by the common law, rights as universal possessions granted by nature, and rights as enactments of positive law documents like constitutions.

RIGHTS AS PROTECTED BY THE COMMON LAW TRADITION

The most prominent view considered rights existing by virtue of the common law. This idea traced its lineage to the belief that English subjects inherited unique legal privileges and immunities from arbitrary governmental action based on whim instead of law. Describing the exact contours of common law is not an easy task, as even its origins are the subject of debate for its greatest practitioners.[8] The phrase itself arose from the many courts in medieval England, where the king's royal courts were in competition from other tribunals—manorial courts, ecclesiastical courts, and local courts—to decide legal matters.[9] With the exception of land cases, a litigant could take their dispute to any number of courts. The king's judges traveled throughout the realm to hear cases and provide justice backed by the authority of the Crown; by the end of the thirteenth century they proved successful in crowding out these lesser tribunals.[10] Unlike the decisions by these competing courts, which affected only local populations, the decisions rendered by the king's judges were held to be common to the entire kingdom and were thus known as the common law.[11] For the common law, custom was key. According to the theory, judges did not decide cases by making new law; instead, they simply declared the law that already existed by virtue of the custom of the land. The custom generally had to be reasonable, long-standing, compulsory, and not in conflict with other customary claims.[12] By recognizing accepted custom as the method by which society would structure its legal order, the common law would reflect the values of the society. Custom also promoted an inherent stability in the law by ensuring that change occurred gradually and only when societal norms evolved.

In the American colonial era, early settlers emphasized that their rights were the same as the rights of those countrymen from whom they had recently departed. For many, this meant claiming the rights entitled to them as Englishmen. A good example is William Penn's 1675 discussion of what constituted "English Rights." For the English, there were certain rights unique to their society: the right to private property; the right to vote on law; and the right to limit or influence the judicial power through the use of the jury trial. Penn traced this last right to the particular Anglo-Saxon heritage of the English, which drew from mythic Germanic ancestors. These rights were not natural and universal but were "the ancient and undoubted rights of Englishmen, as three great roots, under whose spacious branches the English People have been wont to shelter themselves against the storms of arbitrary government."[13] Twelve years later, Penn further refined his view of the Englishness of rights for purposes of informing and reminding the American colonists of their "inestimable inheritance that every Free-born Subject of England is heir unto by Birth-right, I mean that unparalleled privilege of *Liberty and Property*." The freedom from violence or oppression provided by the law was what he called the "Englishman's Liberty." Their representatives in Parliament and their participation in the jury trial system protected this liberty and gave English subjects control not only over the laws but also their enforcement.[14] Maryland echoed Penn's sentiments that the fundamental rights that protected one's person and property were not universal but uniquely English. In 1639, the colonial Maryland General Assembly declared that Christian inhabitants "have and enjoy all such rights liberties immunities priviledges and free customs within this Province as any naturall born subject of England hath or ought to have or enjoy in the Realm of England by force or vertue of the common law or Statute Law of England." Influenced by the Magna Carta, these rights specifically included the right not to be imprisoned or deprived of one's property except in accord with the laws of the colony.[15]

Despite declaring independence from England, the first Maryland state constitution of 1776, still in effect at the time of the *Barron* case, specifically maintained that its citizens retained their entitlement to the English common law as well as to those English statutes that were in effect at the time its citizens emigrated to the colony and were useful in the light of local circumstances.[16] Indeed, between 1776 and 1798, Americans continued the common law tradition as twelve of the original thirteen former colonies passed laws that received the English common law into legal regimes of the new states.[17] As a result, the common law retained its preeminent role as the legal mechanism that guaranteed rights, as many jurists continued to view rights as coming from the wisdom and experience of the English common law. Part of its success was due to the malleability of many of its doctrines. Following independence and into the early republic era, courts, lawyers, and legal thinkers tried to better define what the common law meant for the new nation.

Many wrote influential treatises addressing the role of the common law in the new legal order. Some started as a way to create American versions of the fundamental source of the English common law at that time, William Blackstone's *Commentaries on the Laws of England*. A four-volume work published between 1765 and 1769 and available in the American colonies by the early 1770s, this treatise served as the lodestar from which anyone who needed to address the common law either cited or distinguished.[18] The first generations of postindependence American lawyers and judges continued to rely on English law largely out of necessity. The appeal of Blackstone becomes more apparent if we add to this necessity the difficulty and great expense in putting together a proper law library that would provide the legal community the tools necessary to stay current on the various decisions of the courts.[19] Indeed, importing English legal publications was far cheaper than trying to ship these same bulky works over land between American cities. This began to change by the 1820s, when not only a number of necessary transportation upgrades had taken place, but also an elite section of the national bar had emerged ready to make significant contributions.[20]

One of the most influential lawyers was James Kent. Referred to as one of "the two most significant figures in American legal literature" in the early nineteenth century along with U.S. Supreme Court Justice Joseph Story, Kent is notable as one of the eminent state court jurists of the early republic. After his retirement as chancellor of the New York state chancery court in 1823 because of constitutional age restrictions, Kent began work on his *Commentaries on American Law*.[21] Published in 1826, Kent's *Commentaries* sought to recast the common law for the new nation. For his part, Story began work on his *Commentaries on the Constitution* shortly after his appointment as a professor at Harvard Law School in 1829.[22] In addition to this treatise, Story would author works on conflict of laws, bailments, and commercial law topics like bills of exchange and promissory notes.[23] For Story and Kent, the goal behind these works was not only to create a usable common law for the United States but to do so in in the face of opposition by many who felt that the common law was an English relic that granted too much power to the judiciary.[24]

As a body of law predicated on respect for longstanding custom, the common law raised a number of concerns when it was adapted for a rapidly expanding nation. In the early republic era, the United States underwent a period of enormous growth. At the close of the Revolutionary War, the young nation was home to approximately four million people who were for the most part scattered up and down the Atlantic coastline. Its economy was decimated, not only from the debt incurred in taking on the British but also because it was a colonial economy that had rejected its economic patron. And yet, by the end of the Mexican American War in 1848, the United States was a continental power. In the intervening time, the nation had seemingly remade itself every generation. Cutting through the wilderness to open the interior for world markets and western expansion, roads and turnpikes were surpassed by canals, which were in turn overtaken by railroads. Sailboats shipped American goods overseas and brought in millions of immigrants to swell the population from roughly four million in 1790 to close to twenty-forty million only sixty years later.[25] Natural obstacles were overcome, as steamships conquered the mighty Mississippi, the Erie Canal opened the Great Lakes region to the world, and the telegraph connected the new cities.

How did Americans use law to facilitate these monumental changes? How did they react to the problems that would naturally arise from the building of these canals, roads, and railroads? Who would shoulder the burden of the damages that arose when the farmer lost his property to a new canal? How about the mill owner whose business was decimated when the river that powered his business was dammed upstream? Who would benefit? Morton Horwitz argued that jurists of the early nineteenth century took advantage of the inchoate nature of the common law to purposefully aid in this transition.[26] Other scholars like Charles Sellers struck a more ominous tone, characterizing lawyers of this era as the "shock troops of capitalism" who twisted the common law to serve the needs of a market economy.[27] In contrast, William Novak looked at the dynamic use of common law doctrine to undergird a vigorous state regulatory scheme that would promote the common good.[28] Regardless of the intent of the lawyers or judges, one commonality was that the United States was undergoing fundamental change; the entire machinery of government was involved both in promoting and shaping these changes. In addition to legislative innovations that not only allowed investors to form corporations without the need for a special grant from the state but also limited the liability of those investors to the amount of their investment, the legal system generally conformed its decisions to allow robust development and expansion.[29]

At the Supreme Court, some of John Marshall's most famous decisions gave private entities cover from the overly democratic impulses of state legislatures that could have checked this growth. In *Fletcher v. Peck*, the Court invalidated a Georgia state law that cancelled a prior sale of its western land holdings by the state legislature. Despite the fact that the contract to sell was procured by fraud and bribery, Marshall struck down the state law on the grounds that it violated the contract clause of the Constitution.[30] Similarly, in *Trustees of Dartmouth College v. Woodward*, Marshall held that a royal charter granted by Parliament in 1769 to establish Dartmouth College as an institute to educate and convert Indians was, in fact, a contract.

As a result, the state of New Hampshire could not replace the school's president and board of trustees.[31] Approximately one month later, in *McCulloch v. Maryland,* Marshall struck down Maryland's attempt to tax the Baltimore branch of the Bank of the United States. Through an expansive reading of the "necessary and proper" clause of Article I, Section 8, the Court held that Congress had the constitutional power to charter a national bank, ensuring that Congress would not be limited only to those powers specifically granted to it in the text of the Constitution itself.[32] Through decisions such as these, the Marshall court provided the national framework to keep the states out of the business of interfering with either private corporations or the prerogatives of the federal government.

More noticeably, however, it was in the state courts where the everyday business of the nation took place. In these courts, lawyers and jurists wrestled with the practical questions of settling disputes that came with the nation's growth. For many, the common law provided the answers. An early example is seen in *Lindsay v. Commissioners,* in which a South Carolina court was presented with a case that pitted the city of Charleston against a property owner whose land was taken for the purpose of constructing a new road.[33] The owner sought to prevent construction on the grounds that the enabling law was unconstitutional because it allowed a taking of property without consent, full compensation, or jury trial.[34] The property owner argued the taking violated the South Carolina state constitution, which contained a Magna Carta–inspired provision prohibiting the taking of property except by a judgment of peers or by law of the land, a clause virtually identical to the similar article in the 1776 Maryland constitution applicable in the *Barron* case. The property owner also cited *Vanhorne's Lessee v. Dorrance,* a federal circuit court case from Pennsylvania from a year earlier. There, the court held that the Pennsylvania legislature acted illegally by attempting to settle a land title dispute by passing a law that effectively took property from one party and vested it in another.[35] He also relied on a 1792 South Carolina case, *Middleton v. Bowman.*[36] There, the South Carolina colonial legislature had attempted to resolve a boundary dispute legislatively by confirming title to a contested parcel of property in the name of one of the competing parties. Years later, the purchaser of the adjacent land brought suit and argued that this act by the colonial legislature was void since it violated the principles of the Magna Carta by effectively taking property from the legal heirs without any due process.

The court agreed that the act was against "common right" as well as the Magna Carta since it took the property of one man and vested it in another without compensation or even jury trial.[37]

In response, the city of Charleston admitted that the rules against takings recognized in cases like *Vanhorne's Lessee* and *Middleton* were correct since they violated the Magna Carta and the South Carolina constitution. However, the city argued that the power of the sovereign to maintain roadways for the convenience of society was part of the law of the land well before the Magna Carta or the South Carolina constitution ever existed.[38] Relying on continental theorists like Vattel and Rousseau, the city's legal team argued that a person's power over his property was always subordinate to the right the community has over all property.[39] The team argued from these principles that the state's eminent domain power was a part of the common law of South Carolina.[40] Charleston's lawyers did not interpret the common law as given by the Magna Carta. Rather, they argued for a more common understanding of what were originally considered English liberties. The common law accordingly tracked the wisdom of the ages that formed when the customs of the Saxons, Normans, and Romans mixed with those of the original inhabitants of the British Isles.[41] Thus, the common law could allow the city to take property for a public benefit.

Because the court could not reach a majority decision, the property owner was unsuccessful. Two judges agreed with the city's interpretation that eminent domain was an essential component of sovereignty recognized by the common law and included in the Magna Carta. The Magna Carta did not grant this right; instead, it simply confirmed its existence.[42] Likewise, the South Carolina constitution also declared these "ancient rights and principles" in the same way. For these two judges, the common law provided the basis for the right of the sovereign to take property through its eminent domain power; no individual right could trump this ability. For the other judges, the common law was just as important but for different reasons. These judges held that the power to take property for public purposes was an essential attribute of sovereignty, but that even Vattel argued that it must be done with compensation to the owner. In addition to citing Vattel, they cited the sage of the common law, William Blackstone, for the proposition that the common law required compensation upon the exercise of the takings power.[43] For all the parties in *Lindsay*, the common law was the basis for rights. It contained the basis for the right of the sovereign to take property; it contained the right of the individual to demand payment. All claims to right flowed through the language and concepts of the common law, but the two sides had very different interpretations of what the common law required.

In a later case from New York, a farm owner sought an injunction to stop the trustees of his village from diverting water from his upstream neighbor, thus depriving him of water essential to his farm.[44] In *Gardner v. Trustees of the Village of Newburgh*, the New York chancery court, in an 1816 opinion written by James Kent, cited the common law principle that a landowner had a property right in the water that runs through his land. Kent turned to a common law remedy, the doctrine of nuisance, as the procedural mechanism under which the landowner could vindicate this right. By classifying these damages as a private nuisance, Kent gave the landowner the ability to bring suit.[45] Categorizing the diversion in this way was significant. The nuisance doctrine is defined at common law as one of two types: public or private. A public nuisance is one that is common to the entire community. As such, the sovereign had the ability to use its police power to abate the nuisance without the necessity of payment. A private nuisance inflicts damage on a limited group of people and requires reimbursement. Once Kent classified that the landowner had a property interest in the water and that the diversion of water constituted a private nuisance, he then determined that the landowner's interest could not be "disseised" except by due process, as it was "an ancient and fundamental maxim of common right to be found in the Magna Carta, and which the legislature has incorporated into an act declaratory of the rights of the citizens of [New York] state."[46] Here, Kent was careful to note that the prohibition against taking private property without due process existed as far back as the Magna Carta; as such, its inclusion into state statute was merely a recognition of this fundamental right. Kent was careful to note that the legislature had the power to take property; however, it must be done to serve a public purpose, and the owner must be compensated. Kent located this principle of just compensation in the common law and stated that it was "adopted by all temperate and civilized governments, from a deep and universal sense of its justice," thereby citing sixteenth-century natural-law philosophers Grotius and Pufendorf.[47] The principle could be found in the decisions of the Roman senate, the English government, and in the writings of Blackstone. Furthermore, Kent regarded this principle as so important that it had "frequently been made the subject of an express and fundamental article of right in the constitution of government," noting that similar provisions had been incorporated into the constitutions of Pennsylvania, Delaware, and Ohio, the French constitution of 1795, and even in the U.S. Constitution by way of the Fifth Amendment.[48] While it might seem curious that a New York court judge was citing the constitutions of other states, countries, and even the United States, it is perfectly reasonable if we appreciate that Kent espoused a view of constitutions as containing, and not granting, the first principles of just government. For Kent, the prohibition against uncompensated takings of private property was mandated as part of the common law. However, he was neither locating this right within the common law nor looking at the common law as the source of this right. Rather, Kent echoed a well-accepted appreciation that the common law acted as the mechanism through which these timeless principles were applied.

In 1826, the Pennsylvania Supreme Court considered a very similar question. In *Shrunk v. Schuylkill River Navigation Company*, a state law granted an upstream property owner the right to dam the Schuylkill River, decimating the business of a fishery owner downstream.[49] The owner of the fishery hired William Rawle and his son as co-counsel. In addition to his status as an elite member of the Philadelphia bar, Rawle was a major legal figure of the era whose writings, including his work on the U.S. Constitution, set forth his view that the majority of the Bill of Rights applied to both the federal and state governments.[50] Nonetheless, Rawle viewed this dispute as a matter of common law. He argued that the deprivation of his client's property right in the waters of the Schuylkill was actionable for a number of reasons. Not only did the state law that authorized the company to build the dam require it to reimburse for any injuries it caused, but the common law also recognized a compensable property interest in the claimant's right to fish the river adjacent to his property.[51] Rawle argued that this common law rule was in force in the United States, and he cited the court to the many supporting authorities, including the influential treatise on watercourses by Joseph Angell.[52] However, unlike in Kent's decision in *Gardner* ten years earlier, the Pennsylvania court viewed the issue much differently. It refused to recognize the common law principle and found that the right to claim a property interest in rivers in England applied only if the river was considered navigable, defined traditionally by whether it had an ebb and flow of a tide. In the United States, that distinction was inapplicable. The court noted that the great rivers of the nation, such as the Mississippi or the Ohio, did not move with the tide; however, they were most certainly navigable.[53]

With its ruling against the fishery owner, *Shrunk* presents a good example not only of the differing views of the common law competing during this era, but also of some of the procedural mechanisms that allowed the common law to evolve. The court did not rule against the landowner because, for example, the fishery was not injured or because the defendant was not responsible. Instead, it used the common law doctrine of *damnum abseque injuria*, an injury without a remedy, to deny damages.[54] This common law doctrine is traceable to English jurists beginning in 1792 and was soon in use in American courts in conjunction with the concept of consequential damages, which is the idea that a plaintiff had to prove that the damages suffered were as a direct consequence of the defendant's actions.[55] Considering that the legislature granted the company the right to build the dam provided they compensate for damages, one sees that making such a claim required a fair amount of work on the part of the court. However, even the provision in the company charter that required compensation for injuries allowed the company to reduce the amount it had to pay in damages to property by the amount that property increased in value by virtue of the company's improvements, evidencing that the legislature prioritized the value the company's projects would bring to the state over the rights of individual property owners.[56] By emphasizing a dynamic view of the common law with ample exceptions for damage claims, the *Shrunk* court followed a very similar path.

In *Lindsay* and *Gardner*, the courts viewed the common law as protecting the fundamental rights of property. In *New York v. Goodwin*, a New York court examined another right: the prohibition against double jeopardy, or the act of trying a defendant more than once for the same crime. In 1820, the *Goodwin* court held that the Fifth Amendment double jeopardy rule applied in a state court proceeding but not necessarily because the Fifth Amendment applied to the state.[57] To Chief Justice Ambrose Spencer, that was the wrong question. He wrote, "I do not consider it material whether this provision be considered as extending to the state tribunals or not; the principle is a sound and fundamental one of the common law." However, he added for good measure his belief that the Fifth Amendment "does extend to all judicial tribunals in the United States, whether constituted by the Congress of the United States, or the states individually."[58] Spencer's opinion in *Goodwin* raised two points. First, Spencer set forth a vision of the rights contained in the Constitution that emphasized the declaratory nature of written constitutions themselves. Second, Judge Spencer equated fundamental rights, such as the prohibition against double jeopardy, as protected by the common law. In discussing the prohibition, Spencer cited Blackstone and stated that the prohibition "is grounded on this universal maxim of the common law of England."[59] To Spencer, written constitutions enunciated rights but did not provide them. Accordingly, the extent to which the Constitution applied in New York was wholly irrelevant since it was the common law that recognized these liberties.

In all of these cases, courts predicated their view of rights as tied up with the common law. The idea of rights existing by virtue of the common law is somewhat difficult to entirely pin down since the common law was subject to multiple interpretations in this era. Many viewed the common law as jealously guarding property rights, whereas others transformed its doctrines to suit the realities of the development occurring across the country. For example, in *Shrunk*, the court was not called on to decide an abstract point of law. Rather, the court made its ruling knowing the company's dam on the Schuylkill that ruined the downstream fishery was designed as part of a larger project to tame the river. This was of paramount importance to the state since the project not only would provide access to the Ohio River and the west but also would hopefully help Philadelphia in its race for commercial dominance against New York and Baltimore.[60]

RIGHTS AS PROVIDED BY NATURAL LAW OR NATURAL RIGHT

While many envisioned rights as liberties existing in or secured by the common law, others perceived of rights as based on universal principles of natural law or right. Similar to those who found rights as existing by virtue of the common law, these lawyers and jurists also espoused a view of rights as existing outside of written constitutions. As with the varying interpretations of the common law, there is a similar range when we consider expressions of claims of right as provided by natural law. Just as some courts viewed the common law as providing the basis for the right, others courts envisioned the common law as the vehicle that applied certain timeless principles in practical ways. Likewise, the arguments that envisioned rights as provided by nature were often overlapping. It is important to recognize that there is universal consensus neither on the definitions of natural law and natural right nor even on the difference between the terms.[61] Rather, in much the same way that many lawyers advocated for very different versions of the common law, this chapter interprets rights claims based either on natural law or on natural right as interchangeable. The fundamental distinction to be made concerns those rights' common status as extraconstitutional rather than as grounded in written documents.

We must appreciate the historiographical debate regarding where the generation of the revolutionary era located their rights. One of the major points of contention is the degree to which Americans of that era relied on natural law as supplying the rights they were interposing against the British authorities. For many, the resort to natural-law principles was paramount and evidenced in numerous sermons, pamphlets, and even in the preamble of the Declaration of Independence, where Thomas Jefferson famously invoked the colonists' "unalienable" rights that were "endowed by their creator."[62] For others, reliance on the natural-law arguments expressed in places like the Declaration of Independence is misplaced for a number of reasons: usually the persons making these arguments were not lawyers, but clergymen or laymen (the Declaration is an exception to this); the natural-law arguments were often made by British officials themselves who were using this language to mock colonial claims. Furthermore, these natural-law arguments were almost always coupled with another legal basis and rarely appeared to stand on their own.[63] It is true that many nonlawyers seized on claims of natural right; for example, in 1768, Massachusetts minister Daniel Shute gave an election-day sermon in which he discussed the responsibility of government to ensure to the people "those natural rights and privileges which are essential to their happiness." For Shute, those natural privileges that were "gifts of the creator" were "life, liberty, and property."[64] While Shute was not an attorney, he was a well-respected minister who was later elected to the Massachusetts constitutional convention, where he vigorously supported the proposed federal constitution's prohibition on requiring religious tests to hold public office.[65]

This study does not seek to wade into this debate about revolutionary-era thought on natural law. Rather, what it seeks to do is look at how Americans in the early republic located their rights. Whether the reliance on natural law as a source of right was overstated by modern historians is not relevant except to the extent that Americans of succeeding generations also misread the same evidence.[66] If we go so far as to believe that all persons in the revolutionary generation who made natural-rights arguments to oppose British policy were either naïve or purposefully disingenuous, at the very least there were many in the early republic that took their statements at face value. Indeed, many lawyers and judges in this era continued to attribute the existence of their rights to sources that were in some way grounded in natural law or right, as well as in a view of the common law as the expression of fundamental principle. This was often seen when courts in this era decided takings cases in which state legislatures sought to take the property of one party and grant it to another. Given the haphazard state of recording title to property in the rush westward, this was a common occurrence. When faced with these situations, courts did not rely on the prohibitions contained in many state constitutions or the Fifth Amendment to the U.S. Constitution. Instead, they routinely envisioned that the property owners had valid claims and that this was prohibited by natural law or the common law. Rights against such "naked land transfers" were unanimously accepted as existing outside the constitutions.[67]

Modern concepts of natural law or right are traceable to medieval Europe. To address contemporary concerns, church leaders, canon lawyers, and scholars reengaged classical legal sources that dated to Aristotle. Aristotelian theory separated law into those rules that were considered fundamental because they had their basis in a divine or natural sanction, on the one hand, and laws created by man, on the other hand. The Romans modified but nonetheless largely continued this binary conception.[68] Scholars debate who should be credited as the first to begin the transformation of this classical-rights formula, with some awarding the honor to the 1332 writings of the Franciscan monk, William of Ockham. Ockham articulated a view of a natural right as a subjective possession that invests that person with a type of power to exercise the right, rather than understanding it along the lines of the classical world, which held a right to be a part of an objective universal force and thus fundamentally disconnected from the individual.[69] While the medieval era has generally been accepted as the origin of the modern-rights formula, not all agree. Others argue that the shift occurred earlier as an outgrowth of the revival of legal studies in the new universities of the era.[70] Further minority views attribute the shift to Roman legal scholars, identify Ockham's philosophic heirs like French nominalist Jean Gerson as the critical figure, or claim that modern-rights thought is actually evident in a careful reading of Aristotle.[71] Regardless, in all of these interpretations the critical commonality was that ideas of right and property were fused into one concept.[72]

The seismic upheavals following Martin Luther's 1517 revolt against the policies of the Catholic Church served to promote an intellectual reordering of the concepts of natural law. In the legal philosophies penned in its wake, we see the origins of arguments that predicated rights on inherent, timeless natural law principles. (Barron's attorney, David Hoffman, made just such an argument before the appellate court.) Freed from the ideological boundaries requiring the designation of the divine as the ultimate law giver, philosophers and jurists had the opportunity to set forth ideas of the place of natural law and natural rights in entirely new ways. Most famously, Dutch legal theorist Hugo Grotius considered natural law as discoverable through the exercise of man-made reason.[73] Scholars like Grotius reconceptualized the natural-law doctrine of *jus naturale* as a principle of natural rights, rights that man inherently possessed. As a right possessed by man, the larger society or state could not infringe those rights.[74] In articulating his theories of international law, Grotius premised natural law as a set of rules that were timeless and unchangeable even by God, and he separated natural law from positive law, which were commands enacted by man.[75] Later proponents of the development of international law, such as eighteenth-century Swiss philosopher Emerich de Vattel, similarly emphasized the concept that man maintains inherent natural liberties that cannot be compromised without consent. Like Grotius, Vattel grounded his ideas on the law of nations in the principles of natural law.[76] Building on Grotius' tradition, seventeenth-century German philosopher Samuel Pufendorf similarly discredited the idea of natural law as residing with the divine and accorded those rights to man as an individual being, without relying on the state or the greater society as providing those rights.[77] Similar to Grotius, Pufendorf was writing during the genesis of the modern age of the nation-state following the 1648 Peace of Westphalia and, also like Grotius, charged the state with ensuring the order and well-being of the polity.[78]

While continental theorists Grotius and Pufendorf disconnected the basis for natural law from its divine moorings and placed certain principles ideologically outside the control of human restraint, the

Stuart upheaval of the seventeenth century led to the reevaluation of thought about rights in England. In the English tradition before the seventeenth century, the term "right" simply meant that a person held valid title or owned property, especially realty. Other aspects that we would now consider within the modern definition of a "right" were referred to as "liberties and privileges." Further, these liberties and privileges were effective against the power of the government; however, they were also considered as granted by the government and could be rescinded.[79] The upheaval of the seventeenth century led to an expansion of the idea of a right in two ways. First, a right was to include those qualities previously associated with liberties and privileges. And second, rights were perceived as something that could not be granted or taken away by the government, thereby forming the genesis of the idea of the birthright of Englishmen.[80] In the English tradition, this evolution to the idea of a right as something that an individual owns is generally credited to seventeenth-century political theorists Hobbes and Locke.[81] For example, Thomas Hobbes attempted to discredit the expansive notion of natural law that had been set forth by Grotius and sought to ground those rights with the sovereign.[82] To Hobbes, man's entry into a political community was a bargain whereby the individual designated the state as the exclusive legal authority in the polity. While Hobbes believed in the existence of natural laws that predated the establishment of the commonwealth, once man agreed to enter into the commonwealth and designate a sovereign, the bond was unbreakable.[83] Those natural rights that man had possessed pre-commonwealth were no longer considered separate from the state since the laws of nature and the laws of the sovereign—the exclusive law giver—were considered inseparable.[84]

The political turmoil of the seventeenth century also laid the foundation for the writings of English philosopher John Locke. He wrote his *Two Treatises of Government* (1689) between 1679 and 1681, following his return from France, where he witnessed the persecution of French Protestants.[85] For Locke, man originally existed in a state of nature, prior to the creation of any government. In the state of nature, man possessed natural rights, which included the rights of life, liberty, and property. These rights were not given up once man created government.[86] Rather, the supreme obligation of government was to secure these natural rights.[87] Unlike Hobbes, Locke used rights as a basis by which to measure whether the sovereign honored its duties under the social compact; if not, the compact was broken and the sovereign right forfeited. However, while Hobbes similarly recognized that presocietal man possessed natural rights, he maintained that upon entering into a political society, the individual agreed to merge those rights with the state exclusively. By doing so, the sovereign became the ultimate legal authority; any alleged violation of those rights could not form the basis for recourse against the state since those rights no longer conceptually existed apart from the state.[88]

The 1776 Virginia Declaration of Rights is a good example of the Lockean influence on the colonies. It declared that "all men are by nature equally free and independent, and have certain inherent rights, of which, when they enter a state of society, they cannot, by any compact, deprive or divest their posterity; namely, the enjoyment of life and liberty, with the means of acquiring and possessing property, and pursuing happiness and safety."[89] Similarly, another famous and well-known enunciation of this principle is seen in the 1776 American Declaration of Independence, which presumes the existence of natural and "self-evident" rights that are not granted by any government. Rather, it was the duty and responsibility of any legitimate government to respect these "unalienable" rights.[90]

Much of the reliance on a universal natural-law view of rights coalesced in the early attempts to draft the first state constitutions. Many constitutions contained declarations that enunciated a natural-law type view of rights. Those constitutions that did not do so provided the participants with a platform to debate the basis for rights. An example of this can be seen in the battles over the failed attempts to ratify the 1778 Massachusetts constitution. In the "Essex Result," delegates to the Essex County constitutional convention set forth a view of the proper role of government. Their objection to the proposed state constitution was written by Massachusetts lawyer and future chief justice of the Massachusetts Supreme Court Theophilus Parsons. Parsons echoed the Lockean and Hobbesian view of government as formed voluntarily by persons and their sovereign. He argued, however, that the proper role of a free government was not just to secure the rights that existed in the pregovernmental state of nature but also to promote the greatest happiness of the people. Any government that was destructive of these ends would constitute a tyranny that would reduce the citizens to slaves. Parsons made an interesting and important point in his objections. As an attorney, Parsons was most certainly familiar with Blackstone's *Commentaries.* Thus, on the one hand, he divided rights into the two main categories of the inalienable and the alienable, thereby echoing Blackstone's description of absolute and relative rights. On the other hand, however, whereas Blackstone limited inalienable rights to life, liberty, and property, Parsons described them as rights of conscience. Channeling Locke, Parsons maintained that each citizen, for voluntarily giving up control over his alienable rights by leaving a state of nature and entering society, received the rights of the security of person and property. The inalienable rights, or the rights of conscience, could not, contrary to Blackstone, be controlled by any legislature. These rights were extralegal and not part of any bargain struck between the citizen and the state. The proposed Massachusetts constitution was defective, according to Parsons, because it failed to define clearly those inalienable rights in a bill of rights. The constitution was also deficient since it failed to describe how each man received the security of person and property as consideration for the surrender of part of his natural rights.[91]

The delegates of the town of Beverly, Massachusetts, followed the lead of Essex County in objecting to the proposed 1778 Massachusetts constitution, likewise rejecting it for the lack of a bill of rights. Conceptually, the Beverly delegates split rights into two categories, similar to the inalienable/alienable categories described by the Essex convention or the absolute/relative division described by Blackstone. What was novel in the Beverly split, however, is their description of inalienable or absolute rights as "Natural Rights of Man" inherited from the "Great Parent of Nature." While these rights were so important that they must be contained in a written bill of rights, it is interesting to note the use of the phrase "rights of man" in a document predating the French Revolution and subsequent French Declaration of the Rights of Man and the Citizen, first enacted in 1789 and specifically invoking this phrase.[92] For the Beverly delegates, the rights that were relinquished to society were not properly protected in the proposed constitution, which failed to describe what "Equivalent" the people received in return for parting with such rights.[93]

This widespread concern over rights was remedied in the 1780 Massachusetts constitution, which contained a Declaration of Rights that comprised its first article.[94] Indeed, many early state constitutions reflected this idea that rights existed outside the frame of government. It was important that the constitutions reflect the existence of these natural rights, but there was no idea that those constitutions provided the basis for those rights.[95] For example, in 1776, eight states created written constitutions, with two more adopted the next year.[96] In these constitutions, the states created written constitutions to declare the organization of their body politic once the Declaration of Independence effectively nullified their former royal or corporate charters. Given the headiness of the early days of the Revolution, it is not surprising that many states included written declarations of rights in their constitutions. For example, Maryland confirmed its citizens' right to the English common law and included many familiar rights, such as the freedom of the press; the prohibition against the quartering of soldiers; and the mandate that one's life, liberty, or property could not be deprived except in accordance with law.[97] Similarly, the Pennsylvania constitution majestically declared that all men possessed "natural, inherent and inalienable rights" and that it was the purpose of government to enable them to "enjoy their natural rights, and the other blessings which the Author of existence has bestowed upon man."[98] An obvious omission to a modern reader of these constitutions is the lack of any enforcement mechanisms. This makes sense if we appreciate that these documents were not intended to be the basis on which these rights existed.

A good example of the idea that fundamental rights were declared by the various American constitutions is seen in *Vanhorne's Lessee v. Dorrance*, a 1795 case relied on by David Hoffman during the first trial against the city in Baltimore County Court.[99] In *Vanhorne*, U.S. Supreme Court Justice William Paterson, while presiding over the Federal Circuit Court of Pennsylvania in 1795, was called on to settle a dispute between two parties who claimed land in western Pennsylvania.[100] In the court's charge to the jury, Paterson explored the propriety of the legislature specifically granting title in one party. In the process, he set forth his view of the new state constitutions and the rights they contained. The court discussed the available prohibitions on the actions of a duly elected legislature. According to the court, unlike the unlimited power of Parliament, the United States placed restrictions on the legislative power. The critical key for the court was the written constitution, which did not exist in England where "there is no written constitution, no fundamental law, nothing visible, nothing real, nothing certain, by which a statute can be tested." To the court, the state constitutions were where "certain first principles of fundamental laws are established."[101] The American act of writing down the rules of government into a "constitution" supplied certainty to those preexisting fundamental rights, one of which is the right of property, which the court considered one of the "inalienable rights of man." The court affirmed property as a fundamental right, tellingly stating that the "preservation of property then is a primary object of the social compact, and, by the late constitution of Pennsylvania, was made a fundamental law."[102] As a result, the court held that the Pennsylvania legislature could not divest the party of title to land by legislation and to place title in the opposing party without compensation.[103]

For the *Vanhorne* court, the Pennsylvania constitution was the enunciation of fundamental principle. As a result, the court was required to void the offending property-taking law since it did not comport with the fundamental laws of property contained in its state constitution's Declaration of Rights. However, the court had not yet made the leap to looking solely to the constitution as the lone source of rights, holding that the offending act was unlawful in four respects: it was "inconsistent with the principles of reason, justice, and moral rectitude; it is incompatible with the comfort, peace, and happiness of mankind; it is contrary to the principles of social alliance in every free government; and lastly, it is contrary to both the letter and spirit of the Constitution."[104]

Seven years later, the Virginia courts were faced with the validity of a joint debt where one of the obligors was deceased.[105] In *Elliot's Executor v. Lyell*, three persons jointly agreed to payment of a £600 bond. Four years later, Virginia passed an act specifying that the representatives of a co-obligor of a debt would be jointly and severally liable, meaning they would also be responsible for the entire amount of the debt.[106] This act modified the common law rule that discharged the executors of the estate of a deceased co-obligor upon death.[107] After Virginia's law had passed, one of the co-obligors died. Thus, the question before the court was which law to apply: the common law rule in effect at the time the bond was given, which would release the estate from the debt, or the subsequent 1786 law that would make the estate liable? More important for our purposes, the court was required to determine whether applying the 1768 law would violate any rights held by the parties when they gave the bond. The court held that legislative acts were to be interpreted as operating prospectively only. Otherwise, the subject law would act as an *ex post facto* law if it were criminal in nature. Even if the law did not hold any criminal penalties, it would be contrary to "the principles of natural justice" since it would impair what the parties believed the law required of them at the time the bargain or agreement was struck. The court noted that the U.S. Constitution prohibited the states from passing *ex post facto* laws. That the Constitution was drafted and ratified after the date of the Virginia law in question was immaterial since the Constitution was simply "declaring a principle which always existed."[108]

In 1822, the year that Barron and Craig filed their initial suit against the city, a New York court issued its opinion in *Bradshaw v. Rogers and Magee.* There, a landowner sued the agents of the canal commissioners for trespass after they entered his property and cut down trees to rebuild a portion of a private turnpike road.[109] While the commissioners argued that state law authorized these acts, Chief Justice Ambrose Spencer held them liable because the state law provided for the taking of land only for the construction of the canal, and not to rebuild a road damaged because of the canal, especially a private road.[110] More important, Spencer noted that the act, which allowed the commissioners to take property to rebuild roads interrupted by the canal, disturbingly failed to contain any requirement of compensation for the owner. Such an omission would allow for uncompensated takings in violation of the Fifth Amendment as well as a similar prohibition now contained in the revised New York constitution of 1821.[111] Spencer recognized that the "former related to the powers of the national government, and was intended as a restraint on that government; and the latter is not yet operative," conceding that the Bill of Rights Amendments were drafted to restrain the federal government.[112] Unlike Marshall in his analysis of *Barron,* however, Spencer held this distinction to be irrelevant. The prohibition against taking private property without compensation applied in New York since this principle was declaratory of a fundamental principle of government. Any law violating that rule was void.[113]

In 1831, the Ohio Supreme Court dealt with a very similar matter in *McArthur v. Kelly and Williams.* The court heard an appeal from a property owner seeking to keep the local canal commissioners from digging a watercourse over his property to supply a newly constructed canal.[114] In reviewing the state law that gave the commissioners authority to create these watercourses, the court was guided by two principles. While a government could exercise its eminent domain powers for the greater welfare, it could take property only (1) for a public use and (2) upon a just compensation to the owner, as recognized by the Ohio constitution and the Fifth Amendment. For the court, the obligation to pay for private property taken for a public use is a "fundamental principle of which our constitutions are only declarative, that when the government takes private property for public use, full compensation shall be made to the owner." Citing Vattel, the court declared that "the laws of nations require it."[115]

RIGHTS AS A PRODUCT OF POSITIVE LAW ENACTMENTS

Consistent with the idea of absolute individual ownership of rights was its natural corollary that written documents did not supply the basis for the right, but merely declared their existence, especially in the American colonies. The inclusion of declarations in colonial charters and codes affirmed the existence of the colonists' English rights and liberties, but, as one historian noted, "neither in 1675 nor 1765 would the colonists have believed that such statements created the rights they described."[116] For example, Philadelphia attorney, pamphleteer, and member of the founding generation John Dickinson viewed the rights contained in the colonial charters as "declarations but not gifts of liberties." Channeling natural-law theory, Dickinson argued that the colonists were born with rights founded on larger principles of reason and justice; as a result, written laws only declared and affirmed these rights but did not grant them.[117]

During the early years of the republic, questions of constitutionality more often looked like what we would deem to be political questions. For example, recall the firestorm in Baltimore when the state legislature unilaterally merged two sections of the surrounding county into the city limits. This was a blatant political maneuver by the state—it combined these two pockets of Republican support into like-minded Baltimore while still limiting Baltimore to only two representatives at the general assembly. The city attorney for Baltimore gave his opinion to the mayor in terms of whether the state's actions were constitutional.[118] In the era of the early republic, one thought of constitutions as a type of political settlement among sovereignties rather than as existing to protect individual rights from government overreach. For many, the federal constitution was the evidence of the political arrangement delineating the various rights and boundaries between the states and the federal government. The idea that it protected individual rights was of much less concern.

In some ways, however, the idea of a constitution as the expression of the fundamental principles of government was the first step toward the acceptance of a more positive-law view of rights. Consider the 1803 writings of St. George Tucker, a Virginia lawyer, judge, and law professor.[119] For Tucker, the Constitution was enacted as a compact between sovereign states that, by entering into the agreement, retained their structure and sovereignty.[120] By creating written constitutions that established the form of government and designed limits on those governments, the states set forth declarations of the people's "natural, inherent, and unalienable rights."[121] While Hobbes and Locke described the social contract as an implied agreement entered into when man decided to formally enter civil society, thus giving up certain natural rights in order to live cooperatively, Tucker characterized the Constitution as a written social compact that Americans entered into to create a federal union of states.[122] This was a critical distinction because the Constitution thereby became the evidence of the actual contract made between the people of the United States, as citizens of their respective states, to form a collective government. Further, the distinction did not hinge solely on its written form. Many historians have found that scholars sometimes mistakenly emphasize the act of writing down the Constitution as the essential act in creating the American version of our constitutional system, and Tucker bears this out.[123] The colonists had relied on written documents, specifically letters patent or colonial charters, to enunciate their liberties for generations before charters gave way to constitutions in the Revolutionary era.[124] Similarly, the emphasis on the act of creating written constitutions is misplaced. Much is made of the evolution from the malleable unwritten British constitution, subject to the whim of Parliament, to the fixed American Constitution as the bedrock of fundamental laws. However, historians have noted that much of what was commonly understood to make up the unwritten British constitution—the Bill of Rights, the Magna Carta, and the Petition of Right—was written. The act of writing down the Constitution was not the dispositive change.[125] It was not simply the act of writing down fundamental laws that created this new system. Tucker noted that "there is nothing new or singular in this circumstance, as all national compacts since the invention of letters have probably been reduced to that form."[126] Rather, the unique invention was that this social compact had been entered into at the beginning of a new nation.[127]

The act of creating a written constitution was significant because it marked the birth of this new order and rendered the structure of government and the location of sovereignty plain for all literate persons to read and understand.[128] Thus, Tucker balked at the arguments presented by Federalists that amending the Constitution to add a written bill of rights not only would have been pointless but could, by including limitations on powers the federal government did not possess, also be dangerous.[129] For Tucker, affixing written declarations of rights to the Constitution was important because doing so informed the people of their liberties. "By reducing speculative truths to fundamental laws, every man of the meanest capacity and understanding may learn his own rights, and know when they are violated."[130]

From viewing a constitution as the embodiment of fundamental law that is written down to allow the citizenry to intelligently participate in government, it is only a short step to the counterargument that a constitution alone grants rights. The idea that written constitutions provided the basis for the right in question itself also began to appear in some state courts. In 1824, New York addressed an issue similar to *Goodwin* regarding the applicability of the Eighth Amendment to a state court proceeding. In *Barker v. New York*, the court was presented with a challenge to an 1816 state law that prohibited dueling.[131] The law stated that upon conviction for dueling, a person would be unable to hold any public office.[132] Barker appealed his conviction on the grounds that the Eighth Amendment, in prohibiting cruel and unusual punishment, proscribed the sentence. While not specifically mentioning the *Goodwin* opinion four years earlier, Barker's attorney seemed to try to track former Chief Justice Spencer's logic. For example, Barker's attorney recognized that New York revised its constitution in 1821 and did not include a specific prohibition against cruel and unusual punishment.[133] However, this exclusion was not dispositive—the law in question was against the "spirit" of the new constitution, and the prohibition against cruel and unusual punishment was a "fundamental principle of all free governments" similar to the "rule that the freehold of one man shall not be arbitrarily divested and conferred upon another."[134] The court, however, took the opposite view and methodically set forth the basis for the prohibition against cruel and unusual punishment. The court recognized that the Eighth Amendment prohibited such practice by the federal government, and it further noted that many of the states then amended their respective state constitutions to include the prohibition.[135] The problem for Barker was that New York was not one of those states. The court took a broad view of the powers of the state legislature. It held both that the state constitution gave the court the power to define criminal acts and that the state legislature was the sovereign lawmaking authority, not a body of strict, delegated powers.[136] The court further recognized Barker's argument that certain acts that implicate fundamental rights cannot be regulated or punished by the legislature. However, to determine what acts are deemed indicative of fundamental rights, the court looked again to the constitution itself.

In 1830, the Pennsylvania Supreme Court expressed its view that rights existed as a matter of positive law when it addressed an appeal brought by the owners of a turnpike company.[137] The company had been authorized by the legislature in 1801 to build a road; however, in 1824 the legislature allowed a local municipality to design a town plan and gave them eminent domain powers that encroached on part of the turnpike. Faced with these competing interests, the court held that the original act granting the company the right to build the road was a vested right. In a way that echoed the more dynamic, pro-development view of the common law, the court held that it was "a fundamental principle of all government, that the rights of individuals must yield to the general welfare, and that the only security of the citizen, (and in most cases it is an ample one,) consists in the constitutional provision: 'That no man's property shall be taken or applied to public use, without the consent of his representatives, and without a just compensation being made.'"[138] Citing the words of the Pennsylvania constitution, they allowed damages to the company. This is significant because the court specifically tied individual rights to the terms of the constitution, without discussing or referencing any other natural-law basis, or even mentioning that the constitutional provision was declaratory of any natural or fundamental right. To the court, the right was to be found in the constitution itself.

In his lectures on law given from 1790 to 1791, James Wilson addressed the question of rights. Wilson, a member of the Continental Congress, a framer of the Constitution as a delegate from Pennsylvania, and an original justice of the U.S. Supreme Court, evidenced a view of rights that blended numerous foundations for support.[139] To begin with, when discussing the purpose of government itself, Wilson posited the question of the "principle object" in enacting government: "Was it to acquire new rights by human establishment? Or was it, by a human establishment, to acquire a new security for the possession or the recovery of those rights, to the enjoyment or acquisition of which we were previously entitled by the immediate gift, or unerring law, of our all-wise and all-beneficent Creator?"[140] Wilson argued that the purpose of government was to ensure the latter, to protect those rights that were granted by the divine, combining Lockean concepts of the social compact with early Christian ideas connecting natural rights as emanating from God.[141] For Wilson, government was formed to protect man's preexisting natural rights "to his property, to his character, to liberty, and to safety."[142] Wilson specifically addressed Blackstone's contention that man must give up some of his natural liberties in order to have proper government. Wilson took specific issue with Blackstone's description of the rights of life, liberty, and property as the "'civil liberties' of Englishmen" and especially with Blackstone's conclusion that these natural rights ultimately rested on a human establishment for their existence.[143] He argued that "if this view be a just view of things, then, under civil society, man is not only made *for*, but made *by* the government: he is nothing but what the society frames: he can claim nothing but what the society provides. His natural state and his natural rights are withdrawn altogether from notice."[144]

On the one hand, Wilson espoused a view of rights as natural; for any government to retain legitimacy, it must recognize and protect these preexisting rights. This view was contrary to the concept of rights as particular to Englishmen, a concept that included implicit Blackstonian notions of limitless parliamentary supremacy. However, Wilson clouded this seemingly simple Blackstone/natural rights binary when he discussed the methods by which these natural rights were protected. For example, in discussing the natural right of life, Wilson held that it was partially the common law that protected this natural right. Wilson described a right that found its basis in natural law but grounded its enforcement in the common law, which presented a vision of rights as liberties enjoyed by one's status as an Englishman.[145]

As we have seen, Wilson was not alone in his multilayered analysis of where rights obtained their authority. Indeed, the debates during the founding era evidenced a blend of numerous perceptions regarding this question. Crafted to oppose British colonial policy, these debates revealed that the ideas of where rights originated were subject to numerous interpretations. The era of the early republic continued to locate rights in varied interpretations of the common law, in notions of fundamental principle, or to a lesser extent in the outcomes of positive law. Although many scholars discount as ill-informed the notions of natural law, natural right, fundamental principle, or any other extrasocietal type of right in the Revolutionary era, the fact remains that many in the early republic took those traditions seriously. They continued to consider rights as liberties guaranteed by the common law, as extragovernmental natural or universal freedoms, as enacted by positive law, and in many cases as a blend of these views. As we will see, this variety of interpretations will not last.

4 Trial

> The wharves (for there is no *quai* in Baltimore) are always constructed for the convenience of their owners; because these piers jut out in the water there are, in the direction of the town, marshes dented with wide inlets, while neighboring wharves are just so many breakwaters. All this gives an air of disorder to a place that strict alinement would not only correct but add one charm more.
>
> *Mederic-Louis-Elie Moreau de Saint-Mery (1794)*

The second Baltimore County courthouse was still quite new when Barron and Craig filed their case against the city in 1822. The first courthouse was built at the northern terminus of Calvert Street, which ended at the bluffs overlooking Jones Falls. When the city wanted to extend the street after redirecting Jones Falls, the courthouse found itself in the way. Seizing on an engineering solution that was partly visionary but mostly ridiculous, the original architect persuaded the Maryland General Assembly to allow him to remove twenty feet of soil under the court and replace it with stone arches, essentially creating a court on stilts that residents could pass underneath. While this feat may have impressed tourists, it did not prove a long-term solution. By 1806 the state legislature began planning for a new courthouse.[1] Fittingly, the first courthouse fell victim to the same particular geographic difficulties that plagued early Baltimore and bedeviled Barron and Craig. Its existence in many ways tracked the problems

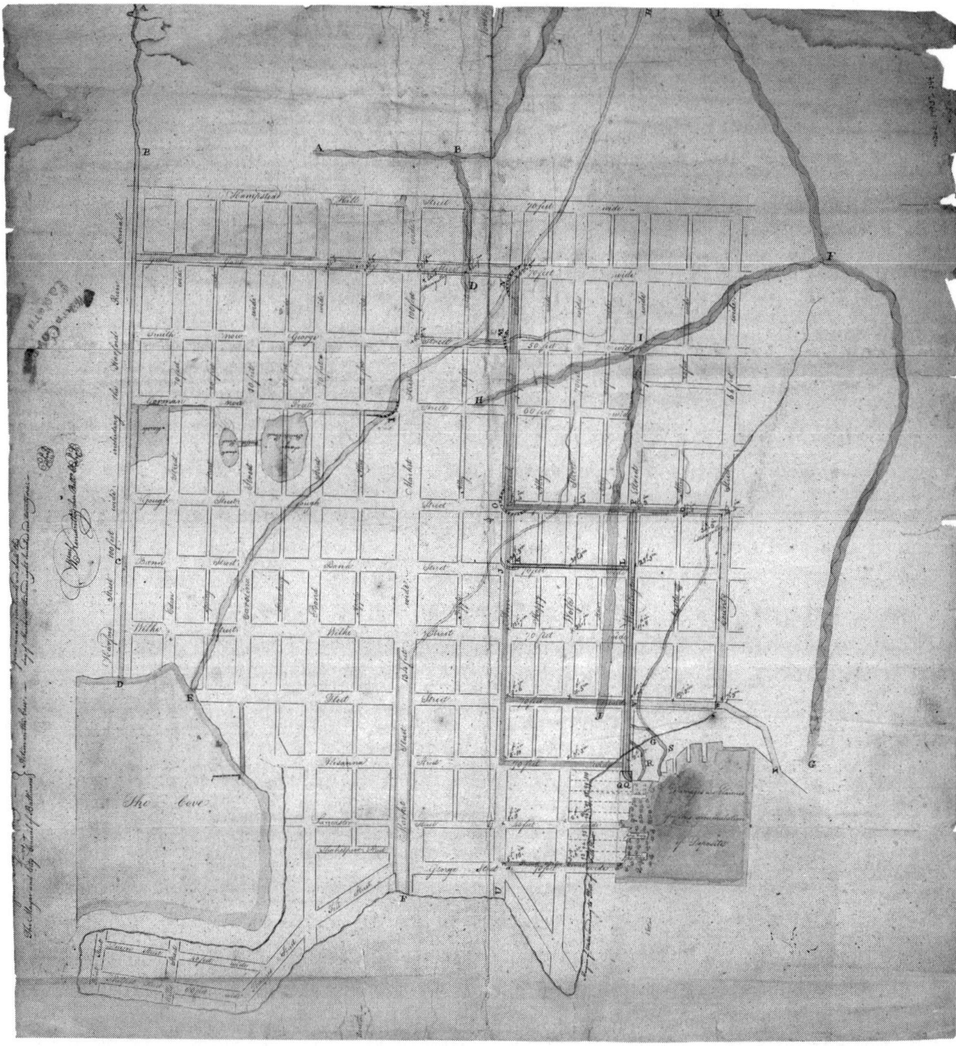

Figure 1. 1826 map of Fell's Point introduced at the trial before the Baltimore County Court. Courtesy of the Maryland State Archives, MSA C2042-168

the city had in trying to deal with exponential growth while butting up against the significant natural obstacles in its way.

Across the street from the new courthouse sat the still-unfinished battle monument commemorating the defense of Baltimore during the War of 1812.[2] The unfinished monument was an appropriate symbol for the state of the city itself. On the one hand, Baltimore was celebrating its place as one of the rising stars of the early republic. Not settled until 1729 nor even formally incorporated as a city until 1796, Baltimore had risen from an insignificant hamlet perched on steep and swampy ground to the third largest American city by the early nineteenth century.[3] The city was creating monuments to its central role in salvaging the nation's honor by repulsing the British attack on the city. On the other hand, the city was still very much a work in progress; it had yet to recover from the postwar aftershocks of the Panic of 1819 as well as the yellow fever outbreak of the same year.[4]

On Thursday, March 21, 1822, Charles Mayer gathered his papers, headed past the incomplete battle monument, and ascended the steps to the Baltimore County Court at the corner of Lexington and Calvert, less than a half mile north of the inner harbor.[5] Once inside, Mayer obtained a subpoena ordering the mayor, John Montgomery, and the city council to appear on the following Monday, March 25, 1822. Unlike modern legal actions, which usually begin with some form of a written complaint, bill of particulars, or statement of claim setting forth all of the facts and causes of action belonging to the party bringing suit, here the procedure was slightly different. Predating the codification of procedural rules, courts still operated largely under common law rules of procedure when it came to the conduct of trials. Thus, the summons issued to the mayor and city council alleged simply that they appear in court to answer to Craig and Barron's plea of "trespass on the case," an umbrella common law cause of action similar to the modern tort of negligence.[6] It sought to recover damages as a consequence of a defendant's wrongful act, where the act was not accompanied by direct force.[7]

The following Monday, Baltimore attorney John Scott appeared before the court on behalf of the city. Scott had only recently been appointed as the attorney for the city by Mayor Montgomery in 1822, but he would continue to represent the city's legal interests in court until 1833, the year the Supreme Court decided *Barron*.[8] Scott demanded that Barron and Craig "declare against them," that is, provide specific facts to support the plea of trespass on the case.[9] While the court agreed, Mayer asked for a continuance. Though the case was initiated in March 1822, it languished in court for years as Mayer repeatedly asked for continuances every six months—September 16, 1822; March 24, 1823; September 15, 1823; March 22, 1824; and September 20, 1824—as a kind of biannual ritual.[10]

On March 28, 1825, Mayer was finally prepared to present his case. This time, however, he was not alone. With him were attorneys David Hoffman and Peter Cruse.[11] They alleged that Barron and Craig owned three lots along with two wharves on the Patapsco River, from which they had the right to collect all profits. They claimed that the city intentionally damaged their property by diverting streams, grading and paving roads, and placing embankments and other dams that caused the water adjacent to the wharves to fill up with sand and dirt.[12] For these actions, Barron and Craig demanded $20,000 in damages.[13] The constitutional principle *Barron* is remembered for today—that the federal Bill of Rights did not apply to the states—was almost completely absent from the trial court proceedings. Mayer, Hoffman, and Cruse kept their theory of the case firmly rooted in common law remedies instead of pursuing a constitutional strategy. If they had chosen the latter approach, they would have had two avenues. First would have been the avenue presented by the Fifth Amendment of the U.S. Constitution:

> No person shall be held to answer for a capital, or otherwise infamous crime, unless on a presentment or indictment of a grand jury, except in cases arising in the land or naval forces, or in the militia, when in actual service in time of war or public danger; nor shall any person be subject for the same offense to be twice put in jeopardy of life or limb; nor shall be compelled in any criminal case to be a witness against himself, nor be deprived of life, liberty, or property, without due process of law; *nor shall private property be taken for public use, without just compensation.*[14]

Bringing a state court claim based on a violation of the Fifth Amendment would not have been the first strategic choice for an attorney in the early nineteenth century. However, a second constitutional avenue would have been found in Article XXI of the Maryland constitution (1776): "That no freeman ought to be taken, or imprisoned, or disseized of his freehold, liberties, or privileges, or outlawed, or exiled, or in any manner destroyed, or deprived of his life, liberty, or property, but by the judgment of his peers, or by the law of the land."[15] The article is similar to Section 39 of the Magna Carta, a bedrock charter of the common law. This section provides that "no freemen shall be taken or imprisoned or disseized or exiled or in any way destroyed, nor will we go upon him nor send upon him, except by the lawful judgment of his peers or by the law of the land."[16] However, these avenues were not initially pursued because no one thought of the dispute as a constitutional struggle. Indeed, as we saw in chapter 3, claims that envisioned rights as constitutionally based were very much in the background in the early republic. Instead, the court served as the arena where competing visions of Baltimore were in competition, and for professional attorneys like Hoffman, Mayer, and Cruse, the rules of the common law provided the most logical remedy.

In many ways the story in the background of the case is not simply one of man versus nature, of early Baltimore trying to make the best of a difficult location. This is also a story of competing factions within Baltimore itself. With most policy decisions there are winners and losers; this case was no different. As the city expanded, dirt paths became roads, and streams turned the formerly green hills of Fell's Point into mud and sludge. In making their decisions about how to manage this growth, the city was forced to consider its priorities. As a prime method of expanding Fell's Point and mitigating negative health consequences, paving roads took on paramount importance for the city. As a municipal corporation, the city of Baltimore had to provide essential services and at the same time find a way to pay for them. To accomplish this, the city relied largely on private entities to carry out these functions.[17] A good example is the duty to provide light for the city. Instead of embarking on the enterprise themselves, by promoting a lottery, taxing the general populace, or taking out loans, the city instead contracted with the Gas Light Company of Baltimore, a private company, to replace the oil lighting by installing gas lines and lamps, as long as they did not disturb the pipes laid by the similarly situated Baltimore Water Company. The mayor was given authority to contract with the company for lighting public areas, while the company could contract with individual owners to light private property.[18]

Similar patterns were followed with other services, including the paving and opening of streets. Paving streets forced the question of who would pay for the improvement: the city or the residents who owned the property adjacent to the road? As we saw from the Pratt Street extension, determining who received the benefit, and thus the expense, was not easy. In addition, the actual paving led to a second issue over who should bear the often-negative consequences of the construction itself. While paving roadways in Fell's Point helped improve the traveling conditions for horses, pedestrians, and carriages, these same smooth surfaces also acted as funnels for redirecting the water that poured through the neighborhood, as Barron and Craig discovered. Before Barron and Craig brought suit for the damage to their wharf, several other aggrieved residents of Fell's Point also sued the city over similar improvements. These cases help show the ways that both the city and other property owners were working through these questions.

A good example of this is *Mayor and City of Council of Baltimore v. Moore and Johnson*. This dispute concerned the authority of the city to pave streets in Fell's Point and to tax the owners of property adjacent to these roads for the construction. When two such owners, Philip Moore and Thomas Johnson, refused to pay the tax assessment, the city filed suit against them for *assumpsit*, a standard common law cause of action that seeks repayment of monies owed.[19] The city, represented at the Maryland Court of Appeals by John Scott and Roger Taney, relied on a mix of state law and municipal ordinances as their authority to tax. First, the city cited the 1796 Maryland state law that incorporated Baltimore as a municipal corporation and gave it general power to "alter and straighten streets, lanes, and alleys" as long as it had the consent of the adjacent property owners. Next, the city introduced a 1797 supplemental act that granted the city power not only to pass all necessary ordinances to pave and maintain streets, but also to tax the property owners in that district if the repairs specifically benefited those residents.[20] Finally, the city placed two 1817 city ordinances into evidence: the first directed the paving of Dulaney Street ("the 1817 Dulaney Paving Ordinance"); and the second ordered the paving of Wilkes, Washington, and County Streets as well as Castle Alley (the "1817 Wilkes Paving Ordinance"), the four street directly north of the wharf.[21] Both of these ordinances sought to redirect all the water that flowed through Fell's Point from its southwestern direction toward the southeast.

After Moore and Johnson won in the trial court, the city appealed the case. Before the Maryland Court of Appeals, Scott and Taney argued that the city was not liable since it acted in accord with these ordinances, a defense the city would raise again in defending the suit by Barron and Craig. However, the court ruled otherwise. The court strictly construed the 1817 paving ordinances by viewing their intent as expressed in their respective preambles. The 1817 Dulaney Paving Ordinance preamble stated the importance of maintaining Dulaney Street, which often served as an entrance to the city. Its poor condition endangered travelers and carriages.[22] The 1817 Wilkes Paving Ordinance likewise mentioned that there had been significant damage to many persons as well as to the navigation of the harbor by virtue of the water pouring into it where it met the southern terminus of Washington Street, which incidentally was directly north of Barron and Craig's wharf. The paving was thus intended to divert some of the water in other directions, hopefully mitigating some of the damage.[23] The court held that taxing Moore and Johnson as the owners of parcels adjacent to the repairs was unauthorized because the repairs did not provide them a special benefit, but instead provided a general benefit for the entire city.[24]

John Barron was likewise assessed with taxes to pay for the same paving scheme as Moore and Johnson. He also contested this assessment on his property located at the southeast corner of Washington and Fleet Streets, one block north of the wharf. As it had done against Moore and Johnson, the city brought a common law claim for *assumpsit* against Barron. The city relied again on the 1796 Incorporation Act, the 1797 Supplemental Act, and the 1817 Wilkes Paving Ordinance. The city also introduced an 1807 ordinance that created the position of city commissioners and described their powers ("1807 City Commissioner Ordinance").[25] This ordinance appointed a committee of three city commissioners—one from east of Jones Falls and two from the west to achieve balance—to carry out the wishes of the city council as expressed in its ordinances. The commissioners were given extensive authority to carry out the directives of the city council ordinances with respect to maintaining the streets, bridges, and sewers of the city.[26] The ordinance gave the commissioners the power to levy tax warrants against the adjacent property owners for payment of the improvement.[27] Although the city filed the case in March 1818, multiple continuances kept it at bay until the county court's March 1822 term, which incidentally was when Barron and Craig filed suit against the city for damages to the wharf.[28] Like Moore and Johnson, Barron was held not responsible for the tax assessment by the trial court. While the city filed a bill of exceptions that formed the record for an appeal, there is no evidence that one took place.[29] It is likely that the Moore and Johnson's appeal, which was for significantly more money, dissuaded the city from pursuing Barron further.

Finally, immediately to the south of Barron and Craig's wharf William and John Price and Hezekiah Waters, respectively, owned two separate wharves. Unlike Moore and Johnson's or Barron's disputes, Price and Waters were not contesting a paving tax assessment but instead were concerned about the city's plan to pave the road that ran perpendicular from their wharf. On June 19, 1821, they collectively filed suit against Mayor John Montgomery and the city commissioners—Joseph Owens, Samuel Boyd, and Henry Stouffer—to enjoin the city from paving Wolfe Street.[30] Price and Waters alleged that the city commissioners were paving the road in a manner that was not in keeping with its original boundaries. While the city argued that it was straightening the road, Price and Waters contended that the city was in fact taking part of their property without compensating them. However, although Price and Waters sought an injunction to stop the city from proceeding, they did not make any constitutional arguments, even though there was an actual physical taking of property at stake. Price and Waters were successful in obtaining two separate injunctions from the trial court, though the ultimate disposition is unclear.

All of these suits between the city and the merchants of Fell's Point show a struggle over the costs of development of an expanding city. Streets needed paving both to meet the growing needs of the expanding population as well as to mitigate dangers to the health of the city. But determining who would shoulder this responsibility was an issue, like other problems inherent in development, that had to be resolved. At its base, Barron and Craig's suit was the same as any of these other cases before the Baltimore County Court in the 1820s. These cases also reflect a routine use of common law remedies and defenses in the courts to review the city's development plans, thus making the decision to bring suit by Barron and Craig a relatively routine matter with an uncluttered legal path to victory, a path that few thought would end up in the constitutional law textbooks of American law students for generations to come.

TRIAL

At the close of Barron and Craig's presentation, the court ordered the city to answer the charges. And again, the litany of continuances resumed. Although the court required the city to present their answer on September 19, 1825, the city sought and received extensions until March 27, 1826, and then again until September 18, 1826. The answer was finally ready for the hearing on March 26, 1827, close to five years after the case was filed.[31] At this point, with both sides perhaps recognizing the gravity of the case, they each brought on additional attorneys for assistance. While Barron and Craig's side had lost Peter Cruse, they added Upton S. Heath and Hugh Evans to the case to assist Mayer and Hoffman. Not to be outdone, the city added to its defense team future Supreme Court Chief Justice Roger B. Taney, John Marshall's successor.[32] In the light of the three lawsuits brought against the city by Barron and Craig, Dawson, and Curtis, respectively, the city council had previously authorized the city to hire an additional attorney to lighten the burden on John Scott.[33]

The city chose well. In 1823, Roger Taney relocated his home and law practice from Frederick, Maryland, to Baltimore.[34] He quickly integrated himself successfully into the local legal community. Within four years of his arrival, Taney was named Maryland Attorney General and held the position throughout the majority of the *Barron* litigation. It appears the appointment caused Taney little conflict since the position resembled more an honorary office at the time. While the pay was low, the position was previously held by lawyers of great esteem, including Luther Martin and William Pinkney.[35] Indeed, Taney continued to represent the city all the way to the conclusion of the *Barron* case in the U.S. Supreme Court in February 1833, well after he had been appointed attorney general of the United States in June 1831.[36] In addition to his many appearances before the Court in his capacity as attorney general, Taney appeared as a private attorney for three additional cases during the Court's 1833 term.[37]

Both sides agreed to an extension to continue the argument, first for six months to September 17, 1827, and again for another six months to March 24, 1828.[38] By the time of this hearing, the delays took their toll; Craig passed away sometime in early 1828.[39] By that time, though, Barron and Craig were parties to the case in name only. Luke Tiernan had taken over the case and long ago claimed any possible recovery. Indeed, Tiernan had been in control the whole time since the suit against the city was filed just over one month after he purchased the wharf at the court-ordered auction.

Economically devastated in their losing battle to maintain the wharf, Craig and Barron were in no position to sustain extended litigation against the city. For example, on November 15, 1822, the year Craig and Barron sued the city, Barron placed a newspaper advertisement for his new rope store. Barron announced that he had just received a quantity of Russian hemp, and he would take orders for cordage under the supervision of a Mr. Chapman. Making rope as a craftsman under the supervision of another is a long way from Barron's position as the co-owner of a successful wharf and strongly suggests that he was forced to return to a trade he likely practiced before his fleeting success.[40] In addition, in 1824 Barron moved north from his residence near the wharf at 10 George Street to a row of apartments on Caroline Street.[41] Meanwhile, Craig fared little better than his former partner and continued to rely on Tiernan for financial support until Craig's death on the eve of trial.[42]

It is obvious that Tiernan, given his financial interest in Barron and Craig's recovery of damages against the city, was driving the litigation. He was properly secured and would recover any potential damages granted in the case. With Tiernan likely financing the litigation, it is reasonable to conclude that he selected the attorneys as well. To take on the city, Tiernan hired the best. Attorneys David Hoffman, Peter H. Cruse, Upton S. Heath, Hugh D. Evans, and Charles F. Mayer all appeared on behalf of Barron and Craig at various points in the case and represented the elite of the Baltimore bar.[43] While all of the attorneys were well-regarded members of the Baltimore legal community, David Hoffman was a national legal figure. Not simply a practitioner who had appeared before the U.S. Supreme Court, Hoffman was also famous as a legal educator, unusual in the age of the apprenticeship. In 1813, Hoffman was named as the first law professor for the new law school of the University of Maryland, itself founded only one year earlier.[44] In 1822, when the death of local judge Walter Dorsey caused the closing of Dorsey's private law institute, Hoffman's school finally commenced at long last.[45] His lectures relied on a more formal course of study rather than the attorney/apprentice model that characterized most legal education and culminated in an apprenticeship period and the taking of an oath before a local judge.[46]

In Maryland, colonial legislation required simply the approval of the justices of the Maryland courts, but over time an uneven pattern of admission had evolved in each county.[47] In 1831, the legislature standardized the requirements. A candidate who was at least twenty-one years old and a "free white male citizen" could practice law after he had completed two years of study and passed an examination of his character and competency before a judge.[48] Of course, while the two years of apprentice legal study gives the process a feeling of structure, the reality was much more uneven. As Lawrence Friedman has more aptly described legal apprenticeships in this era, "For a fee, the lawyer-to-be hung around an office, read Blackstone and Coke and a miscellany of other books, and copied legal documents."[49] In contrast, Hoffman was a proponent of the study of law as a natural science that required a more expansive and vigorous study than a law-office apprenticeship would normally provide.[50]

Hoffman published his most famous work, *A Course of Legal Study*, in 1817. Seeking to elevate the capabilities of American lawyers, Hoffman's text demonstrated that candidates must rigorously engage the great works of literature, philosophy, and political theory to arrive at certain universal truths that all just legal systems would one day share.[51] This work is credited as the first outline of law in the United States and was praised by Supreme Court Justice Joseph Story, who agreed with Hoffman's perception of law as a science that deserved to be taught in the same university format as other disciplines.[52] For Hoffman, "To be great in the law, therefore, it is important that we should be great in every virtue; skilled in many, and somewhat improved in most of the departments of knowledge..."[53] While at times his work, and more often his personality, was criticized for its impenetrable and arrogant qualities, Hoffman was nonetheless recognized as a trailblazing legal educator and attorney.[54] As we will see, Hoffman's appreciation of law as emerging from a classical liberal education informed his legal arguments regarding the sources of Barron and Craig's property rights, most notably during the appellate trial.[55]

Given the composition of the lawyers assembled to handle the case, Hoffman was most certainly involved in the selection of the other attorneys. Some of Hoffman's choices for co-counsel are fairly obvious; for example, Peter Hoffman Cruse was his nephew.[56] In addition to Cruse, Hoffman was joined by Upton S. Heath and Hugh Davey Evans. Heath was later appointed by President Martin Van Buren to serve as a judge at the federal district court level, a position he held for fifteen years. Evans was a similarly well-regarded member of the bar who later served as Baltimore city counselor.[57] Rounding out the legal team was Charles Mayer, a highly regarded Baltimore attorney who practiced for forty years in Baltimore and served one term as a Maryland state senator.[58] More so than any of the other attorneys, Mayer did the most work on the case, from the initial filing in 1822 to the final argument before the Supreme Court in 1833.

BARRON AND CRAIG'S CASE

After years of delay, the court finally ordered the sheriff to empanel a jury. With each side given four juror challenges, a final jury of twelve men prepared to hear Barron's case.[59] The trial began on Monday, March 24, 1828, before Chief Judge Stevenson Archer and Associate Judge Charles Hanson.[60] The third judge, Thomas Kell, withdrew at the start of the trial.[61] Though the court's records simply noted that Judge Kell withdrew at the start of the trial, he may have done so because of his extensive background in local and state government.[62]

Barron's attorneys began by introducing a diagram (Figure 1; Map 1 is a more legible reproduction) of Fell's Point that showed the various locations where the water flowing throughout the district was gradually redirected and ultimately funneled into the Patapsco directly north of Barron and Craig's wharf.[63] They then introduced several city ordinances to establish a causal chain between the actions of the city and the damage to the wharf, many of which were also the subject of the disputes between the city and Moore and Johnson, Barron, and Price and Waters. For example, they introduced the 1807 City Commissioner Ordinance as well as an 1813 ordinance that provided for the appointment of port wardens.[64] They then presented several more ordinances and resolutions that led to the damages, including the 1817 Dulaney Paving Ordinance and Wilkes Paving Ordinances, which together demonstrated the city's gradual design to divert the waterways entirely, as well as the 1821 ordinance that paved the remaining streets north of the wharf. Finally, they presented the obligatory evidence showing that Craig and Barron were the legal owners of the wharf property by entering into evidence the deed from Frederick Mackubin.[65]

After introducing these statutes and ordinances into evidence, Barron's attorneys began their testimony, calling nine witnesses. They led with Ephraim Smith, a longtime resident of Fell's Point and a former street superintendent.[66] Smith asserted that the drainage situation in Fell's Point went back decades. He testified that the water that flowed through Fell's Point originated primarily from two sources: Gile's Old Spring and the area between Hampstead and Loudenslager's Hills. Since these were both north of Fell's Point, the downward elevation created a drainage situation where a stream flowed directly through the neighborhood, ran southwest across Dulaney Street (later known as Baltimore Street), and emptied into the harbor at location "E" of map 1. Smith testified that in 1809, the city council attempted to address this stream that cut directly through Fell's Point. They decided to divert the water at Pratt Street to an unimproved lot bounded by Gough Street to the south, Pratt Street to the North, Caroline Street to the west, and Bond Street to the east. Residents called the resulting creation the "Brick Pond." Smith recalled that the water flowed through a "deep gully or ravine" across his neighbor's vacant lot and directly in front of his door.[67]

After the war, when the Brick Pond was nearly overflowing, the city paved Pratt Street in Fell's Point. While this largely kept the water from collecting in the Brick Pond, the Pratt Street improvements simply created another headache. Now the water that used to collect in the Brick Pond was redirected southward and began to cascade down Market Street, a large thoroughfare, and into the harbor, noted in map 1 as location"F."[68] Shortly thereafter, in 1815 the city dammed Ann and Dulaney Streets at location "N," which diverted the water from Market Street and caused it to flow into the harbor south along Ann Street at location "U." In 1822, the dam at Ann and Gough Streets was put up (noted as location "O"), which redirected the water down Washington Street.[69] Smith testified that

Facing page: Map 1. Fell's Point, Baltimore. The letters are the same ones used in the exhibit (Figure 1) introduced during Barron and Craig's trial in Baltimore County Court and correspond to significant locations in the city's many attempts to redirect the water pouring across the district. Map drawn by Will Fontanez based on the *Barron* trial exhibit (Figure 1) and a series of maps held at the Maryland State Archives and reprinted in the Maryland State Archives, *Atlas of Historical Maps of Maryland, 1608–1908*, edited by Edward C. Papenfuse and Joseph M. Coale III (Baltimore: Johns Hopkins Press, 2003), 165–67.

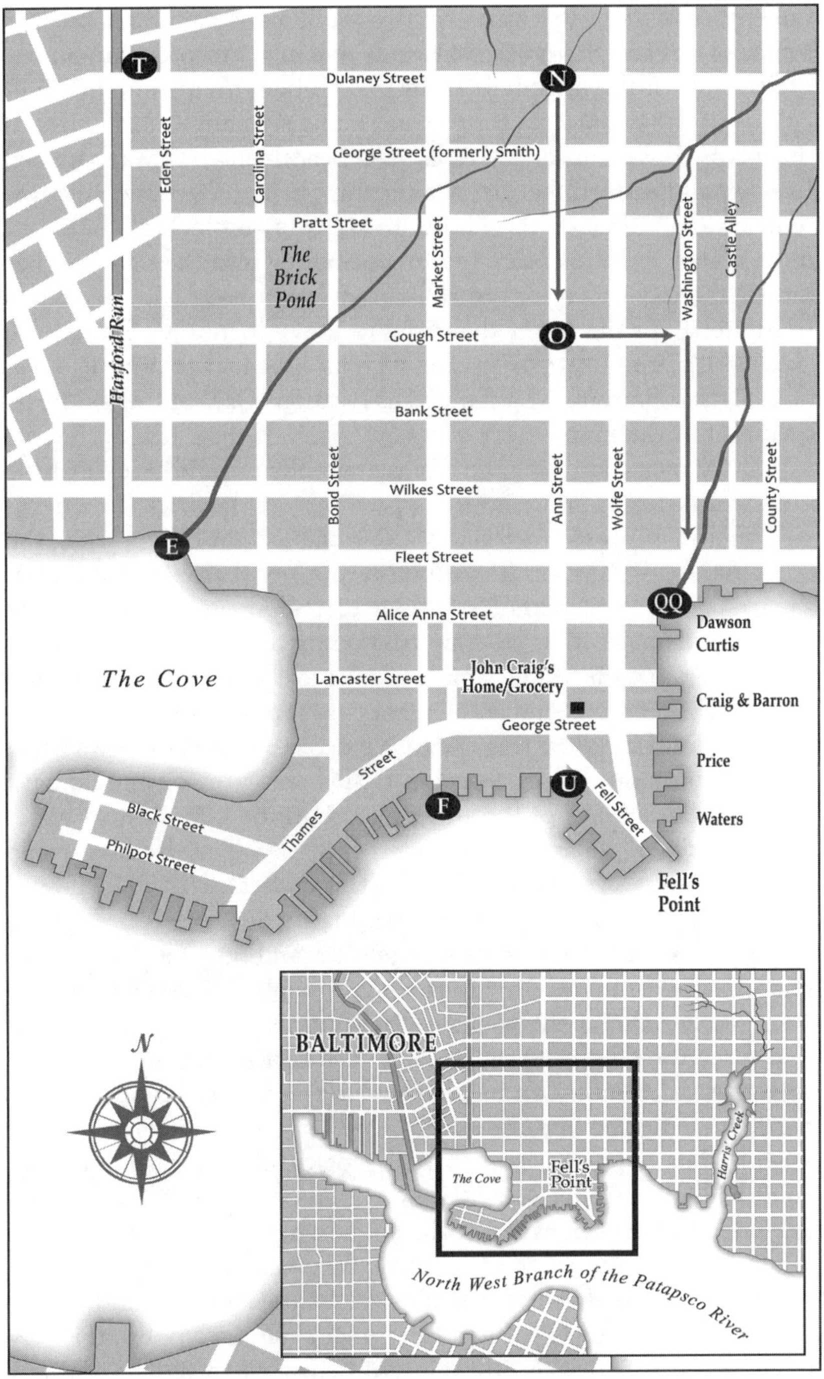
Dulaney Street
George Street (formerly Smith)
Pratt Street
Eden Street
Carolina Street
Harford Run
The Brick Pond
Market Street
Washington Street
Castle Alley
Gough Street
Bank Street
Bond Street
Wilkes Street
Ann Street
Wolfe Street
County Street
Fleet Street
Alice Anna Street
Lancaster Street
John Craig's Home/Grocery
George Street
The Cove
Thames Street
Black Street
Philpot Street
Fell Street
Dawson
Curtis
Craig & Barron
Price
Waters
Fell's Point
T
N
O
E
QQ
U
F
N
BALTIMORE
The Cove
Fell's Point
Harris Creek
North West Branch of the Patapsco River

the city, to redirect the water southward along Washington, created a bank of dirt and gravel at least twenty feet high. According to Smith, the run-off of the sediment from this embankment was the chief culprit of the damage to Barron and Craig's wharf. Smith believed that before this diversion in 1822, water near their wharf was between twelve and fourteen feet deep; after this change, the same area was "entirely dry."[70] Finally, the various road-paving projects also allowed more water, and thus more sediment, to flow into the harbor.[71] For Smith, the city's plan for the Fell's Point water issue was ultimately to funnel all of the water that used to flow separately through the entire Fell's Point district and channel it into the harbor directly north of Craig and Barron's wharf, noted as location "QQ" in the southeast quadrant of the map.[72]

Thus, since addressing the drainage problem would certainly have been welcomed by Smith given his proximity to the Brick Pond debacle, much of his testimony did not so much center on opposing the city's actions. Rather, Smith emphasized a key theme of the case at the trial court level, namely, that Barron and Craig suffered unique or special damages that were not shared by the rest of the community. To support this claim, Smith addressed the second dam erected at the intersection of Ann and Dulaney (at location "N"). In his opinion, instead of building this expensive dam to redirect the water all the way south down Ann Street into the harbor, the city could have simply regraded part of the street and continued the flow of water westward down Dulaney at much less expense.[73] This decision would have led to two significant results. First, as the water naturally flowed in a southwesterly direction, redirecting its flow westward would more or less continue it in its natural flow and prove a much easier solution than building numerous embankments across Fell's Point to completely redirect the water to the southeast.[74] Second, it would also force the stream to drain into Harford Run (at location "T"), which carried water from a separate source located much farther north and emptied into the harbor west of Fell's Point, closer to the inner harbor.[75] For Smith, this was the logical choice given that Fell's Point had begun to overtake the inner harbor as a desirable location for wharf services because of the shallowness of the inner harbor. Smith noted that the city was trying to fill up and create more land at the western cove of Fell's Point at its great expense, while at the same time it was diverting to the east water that could accomplish this very purpose. Further, for Smith, the sediment that would accompany the water would be of less concern since the western cove was much larger and could more easily handle the deposit.[76]

Following Smith, surveyor Jehu Boulden took the stand. Boulden was a well-regarded and experienced practitioner who had been actively mapping Baltimore since the mid-1790s.[77] Instead of the westerly route proposed by Smith, Boulden testified that the city could have redirected over two-thirds of the water farther east to Harris's Creek, located on the eastern border of Fell's Point.[78] Boulden testified that the city even hired him to determine the feasibility of the Harris's Creek route, which he estimated at $10,000, but that the city never began the project. Instead, he confirmed Smith's testimony that the city went ahead and built dams to artificially redirect all the water toward the southeast to empty into the harbor directly north of the wharf.[79]

The next witness, Colonel Thomas Shepard, a former member of a committee empaneled by the city to study the drainage problem, testified that the committee recommended the waters flowing down the streets could easily be redirected to their natural streams, which deposited in the western part of the harbor, a solution similar to what Ephraim Smith proposed. Shepard further testified that it "was a matter of great astonishment to him and others" that the city did not do so but instead dug ditches and further dammed the streets, actions that "produced all the mischief." Shepard additionally commented on the ineptitude of the city's costly plan to fill up the western part of the harbor, which apparently was in need of sediment and debris.[80]

William Barker testified next. He lived near the wharf for thirty-two years and was one of Barron's neighbors. Barker told the jury that before the current alterations of the drainage pattern in the eastern cove of Fell's Point, there had not been any drainage issues. Barker advised that the hills were covered with grass and the water in the eastern cove was "very deep, by far the best in the city."[81] Barker noted that, for example, in 1809, a ship could easily dock at William Dawson's wharf since it had twelve feet of water. Barron and Craig's wharf, which lay directly to the south of Dawson's, was even better since it measured nineteen to twenty feet and routinely unloaded ships upwards of 450 tons. Barker noted that at the time of his testimony Dawson's wharf was completely dry land. Further, Barron and Craig's wharf was not much better given the deposit of sediment.[82]

Following Barker's testimony, James Beacham was offered as the fifth witness. Like Barker, Beacham testified to the depth of the water surrounding the wharf. Beacham was in a good position to know as he had rented Barron and Craig's wharf, excluding the piers, since 1820, and the entire wharf since 1825.[83] In 1816, it measured at a depth of at least seventeen feet, while by 1826 it had dropped to fourteen feet.[84] The problem, according to Beacham, was that while there was still a good amount of water surrounding Barron's wharf, it was useless because a sandbar blocked access to it. Beacham testified that in June 1826, he tried to launch a frigate from the wharf but had to hire a mud machine from the city to clear a channel first. Worse, this channel had filled up with approximately five feet of sediment per year since then.

Beacham's testimony gives us insight on how Barron and Craig dealt with the loss of the wharf. Beacham testified that after they had suffered the sediment damage, Barron and Craig rented another wharf. They spent about $4,000 in 1824 and 1825 converting this second wharf to one that would focus on maintenance and repair instead of loading and unloading.[85] Beacham estimated Barron and Craig's original wharf, purchased in 1815 for $25,000, as a "very great bargain," but noted that it was currently worth no more than $10,000 or $12,000.[86] Beacham's testimony also helps Barron and Craig prove that their damages were special, a proof required to overcome the city's public-nuisance defense. In keeping with the theme of the case, Beacham helped show that it was specifically Barron and Craig that suffered in order to keep the streets of Fell's Point dry. His testimony also speaks to the inconsistent message the city was sending. On the one hand, the city was desperately trying to keep the harbor clear for maritime navigation, a problem it had faced since its founding. Indeed, before Baltimore was even incorporated as a separate municipality, the state of Maryland created a five member board of wardens in 1783 for the upkeep of Baltimore Harbor.[87] On the other hand, the city was exacerbating this same problem when it addressed the Fell's Point drainage situation.

Following Beacham came Hezekiah Waters, who owned the wharf directly to the south of Barron and Craig's wharf. Like Beacham, Waters attested to the value of Barron and Craig's wharf, stating that it "was always considered the best and most valuable water lot in the city" until the damage. He estimated the water depth at their wharf to be in excess of twenty feet.[88] Describing the city's actions as "ruinous work" that was "done against our remonstrances," Waters was more direct than the other witnesses. He argued that Barron and Craig's wharf had been rendered valueless. While the wharf could service small ships, none came, and large ships could not reach the wharf since the sediment created an artificial channel and sandbar that blocked access.[89] The next witness, Colonel Thomas Tenant, similarly attested to damages, stating that if the wharf had "good water," it might sell for $26,000. But, given its present circumstances, it might bring only $18,000 or $20,000. Perhaps sensing that this valuation was still too high, Tenant quickly corrected himself by adding, "It is difficult, however, to say; I may have overrated the plaintiff's property at this day, at $18,000, for if the deposites [*sic*] continue, the property must become wholly worthless, as wharf property, for it fills up rapidly."[90]

William Price also confirmed that the water near the wharf was twenty feet deep at one time, capable of loading and unloading any size vessel, but that now only small ships were able to reach the wharf because of the sandbar.[91] This was even more problematic because small ships did not sail to the eastern cove of Fell's Point, and large ships could not. As the owner of a wharf directly south of Barron and Craig's, Price was quite aware of the problems in the eastern cove. He established that during the prewar embargo, his wharf received approximately $14,000 per year in wharfage fees alone, but he insisted that Barron and Craig's wharf could not seek to ever get that amount since it was "wholly forsaken" other than for maintenance on small crafts or for shipbuilding.[92] Witness Jacob Dunham confirmed this decline, stating that roughly nine or ten years prior, the *Franklin*, a ship that drew approximately seventeen feet of water, docked at Barron and Craig's wharf, as did many others. In contrast, no large ships had been present at their wharf for several years.[93]

Before finishing their case, Barron's attorneys brought back their first witness, Ephraim Smith. Smith again criticized the city not so much for addressing the drainage problem as for their clumsy way of doing so. Living in Fell's Point for forty years, he told the court that if the drainage plan would have been slightly altered to turn the stream into Harford Run and into the western cove, as it more or less naturally flowed, Fell's Point would not have suffered any damage. Further, after Pratt Street was paved, which stopped the water from flowing into the Brick Pond, the drainage problem was more or less solved. At that time, according to Smith, the Pratt Street paving caused the water to flow in four separate directions, thus keeping the water flow from becoming too great on any one street and ensuring that the harbor did not fill up in any one location. But a subsequent street project turned the water down Ann Street north of Barron and Craig's wharf. Smith believed this change affected the health of the people in Fell's Point, especially the yellow fever epidemic of 1819; the court reporter made sure to note that this point was contested as simply Smith's opinion.[94]

With Smith's testimony, Mayer and Hoffman rested their case. They were able to enter into evidence the city ordinances that explicitly laid out the gradual redirection of the water to enter the harbor directly north of the clients' wharf. This was not the difficult part. No one, including the city, ever argued that the water was not directed in this way. Rather, most of the witness testimony focused on anticipating the city's defenses. Mayer and Hoffman needed to show that the damages suffered were unique to their clients. Without this, the city's argument that it was abating a nuisance by correcting the drainage problem could prevail.

BALTIMORE'S PRESENTATION

After sitting through nine witnesses, each describing an incompetent or vindictive city government that targeted and destroyed the lives of two local merchants, John Scott and Roger Taney finally got the chance to respond. Whereas Mayer and Hoffman led the court through a litany of offenses their clients had suffered at the hands of the city, Scott and Taney's response was mostly premised on reminding the court of the finer points of agency and nuisance law. They did not deny that the city's actions damaged Barron and Craig's wharf. Instead, they relied generally on two legal points. First, they claimed that because the paving was done without malice, in accord with the enabling ordinances, and within the scope of their authority as public agents, the mayor and city council were not responsible for the damages.[95] Second, they characterized the city's actions as an attempt to abate a nuisance. This is significant because abatement of a nuisance generally does not allow for a private right of action, as opposed to an impairment of private property, which would. According to nuisance law, Barron and Craig could not recover damages as a result of the paving projects if the court viewed the city's actions as remedying a public, rather than a private, nuisance.[96]

The general legal scheme under which the city operated requires us to distinguish between types of governmental actions that affect private property. To a great extent, language is key. For example, there is a world of difference between calling an impairment of private property a "taking" versus an "abatement of a nuisance." If it is considered a taking, the law considers it to fall under the rubric of eminent domain; since the government has to allege the necessity of the taking and show that the property is being taken for a public purpose, the presumption in such cases is more in favor of the property owner. Conversely, if the impairment is conceived of as an abatement of a nuisance, the act falls under the inherent police power attributable to the government. In this case, the property owner must show that his damages were unique from the public and that the government acted in excess of the law under which it proceeded. Since a taking usually will require compensation, whereas an abatement of nuisance usually will not, determining what makes an impairment of property a taking versus an abatement of a nuisance becomes the key issue.[97] If the damage to their wharf was classified as an attempt by Baltimore to address a nuisance, Barron and Craig could not recover damages unless they could show that they were uniquely damaged. Scott and Taney argued that Barron and Craig's damages were common to the rest of the public. Hoffman and Mayer knew they had to prove that Barron and Craig suffered unique damage; this helps explain their heavy reliance on witnesses that testified about Barron and Craig's losses. Further, even if Barron and Craig could show special damages, Baltimore might escape liability if the city could show that it did not exceed its legislative authority or carry out that authority wantonly or oppressively, as Scott and Taney also argued.

To carry out this defense, they began by citing legislation from the state of Maryland directing and empowering it to take these steps. They also argued that all remedial measures complained of by Barron were done in compliance with those laws.[98] The city then called six witnesses, mostly made up of former city commissioners and port wardens. Eager to justify their actions, the city's witnesses testified that following the original paving of Pratt Street in 1813, which diverted water away from Brick Pond and down Market Street, the city had to take some action for the "general interests and prosperity of the city."[99] The city's lawyers began with former city commissioner Henry Stouffer.

In Baltimore, the elected officials of city government were the mayor and the city council. City commissioners were employees of the city and were responsible for carrying out the decisions made by the city council. To that end, commissioners entertained petitions from the public seeking a number of actions: settling boundary disputes, wanting appointment to minor city posts, and requesting the commissioners take care of nuisances like the horses and wagons clogging the markets. The act of paving streets was one of their more common tasks. Paving was initiated sometimes by the city via ordinance, as was the case in *Barron*, but more often it was undertaken when property owners collectively petitioned the commissioners.[100] If approved by the city, the commissioners were then responsible for finding someone to perform the actual paving. The commissioners would entertain offers from those seeking to do the work and would sign contracts with the successful bidder.[101] The commissioners would also keep track of which property owners did not contribute their payment to the paving of the road, the idea being that those who would benefit most directly from the improvement, namely, the adjacent property owners, should bear most of the responsibility for payment.[102] Thus, while Stouffer and his colleagues were not responsible for the decisions that caused the damage to the wharf, they were in charge of the actual execution of the drainage plans.[103]

Stouffer testified that his concern was with the stream that cut through Fell's Point from the north and emptied into the western cove at location "E." Stouffer admitted that previous city council members decided to lower Dulaney Street as it ran westward toward Harford Run; however, Stouffer felt that taking the runoff ultimately into the western cove was unwise as it would have filled up that part of the cove and affected the navigable channels between Baltimore and Fell's Point. As a result, the city council decided to redirect all the water eastward. To accomplish this express purpose, in 1813 the city council authorized the paving of Pratt Street, which sent the water south down Market Street. When this proved unsatisfactory, the city in 1815 began to divert the water south down Ann Street, east to Bank Street, and south again down Washington Street, from which it would empty into the eastern cove just north of Barron and Craig's wharf, at location "QQ."[104] Stouffer's testimony did not differ factually from the evidence given by Barron and Craig's witnesses about the steps taken to turn the water toward the east. However, Scott and Taney intended to make their point when Stouffer addressed the testimony of Barron and Craig's witness Jehu Boulden. Recall that Boulden felt that instead of redirecting the water west toward Harford Run and into the inner harbor, the city should have simply redirected it much farther east into Harris's Creek. Stouffer admitted that although such a route toward Harris's Creek would not be impossible, it would have been impracticable, reminding the court that it was over a half mile to the creek. Stouffer revealed that the city had tried to take measures to relieve the damage that diversion was having on Barron and Craig's wharf. They had cut a small channel to divert some of the water that was pouring down Washington Street to enter the eastern cove.[105] Stouffer never denied that the rerouting of the stream would carry large amounts of dirt, gravel, and other sediment into the harbor; indeed he admitted as much. He also admitted that the water naturally flowed westward. Nonetheless, in his opinion, it would be less damaging for the city if the water was redirected eastward and poured out largely at one spot, as a westward location would have "injured the navigation" in the inner harbor.[106]

Stouffer's former colleague, city commissioner Nathaniel Hynson, agreed that directing the water east toward Barron and Craig's wharf instead of west toward Baltimore was the preferable course of action. Hynson indicated that the final decisions on where to divert the water were the result of a political battle between factions of residents. For example, Hynson testified that the "town interest" wanted to divert the water toward the east, whereas the "Point interest" wanted it to go west, with the city commissioners and port wardens finally deciding on an easterly direction because the westerly direction faced a more uphill grade.[107] Indeed, this battle seems to mirror much of the same decades-long tension between residents of Baltimore and Fell's Point. For example, attempts to incorporate Baltimore as a city were stymied by Fell's Point residents who feared that they would be forced to pay to dredge the inner harbor.[108] The act of incorporation for the city of Baltimore specifically included a provision excepting residents of Fell's Point from paying any direct or indirect tax on preserving the navigation of the inner harbor.[109]

The next witness, former port warden William McDonald, echoed Hynson's sentiment about redirecting the water away from the western cove. McDonald confirmed that the navigability of the harbor was the primary goal for all concerned.[110] Given the continuous battle to keep the inner harbor clear of sediment and to maintain a sufficient depth, this claim seems reasonable, especially since McDonald's job as port warden included such a charge. In fact, Fell's Point was attractive for development because it was roughly one mile east of the inner harbor and had access to much deeper water. These tensions between

Baltimore and Fell's Point were apparent in the decisions to redirect the water, as the witnesses collectively described the city sacrificing the depth in the eastern cove of Fell's Point to preserve the depth for Baltimore's inner harbor.

After the testimony of the former city commissioners, the city brought in several local residents who agreed with the city that the drainage should have gone east. Again, all these witnesses spoke to the underlying tensions over exactly who should pay to fix the drainage problem in Fell's Point. Longtime resident Frederick Schaeffer agreed that in turning the water to the east, "the city did the best that could be done for the town."[111] David Williamson added that the idea of redirecting the water west into Harford Run would have damaged the inner harbor since it would have added to the sediment already flowing into it from Jones Falls.[112] John Hillen was more circumspect, noting that the decision over which way to turn the water was simply one of opinion, but in his view the direction the city chose was in the general interest.[113]

Before finishing their presentation, the city brought back the port warden William McDonald, who alluded to another problem with Barron and Craig's case. As port warden, it was part of McDonald's duties to keep the harbor clear of obstructions. As McDonald testified, one of the main obstacles to this was the city's steep topography, which washed sediment into the harbor from all the surrounding areas. The city did not simply sit idly and watch this occur, however. McDonald testified to the city's use of the mud machine in every part of the harbor to battle the rising harbor floor. McDonald noted that while the city used the mud machine to clear out around the public wharves, private wharf owners were expected to incur this expense personally, a not too lightly veiled shot at Barron and Craig.[114]

With this, the city rested its case. Scott and Taney sought to have Judge Archer instruct the jury on four points: first, the city acted as mere public agents in the discharge of a duty required of them by law; second, because the city was a corporation comprised of Baltimore residents, it was not liable for damages resulting from acts done by its agents; third, since the harbor and underlying soil were the property of the state of Maryland, and the city was an agent of the state responsible for preserving the navigation of the water, the city was not liable; and fourth, any damage suffered because of the filling up of the harbor was a noncompensable public nuisance that did not give rise to a private cause of action. In addition to these points, the city argued that it could not be held liable for damages to the wharf if the jury found that the city's agents, in grading and paving the streets, acted impartially, without malice, and with the exercise of their best judgment within the scope of their lawful authority.[115] Judge Archer refused to give these instructions and instead substituted his own, which in many ways guaranteed a verdict for Barron and Craig. Archer instructed the jury "that the plaintiff will be entitled to a verdict, if the jury believe from the testimony that the plaintiff's property was injured by the washings occasioned by the diversion of the waters from flowing into the western cove and turning them into the eastern cove."[116] Given that the city admitted as much, these jury instructions proved devastating to their defense. Archer's instructions revealed his view of the case—the jury should decide in favor of Barron if they believed the actions of the city caused injury to Barron, even if they believed those actions

> Neither malicious, negligent, or careless, but . . . even beneficial to the general interests of the city, made with the best advice, and with due circumspection, consulting the general prosperity of the city and its inhabitants, either for securing the health of the city, or of preserving more effectually its navigation, still, notwithstanding the jury should believe these facts, the plaintiff is entitled to damages for the injury the jury shall find the plaintiff may have sustained, in as much as this general improvement would, in such case, be made for the benefit and advantage of the inhabitants of Baltimore, and it would be unjust that the property of the plaintiff should be deteriorated, (and to the extent of such injury,) deprived of his property without remuneration.[117]

Judge Archer viewed certain rights, including nondeprivation of property without due process or proper reimbursement, as paramount liberties that could not be infringed regardless of intent or motive. Following the close of evidence and Archer's instructions, on May 5, 1828, the jury returned with a verdict in favor of Barron. However, instead of the $20,000 sought, the jury ordered only $4,500. They likely based this figure on Archer's instructions to consider damages as the amount the wharf had depreciated as a result of the city's actions.[118] Likewise, Dawson and Curtis were also successful in their claims against the city later that week, but they too received far less than they wanted, as Dawson was awarded $2,000, while Curtis received only $900.[119]

THE DECISION

While Barron and Craig pled the matter as a trespass on the case and set forth evidence to support what is essentially a forerunner of a modern negligence action, the city argued that its delegated police power allowed it to correct the nuisance in Fell's Point, regardless of the incidental damage to Barron and Craig's wharf. Judge Archer, however, bypassed a strict determination of whether the damage to the wharf constituted a taking or a permissible exercise of the city's police power to remedy nuisances. He reframed the issue as one that could be decided by relying on common law principles concerning damage to property more generally. In support, Archer cited several instances where persons were held liable for nonintentional damages to the property of others. His examples show that he perceived the dispute as requiring an evaluation of the rights and responsibilities of equal property owners, and not as a matter of the circumstances under which the government could take or regulate property. Archer cited the "undeniable principle that *ex jure naturae*," or according to natural law, every man has a right to divert a watercourse from its natural flow to protect him from injury. However, this principle carried with it a consistent obligation to indemnify those who were injured by the diversion, regardless of whether the damages suffered were a direct result of the diversion or were merely consequential. He further cited the common law principle that every man must use his property with caution so as to not affect the property rights of others, referring to the prevailing common law property maxim *sic utere tuo ut alienum non laedas.*[120] Further, this common law principle applied to watercourses. Archer conceded that the common law rule of *damnum abseque injuria,* those injuries that have no remedy, can limit losses when the lawful use of your property causes damage to that of your neighbor; however, he considered this rule to be limited.[121] As examples of its application he referred to situations such as when a farmer's tilled soil washes over the crops of his neighbor's field in a heavy rain, or when a property owner erects a mill that injures the mill of an owner downriver by virtue of the decrease in the speed of the water. In both such situations, the *damnum abseque injuria* exception would apply since both property owners used their property in a lawful manner and the resulting damage to their neighbor's property did not constitute a permanent or significant injury.[122] Unlike these situations, however, Archer ruled that an individual who caused the types of damages sustained by Barron and Craig would clearly be liable.

Archer was thus incredulous that because the party that caused the damage was the city, the outcome would be any different. The city unquestionably had the legal authority to take action to abate nuisance, such as the water pouring through Fell's Point. However, the question of whether this authority was exercised properly or done with malice was absolutely immaterial. To Archer, if the water was diverted to benefit the residents of Baltimore, and the effect of the benefit was to permanently injure Barron and Craig's wharf, "justice seems to demand that he whose property has fallen a victim to the public service should be compensated in some way."[123] Next, Archer clarified his opinion to overcome a main conceptual problem with the case, namely, that the wharf itself was not physically damaged or injured. To address this, Archer had to expand Barron and Craig's property interest in excess of simple ownership of the wharf. Archer conceded that the soil in the Patapsco River as well as the water covering the soil belonged not to Barron and Craig but to the state. Barron and Craig's property interest included only the wharf itself. Nonetheless, Archer held that this property interest was sufficient to bring suit by expanding the property interest of the wharf to include an implied easement. Archer noted that the plaintiff was indeed "disseized, or, more properly speaking, deprived of an easement appurtenant to his land, which constituted a great portion of its value."[124] Moreover, Archer added that "it would be in vain to guard with such vigilance the freehold itself, if the liberties and privileges appurtenant to it were not also the subject of constitutional guardianship."[125] Archer held that the "liberties and privileges appurtenant" to the wharf included an implied easement that required the wharf be clear of obstructions. Citing the language contained in both the Magna Carta and the Maryland constitution, Archer insisted Barron and Craig could not be deprived of this easement except upon "judgment of his peers or by the law of the land."[126] Parenthetically, with the exception of a brief reference by Taney in his appellate argument, the obvious question of whether the run-off that damaged the wharf actually constituted a physical taking remained unasked during the litigation. Its absence shows that for much of the case the dispositive question concerned liability for more routine allegations of damage rather than whether the remedy would lie in the Fifth Amendment's taking clause.

Archer then addressed the city's argument that Barron and Craig's damages were noncompensable since the city was simply exercising its obligation and power to abate nuisance. According to this argument, their damages were not specific but shared by all members of the public; therefore, Barron and Craig lacked standing to bring a claim. To refute this, Archer ruled that Barron and Craig did suffer unique damage, namely, the right to collect wharfage, or the monies charged to load or unload ships, which was destroyed by the city's actions.[127] Barron and Craig's easement was also destroyed by the actions of the city, which decimated their profits. These damages were special as not all residents of Baltimore suffered similarly; rather, these damages were borne only by wharf owners in the vicinity.[128] As Barron and Craig had a property interest that was uniquely damaged by the acts of the city, the city owed reimbursement regardless of its inherent powers.

Ultimately, Archer viewed the city's actions as infringing on fundamental rights that were protected by generations of wisdom expressed in the common law and recognized by constitutional documents like the Magna Carta and the Maryland constitution. Archer also cited the similar provision in the Fifth Amendment. He conceded that there was a dispute regarding whether the Fifth Amendment applied to the states; however, he argued that the general prohibition against simply taking private property was so fundamental that it had "a deeper foundation in all free governments than constitutions or laws; it rests upon the universal sense which all mankind feel of its equity and justice."[129] To Archer, the critical point was not the applicability of the state or federal constitution that contained these private-property protections. Rather, these rights existed independently of any written constitution. For Archer, the Maryland constitution's prohibition on the deprivation of private property except by the law of the land was "merely declaratory of the common law of England."[130] Archer agreed that while some of the amendments to the U.S. Constitution were intended to apply only to the federal government, many were created to ensure that all citizens of the United States were guaranteed certain freedoms regardless of which state they resided in. In particular, Archer cited the Second, Third, Fourth, Fifth, and Eighth Amendments as applying to both the federal government as well as state governments.[131] Archer not only relied on his own view of the extraconstitutional nature of certain rights but also cited William Rawle's contemporary treatise *A View of the Constitution of the United States of America,* where Rawle maintained that the amendments to the Constitution simply declared preexisting rights of the people and thus bound both the federal and state governments.[132]

Archer recognized the potential criticism that his *Barron* ruling could bring from those concerned about judicial interference in the growth essential to cities like Baltimore. However, he predicted, "I perceive no danger of an infinity of suits growing out of these doctrines. The exercising of the right of cutting down streets and diverting water-courses into particular parts of the basin, for the benefit of the navigation, does not necessarily lead to a loss for which a suit may be maintained."[133] As support, Archer cited the earlier 1805 New York state case *Palmer v. Mulligan,* where the court refused to hold an upstream mill owner liable for damages by the owner of the downstream mill resulting from the diversion of water.[134] That Archer felt it important to distinguish *Palmer v. Mulligan* at the end of his opinion is important. *Palmer* has been described as a critical moment in the evolution of the concept of the paramount attributes of property ownership.[135]

In *Palmer,* Justice Spencer held that all mills would necessarily injure any other mills downstream on the same river; thus, the damages were *damnum abseque injuria,* an injury without a remedy.[136] In a concurring opinion, Justice Henry Brockholst Livingston agreed and chipped away at the common law rules regarding riparian rights, or the rights of those who own property that contain or abut waterways.[137] Livingston classified the damages to the downstream owner as merely an inconvenience that would always attend the building of additional mills or dams on a river. In a signal that he intended to bend common law rules to fit with the expansionist needs of a growing nation, Livingston wrote, "Were this not permitted for fear of some inconsiderable damage to other persons, the public, whose advantage is always to be regarded, would be deprived of the benefit which always attends competition and rivalry."[138] In contrast, Justice James Kent, joined by Smith Thompson in dissent, argued that the downstream mill was "materially and permanently" injured by the disruption of the current. *Damnum abseque injuria* can limit certain claims;

however, it would apply only to those for the "insensible evaporation and decrease of water by dams, or the occasional increase or decrease of the velocity of the current, and of the quantity of the water below." For Kent, the downstream mill owner should collect damages in this matter, and he proffered eight witnesses who set forth uncontroverted evidence that the placement of the upstream mill injured his property, including one who estimated the loss at close to a hundred dollars per year.[139]

Archer cited *Palmer* to support his claim that his *Barron* ruling would not lead to an explosion of cases against municipalities. For Archer, the critical difference was that Barron and Craig suffered permanent injury. In reading *Palmer* this way, Archer relied more on Kent and Thompson's dissents than the actual majority opinion. This is not altogether unsurprising, as Archer in many ways echoed Kent and Thompson when he drafted his opinion explaining his decision to rule against Baltimore. For example, Archer did not state that municipalities could never divert waterways or alter drainage to provide a public benefit. Rather, like Kent and Thompson's dissenting opinion, Archer sought to reign in an overly expansive use of the common law exception, *damnum abseque injuria.* If the state sought to abate nuisance through the use of its police power, it was entitled to do so. What the state could not do is damage property and in the process rely on a tortured interpretation of the common law to escape its responsibilities.[140]

If we compare the *Palmer* majority and dissenting opinions, we see a dynamic occurring in a very similar way to *Barron*. Justices Spencer and Livingston were implicitly asserting the primacy of the state over the river by disallowing two private entities to fight over the superior right to the use of a public river. Similarly, in *Barron*, the city argued that it was within its lawful authority to redirect the water flowing through the Fell's Point district. Any damage incurred by private actors as a result of the city's actions was non-compensable because the city had acted pursuant to its delegated police power from the state of Maryland. The city did not contest Barron and Craig's damages, and it defended the case on the basis that exercising its police power within its mandate and without malice constituted an absolute defense. In contrast, Justice Kent in dissent clung to an older view that did not see the powers of the state in such an expansive manner. Kent grounded the plaintiff's right of recovery in his property rights inherent in his thirty-year ownership of land on the river, which he held nonnavigable at common law. Under the English common law tradition, the question of navigability of a river determined whether it was a common public highway. If it did not have an ebb and flow, it was a nonnavigable inland river and thus belonged to the owners of the adjacent land.[141] According to Kent, the Hudson River at the point of the plaintiff's land was nonnavigable. Thus, he had a recognizable property right for which the court should have provided compensation.[142] Similarly, in ruling in favor of Barron and Craig, Judge Archer held that the city, regardless of its inherent police power, must provide compensation for the damage to their property.

Archer's logic was followed by many jurists of the era. Archer felt that constitutions declared rights that existed at common law, entirely separate from the documents themselves. In addition, Archer held the rights set forth in the Bill of Rights as those secured to the people, not the respective state governments. He continued a line of thought that began at the Constitutional Convention, where many felt that a national sovereign people were creating a new government of the "United States" that would fundamentally alter the prior confederation of wholly separate sovereign states. These jurists maintained the ideological tradition of holding certain rights fundamental to the people and outside the realm of the government. Whether the Bill of Rights applied to the states did not get to the heart of the matter. Many jurists entertained doubts about whether the Bill of Rights applied to state action.[143] However, that question was immaterial. Placing the right to compensation for takings of private property did not mean that this right existed in the Constitution exclusively. Rather, they viewed the Fifth Amendment as simply recognizing the existence of the right. What we see in the trial court is a different framing of the central issue of *Barron* than is commonly remembered. Before the U.S. Supreme Court, the dispute was viewed as one answerable by examining whether the federal Bill of Rights could bind the actions of the state governments. However, before the trial court, the parties largely fought within the confines of the common law. The court agreed, also viewing this as a matter decided by the common law or, to a lesser extent, fundamental or natural-law principles. Both sides, however, had differing views of what the common law required when a municipality like Baltimore undertook certain development projects that injured private property owners like Barron and Craig. The city advanced their vision of a common law that was dynamic and had innovated doctrines that would allow property owners, businesses, and municipalities the space to develop the canals, fields, and rivers that would give Baltimore latitude to expand and improve without the threat of continual lawsuits. In contrast, Barron and Craig and, most importantly, Judge Archer embraced a common law tradition that retained more static rules of property. These competing interpretations of the common law would continue, as immediately after the court's decision, the city "prayed leave to except," an early method of preserving an objection for appeal. By seeking leave of the court to prepare a bill of exceptions, the city was memorializing Archer's ruling on the jury instructions by creating a written statement, signed by the court for accuracy, that they could then appeal to a higher court.[144]

Two years later in Annapolis, the city had a second chance to convince the Maryland Court of Appeals that it should not be held liable for these damages, either to Barron and Craig or to William Dawson. Parenthetically, despite the loss to James Curtis, it appears that the city did not pursue an appeal but simply awaited the result of the *Barron* case.[145] However, this time neither the city nor Barron and Craig limited their views of the rights at issue to simply strict versus expansive readings of the common law. Rather, John Scott, Roger Taney, David Hoffman, and Charles Mayer expanded their arguments in ways that more closely tracked the wider range of interpretations about where rights originated.

5 Appeal

> If the legislature has the power to do so, then if they pass a law to that effect, it is the law of the land. . . . There is no restraint upon the exercise of the state governments . . . such as found in the Constitution.
>
> Roger Taney, before the Maryland Court of Appeals

Less than one month after the trial, John Barron awoke in the middle of the night in a violent coughing fit. He had been sick for some time, likely with terrible chest pain, fever, and never-ending coughing spells. Barron had tuberculosis, the most lethal disease in America at the time. And although the disease was not yet known by that name, those around him were certainly aware of its symptoms.[1] Shortly after 3 A.M., Barron died. He was forty-seven years old.[2] Barron left a wife, two sons, and one daughter.[3] His partner John Craig had died shortly before the trial began. Given the proximity in time of their deaths, it is very possible that Craig and Barron contracted the disease at the same time or even from each other. Perhaps aware of a fatal illness, Craig had drafted his will the summer before.[4] But what could either man leave his family given that he was so heavily in debt? This was a critical question for the Craigs: his wife Peggy, two sons John and Robert, and two daughters Margaret and one unknown were still very much reliant on the patriarch for support. Indeed, although his daughter Margaret was married, she and her husband were nonetheless still financially reliant on Craig. Far from the wealthier sections of town to the west, Fell's Point was home to scores of people who were only one lost job or one lost spouse away from economic disaster. In his study of working-class Baltimoreans in this era, Seth Rockman noted that close to 20 percent of the households in Fell's Point in this era were headed by women. Far from a declaration of economic or personal independence, these households were deprived of men's wages and existed as female-headed households out of sheer necessity.[5] Since Robert Craig was still a minor, either the younger John Craig had to provide support, or his mother would need to find a new marriage partner. Otherwise, the indignity of the Baltimore almshouse awaited, which the year after Craig died admitted an all-time high of 1,100 persons.[6] In his will, Craig divided the remnants of his estate between his son John and his son-in-law, John Staples. They would likewise share guardianship over Robert Craig. To see that his will was faithfully carried out, Craig appointed his son John and Luke Tiernan as co-executors of his estate. However, on November 14, 1827, approximately five months after the will was executed, Craig's son renounced all rights as an executor of his father's estate, leaving Tiernan as the sole executor.[7]

Tiernan pursued the case against the city all the way to the Supreme Court before finally accepting that the wharf damages would not be recognized, posting bonds and likely paying the legal fees the whole way to keep the case alive. Certainly, as Craig's executor, Tiernan had a legal obligation to pursue any monies or other assets that could belong to his estate. However, it seems that a sense of loyalty to Craig was not Tiernan's prime motivation for keeping the case going and upholding his fiduciary duty as executor, nor was it even a desire to see the high Court vindicate the right to receive reimbursement for governmental takings of private property. Instead, it appears that Tiernan was motivated primarily because Craig owed him a significant amount of money. As chapter 1 shows, Tiernan had made regular loans to Craig as he and Barron desperately tried to save the wharf. According to a ledger acknowledged as accurate by Craig on February 21, 1826, approximately two years before his death, he owed Tiernan's firm $8,846.76.[8] However, an inventory of Craig's estate taken shortly after his passing in 1828 listed his assets as totaling only $1,199.20.[9]

Tiernan did not passively allow these debts to accrue. Well before Craig and Barron passed away, Tiernan had positioned himself to recoup these losses. In January 1822, Tiernan successfully purchased

Barron and Craig's wharf at auction for $16,000.[10] Approximately one month later, Craig and Barron brought the *Barron* case against the mayor and city council, with Tiernan's essential financial backing. After Craig died, and while the appeal was pending, Tiernan picked up the pace. Tiernan targeted Craig's home and business at the corner of Ann and George Streets in Fell's Point, a prime location only one block north of the water and two blocks east of the wharf. The property comprised two contiguous parcels. On July 16, 1829, Tiernan sued Craig's wife, daughter Margaret, and son-in-law John Staples to foreclose the brick house on the southernmost parcel that Craig had mortgaged to him in 1820 in return for a much needed loan of $3,000.[11] As the remaining Craig family did not contest the suit, the court ordered the property auctioned to satisfy the debt. The court appointed Tiernan's son William as trustee to conduct the auction.[12] On May 13, 1830, William Tiernan auctioned the property, which sold for $1,795 to the highest bidder, which was again Luke Tiernan.[13] Tiernan was able to acquire the northernmost parcel much more easily. One month earlier, Craig's son-in-law assigned to Tiernan the lease he in turn had received from Craig in 1827.[14] Only a few months later, Tiernan likewise sought to claim the proceeds from a lawsuit that Craig had filed before his death. In 1826, likely seeking to call in any debts that he could use to pay off Tiernan, Craig filed suit against Thomas Cowart seeking his share of profits from the sale of a schooner that they purchased together three years earlier. While Craig obtained a legal judgment against Cowart, it was left unsatisfied by the time of Craig's death one year later. Tiernan hired John Scott, whom he knew as councilor for the city in the *Barron* case then on appeal, to file an appearance in *Craig v. Cowart* in December of 1829 and succeeded in having the court issue the appropriate writ to collect the judgment from Cowart.[15]

All of these claims paled in comparison to the suit against the city of Baltimore, however. The trial court had handed Tiernan a victory, but the city filed the necessary bond to appeal the case and, more important, to delay paying the judgment. The city appealed the decision to the court of appeals for the Western Shore of the State of Maryland.[16] Traveling from Baltimore to the Maryland coast, the attorneys—Charles Mayer, David Hoffman, Roger Taney, and John Scott—arrived in Annapolis, home of the state capitol and court of appeals. As train service would not link the two cities until 1840, by this time the attorneys of the Baltimore bar often traveled together to Annapolis by steamship.[17] Likely gathering in the City Hotel, a semi-communal home away from home for out-of-town attorneys where they and the judges would often socialize and dine together while court was in session, the attorneys prepared their arguments.[18] On Friday, December 17, 1830, Scott, Taney, Mayer, and Hoffman left their accommodations at the City Hotel and walked to the Maryland State House, where the court of appeals occupied a room on the second floor. The appeal was scheduled to take place during the court's winter session, when the weather would provide a desired break from the summer terms' stifling atmosphere.[19] Instead, a fireplace on the northwest wall provided heat. On the opposite wall, six individual desks for the judges sat on a two-foot-high raised platform in the shape of a semicircle. Between the fireplace and the raised platform were desks for the attorneys and a few seats for spectators.[20] Whereas the parties at the Baltimore County Court had only Judge Archer and Associate Judge Hanson to persuade, at the appellate trial they would have to persuade a panel of five judges: Chief Judge John Buchanan of Washington County; Richard Tilghman Earle of Queen Anne's County; Thomas Beale Dorsey of Anne Arundel County; William Bond Martin of Dorchester County; and John Stephen of Prince George's County.[21] The sixth justice, representing Harford and Baltimore counties, was not present. Stevenson Archer, who had ruled in Barron and Craig's favor at trial, was absent, likely recused.[22]

Barron v. Baltimore is generally recognized for little more than its brief ruling that the Bill of Rights did not apply to the states. However, as we saw in the lower court trial, the Bill of Rights was absent from the arguments. The Baltimore County Court did not witness a grand display of constitutional arguments but instead served as a forum for a conflict fought within the parameters of the common law. The dispute as framed at the trial court pitted the rights of an individual property owner versus the police power of the city to provide for the health, safety, and welfare of the community. The remedies invoked all around traced their lineage to the common law. On appeal, however, Mayer and Hoffman broadened their interpretation and expressed a view of Barron and Craig's property rights as existing not only in a static version of the common law, but as a fundamental principle of all free governments expressed in the federal and state constitutions. It is unclear whether Mayer and Hoffman failed to appreciate the larger rights-based constitutional argument during the initial trial, or whether they were simply constrained by the rules of pleading to fit the case into an accepted cause of action. What is clear is that the parties, apparently encouraged by Judge Archer's opinion, began to address the larger issues of the role of the Maryland and U.S. constitutions. The characterization of rights evolved before the court of appeals. As we will see from the arguments before the court, the city reemphasized its view that an expansive version of the common law gave it ample room to use its police power. Hoffman and Mayer not only reasserted their reliance on an interpretation of the common law that was more protective of property rights, but they now began to incorporate a view of these property rights as provided by natural law or as an essential requirement of free governments.

Since the city was appealing the decision, its attorneys were allowed to argue first, followed by a reply from Barron and Craig's legal team, which then gave the city a chance for a final rebuttal. John Scott began on behalf of Baltimore.[23] Scott recognized that while Barron and Craig "may have been damaged," they nonetheless did not have a valid cause of action against the city. As in the trial court, Scott cited the various state laws, local ordinances, and resolutions that, he argued, collectively granted power from the state to Baltimore and allowed it to take all actions necessary to address the drainage problems in Fell's Point. Scott linked the city's general power to prevent nuisance to the power to pave and grade streets. In addition to the statutory authority, Scott moved to his larger argument that the common law exempted the city from damages. In so doing, Scott again relied on a more expansive interpretation of the common law that gave municipalities much wider latitude to exercise their police power. Scott structured his argument around two main points, emphasizing both the limited liability of the persons that made up the corporation as well as an expansive view of the law of damages that freed those entities from liability for most claims.

First, Scott relied on a line of cases that held that officers and directors of a corporation—and indeed the corporation itself could not be held liable for damages incurred in following legislative directives unless their actions exceeded the scope of the law. Scott could rely on a wealth of cases that supported his position; there was ample case law during this era that specified the nonliability of agents as long as they acted pursuant to the enabling law and without malice.[24] Scott also cited a number of more recent English cases that specifically exempted appointed agents of municipalities, agents like the

Baltimore city commissioners. In the case of *British Plate Glass v. Meredith*, the court found that agents were not liable for actions that damaged private property because they did not exceed their authority; in *Sutton v. Clarke*, the court exempted a road commissioner from liability for flood damages resulting from defective construction of a ditch because the commissioner had relied in good faith on a surveyor's report.[25] Scott argued that because Baltimore's corporate form exempted the mayor and city council from liability, Judge Archer erred by viewing them as individuals. While this is a well-accepted principle of corporation law today, many features that are often considered essential to corporations, such as limited liability, were not fully accepted in the early nineteenth century.[26] Indeed, many of Scott's claims that are now more-or-less routine aspects of black letter law were highly contested points at the time. In fact, Scott's claims met without success at trial, and Judge Archer found that the sort of rulings in *Sutton* and *British Plate Glass* were "utterly untenable, and are in violation of first principles," as they would allow private entities chartered by the state to inflict damage with impunity.[27]

After making his point that the persons making up the municipal corporation were not liable, Scott turned to his second main argument, namely, that the municipal corporation of Baltimore itself was not responsible. Scott doubled down on his view that the common law allowed states and municipalities wide latitude to exercise their police power. He argued that the maxim of the common law—*salus populi est suprema lex*, or the welfare of the people is the supreme law—meant that Baltimore was not responsible for damages incurred in carrying out this mission.[28] To this point, Scott cited *Lansing v. Smith*, an 1828 New York state case that contained facts remarkably similar to those in *Barron* and emphasized the pro-development line of common law cases that were emerging in this era.[29] In *Lansing*, a wharf owner brought suit against the commissioners of a private company chartered by the state to construct a basin in the Hudson River. As the construction impeded access to his wharf, the owner sued for the depreciation in its value, relying partially on an explicit provision in the state constitution that prohibited the taking of property.[30] Described as a "classic public *damnum abseque injuria* case," the *Lansing* court ruled that the wharf owner's damages were not special to him, but common to the entire community, aligning its decision with a body of cases that required special or unique damages in order to bring a private lawsuit resulting from a public nuisance.[31] As a result, since the court held that the wharf owner's damages were suffered only as a consequence of the construction, they were *damnum abseque injuria* (an injury without a remedy) and must "be bourne as a part of the price to be paid for the advantages of the social condition. This is founded upon the principle that the general good is to prevail over partial individual convenience."[32]

As *Lansing* did not consider the specific takings clause of the New York constitution as sufficient to overcome the power of the state over the Hudson River, Scott then compared this to the case at hand. Article XXI of the Maryland constitution was a virtual copy of a similar provision in the Magna Carta, and provided that no one could be deprived of "life, liberty, or property, but by judgment of his peers or by the law of the land."[33] Scott claimed that the state bill of rights did not alter the common law of Maryland and that Article XXI did not apply because Barron and Craig's property was not physically taken; rather, their injuries were similar to those suffered by the rest of the public. Here, Scott took the existence of a written-rights provision and found a way to eviscerate it through a variety of common law techniques, ultimately turning a textual constitutional-rights claim into a noncompensable nuisance action. It is important again to note that Scott was seeking the court of appeals to embrace a particular interpretation of the common law. For example, Scott recognized that the Massachusetts Supreme Court ruled that the common law provided a remedy for a property owner who suffered flood damage. In 1815 in *Stevens v. Middlesex Canal Company*, Chief Justice Parker held a state-chartered canal company liable to a property owner for flood damage. There, the state passed a law allowing the company to dig a canal, but it did not provide a mechanism in the law to pay damages to affected owners. As the state constitution contained a provision that property could not be taken without compensation, Parker held that the owner would have a common law cause of action to sue the company. Faced with this, Scott argued that this case would not apply in Maryland, as its takings clause, Article XXI, did not contain a specific statement requiring compensation.

After arguing that the individuals that made up the municipal corporation of Baltimore were not liable, and that the corporation itself was likewise not responsible since it was exercising its duty to public, and finally that even a specific takings provision could not impart liability to the city for their actions, Scott concluded his argument. Charles Mayer presented the first reply for Barron and Craig. In response to Scott's characterization that the city should not have to pay for the damages since it acted in accord with its lawful authority, Mayer argued that because the Baltimore authorities willfully damaged his clients, "principles of truth and justice" obligated it to pay for the injury.[34] Because Barron and Craig were suing the mayor and city council only in their collective corporate status, Mayer characterized as a false argument Scott's claim that they could not sue the city officers individually.[35] He clearly tailored his argument in the light of the many examples given by Scott that exempted agents carrying out improvement projects unless they acted "wantonly and oppressively."[36] Mayer noted that the city was not serving as an agent of the state when it paved the streets of Fell's Point and diverted the waters toward the wharf. Since the city was acting for its own benefit, it could not be considered as simply relying on lawful directives. Rather, the city's powers had to be interpreted in the light of the 1796 Act that created the municipal corporation, which specifically prohibited the city from taking any actions repugnant to either the Maryland or U.S. constitutions.[37] In a way, Mayer conveniently overlooked Scott's argument that no actual taking took place, focusing more on a simple argument that private property was taken for public use. As a result, indemnity was required.

Mayer closed by addressing Scott's expansive view of the city's powers under the common law. Mayer argued that the damages to the wharf were not *damnum abseque injuria* but instead compared them to those incurred by a homeowner whose house was pulled down by order of a local law. Equity would require that the public authority making such an order provide compensation to the owner. Attempting to distinguish Scott's argument that acts made to remedy a public nuisance could not give rise to a private cause of action, Mayer contended that it was possible during the abatement of a public nuisance for special damages to arise, as was the case for Barron and Craig.[38] Mayer attempted to collapse the public/private nuisance distinction by arguing that simply because an act was deemed a public nuisance did not mean that it could not also operate as a private nuisance with the requisite special damages necessary to allow a private right of action.[39] However, the existence of cases like *Lansing*, decided after *Barron* was filed in 1822 but before the appellate arguments in 1830, may have pushed Mayer and Hoffman to stress the constitutional- and fundamental-law arguments so forcefully on appeal. Specifically, Mayer sought to redirect the court's focus from more recent cases like *Lansing* and toward older decisions like *Vanhorne's Lessee v. Dorrance*, which upheld the sanctity of private property as a fundamental right of man declared by our constitutions.[40]

Mayer concluded his argument and returned to his counsel table in the middle of the courtroom. Hoffman rose, adjusted his coat, and began to address the court. Whereas Mayer's presentation was mostly limited to rebutting Scott's claims, Hoffman put on a performance. Not only a nationally recognized attorney but also one of the country's first legal educators, Hoffman decided to lay out every reason why the trial court was correct.[41] In his *Course of Legal Study*, Hoffman compiled lists of readings he felt would prepare well-rounded students for the practice of law by stressing its ethical, moral, and historical antecedents in ways that the simple practice of reading Blackstone and apprenticing in a law office would not. To that end, Hoffman's *Course* contains numerous lists with multiple parts, subparts, and extensive commentary to fully map out the genealogy of the law for his students. Hoffman took a very similar approach with the court of appeals, structuring his lengthy oration around twenty-one separate points of law. For clarity, we can sort them into five general categories.[42]

First, Hoffman concentrated on eminent domain, or the power of the state to take private property for public purposes. He conceded that the city was within its authority to pave and grade the streets to protect the health of the residents but did not possess the power of eminent domain, which allowed the taking of private property for the benefit of others. Eminent domain was an extraordinary attribute possessed solely by the sovereign. It could not be delegated to lesser entities by mere implication. If the state of Maryland intended to allow Baltimore to exercise this power, it had to be done in express terms.[43] Otherwise, if the city caused damage while making street repairs, it had the duty to provide compensation.[44] In support, Hoffman cited Joseph Angell's *Treatise on the Common Law in Relation to Water-Courses*, which was also relied on by Judge Archer in his trial court opinion. First published in 1824, it provides an excellent primer on the contemporary remedies provided by the common law for all manners of damage to and by flowing waters.[45] Hoffman particularly relied on Angell's principles that watercourses were included in the "well established principle of natural equity" and that the governmental taking of private property can be had only upon compensation, citing natural-law theorists Grotius and Pufendorf in support. A taking of property without compensation, wrote Angell, would be "not only contrary to the first principles of civil government, but in opposition to (what is of higher authority and absolutely decisive of the sense of the people of this country) an express article of the constitution." Angell cited the Fifth Amendment as well as noted similar provisions in many state constitutions.[46] His treatise restated the well-established orthodoxy of the common law as it related to riparian, or water, rights. In many ways, Mayer and Hoffman's reliance on treatises like Angell's was an attempt to hold onto a rapidly evolving view of the common law. Angell's position that any acts that redirected or obstructed watercourses would give rise to a claim for damages was increasingly outdated and becoming eclipsed by decisions that permitted much more flexibility.[47]

Second, Hoffman countered the city's claim that their actions did not constitute a taking but were done to remedy a public nuisance by asserting that the question of whether the public was injured was absolutely immaterial to the case.[48] The law did not recognize a distinction between direct and indirect damage to private property when taking actions for the public good. In fact, Hoffman argued that the "greater the good, the stronger the claim for compensation."[49]

Third, Hoffman confronted the city's argument that the mayor and the city council could not be held liable since they acted within the scope of the powers granted by the enabling laws passed by the Maryland legislature. Hoffman argued that the city was not an agent of the state of Maryland but an entity that could be sued. While the state would have sovereign immunity, the city would not. Hoffman then asked the court what the liability would have been if a private individual owned the Fell's Point stream and diverted its course.[50] Under general common law principles, such an owner would be liable for the resulting damage. Like Mayer, Hoffman also addressed the several cases cited by Scott that held that government agents acting pursuant to their legal mandate could not be held liable for damages, like the 1815 English case *Sutton v. Clarke*.[51] In *Sutton*, a property owner sued trustees who were empowered by law to widen a road and to cut any watercourses in order to keep the road from flooding. In doing so, the trustees dug a drainage canal that was too shallow, allowing the water to overflow and damage his property.[52] The court ruled that the trustees were not liable as they were not private individuals taking these actions for their own benefit but were carrying out a duty prescribed by law for a public benefit. If the trustees were private individuals, they would be liable for these damages, even if they had exercised all due care.[53] As they were acting under color of law, the only way they could be held liable would be if they acted in an arbitrary manner, or if within their jurisdiction they behaved "wantonly or oppressively."[54] Hoffman distinguished *Sutton* in an attempt to show that the city in fact exceeded its authority in the manner it redirected all the water pouring through Fell's Point. Certainly, in the trial court, this would explain his emphasis on calling numerous witnesses who contested the methods taken by the city to resolve the drainage problem. Judge Archer was receptive to this argument. He also disregarded *Sutton* in his trial court opinion wherein he addressed the holding that persons acting pursuant to legal mandate for the public good could not be held liable for damage. Archer took this point stressed by *Sutton* to be completely inapplicable, and he delved further into this question. He asked, "Who are the defendants? They are trustees for the public; but what public? Themselves. They are trustees of the public interests *for their own benefit*, and ought to answer as an individual to the person at whose expense they are benefited" (emphasis in original).[55] Archer collapsed the distinction between an individual acting for his own benefit and a person acting solely for the public good out of public-policy reasons. He argued that a contrary result would allow any private company that was chartered by the government to cause damage with impunity.[56] Given the number of major improvement projects undertaken by private entities chartered by the state that took place during this era, this concern was not unfounded.

Fourth, Hoffman echoed Judge Archer's opinion to argue that at common law, Barron and Craig had a property interest not only in the wharf, but also in the adjacent soil and water that covered it.[57] That the actual wharf was not taken or even physically damaged represented a hurdle that Barron and Craig had to overcome in some way. Judge Archer avoided this problem by classifying Barron and Craig's interest in the water near the wharf as an implied easement that ran with their ownership of the wharf. Hoffman attempted to refine this analysis and argued that Barron and Craig's property interest in the soil and water was an incorporeal real hereditament.[58] An incorporeal hereditament is any right that accompanies the ownership of property itself and can be inherited along with the property itself, in this case realty. For example, a corporeal (meaning physical) real hereditament would be land, whereas an incorporeal (meaning intangible) real hereditament would be the right to rents from tenants occupying the land. The incorporeal hereditament arises out of the corporeal hereditament.[59] In making this argument, Hoffman may have tried not only to overcome the allegation that his clients did not suffer unique damages but also to have the court of appeals appreciate that the damage to the wharf constituted a taking by the city and was not the city merely acting to abate nuisance. However, to refocus the court on the taking argument, Hoffman had to expand the scope of Barron and Craig's property interest to include more than just the wharf itself.

Finally, unlike Mayer, Hoffman did not argue that the damage to the wharf constituted a violation of the Maryland or U.S. constitutions. Rather, Hoffman predicated Barron and Craig's right to recover on an extraconstitutional appreciation of rights. Hoffman argued that the law made no distinction between direct and indirect injuries to private property caused by improvement for the public good. In all such situations, the "social compact"—a concept that echoed Locke or Hobbes and their belief that society was based on a fictional agreement to protect the rights of man that existed in his natural state—required that just compensation be made.[60] For Hoffman, an injury suffered by the owner of private property demanded reimbursement, regardless of whether it was a governmental entity that damaged the property, it was done for a public good, or the damage was direct or incidental. Like Mayer, Hoffman also cited cases like *Vanhorne's Lessee* that held the Pennsylvania constitution as the enunciation of preexisting fundamental law.[61] However, Hoffman went much further. Relying on natural-law theorists Vattel, Grotius, and Pufendorf, and even the Roman historian Livy, Hoffman argued that in such cases, eminent domain could be justified only in situations of "great public emergency and for the public good" and, most important, accompanied by just compensation to the owner.[62] For Hoffman, Livy showed that as far back as Rome, the state could not keep the private property of its citizens without their consent, or at least not without providing some reasonable compensation or indemnity for its return, even during times of war.[63]

Following his twenty-one-point oration, Hoffman yielded the floor. In response, Roger Taney rose to give the city's rebuttal. The arguments before the court of appeals witnessed a debate between two legal heavyweights of the era. Hoffman was famous not only as an attorney but also as a pioneering legal educator. For his part, Taney's best and worst years were still ahead of him. Taney is remembered mostly as John Marshall's replacement and the chief justice who brought shame on the Supreme Court through his explicitly political, legally suspect, historically inaccurate, and obscenely racist *Dred Scott* decision. To a lesser extent, many may recall his inept rage and partisan crusade against the Lincoln administration in *Ex Parte Merryman*, while others may remember that he largely owed his Supreme Court career in the first place as a political lapdog to Andrew Jackson, faithfully removing the deposits from the Bank of the United States when others refused.[64] However, despite these later failings, the younger Roger Taney was widely considered one of the best attorneys in the nation. Though noted as a bit gangly and round-shouldered in appearance, his oration style was first rate. While he spoke softly, Taney impressed listeners with his exceeding ability to relate complex issues in a clear and understandable manner.[65]

In his opening statement, Taney went right after a major part of Hoffman's argument, namely, that the city did not possess the power of eminent domain. Taney quickly conceded that the city indeed did not possess this eminent domain power, but he then argued that this deficiency was wholly irrelevant since the city did not take property. Instead, Taney contended that Barron had "no right of property in the water that passed by his wharf" any more than the general public did.[66] Taney was hoping to refocus this case as one where the city abated a public nuisance, which did not require reimbursement, and not as one where the city took private property, which did. Taney was likely less hopeful that the court would simply rule that Barron and Craig had no property interest at all in the case, as scholars have noted that courts in the early nineteenth century routinely awarded compensation to persons whose property rights were affected in some way, even though the property was not fully physically appropriated.[67] Rather, by paving the streets of Fell's Point, the city was remedying a nuisance, and it was perfectly lawful for the state to delegate to the city the power to help protect the depth of Baltimore harbor.[68] Next, as the city could be considered as an agent for the state in protecting the harbor, Baltimore could not be held liable for damages unless they acted oppressively or wantonly, as the case law required.[69]

Revisiting Hoffman's claim that the city did not possess the power of eminent domain, Taney finished by posing a bold counterfactual. He queried why the state legislature couldn't delegate that power to the city if it so chose. Taney curiously claimed that the Maryland constitution gave the legislature the power to take private property for public purposes without any limitations.[70] As an absolute attribute of sovereignty, the courts could not restrain the legislature's eminent domain power. He recognized that Article XXI of the Maryland constitution provided the Magna Carta–inspired right that no freeman could be "disseized of his freehold, liberties, or privileges, or outlawed, or exiled, or in any manner destroyed, or deprived of his life, liberty, or property, but by the judgment of his peers, or by the law of the land."[71] While Judge Archer cited this provision as partial support for his ruling that Barron and Craig had been wrongfully deprived of their property without due process, Taney found just the opposite and argued that this provision was inapplicable.[72] Taney reversed Archer's reasoning and argued that since the provision was copied from the Magna Carta, the Maryland legislature should then be able to operate the same way as Parliament. And, since Parliament could take private property without payment, the same rule should apply in Maryland.[73] Rejecting Mayer and Hoffman's view of legislative power as limited by fundamental and extraconstitutional principles, Taney argued that "if the legislature has the power to do so, then if they pass a law to that effect, it is the law of the land."[74] To make this extraordinary claim, Taney had to distinguish the scores of cases cited by Mayer and Hoffman that placed limits on the state legislatures, including Justice Marshall's opinion in *Fletcher v. Peck*.[75]

Following the wholesale bribery of nearly every one of its member, the 1794 Georgia legislature sold thirty-five million acres of the state's holdings located in modern-day Mississippi and Alabama, referred to as the Yazoo lands, to four companies for only 1.5 cents per acre. When the 1796 Georgia legislature passed a law rescinding the sale, a purchaser, Fletcher, and his seller, Peck, concocted a lawsuit to test the law. [76] Before the Supreme Court, Justice Marshall prefaced his opinion with an obligatory statement of deference to the legislature but then ignored the fraud and instead held the subsequent law rescinding the land grants unconstitutional. According to Marshall, the legislature was incompetent to void the earlier land grants since they were, in effect, contracts that the state legislature could not later unilaterally modify.[77] As we will discuss in more detail later, Marshall struck down the rescission law not only as contrary to the contract clause of the U.S. Constitution but more importantly as violating the larger principles that restrain all legitimate government. Marshall wrote:

> It is, then, the unanimous opinion of the court, that, in this case, the estate having passed into the hands of a purchaser for a valuable consideration, without notice, the state of Georgia was restrained, *either by general principles which are common to our free institutions, or by the particular provisions of the constitution of the United States,* from passing a law whereby the estate of the plaintiff . . . could be constitutionally and legally impaired and rendered null and void.[78]

For Marshall, the property rights in the Yazoo land vested in Fletcher, and the legislature could not repeal those rights.[79] The legislature had limits to its powers and vested property rights provided a boundary line. To overcome this, Taney cited *Satterlee v. Matthewson,* an 1829 U.S. Supreme Court case that largely contradicted *Fletcher v. Peck* without overruling the decision.[80] In *Satterlee,* Justice Bushrod Washington held that a Pennsylvania law passed to specifically overrule a decision of the Pennsylvania Supreme Court concerning a land title dispute was not unconstitutional since it applied only retrospectively. This type of reasoning was difficult to maintain in the light of decades of federal court decisions. For example, recalling John Marshall's famous *Fletcher* opinion, Washington recognized that "it might well be doubted, whether the nature of society and government do not prescribe some limits on the legislative power."[81] Regardless, the actions of the state legislature were permissible since they did not violate any of the explicitly textual provisions in the U.S. Constitution and it was not an *ex post facto* law, which Washington believed applied only to criminal cases and did not impair the obligation of contract as prohibited by the contract clause.[82]

Washington also recognized the existence of federal cases like *Vanhorne's Lessee,* decided in 1795 by Supreme Court Justice Paterson in Pennsylvania Circuit Court and relied on by Mayer and Hoffman in their arguments.[83] In *Vanhorne's Lessee,* Paterson ruled that a law passed by the state legislature that settled a land dispute by simply confirming proper title to one party in the dispute constituted a taking of property without compensation. Paterson considered state legislatures as constrained by their constitutions. However, Paterson was not arguing for a view of constitutions as the source of rights; rather, he viewed constitutions as places where "certain first principles of fundamental laws are established."[84] For Paterson, the right of protecting one's property "is one of the natural, inherent, and unalienable rights of man." Preserving property was one of the main goals of the "social compact" and was made a fundamental law by virtue of its inclusion in the Pennsylvania constitution.[85] Washington distinguished *Vanhorne's Lessee* by summarily deciding that its decision was based on the Pennsylvania state constitution. He did not address the view of that constitution as the place where fundamental principles were announced, not provided.[86]

Further, Taney added that the Fifth Amendment of the U.S. Constitution did not apply since the Bill of Rights restricted only the activities of the federal government and not those of the states. For this proposition, Taney cited *Bradshaw v. Rogers and Magee*, an 1822 New York state case cited also by Charles Mayer in his oral argument, but for a different reason.[87] The very different interpretations of *Bradshaw* by Mayer and Taney show how both approached the question of where property rights existed in the American constitutional order at the time. In *Bradshaw*, the plaintiff sued for trespass to his land after agents of the local canal commissioners cut and removed an amount of timber.[88] The defendants asserted that they were not liable since their actions were pursuant to their road construction contract with the local canal commissioner. Justice Spencer, writing for the court, held in favor of the plaintiff because he was incredulous that the latter's land could be entered for the purpose of removing the timber without consent.[89] Spencer conceded that the Fifth Amendment applied only to the federal government and that the parallel provision of the New York constitution was not yet operable since it had not been ratified as of the time of his decision. Nonetheless, the lack of a textual provision was irrelevant because Spencer held that both provisions were "declaratory of a great and fundamental principle of government; and any law violating that principle must be deemed a nullity, as it is against natural right and justice."[90] For Spencer, the requirement of just compensation for the taking of private property was not a right that existed by virtue of its inclusion in a written constitution. Spencer's view of constitutions was similar to that set forth by Mayer and Hoffman, as well as Justice Paterson in *Vanhorne's Lessee:* a constitution recognizes preexisting rights; it does not provide their basis. Taney took the opposite approach and lifted the one line where the court recognized that the Fifth Amendment did not apply to the states to support a purely textual view of where the right existed.

Taney closed his presentation with a practical point. Considering the pace of expansion and growth in Maryland and in the rest of the United States at the time, this may have been his most persuasive argument of all. Bear in mind that within three years of this hearing, the Baltimore and Ohio and the Baltimore and Susquehanna railroads were chartered and began construction, as had the Chesapeake and Ohio Canal.[91] Taney argued that if Baltimore's actions in paving the streets, which had the effect of lowering the depth of the harbor, could now be considered an injury requiring compensation, the city would face endless lawsuits. In this way, many of these cases make more sense. For example, if we consider *Vanhorne's Lessee*, we note that Justice Paterson ruled in 1795 that the act of a state legislature divesting one party of property and placing title in the other was contrary to natural right. The principle was fundamental to the basic social compact and was contained in the state constitution as an expression of its importance. Fifteen years later, in 1810, Justice Marshall ruled in *Fletcher* that the act of the Georgia state legislature in voiding a land scale procured by massive fraud was contrary to the "general principles which are common to our free institutions" as well as in violation of the contract clause of the U.S. Constitution.[92] Thirteen years later, in *Green v. Biddle* in 1823, the Supreme Court heard a dispute between Kentucky and Virginia that dated to Kentucky's separation from Virginia in 1789.[93] While their compact stipulated that Kentucky would continue to recognize all existing land claims in accord with Virginia law then in effect, Kentucky passed two subsequent laws that attempted to ameliorate the effects on Kentuckians that had lived on and improved lands, only later to face ejectment by absentee Virginia landowners. These laws did not seek to void the claims of the Virginia owners; it simply allowed for a less draconian treatment as they appointed neutral commissioners to hear eviction disputes and assess the amounts payable to the Kentuckians for improvements made on the lands. There, Justice Bushrod Washington ruled that the original compact between Virginia and Kentucky controlled the question. While the Kentucky laws did not attempt to take land titles from one party and give it to another, as was the case in *Vanhorne's Lessee*, or seek to void private land sales altogether, as in *Fletcher*, the court ruled in favor of Virginia since it considered the Kentucky laws as taking private property without compensation. This violated not only the Virginia common law but also "the universal law of all free governments."[94] While the Court did not apply the Fifth Amendment takings prohibition to this case, it nonetheless viewed rights as fundamentally extraconstitutional, as the Virginia constitution of 1776 in effect at the time did not contain a takings clause. However, six years later, in *Satterlee*, Justice Washington was again presented with a fact pattern very much like that seen in *Vanhorne's Lessee*. When the Pennsylvania state legislature passed a special law vesting one side in a property dispute with valid title, Justice Washington held this law valid by looking at the property right as explicitly textual.

In many ways, Taney's argument before the appeals court tracked this progression and foreshadowed much of his jurisprudence while a member of the Supreme Court. As Chief Justice, Taney authored decisions that gave the states much more space in the federal system to exercise their sovereign power. The primary vehicle through which states could do so was their inherent police power. For example, when Taney claimed that the state's right of eminent domain could not be limited, even by the courts, he relied on *Willson v. Black Bird Creek Marsh Company*, an 1829 case in which the Marshall court allowed states to exercise commerce power—a privilege constitutionally reserved to Congress—if the federal government had not passed any direct legislation on the matter.[95] Scholars have recognized that Marshall's decision in *Willson* was not only out of character with his prior commerce clause decisions that claimed this power for the federal government, but also that it is partly explained by the doctrine of state police power that was gaining strength in the late 1820s.[96] Over the course of the case, the city argued that the courts should not hold it liable for damages since it was exercising its duty to use its police power to provide for the health, safety, and welfare of the residents of Baltimore. The Marshall court recognized the existence of the state police power in 1827 in *Brown v. Maryland* and implicitly referred to it as a prerogative of the states in *Willson* two years later.[97]

Consider the city's arguments before both the trial and appeals court. The city tried to persuade the courts to use an expansive interpretation of the common law that would allow them to evade Barron and Craig's damage claim. The city relied on case law that exempted agents of states and municipalities from all development-related claims of damage, even if the injury was suffered through the agent's negligence. The city argued for the courts to embrace common law notions of consequential damages and to view Barron and Craig's injuries as *damnum abseque injuria*, an injury without a remedy. All of this would allow Baltimore the space to use its police power without interference from individual rights claims like Barron and Craig's. At the same time, Mayer and Hoffman relied on older understandings of the common law or of constitutions as enunciating property rights as timeless fundamental principles, understandings that were becoming less tenable by the late 1820s.

Following Taney's argument, the hearing concluded and the court took the case under advisement.

Less than one month later, on January 6, 1831, the court released its terse opinion, reversing the respective trial court judgments in favor of Barron and Craig and William Dawson. Without issuing a lengthy written opinion, the appeals court overruled the judgment against Baltimore, finding that the trial court "manifestly erred." The court ordered Barron to pay the city $374.88 for their costs in defending the lawsuit.[98] The *Baltimore Patriot* hailed the decision as a great moment for the city, as it would release Baltimore from all liability from their Fell's Point improvement plan.[99]

Meanwhile, Luke Tiernan, David Hoffman, and Charles Mayer plotted their next step. As the highest court in the state, the adverse ruling by the Maryland Court of Appeals in Annapolis meant they were out of options in the state system.[100] The obvious question remained: should they cut their losses or try to press on in the federal courts? They very quickly chose the latter. On January 10, 1831, just four days after the appeals court ruling, U.S. Supreme Court Chief Justice John Marshall personally signed the documentation that signified the Court's intent to hear the case.[101] Just over two years later, Charles Mayer traveled to Washington, D.C., to plead Barron's case.

What might Mayer and Hoffman have thought about their potential chances and the hurdles that they would have to overcome in the nation's highest federal court? As noted in chapter 3, state courts across the country commonly decided rights claims through an interpretation that the liberties in question were extraconstitutional in some fashion. Most courts did not view the state or federal constitutions as the foundation of rights, nor did they find them a bar to recovery. In taking the case to the Supreme Court, Mayer and Hoffman were likely heartened that many of the justices' past rulings seemed to indicate that they might be sympathetic to their claims. Most important, based on his close to three decades of decisions that announced the right of the federal judiciary to forcefully protect and expand the powers of the federal government over that of the recalcitrant states, Chief Justice John Marshall would seem receptive. Further, his early decisions like *Fletcher v. Peck* viewed the Constitution as enunciating fundamental principles that existed outside of its written text. Whereas Marshall became significantly more textual in his interpretations after *Fletcher*, his ally Joseph Story continued to base many of his decisions on a view of the Constitution as the enunciation of fundamental principles that preceded its framing.[102]

If they could convince Marshall and Story, they could gain the necessary majority of the seven-member Court with two more votes. Two likely choices were Justices Henry Baldwin of Pennsylvania and William Johnson of South Carolina. Baldwin was appointed earlier that year by Jackson to replace Bushrod Washington, while Johnson had been a fixture of the Court for twenty-five years.[103] In prior decisions, both Baldwin and Johnson signaled they would be receptive to a claim that the Fifth Amendment applied to the states. For example, in 1819, the Supreme Court held the Seventh Amendment guarantee of a civil jury applicable in a state court proceeding.[104] In *Bank of Columbia v. Okely*, the Maryland legislature incorporated a bank and gave it the right to use an expedited collection procedure to levy on assets of borrowers who fell in default. The parties argued whether the law violated either the Seventh Amendment right to trial guarantee or Article XXI of the Maryland constitution, which codified the Magna Carta's prohibition against the taking of one's life, liberty, or property except in accord with the due process of law.[105] Writing for the Court, Johnson held the Maryland constitution inapplicable since the section of the Magna Carta it was based on meant to restrain governmental actions and not transactions between private individuals.[106] However, Johnson held the Seventh Amendment applicable but ruled against the defendant since the Court held that he properly waived its protections.[107] In addition, the basis for this view of the applicability of the Seventh Amendment is a bit uncertain as the bank was located in the District of Columbia. While the laws of Maryland continued to apply following the transfer of the D.C. lands from Maryland to the federal government after 1801, the fact remains that the case occurred in a federal district and not a state.[108] However, one year later in *Houston v. Moore* (1820), Johnson had another opportunity to address the applicability of the Bill of Rights Amendments to state action. As a private in the Pennsylvania militia, Houston failed to muster during the War of 1812 in violation of state law.[109] Following a state court-martial, Houston was convicted and fined. Houston appealed to the Supreme Court on the ground that the Pennsylvania statute was unconstitutional since the state did not have the authority to punish his failure to report for duty for service to the federal government.[110] At the Supreme Court, Johnson held the statute constitutionally valid and ruled against Houston in a concurring opinion. However, in dictum, Justice Johnson, apparently referring to the Fifth Amendment, argued that prohibition against double jeopardy was applicable to both the federal and state governments.[111]

Likewise, Henry Baldwin tipped his hand when deciding a matter while on federal circuit court earlier that year. In 1830 in *Bonaparte v. Camden & A.R. Co.*, Baldwin heard a dispute brought by Joseph Bonaparte, the older brother of Napoleon Bonaparte and the former king of Naples and later king of Spain.[112] After Napoleon's defeat at Waterloo in 1815, the elder Bonaparte left for America and eventually settled outside Bordentown, New Jersey on a two-thousand-acre estate. To transform rural New Jersey into a home befitting a former king, Bonaparte spent over $300,000 installing parks, walkways, gardens, a lake, and other similar improvements.[113] The problem was that the state of New Jersey incorporated a private company to build a rail line through his immaculate estate. After the company's workers began to mark the proposed route, Bonaparte sought an injunction to halt construction. Baldwin conceded that the applicability of the Fifth Amendment's prohibition on takings without just compensation against the states was in some doubt. However, the question was immaterial because the principle expressed by the Fifth Amendment was a declaration of the existing rights of citizens, stating that "though it may well be doubted whether as a constitutional provision, this applies to the state governments, yet it is the declaration of what in its nature is the power of all governments, and the right of its citizens; the one to take property, the other to compensation."[114] In support for his position that the Fifth Amendment might not apply, Baldwin cited the decision by New York Chief Justice Spencer in *Bradshaw v. Rogers and Magee*, in which the court held that the fundamental obligation to compensate for a taking of property existed notwithstanding any constitutional provision as a matter of fundamental principle.[115] Like Barron's attorney David Hoffman, Baldwin invoked natural-law theorists Grotius, Pufendorf, and Vattel for the principle that while the right to take property for public use is an attribute of sovereignty, the right to make just compensation was an absolute corollary to that right.[116]

In the trial court, Mayer and Hoffman expressed their client's claim for damages as required by a largely static view of the common law. The right that property could not be taken except upon payment of just compensation applied regardless of the city's claim that they were simply following the law, exercising their police power, or abating nuisance. Before the court of appeals, they transitioned their argument. While they still considered this right as extraconstitutional, they now framed it as provided by the social contract, by natural law, and as required as a fundamental principle of legitimate government since classical times. Preparing an argument before the Supreme Court presented a different challenge. While Marshall's court would seem receptive to a claim that favored the federal constitution over the power of the states, Mayer and Hoffman were largely victims of poor timing. When they decided to appeal the case to the Supreme Court in January 1831, they were pressing this issue at the worst possible time.

6

A Question of Great Importance

Barron at the Supreme Court

We are up to the chin in politics.

John Marshall to Joseph Story, August 2, 1832

On a cold Friday, February 8, 1833, Mayer walked up the hill to the U.S. Capitol and climbed its steps.[1] Once inside, he headed north toward the Senate before taking the stairs down to the Supreme Court.[2] Until the Court moved into its own building in 1935, it met mostly wherever it could find space. In February 1833, when *Barron* finally arrived on its docket, the Court met in a space directly beneath the old Senate chamber.[3] As Mayer made his way to the courtroom, he was surely running through the argument in his head. Oral arguments in the early Supreme Court, which enforced no time limits, were often grand displays of oratorical skill. In contrast to the more modern tradition of verbal sparring between counsel and justices, the Marshall court allowed attorneys to argue uninterrupted. Other than an occasional question from Justice Story, observers noted that the justices sat silent and almost completely motionless during argument.[4] Perhaps Mayer hoped to emulate the success of some of the more famous advocates of the age who had argued before the Court in this grand style: Daniel Webster, William Wirt, John Sergeant, Roger Taney, and even Henry Clay.[5]

Despite the magnitude of the hearing, Mayer sat at the counsel table alone. His more experienced colleague David Hoffman had disappeared.[6] Hoffman was a major legal figure in the early republic era as a practicing attorney and, more important, as a pioneering law professor. His *Course of Legal Study*, first published in 1817, received praise from the elite of the early American legal and political profession, including giants like sitting U.S. Supreme Court Justices Joseph Story and Gabriel Duvall, New York Governor DeWitt Clinton, Chancellor James Kent of New York, and even Chief Justice John Marshall.[7] Even more important, Marshall not only respected Hoffman's written work but also personally attested to his abilities as an attorney. The year *Barron* came before the Supreme Court, Marshall penned a testimonial describing the legal aptitude of David Hoffman, who with his law partner republished the endorsement as part of a newspaper advertisement. The advertisement noted Hoffman's status as an attorney authorized to practice before the Supreme Court. Printed in a D.C. newspaper, it clearly aimed at attracting clients with cases before the Court.[8]

Mayer must certainly have felt the added burden of appearing before the Court without his more famous, more experienced, and better-connected counterpart. The absence of Hoffman not only would have subtracted significant prestige from their legal team but also would have sheared much of the natural law–based arguments that were so prominent in their case before the Maryland Court of Appeals. Hoffman's biographer argues that his well-known difficulties, both real and self-inflicted, with the trustees of the University of Maryland were to blame for the absence. Embroiled in a dispute with the trustees over legal fees Hoffman felt the school still owed him, he spent the early part of 1833 preparing to depart for an extended tour of Europe. For their part, on April 16, 1833, the same month that Hoffman left Baltimore, the trustees sued him for the return of books, furniture, and other items they felt belonged to the school. Staying true to form and maintaining that these items were purchased with his personal funds, Hoffman kept the items and sailed to England.[9] Instead of assisting Mayer with the presentation at the Supreme Court, Hoffman instead spent February 1833 corresponding with American elites like James Madison and seeking letters of reference that would help his introduction into polite European society.[10]

Not only did Mayer face the Court alone, but he again had to match the exceedingly formidable skills of Baltimore's attorneys, Roger Taney and John Scott.[11] Since their last meeting at the Maryland Court of Appeals in December 1830, Taney was appointed attorney general of the United States, though he appeared before the Court in *Barron* as a private attorney. While no one yet knew that Taney would ultimately replace John Marshall as chief justice of the Supreme Court, he nonetheless supplied significant legal heft to the city's cause and certainly exuded a strong presence at the Court. For example, Taney appeared before the Court as counsel in eighteen of the forty-one reported cases heard before the Supreme Court during the 1833 term.[12] Luke Tiernan was well aware of the task ahead of Mayer; only two years earlier, Scott and Taney successfully represented Tiernan before the Supreme Court in an unrelated commercial case. Perhaps seeking to emulate those past results, Tiernan posted the $500 bond needed to appeal *Barron* to the Supreme Court just five months after the successful conclusion of that matter.[13]

MAYER'S ARGUMENT

In the darkened chamber, Mayer faced the justices. The Supreme Court occupied a modest semicircular room. The justices sat behind seven individual desks with their backs to the outside wall and faced the lawyers' desks and, behind these, a few rows of seats available for spectators. Justice Marshall sat in the middle with the associate justices—Joseph Story, Gabriel Duvall, Smith Thompson, John McLean, and William Johnson—to his left and right. Henry Baldwin's desk was unoccupied. The justices' desks were separated from counsel by a railing. Three arches behind the justices framed heavily curtained windows that provided the only source of natural light in the entire courtroom. There were neither contiguous offices for the justices nor any private rooms. Indeed, the justices would put on their robes and enter the Court from a small room that was in full view of the main courtroom.[14] We can only guess what Mayer thought as he took a deep breath and prepared to begin. It had been eighteen years since Barron and Craig had bought the wharf and eleven since Mayer had filed the lawsuit in Baltimore County Court. Since then, his nominal clients had lost the business and their fortunes before both passing away. Was he thinking about them? Was he concerned about pleasing his true client, Luke Tiernan, who owned the right to any damages that might come from a successful appeal? Since Tiernan was most certainly paying his legal fees, Mayer likely felt the expectations that come with representing a well-connected client. Or, was Mayer preoccupied with thinking about his claim? He was arguing that the

Court must recognize that the Bill of Rights applied to the states. While judges across the country had recognized this principle, this was the first time the issue had come before the Supreme Court.

In the end, the final act of the *Barron* drama was a letdown. Neither Mayer's preparation, Hoffman's exit, or Taney's prestige made much of a difference. Before Mayer could begin, Marshall interrupted. Rather than allowing an extended oration on the applicability of the Bill of Rights or the nature of rights themselves, Marshall advised Mayer to confine his argument to the question whether, under the Fifth Amendment, the Court had jurisdiction to hear the case.[15]

Strictly speaking, the Judiciary Act of 1789 set forth the Supreme Court's authority to hear the case. The first Congress passed the act to set up the federal judiciary and to help specifically define the functions of the Supreme Court as more generally outlined in Article III of the Constitution. Section 25 of the act set forth the scenarios under which the Supreme Court could review the actions of state courts, including when the latter ruled against the validity of a U.S. statute or treaty or against any privilege or right claimed under the Constitution, federal treaty, or federal law. It also included the scenario put forth in the *Barron* case, namely, when a party argued that a state law or action was repugnant to the U.S. Constitution and a state court ruled in favor of the state.[16]

By admonishing Mayer to discuss only whether the Court had jurisdiction under the 1789 Judiciary Act, Marshall effectively kept him from arguing most of the points made at the Maryland Court of Appeals. During his appellate argument, Mayer and Hoffman found precedent for their claims of compensation in a wide range of sources, including the common law, fundamental or natural law, and even in Roman history. However, instead of allowing extensive oratory on the nature and source of rights, Marshall framed the argument for him. Mayer began within these narrow confines and continued over the course of that Friday, resuming the following Monday.[17] Before starting on the main body of his argument, Mayer tackled one of the most critical problems with the case, namely, identifying the property that was actually taken. The facts of the case would prove tricky on this point. As a technical matter, the city did not physically "take" or appropriate the wharf property itself; rather, it took actions that destroyed the wharf's intended purpose. Mayer had his work cut out for him because Fifth Amendment takings jurisprudence in 1833 had not evolved to the point that recognized the ways that lawyers could expand their views of takings. For example, Mayer could not yet rely on the modern concept of a regulatory taking, or the concept that governmental actions, like zoning laws, were so burdensome to the intended use of the property that the regulations effectively "took" the property, though no physical appropriation occurred.[18] However, that the wharf property was not physically taken by the city was not fatal to the claim. Mayer repeated the argument made by David Hoffman before the appeals court, namely, that use of the water around the wharf was an incorporeal hereditament, a common law doctrine. In making this claim, Hoffman and Mayer claimed that the water surrounding the wharf was part of the property interest that they gained when they purchased the wharf, similar to the right of a landowner to collect rents from tenants.[19]

Once he identified the property interest that was taken by the city, Mayer then transitioned to the body of his argument, structured around main five claims. His first two points were generally routine elements of any suit against a governmental entity. For example, Mayer first alleged that the mayor and city council, despite their status as agents of the state clothed with sovereign immunity, were nonetheless liable for their tortious acts.[20] Mayer had to address the legal rule that the sovereign, or government, cannot be sued without its consent. The concept of sovereign immunity in the United States is most notably tied to the Eleventh Amendment to the Constitution. This amendment provides that the federal courts cannot hear cases against any state by a citizen of another state or foreign nation.[21] Ratified in 1795 and constituting the first amendment of the Constitution after the inclusion of the Bill of Rights, the Eleventh Amendment was drafted to overrule the early Supreme Court decision of *Chisholm v. Georgia* (1793). There the Court interpreted its powers as including the right to hear a case between a citizen of one state (here, South Carolina) and the state government of another (here, Georgia).[22] However, this was not fatal for Mayer's argument. Indeed, a textual reading of the Eleventh Amendment shows that it would not apply since his clients, Barron and Craig, brought a claim against their own state of Maryland. However, there was more in Marshall's own jurisprudence that should have helped. For example, Marshall routinely decided Eleventh Amendment cases that came before him in ways that would allow the Court wide latitude to hear state law cases. In *Osborn v. Bank of the United States* (1824), the Court heard a dispute from Ohio where that state taxed and then seized funds from the local Bank of the United States branch, actions in clear violation of the Court's grand pronouncement in *McCulloch v. Maryland* (1819) that the "necessary and proper" clause of Article I, Section 8, gave the federal government the implied authority to charter this bank. Not only were the Ohio laws that ordered the taxing and removal of the federal deposits unconstitutional, but the state officers who carried out the law were held personally responsible for their actions.[23]

Second, Mayer needed to prove that the actions that caused the damage to Barron and Craig's wharf were done by the state. Mayer pointed out that the acts in question were exercised under the authority of the state of Maryland pursuant to the enabling legislation granted to the city by the Maryland legislature.[24] Here, Mayer established a connection between the acts of the city and the state of Maryland. Since Baltimore was a municipal corporation created by the Maryland General Assembly, all of the actions taken by the city, including those that damaged the wharf, were legally attributable to the state of Maryland.

With the predicate points out of the way, Mayer's next argument got to the heart of the matter. Parroting the necessary language of Section 25 of the Judiciary Act, Mayer claimed that because Maryland's actions effectively took Barron's property without compensation, its acts were repugnant to the Fifth Amendment. To show that Maryland was required to observe this Fifth Amendment requirement, Mayer relied on an expansive view of rights. He argued that the Fifth Amendment was enacted to protect the people in every state. The states were thus required to observe the Bill of Rights since they were designed to protect them as citizens as the United States. Here, Mayer implicitly recognized that just as the federal system allowed for two sovereigns over the same geographic area—state and federal—it naturally extended to the people. While Mayer did not engage the larger question about who created the Constitution—the states or a collective national people—he implied that every American was a member of a state but also a citizen of the United States. The states had the power to create their own rules regarding the matters within their jurisdiction, but they had no power to infringe on the rights of those same people that were protected in their dual capacity as U.S. citizens.[25]

Fourth, Mayer then returned to Marshall's question of jurisdiction. Mayer again cited Section 25 and reminded Marshall that it gave the Court the authority, first, to hear cases decided from the highest court of a state and, second, when there was a question of whether a state statute, or state authority more generally, was in conflict with the Constitution. Here, both grounds were met.[26]

Finally, Mayer used his fifth point to expand his argument despite Marshall's limitations. Mayer advised that the Court was not limited to simply determining questions of jurisdiction, hoping to break free of the restraints laid down by Marshall at the start of the oral arguments. Mayer reminded the justices that they sat as an appeals court; as such, it was "not confined to the establishment of an abstract point of construction" but could take into account other factors to determine the rights of the parties. First, Mayer contended that the Court had the power to settle the nature of Barron's ownership in the water in which the wharf was located, likely hoping to preempt a ruling denying his Fifth Amendment claim on the grounds that Barron and Craig's property was not actually taken. Second, Mayer sought to turn the Court's attention away from looking at the matter as a simple all-or-nothing jurisdictional question and to consider the common law merits of the case. For example, Mayer contended that the Court could determine whether Baltimore's actions constituted a private nuisance, thus allowing a valid cause of action against the city by his clients. Not only had Mayer spent eleven years framing the case in this way, he also had generations of precedent on which to draw. Barron and Craig's claim makes a great deal of sense under the logic of the common law of nuisance.[27] Given Marshall's limits, Mayer used this last point as an attempt to introduce as much of his remaining argument as possible, as would be expected from an experienced attorney.

Mayer could have saved his breath. Following his argument, Marshall incredibly stopped Taney and Scott from even presenting their rebuttal and concluded the hearing.[28] Would Marshall have been so curt if David Hoffman had been presenting the case for Barron? Conceivably, Marshall might have made the city at least go through the motions of presenting a rebuttal. Nonetheless, it was clear in the Court's opinion that by February 1833, Marshall had already decided that the states did not have to observe the Bill of Rights even before Mayer walked into the courtroom. Marshall's certainty is evident in the Court's opinion issued on Saturday, February 16, 1833, only five days after the oral arguments.[29]

THE END OF THE LINE

In the eleven years before the case reached the Supreme Court, all the parties aggressively debated the role of rights. Their varied arguments exposed the many competing views that were competing for primacy. They engaged in a rich debate that revealed the unsettled nature of rights at that time. For example, we saw the interplay between rights as an individual possession and rights enjoyed by a community, echoing Blackstone's absolute versus relative rights binary. In addition, the players all enunciated different strands of thought regarding the location of rights themselves: Hoffman espoused individually based natural rights; Taney argued for community-based rights to ensure harmonious order; Archer held that compensation was required by the principles of the common law; and Mayer initially pled that Barron and Craig's claim for reimbursement was predicated on the accepted and routine procedural remedy classified under trespass. Instead of engaging this lively debate, the Court's unanimous decision viewed the right that the government could not take property without some sort of due process as hinging solely on the explicit language of a written constitution. It then used this interpretation to demolish Barron and Craig's claim. While Mayer urged the Court to view the Fifth Amendment as protecting the right of all citizens from all governmental encroachment, Marshall's court reframed the issue as a jurisdictional question of whether the Fifth Amendment applied to state governments. After posing the question in this way, the Court answered that the "question thus presented is, we think, of great importance, but not of much difficulty."[30] True to its word, the Court disposed of Barron's case and altered the course of constitutional history in an opinion spanning just under five pages.

The Court structured its terse opinion around three main points. Writing for the Court, Marshall first expounded on the question of who created the Constitution. He noted that it was produced not by the states but by the people of the United States to establish a government for their benefit. The question regarding who created the Union, the states or a national American people, was as old as the Union itself. One view considered the Constitution as a compact of the various states. Indeed, during the decades before the Civil War, the various movements to secede from the Union rationalized their efforts by viewing the Constitution as a political agreement between sovereign states. The concept that a state can secede in the prewar constitutional order makes sense if one believes in this compact theory of the Constitution, as parties to a contract or a treaty can cancel the agreement under certain circumstances. However, if one believed, like Marshall, that the Union was created by a national people, secession is illogical. A state cannot break apart an agreement to which it is not a party. This view that a national people breathed life into the United States is evidenced textually in the very first words of the Preamble to the Constitution that framed the document: "We the People of the United States, in Order to form a more perfect Union." In addition, this view also looked at the way the Constitution was ratified. Instead of the state legislatures ratifying the Constitution, which would make it a compact of those states, the Constitution was approved by special constitutional conventions of men specifically elected for this sole purpose. That these conventions were elected on a state-by-state basis and were largely composed of the same men who served as state legislators makes this a bit of a fine point, but it is an important distinction nonetheless. This view of constitutional authorship was similar to the view espoused by its contemporaneous proponents, such as James Madison or Alexander Hamilton, as well as disparagingly noted by its opponents, such as Patrick Henry or the antifederalist treatise writer, Brutus.[31] This same debate was still raging in 1830 in the famous debate between Daniel Webster of Massachusetts and Robert Hayne of South Carolina.[32]

While Marshall began with this proposition, he quickly qualified its potential. In *McCulloch v. Maryland* Marshall's court, before holding Maryland's tax unconstitutional, had asserted that the constitution was a creation of a national people and not a compact among sovereign states. In *Barron*, however, the Court made a comparatively milder point.[33] Marshall's court recognized that all Americans were citizens of both state and federal governments. As a result, the rights they enjoyed depended on the constitutional arrangement those citizens had with each government. According to Marshall in the Court's decision, "the Constitution was ordained and established by the people of the United States for themselves, for their own government, and not for the government of the individual states."[34] Each state had also established their own constitution, created by the citizens of the respective states. In those various state constitutions, the people of each state provided their own protections against their respective state governments. As such, the Fifth Amendment restrained only the federal government.

Second, the Court addressed Mayer's view that the Constitution was intended to secure the rights of these national people against infringement by any government. To support the claim that the Fifth Amendment applied only to the federal government, Marshall's court transitioned to a textual reading of the Constitution. Other that the First Amendment, there is no language specifying whether the Bill of Rights apply exclusively to the federal government, to state governments, or to both.[35] To remedy this omission, the Court examined Article I of the Constitution, which details the powers of Congress, and focused specifically on two sections: Article I, Section 9, which specifically limits the power of Congress; and Article I, Section 10, which restricts the state governments. The Court explained that these restrictions on the states, such as prohibiting them from entering into foreign treaties or coining money, existed because they related to common national interests that would prove chaotic if attempted individually by each state.[36] The Court noted that these restrictions on state authority were permissible since they were "averred in positive words." As a result, if the liberties set forth in the Bill of Rights were also to restrict the states, they must likewise contain specific limiting language, which they did not.[37]

Marshall's court ended the opinion with a nod toward history. They posited that if the people of each state had wanted more limits on their respective state governments, they had the power to enact such limits in their own state constitutions. Further, if Congress had intended the Bill of Rights to bind the states, they would have made this clear, writing that had it "engaged in the extraordinary occupation of improving the constitutions of the several states, by affording the people additional protection from the exercise of power from their own governments . . . they would have declared this purpose in plain and intelligible language."[38] Here, the Court was attempting to buttress its second, more textual interpretation by using history to help prove its point. The Court invoked the state constitutional ratifying conventions held to determine whether they would indeed ratify the Bill of Rights. Marshall's court noted that in the various ratifying conventions, almost every state "demanded security against the apprehended encroachments of the general government—not against those of the local governments."[39]

As a result, the Court held that the Fifth Amendment applied solely to limit the power of the federal government, and not the states.

Since this meant that there was no repugnancy between the actions of the city of Baltimore and the Constitution, as required by the Judiciary Act, the Court did not have jurisdiction. The case was dismissed.[40] In many ways, the Court's ruling in *Barron* is widely considered common sense or accurate by modern commentators because its view of law so thoroughly comports with existing notions of legal practice. It would be unthinkable for an attorney to argue a rights case before a tribunal without pointing to the constitution, statute, or rule where the right existed. Indeed, the vast majority of the rights revolution of the twentieth century concerns the ways that lawyers were successful in convincing courts to recognize that the liberties written in the Bill of Rights were also incorporated into various clauses of the Fourteenth Amendment and thus made applicable against the states. Virtually this entire endeavor is predicated on envisioning rights as textually based; ask any professor who has tried to explain why we read the Sixth Amendment's right to counsel as incorporated against the states through the due process clause of the Fourteenth Amendment or any student who has had to wrestle with this clunky and seemingly archaic method. *Barron* is unquestioned because it reflects a view of rights as existing by virtue of their existence in written documents. It is also the classic starting point for the story of the incorporation of rights and exemplifies the pre–Civil War constitutional order that the Fourteenth Amendment was designed to remedy.

Compare Marshall's logic in *Barron* to some of his opinions from earlier decades. If we return to the beginning of Marshall's judicial career in *Marbury*, we see Marshall asserting the right of the Supreme Court to hold legislative acts unconstitutional.[41] Marshall eloquently described the basis for this power by describing the purpose of a constitution:

> That the people have an original right to establish, for their future government, such principles as, in their opinion, shall most conduce to their happiness, is the basis, on which the whole American fabric has been erected. The exercise of this original right is a very great exertion; nor can it, nor ought it to be frequently repeated. The principles, therefore, are deemed *fundamental*. And as the authority, from which they proceed, is supreme, and can seldom act, they are designed to be permanent.[42]

With respect to altering the Constitution, "there is no middle ground. The constitution is either a superior, paramount law, unchangeable by ordinary means, or it is on a level with ordinary legislative acts, and like other acts, is alterable when the legislature shall please to alter it."[43] The language in this famous opinion is well known. We can compare the language used in *Marbury* to *Barron*, written thirty years after *Marbury*. In *Marbury*, Marshall bravely and radically set forth the equality of the judiciary in order to act as a guardian against encroachment from the legislature. However, thirty years later in *Barron*, Marshall veered sharply into the perspective of rights as given or taken away by positive enactments of legislators. After reading sections 9 and 10 of Article I, which place limitations of the powers of the federal and state governments, respectively, Marshall determined that all limitations on the states must be specifically set forth in the Constitution, strictly construing that "if, in every inhibition intended to act on state power, words are employed, which directly express that intent; some strong reason must be assigned for departing from this safe and judicious course, in framing the amendments, before that departure can be assumed. We search in vain for that reason."[44]

If we examine the *Barron* decision, we can see that Marshall's analysis as expressed in the Court's opinion is incomplete in many places. Consider the second part of the ruling, which held that the Fifth Amendment did not apply to the states because the constitutional framers failed to specifically assert that it did. As a member of both the Virginia convention that ratified the Constitution in 1788 and a delegate to the Virginia legislature that ultimately ratified the Bill of Rights in 1791, Marshall knew that the two provisions were enacted at different times and under very different circumstances. Indeed, the opposite argument—that the lack of limiting language in Article I means that the amendments have universal application—is actually more reasonable from a purely textual analysis. If the amendments were meant to apply only to the federal government, they would contain the same prefatory qualifications as Article I, Section 9. By failing to recognize the historical context of these two very different moments of constitutional drafting, Marshall's thinking shows a common defect with textual interpretation.

Similarly, consider Marshall's third point in which he looked to history to support his view that the constitutional framers did not intend the Bill of Rights to apply to the states. As Marshall rightly noted, the Constitution itself was not intended to restructure the state governments. Marshall may be the last American jurist that could plausibly use an original-intent interpretation without any dissent; indeed, he could claim authoritatively that Virginia, by demanding a bill of rights to limit the new federal government, did not intend for those demands to be read as later binding the state.[45] From a purely textual reading of the Constitution and the ratifying debates, Marshall's position is certainly quite reasonable. Based on this logic, if the Fifth Amendment was meant to apply to the states, it was up to the framers of the Constitution to ensure that it was drafted in such a manner. For the Fifth Amendment and the rest of the Bill of Rights to apply to the states, history would have to wait for the Civil War, the resulting Fourteenth Amendment, and the selective incorporation process that would proceed piecemeal over the following one hundred and fifty years. However, if we view the same question with an appreciation that constitutions simply declared preexisting rights, did the insertion of those rights into the U.S. Constitution mean that liberties such as the private property rights at issue in *Barron*, which trace their recognition to the Magna Carta, now no longer apply because they were not explicitly mentioned as also applying to the state governments? Marshall's point works if we appreciate rights as applicable only if contained in written constitutions. As we saw in chapter 3, Marshall's positivist interpretation of rights was not a tenable option for those from the colonial and founding generations and was a very debatable interpretation during the early republic. Fundamentally, Marshall approached the rights question from a different perspective than Mayer or even the trial court. Looking at *Barron* from their perspective makes Marshall's opinion illogical. How could these rights that predated the Constitution now not apply?

The ultimate effect of the Court's ruling meant that the right to compensation for a taking could not be violated by the federal government, but it could be done by the states if they so desired. Citizens could keep their state governments from doing this only by changing their state constitutions. In making rulings of this sort, Marshall's court enunciated a view of rights as emanating from written documents. The right at issue in *Barron* existed in some form as far back as Magna Carta. Instead of viewing this right, and indeed all rights, as simply declared by written constitutions, Marshall's court reclassified them as effectively existing only to the extent that they were recognized by written constitutions. By characterizing rights as creatures of positive law, they could now be subject to the same legal rules as ordinary statutes. In this light, rights were not timeless liberties that existed independent of any government; instead, they could be obeyed or disregarded dependent on the governmental entity in question.

EXPLAINING *BARRON*

So why did *Barron* turn out this way? For many historians, *Barron* is the odd piece of the puzzle, a strikingly pro-state decision that does not fit with the rest.[46] As we saw in chapter 3, the Court's opinion locating the source of rights in the written constitution was a minority view for the era in which it was penned. The ruling is also out of joint with respect to Marshall's own jurisprudence. It is an article of faith for Supreme Court watchers that Marshall was not only an excellent jurist, but also a masterful politician who through force of will and persuasion established the Court as a prime agent for strengthening the federal government. Similarly, much of Marshall's jurisprudence also reflected personal and historic connections to contemporary events, but *Barron* seems out of place. The holding that the Bill of Rights did not bind the states has puzzled many, including one historian who viewed it as "an extraordinary concession to state autonomy not compelled by the language of any of the original ten amendments except the first."[47] Marshall's *Barron* opinion is usually considered an uncharacteristic outlier.[48]

The *Barron* anomaly is best explained by thinking about the case historically. If we try to understand the decision by placing it within three decades of Marshall's jurisprudence, we will continue to miss the signs that led to *Barron* emerging the only way it could. Let's return to January 1831, the month that John Marshall decided he wanted *Barron* before the Supreme Court. In 1831 the Court did not have the luxury of selecting the cases it wanted to decide, as the Court was not first invested with discretionary power until 1891.[49] Nonetheless, some scholars argue that modern observers sometimes make too much of this fact. The Court was able to exercise a degree of discretion over its docket through aggressively seeking to sign the appeals documentation in cases it sought to hear. In cases where a party sought to appeal a judgment of the highest court of a state, a writ of error would be drafted by the appealing party's attorney and could be approved either by a justice of the state supreme court or by a justice of the U.S. Supreme Court. State courts often did not want to sign writs of error to grant the Supreme Court jurisdiction to overrule their decisions.[50] In Barron's case, however, Marshall personally signed the writ of error in January 1831, when he seemed intent on hearing the case. However, while the underlying record was received by the Court in August 1831, the case was not scheduled for the 1832 docket. By the time *Barron* was ready for hearing in February 1833, two years had passed since Marshall's signing of the writ of error, and quite a bit had changed.

Personally, professionally, and almost existentially, Marshall was confronted with crises after he signed the *Barron* writ of error that he had never faced before. Despite leading the federal judiciary for nearly three decades, he now faced challenges that tested the core of his character. The year 1831 was devastating personally. After returning to Virginia in March after the 1831 Supreme Court term, Marshall began to experience excruciating pain, which was later discovered to be caused by bladder stones. He spent much of the remainder of the year in extreme discomfort. Marshall was ultimately forced to travel to Philadelphia in October 1831 for surgery. After undergoing a procedure that is painful even to read about, the surgeon removed close to one thousand stones from Marshall.[51] He miraculously survived the operation and would live largely pain free for another four years. Although Marshall was able to return to his federal circuit court responsibilities in Richmond for the opening of the November 1831 term, his good fortune soon ran out. In mid-December, his wife Polly fell ill. Just short of their forty-ninth wedding anniversary, Polly passed away on Christmas Day, 1831.[52]

Professionally, Marshall's working relationship within the Court was also changing. When in Washington, D.C., for the Court's term, the justices had most recently resided together at Brown's Indian Queen Hotel on Pennsylvania Avenue. Being near the foot of the U.S. Capitol, the justices could dine together, socialize, and conveniently walk to the Court. Recent Jackson-appointee Henry Baldwin replaced Marshall's longtime ally Bushrod Washington and instantly upset the chemistry of the Court. Not only did Baldwin dissent seven times in 1831, further shattering the Marshall court's practice of issuing one opinion, but he also proved personally volatile.[53] During the 1831 term, he unexpectedly and inexplicably advised Marshall that he did not like staying at the Indian Queen, despite its good reputation.[54] Seeking to maintain harmony on the Court, the Chief Justice placated Baldwin and agreed to allow him to find alternate communal lodgings for the 1832 session. By the start of the 1833 session, Baldwin had lapsed into a mental illness that would force him to miss the entire term.[55] Charles Hobson argues that Marshall endured this drastic inconvenience because he believed he would likely retire soon if, of course, Andrew Jackson was no longer president after the 1832 election.[56] All he had to do was wait until the end of 1832 to make sure. Events in Georgia would ensure that his anticipated final year was one of his worst.

Hundreds of miles south of Washington, D.C., the state of Georgia prepared to settle old scores. Within the state borders lay a good portion of the ancestral homeland of the Cherokee Nation. One of the so-called Five Civilized Tribes of the Southeast, the Cherokees occupied a prime location in northwest Georgia. Like many native nations, the Cherokees had learned hard lessons. Beginning in 1819, the Cherokees set in motion a series of reforms that were consciously directed toward adopting the methods of the Americans in order to revitalize their nation and become less economically and politically dependent on the United States.[57] Much of this transformation depended on outwardly embracing the Americans' ideologies regarding the role of native peoples in the expanding republic. One view, shared by persons like Thomas Jefferson and George Washington, saw native peoples as capable of assimilation into American society if they embraced Christianity, education, and individual land ownership for western-style agriculture.[58] Of course, while this belief was beneficial on its face, it still mirrored the limits of tolerance of the age. Assimilation meant cultural destruction in order to survive. The opposite view did not need to wrestle with these fine points, however. It reserved no place in the American republic for native peoples, neither figuratively and certainly not physically; native peoples were to make way for American progress.[59] For Georgia, the continued presence of the Cherokees, who occupied increasingly valuable land, was not only an irritant but was also a constant reminder of an unfulfilled agreement by the federal government going back decades.

In 1802, Georgia deeded its western lands to the federal government in return for its pledge to extinguish Native American land claims within the state.[60] Over twenty-five years and four presidential administrations had come and gone, and yet the Cherokee Nation remained. Making matters worse, many Cherokees had wholeheartedly embraced the assimilation model. They allowed missionaries to establish schools for the education of their people. Sequoia translated the Cherokee language into writing, the first for a Native American tongue. The subsequent creation of *The Phoenix*, a bilingual Cherokee-English newspaper, aptly captured the rising fortunes of the Cherokee Nation. Many Cherokees became virtually indistinguishable from their fellow Georgians, owning vast farms worked by slaves.[61] Finally, in 1827 the Cherokees created a constitution, announcing their status as a sovereign independent nation with their own laws and court system, and specifically delineating their boundaries.[62] Not only was the federal government not honoring its agreement to remove the Cherokees, but the Cherokees seemed to become more entrenched by the year. By December of the same year, Georgia passed a resolution that announced its legal jurisdiction over Cherokee territory, in effect treating the Cherokee Constitution and its pronouncement of sovereignty as a nullity. For Georgia, "the Indians are tenants" and possessed their land by the consent of the state.[63]

While the resolution did not force the hand of the Adams administration, everything changed after the 1828 election of Andrew Jackson.[64] In December 1828, shortly after Jackson's electoral triumph, Georgia formally annexed the Cherokee lands lying within the state. In a signal that they had faith in Jackson to come to their aid, the Georgia law was not scheduled to take effect until June 1, 1830.[65] Jackson did not disappoint. Georgia rightly anticipated that Jackson would force the issue that decades of federal officials had ignored. In a perverse twist on the assimilationists' emphasis on civilization as a means toward entry into American society, Jackson famously argued in his first message to Congress that he was concerned with the preservation of Native America culture. If the Five Civilized Tribes remained in the southeast, their culture, like that of the Mohegan, the Narragansett, and the Delaware in the north, would be forever lost. If, however, they agreed to voluntary remove themselves to the Oklahoma Territory as he demanded, they would be able to preserve their heritage.[66] This was just the type of rhetoric the state of Georgia was counting on from the Jackson administration.

Jackson viewed the Cherokee declaration of sovereignty as unacceptable and successfully navigated through Congress an Indian Removal Act that would relocate all five of the civilized tribes west of the Mississippi. Signed into law by Jackson on May 28, 1830, only four days before the Georgia law went into effect, this act signaled to the Cherokees that their treaty partner, the U.S. government, had abandoned them.[67] As anticipated, Georgia extended its laws over the Cherokee territory and outlawed the meeting of Cherokee government, the sitting of its courts, or the enforcement of its laws. Surveyors streamed into Cherokee land and laid the practical groundwork to carve up their nation. By October 1830, the recipients of Cherokee land under the Georgia lottery system began forcibly removing the Cherokees from their homes.[68]

Since the president and Congress had failed them, the Cherokee Nation turned to the federal courts to stop Georgia. John Marshall's Supreme Court would appear to provide a measure of hope. In his three decades leading the Court, Marshall had proven himself a tireless supporter of a vigorous federal government. In an age filled with talk of sovereignty by the men of Georgia, South Carolina, or his native Virginia, Marshall was of another generation: he was a member of the Virginia convention that ratified the Constitution; he served as secretary of state under the first Adams administration. In short, he was a Federalist that clung to his ideals long after his party ceased to exist. Marshall remembered the turmoil of the 1780s, the long decade between the end of the Revolution and the framing of the Constitution. He saw how the states refused to fund the central government; he remembered the states closing their courts to creditors and printing worthless paper money; he recalled how Daniel Shays and his army surrounded the armory in western Massachusetts in the winter of 1787, an act that finally convinced the states to send delegates to Philadelphia to discuss amending the Articles of Confederation.

To place their plight before Marshall's court, the Cherokees hired some of the most prominent attorneys of the age, retaining former U.S. Attorney General William Wirt and John Sergeant to craft a legal strategy to save their nation from destruction. Both were opponents of Jackson; indeed, Wirt resigned in 1829 after Jackson's election and unsuccessfully ran against him for president in 1832 on the Anti-Masonic ticket, while Sergeant served as Henry Clay's running mate for the National Republicans in the same contest.[69] Their first opportunity quickly presented itself. In December 1830, Marshall ordered the state of Georgia to appear before the Court regarding a Georgia court's trial, conviction, and death sentence of George Tassells, a Cherokee accused of killing another Cherokee on Cherokee land. Wirt appealed Tassells' conviction to the Supreme Court under the theory that Georgia lacked any jurisdiction to punish this crime. Georgia characteristically viewed Marshall's order to appear before the Court as an affront to the rights of the state. Not only did the state disregard Marshall's command, but it purposefully rushed Tassells to the gallows within two days of the legislature's receipt of his order.[70]

At issue in the Tassells case was a question of sovereignty. Could Georgia extend its jurisdiction over Cherokee land and citizens? While Tassells' execution made this question moot, the underlying problem of sovereignty had to be addressed. The Cherokees had to obtain a legal ruling that Georgia could not claim jurisdiction over the Cherokees, since it was recognized by its treaty partner, the United States. The Cherokees needed to show that Georgia had no standing to interfere with this relationship. With the Tassells' appeal foreclosed, Wirt chose to file an injunction in the Supreme Court challenging the right of Georgia to negate Cherokee sovereignty and extend its laws. Wirt served the injunction on the Georgia governor three days after Tassells' hanging.[71] On March 18, 1831, Marshall delivered his opinion in *Cherokee Nation v. Georgia* (1831).[72] While he ruled against the Cherokee Nation, he did so only on procedural grounds. Article III of the Constitution sets forth the types of cases that the Court can hear. In addition to those cases that naturally implicate the federal courts—such as disputes concerning U.S. laws, admiralty cases, or those suits where the United States was a party—Article III also provides the Court with the ability to hear cases under what is referred to as its diversity jurisdiction. Diversity jurisdiction is a way for federal courts to hear cases that might not get an impartial hearing in state tribunals, such as lawsuits between two states, between a state and a citizen of a different state, or between citizens of different states. The same article also gives the Court the ability to hear cases between a state and a foreign state.[73] If the Cherokee Nation could not successfully argue that they were a "foreign state," the Court could conceivably refuse to hear their appeal. Marshall, who authored the majority opinion, did just that. In so doing, he presented both an obstacle and an opportunity. He held that the Cherokee Nation was not a foreign state and thus could not bring suit in federal court, yet it was not without its own sovereignty. Rather, Marshall identified the Cherokees as a domestic dependent nation.[74] Though this sounds to modern ears as simultaneously condescending and a bit of an oxymoron, it did signal to Wirt and Sergeant that they should return to the Court if they could find a case that could overcome the Article III issue.

When the state of Georgia arrested missionaries Samuel Worcester and Elizur Butler for violating one of its state laws extended over Cherokee territory, that opportunity arrived. Notorious for their opposition to removal, missionaries were a particular irritant. The Georgia legislature had provided a way to neutralize outsiders like Worcester and Butler by requiring all persons living among the Cherokees to first obtain a permit and swear an oath to Georgia. Failing to do either, Butler and Worcester were arrested. On July 7, 1831, the men were sentenced by a Georgia court to the wildly disproportionate sentence of four years' imprisonment at hard labor in order to force them to accept pardons in exchange for their recognition of Georgia's authority over the Cherokees.[75] As missionaries of sturdy conviction, Georgia's plan backfired. Worcester and Butler refused to accept pardons and instead appealed their sentences to the U.S. Supreme Court, led again by Wirt and Sergeant. Unlike the jurisdictional problem that stymied *Cherokee Nation v. Georgia*, Worcester and Butler as American citizens were unquestionably entitled to use the federal courts to contest Georgia.[76] In *Worcester v. Georgia* (1832), Marshall again authored the majority opinion for the Court, which ruled against Georgia on all counts. Marshall held that the Cherokees, like other Indian nations, were a distinct and separate entity that retained all of its natural rights, excepting the right of negotiation and trade. Hinting at a much more narrowly tailored view of his prior opinions dealing with native land rights, Marshall held that Indian nations were bound to treat and ally only with the initial conqueror, in this case the United States. The Cherokee Nation was a distinct entity with treaty rights and obligations to its treaty partner, the United States, and as such Georgia had no standing to nullify Cherokee sovereignty. Georgia's laws over Cherokee territory were void and their convictions of the missionaries were reversed as unconstitutional.[77]

However, in many ways Marshall's political compass began to fail him. Having decided *Worcester* in March 1832, Marshall likely intended that his ruling in favor of the Cherokee Nation would place Jackson in a bind during a reelection year. For example, if Jackson enforced the order against Georgia, he would provoke outrage in the south. However, if he refused to enforce a court order, he would reinforce the view of many in the north and northwest that Jackson was an unprincipled tyrant.[78] Very quickly, the rumors flew in the press that Jackson had no intent to enforce the order, and Jackson took no action that would lead anyone to believe to the contrary.[79] Procedurally, since Marshall reversed the conviction, the matter went back to Georgia where Worcester's attorneys desperately tried to translate Marshall's edict into action. With the ruling in hand, local counsel for the Cherokees raced back to Georgia to secure the release of Worcester. The state court refused counsel's motion to issue a writ of habeas corpus to the prison where his clients were kept. The court even refused to allow the *Worcester* ruling into evidence. After denying both motions, the judge quickly left the bench to attend to his caseload presiding over the former Cherokee lands.[80] The Supreme Court also sought to obtain information that Georgia had failed to act on the *Worcester* ruling that invalidated the conviction, but these findings were not collected before the end of the Supreme Court's term, which concluded its 1832 session on March 17, 1832, only two weeks after its *Worcester* decision.[81] Since the Court did not release an order that directed a specific action, such as a granting of a habeas corpus petition that ordered Georgia to release the prisoners, Jackson was not necessarily in violation of any obligation to enforce federal law.[82] There was nothing for the Court to do until its next session commenced in January 1833.[83] In the meantime, Jackson won reelection, and his new vice president Martin Van Buren diffused the standoff by persuading Georgia governor Wilson Lumpkin to issue pardons to the missionaries and, more importantly, for Worcester and Butler to accept them.[84]

Why did Jackson cede control over the Cherokee lands to Georgia? Was it his personal views about the incompatibility of native peoples in the expanding nation, or was it his constitutional ideology that prohibited a sovereign Indian nation from existing within the boundaries of a likewise sovereign state?[85] While these are good explanations, any accurate answer has to also take into account more pragmatic reasons. Jackson was not going to take any actions that could possibly cause Georgia to exacerbate what he felt was an infinitely larger crisis occurring at the same time: nullification. Jackson was not going to allow Georgia to interfere, or possibly ally, with South Carolina during the Nullification Crisis of 1832.[86] We must examine and appreciate nullification as the immediate context to Marshall's *Barron* decision.

While the ostensible roots of the crisis between South Carolina and the federal government concerned the national tariff on manufactured products from England, the larger story was more complicated. In the heady days following the close of the War of 1812, South

Carolinians imagined that their plantation-based economy would continue to allow them access to fabulous wealth. Protectionary tariffs not only would allow American manufacturing to mature, but would help raise the revenue for the federal government to fund the roads, canals, and other internal improvements that were too important to be left to the will of the particular states.[87] However, in a little over a decade, the state would see the price of its staple crop of cotton plummet from $0.31 per pound in 1818 to $0.08 in 1831.[88] When Congress passed a new tariff in 1828 that added duties, thereby raising the price of imported goods like iron, steel, wool, hemp, flax, and molasses, South Carolina reacted.[89] The 1828 tariff was designed not only to protect fledgling American industries but also to help elect Jackson that year, and the final product had election written all over it. Jackson supporters engineered a tariff that would allow Jackson to steal the tariff support from President John Quincy Adams. Knowing that Jackson would carry the South but not New England, the tariff promoters sought to win support in the pro-tariff regions of the Mid-Atlantic and the West. Although the tariff satisfied the demands of these regions, it inflamed the South and New England, who were being asked to shoulder the burden. The 1828 tariff protected products that were not produced in the South, angering southerners upset over the natural price increases. The tariff also raised the cost of raw materials that many New Englanders relied on, such as the iron, molasses, and hemp that were essential to shipbuilders, distillers, and other craftsmen.[90]

John C. Calhoun, Jackson's first vice president, was able to retain support in his home state of South Carolina since his first days in Congress. However, his early advocacy for a national program of federally funded improvements and tariffs, which was considered not only reasonable but necessary given the lessons learned in the War of 1812, was significantly out of step with the mood of the state by the late 1820s.[91] Calhoun's political evolution in many ways mirrored the transformation of South Carolina itself. In the fall of 1828, Calhoun secretly authored the South Carolina Exposition, a treatise that not only laid out his restrictive views on the ability of the federal government to collect tariffs but also articulated that his remedy resided in the rights of states to effectively veto unconstitutional actions of the federal government as an essential attribute of their sovereignty.[92] By 1831, well aware that he was being passed over by Jackson as his successor in favor of Van Buren, Calhoun changed his focus. In July

1831, Calhoun decided to openly publish his views on the tariff debate. In his Fort Hill Address, Calhoun laid out his belief in compact theory, or the idea that the Union was created through an agreement of states that retained a large measure of their sovereignty. As such, the states retained their rights to "interpose" or judge whether the actions of the federal government exceeded its bounds as delineated by the Constitution, the concept of interposition a tipping of his hat to Jefferson's use of the term in the Virginia Resolution of 1798.[93]

Seeking a legislative solution, by July 14, 1832, Congress passed a compromise tariff that would take effect March 3, 1833. Years of agitation against the tariff led to its natural end in the state, despite its being hailed as an achievement. In the state elections of October 1832, the nullifiers had gained enough seats in the legislature to call for a state convention.[94] As expected, on November 24, 1832, the convention passed the Nullification Ordinance, which declared both the 1828 and 1832 Tariff Acts null and void within the state. No officer of the state or the federal government could lawfully enforce the tariff act in the state after February 1, 1833. All state officers were directed to take an oath to uphold the Nullification Ordinance; those who refused were to be removed from office. No cases that concerned the ordinance in any South Carolina court could be appealed to the U.S. Supreme Court. Those who attempted to seek relief in the Supreme Court were to be held in contempt of court. Finally, any attempt by the federal government to use force against the state would result in South Carolina dissolving its political connection with the other states; it would immediately organize a new government by its right as a "sovereign and independent" state.[95]

At roughly the same time, Jackson issued his Proclamation on Nullification, where he not only outlined his views on the idea of nullification but more importantly set forth his interpretation of the constitutional relationship between the states and the federal union. Jackson began by letting South Carolina know that he intended to enforce the tariff since it was part of his duty as chief executive to not only enforce federal law but to preserve the Union. South Carolina was wrong to claim that they could nullify federal law since other options to challenge the tariff were available, such as seeking redress in Congress or in the federal courts. With that in mind, Jackson denied that South Carolina, or any state for that matter, had the right to declare a federal law unconstitutional or to prohibit its enforcement.

For Jackson, such a proposition was illogical given the nature of the federal union. As the Constitution was ratified by a national American people, sitting in their respective conventions, as opposed to representing a compact of the states, a state could not secede from this political order.[96] On December 28, 1832, Calhoun formally resigned as vice president and was immediately appointed by South Carolina to represent it in the Senate.[97]

Thus, by the time the Court reconvened for the January 1833 term, Marshall returned to D.C. to face not only the indignity of his still unenforced decision in *Worcester* but also the return of Calhoun to Washington, this time as a senator prepared to do battle with the administration.[98] Calhoun wanted confrontation, but he was content to allow Jackson to play his familiar role of the aggressor. Indeed, Calhoun continued to use Jackson's positions as evidence of the tyrannical nature of the federal government.[99] On January 16, 1833, only one day after the Supreme Court heard oral arguments in the first case of its 1833 term, Jackson transmitted his message to Congress where he picked apart the legal and constitutional claims made in the Nullification Ordinance. He asked Congress for authority to move the collection posts away from the control of the South Carolina authorities.[100] In a speech to the Senate that same day, Calhoun countered Jackson's claims that South Carolina was openly hostile to the authority of the United States. Rather, for Calhoun, it was the U.S. government that was marshaling troops to confront South Carolina. Calhoun mockingly rejected Jackson's suggestion that South Carolina submit this dispute to the U.S. Supreme Court, noting the obvious hypocrisy of such a suggestion in the light of the Cherokee cases. For Calhoun, Jackson "had not held this opinion in reference to the resistance of the State of Georgia. A narrow river only divides the territory of Georgia from that of South Carolina; yet, on the one side, the power of the Supreme Court, as the arbiter in the last resort, is to be sustained; while, on the other side, the will of the Executive is to be supreme."[101]

Six days later, Calhoun upped the ante by proposing a series of resolutions in the Senate that would confirm his unique view of the nature of the Union. First, he sought a resolution in line with his constitutional theory delineating that it was the people of each state that created the Union, a clever point that sought to maintain the preeminent role of the states by coopting just enough of the theory that a national people created the U.S. through state ratifying conventions.

A second resolution maintained that, in giving life to the United States, the people of each state expressly delegated power to the federal government and reserved all others to themselves. In the event that the federal government exercised any power not delegated to it, that power would be considered unauthorized and void. Finally, Calhoun wanted a resolution declaring that arguments against South Carolina's position—such as that a national people created the Union, that states cannot punish treason, or that states cannot determine the powers delegated or reserved to the federal government "in the last resort"—were "without foundation in truth."[102]

Six days later, when fellow senators sought to introduce their own substitute resolutions or at least postpone Calhoun's resolutions so as to allow more time to resolve the tariff dispute and hopefully negate the necessity of needing to debate the proposed resolutions, Calhoun exploded. Intending to head off the substitute resolutions offered by Felix Grundy of Tennessee, Calhoun offered an amendment to Grundy's resolutions.[103] After parroting the language of the Tenth Amendment stating that the federal government possessed only the powers expressly granted to it by the Constitution while the remaining powers resided in the states or the people, he moved to the tariff issue at hand.[104] For the next two days, Calhoun sparred with William Wilkins of Pennsylvania over the extent to which South Carolina was readying itself for military action, and he clarified his constitutional position on the persons who created the Constitution with Theodore Frelinghuysen of New Jersey. As Calhoun reminded Frelinghuysen, the Constitution was not created by a national American people, nor was it devised by the states, as Frelinghuysen characterized Calhoun's position. Rather, Calhoun argued that the Constitution was the product of the people of the individual states.[105]

In the middle of this vortex, John Marshall reconvened the Supreme Court for its 1833 term. The Court heard its first oral arguments on January 16, 1833, one day after Jackson asked Congress for the authority to use military force against South Carolina and only two days after Georgia governor Wilson Lumpkin issued pardons to missionaries Worcester and Butler.[106] As the debate regarding the tariff, the use of force, the powers of the federal government, and indeed the nature and continued existence of the Union itself raged in the Senate, John Marshall's Supreme Court quietly went back to work downstairs. Consider how these twin crises were playing out across the nation. For example, on January 17, 1833, the day after the Court opened its 1833 session, the *New-York Spectator* carried an article that discussed both the still-unresolved issue of the missionaries languishing in a Georgia prison despite the Supreme Court's order as well as the actions of South Carolina in nullifying federal law. The *Spectator* did not mince words when it described the gravity of the situation to their readers: "All men must see, and it is idle to disguise it, that unless both South Carolina and Georgia can be driven from the positions which they respectively have assumed, THE UNION IS DISSOLVED."[107]

Charles Mayer had the unfortunate luck to argue that the states must be forced to observe the Bill of Rights just as the Georgia controversy came to a whimpering end and the South Carolina dispute was intensifying. The *Barron* oral arguments were held February 8 and 11, 1833, and the decision was issued less than a week later.[108] In fact, on the day the *Barron* opinion was issued, February 16, 1833, nullification reached a crescendo in the Senate. Calhoun was in the middle of a two-day speech—considered by some as one of the most important of Calhoun's storied career—against Jackson's request to Congress to move the collection sites, dubbed by opponents as the Force Bill.[109] While Calhoun launched into an extended treatise on the unconstitutional nature of the tariff and on the right of the states to determine this question, he also got personal. Calhoun accused Jackson of turning his back on the state that helped him get elected. He dredged up Jackson's tawdry Eaton-affair scandal. Calhoun also made sure to defend himself against accusations that he led this charge out of spite for his unrequited ambitions to succeed Jackson as president. Point by point, he rebutted the charges made against himself, his state, and the Nullification Ordinance. Notably, Calhoun introduced his constitutional theory that it was not the state of South Carolina that nullified federal law but the people of the state sitting in convention, the same theoretical people that ratified the Constitution.[110] His rhetoric was limited not simply to dry theories of the proper balance between the state and federal governments, the difference between revenue-generating and revenue-protective tariffs, or the proper remedies to resolve constitutional questions. Calhoun continued the first day of his speech with fire, arguing that the Force Bill did not merely declare war against South Carolina but instead "decrees a massacre of her citizens!" It would allow Jackson, "without the intervention of a court or jury, to kill without mercy or discrimination!"[111]

Calhoun concluded his first day by reiterating his concept that since the only sovereignty in the United States existed in the states themselves, divided sovereignty was not possible. The Constitution did not create a government consolidated in Washington, D.C., but created a federal system. This federal system, where sovereignty remained with the states, was the most important part of the Union. Before adjourning for the day, Calhoun compared the nullification crisis to the great conflicts in history, which he saw as a struggle between liberty-preserving federal systems and consolidated governments that led to tyranny.[112]

The next morning, Calhoun returned to the Capitol and resumed his speech in the Senate. That same morning, Marshall also climbed the Capitol steps and likewise headed to the Senate chamber, but of course he took the stairs to the basement to release the Court's opinion in *Barron*. As Marshall announced the decision, Calhoun continued in the chambers above. After speaking for more than an hour, Calhoun finally rested. Immediately, Daniel Webster began to rebut Calhoun's charges. Before a Senate chamber packed to capacity, with men and women overflowing the galleries and with the lobbies and even the Senate floor itself overrun with spectators, Webster held the floor until 3:00, when the assembly broke for a two-hour recess. Resuming at 5:00, Webster continued until after 8:00, when his speech was met with roaring applause.[113] Noted by one scholar as a masterpiece, Webster's speech was reprinted and widely circulated within a month.[114] Webster took apart Calhoun's view of the Union as a creation of states that retained their sovereignty and thus could determine whether federal laws violated their compact. Webster argued that the Constitution created not a league or confederacy of sovereign states but a new government that had a direct relationship with a national American people. As a result, no state had the authority to interfere in this relationship. Since the relationship between the people and the U.S. government could be terminated only by revolution, the idea of secession without a revolution was not possible. The Constitution and the laws of Congress were supreme, with the Supreme Court serving as the final judge of constitutional questions. Lastly, any attempt by a state to nullify a federal law within its boundaries was not only unconstitutional but tantamount to promoting revolution.[115]

The spatial irony of this moment should not be lost. As Calhoun and Webster, two political giants of the early republic, thundered upstairs in the Senate, the Supreme Court sat directly below hearing arguments and deciding cases. Despite the snowstorm that began the day before, the street outside was jammed with carriages and the Senate was overflowing with spectators that had waited hours.[116] Directly below, Marshall prepared to announce the Court's decision in *Barron*. In contrast to the grand show upstairs, the Supreme Court chambers were cramped and the ceiling was low, giving many observers the feeling that it was more akin to a cellar than a courtroom.[117] If we read *Barron* with an appreciation for this constitutional crisis as a backdrop, the opinion makes sense as an attempt to provide stability to the federal and state balance that seemed to be unraveling before Marshall's eyes.

Indeed, Marshall was not the only one thoroughly distracted by events taking place upstairs in the Senate. The legal community viewed the nullification crisis as a monumental incident. Scholars have noted that in the two years following the crisis, more new treatises on the Constitution were published than in any prior period.[118] More important for Mayer, recall that the *Barron* decision in favor of the city was unanimous, save for Henry Baldwin who missed the term. It is important to note that Marshall, although still the leader of the Court, was no longer able to enforce unanimity among his judicial brethren.[119] Before bringing the appeal to the Court, Mayer and Hoffman most certainly thought about their chances of success and would have considered the chances of persuading each justice. Based on prior decisions, Marshall, Story, Johnson, and Baldwin could have been sympathetic to their arguments. Again, Barron and Craig were victims of bad timing, and Baldwin's absence from the Court during the *Barron* decision proved especially unfortunate. When Baldwin returned to his judicial duties later that year, he held the Bill of Rights applicable to state action while sitting as a federal circuit court judge in Pennsylvania.[120] In *Johnson v. Tompkins*, Baldwin took an expansive view of their applicability, ruling that the Second (right to bear arms), Fourth (rights against unreasonable searches and seizures), Fifth (rights of due process) and Sixth (right to confront accusatory witnesses) Amendments applied to the states before holding that all the amendments applied.[121] Baldwin maintained his view that both the Pennsylvania and federal constitutions were "not the source of these rights, or the others to which we have referred you, they existed in their plenitude before any constitutions, which do not create but protect and secure them against violation by the legislatures or courts, in making, expounding or administering laws."[122]

Had Baldwin been present during *Barron*, Mayer could have salvaged a bit of pride with a six-to-one decision. Though this would not have helped his clients, it could have deflated some of the sense of inevitability with which many consider the decision today. Instead, the remainder of the Court fell in line with Marshall.

As seen in his correspondence to Marshall, Joseph Story was just as distracted by the seemingly never-ending tumult of the last few years. Indeed, as scholars have noted, Story began his famous *Commentaries on the Constitution* in 1831 mostly to respond to the spate of pro-nullification legal theories that seemed to gain more traction by the day.[123]

William Johnson likewise failed to follow his earlier precedents in *Bank of Columbia v. Okely* and *Houston v. Moore*, where he viewed the Constitution as declaring, but not providing, fundamental principles of free government.[124] Indeed, in the same term that the Supreme Court heard *Barron*, Johnson authored *Livingston v. Moore* (1833), wherein the Court was asked to decide the constitutionality of a Pennsylvania statute that allowed the state to lien and sell land owned by a former state comptroller who mishandled state funds.[125] Years after the property was sold, the heirs of the disgraced comptroller brought an action for ejectment against the new owners who purchased the property. Interestingly, in *Livingston*, the plaintiffs were represented by Roger Taney and Pennsylvania attorney and legislator Charles J. Ingersoll. Although Ingersoll made the argument before the Supreme Court instead of Taney, the legal team nonetheless relied partially on the same argument made by the plaintiffs in *Barron*. The Court ruled on *Livingston* nine days after *Barron*, and Ingersoll and Taney were likewise unsuccessful. Their legal argument to recover the property was quite similar to that crafted by Hoffman and Mayer in the *Barron* litigation. For example, they argued that the acts of the Pennsylvania legislature that resulted in the sale of the property violated the Pennsylvania constitution and the U.S. Constitution—specifically the contract clause of Article I, Section 10, barring a state from impairing the obligations of contract, the Fourth Amendment prohibiting unlawful search and seizure, and the Seventh Amendment guaranteeing the right to jury trial—and contravened natural-law principles that were partially recognized in documents like the Magna Carta. The plaintiffs argued that "the obnoxious acts violate, 1st, universal law or common justice; 2d, the constitutional or organic law of this federal union of the states; 3d, the constitutional or organic law of the state of Pennsylvania. In other words, they violate natural, federal and municipal law."[126] Relying heavily on Justice Paterson's 1795 fundamental-law decision in *Vanhorne's Lessee v. Dorrance*, they argued that legislation that takes private property without just compensation was contrary to "the common law of all nations."[127] But Johnson relied on a strictly textual interpretation of the Constitution to dispose of the claim. He evidenced a view of the legislature as supreme except where explicitly restricted by the written prohibitions of a constitution, writing "that the legislature possess all the legislative power that the body politic could confer, except so far as restricted by the instrument itself."[128]

Regardless, the *Barron* decision has Marshall's fingerprints all over it. Its use of history to justify the rule that the Bill of Rights did not apply to the states came directly from Marshall's own earlier experience in framing Virginia politics. The tenor and brevity of the opinion directly reflects his actions during the oral arguments, both in limiting discussion to the jurisdictional question and by not even wanting to hear the rebuttal from the city. This was Marshall's case, and it was unquestionably informed by the political storm that was raging above the courtroom. We do not, however, have to rely solely on spatial and chronologic coincidence to appreciate why *Barron* was decided in the way that it was. Marshall's personal correspondence bears out much of his concern over the continued existence of the Republic. On August 9, 1831, two weeks after Calhoun's Fort Hill address, Marshall wrote to ex-president and current congressman John Quincy Adams. Adams had recently sent Marshall a copy of a Fourth of July speech he gave in Quincy, Massachusetts, about the dangers of the constitutional heresy of nullification as well as the idea pushed by men like Calhoun that the sole sovereignty in the U.S. resided in the states.[129] Likewise concerned about constitutional theories that viewed the Union as a state creation, Adams placed the genesis of U.S. nationhood not with the creation of the Constitution but in 1776 with the Declaration of Independence. Adams argued that the Declaration was the act of a united people coming together to notify the world that they were no longer dependent on Great Britain but instead had created a new social compact among themselves. The union of these people occurred before independence; as such, independence was inseparable from their union.[130] The idea that the Declaration also recognized the preexisting union of a national American people struck Marshall as particularly interesting, especially as it led Marshall to a view that the "independence of the states is a graft on the stock of the union of the states, and is nourished by that stock. I believe that they exist, flourish, and must perish together." Marshall also admired Adams's views on sovereignty, the concept in which nullification and many of the other "extravagancies of the day" found their basis. Marshall especially appreciated how Adams compared the current claim of proponents of state sovereignty to those made by the British parliament to tax the colonies.[131]

As the nullification crisis grew, Marshall's letters to Joseph Story during 1832 and 1833 evidenced an ever-growing anxiety and sense of resignation. After exchanging pleasantries in his August 2, 1832, letter to Story about recommending books to shelve the law library in Congress, Marshall got down to business, noting that "we are up to the chin in politics." He expressed regret that his home state of Virginia was "insane enough to be opposed to the bank of The United States, and therefore Hurra's for the veto," referring to Jackson's veto of the renewal of the Bank's charter less than one month prior.[132] He likewise lamented Virginia's approval of Jackson's pocket veto of a federal bill designed to help dredge the waterways leading to Richmond, which could aid in bringing in larger ships. For this failure, he again blasted the Virginia politicians, noting "our sagacious politicians are thankful. We seem to think it the summit of human wisdom, or rather of American patriotism, to preserve our poverty." Marshall concluded the letter to Story with his concern over the actions by the leaders of the southern states, who "are determined to risk all the consequences of dismemberment." Marshall continued with the possibility that "I cannot entirely dismiss the hope that they may be deserted by their followers—at least to such an extent as to produce a pause at the Rubicon," comparing the choices before many southern leaders in 1832 to those presented to Julius Caesar regarding whether to cross the Rubicon and start a civil war.[133]

Marshall was less circumspect in his next letter to Story, which he penned on September 22, 1832, less than five months before the *Barron* hearing. Marshall congratulated Story on the imminent completion of his magisterial, three-volume *Commentaries on the Constitution of the United States.* In a nod to the political climate that existed at the end of 1832, Marshall assured Story that he "shall not be among those who bring on you the charge of '*apostasy*' and *ultraism.*" Marshall also continued in his belief that much of the ideological support for the dangerous yet prevalent views of the Union as a confederacy of states was traceable to the influence of Jefferson. Marshall noted that he hoped to see how Story's use of quotes from Jefferson, whom he referred to solely as "the sage," could "imitate the bee in extracting honey from poison." After stinging Jefferson yet again as he had done with great vigor over the course of his long career, Marshall turned more resigned. He ended his letter to Story on a heartbreaking note, lamenting that "I yield slowly and reluctantly to the conviction that our constitution cannot last. I had supposed that north of the Potowmack a firm and solid government competent to the security of rational liberty might be preserved. Even that now seems doubtful. The case of the south seems to me to be desperate. Our opinions are incompatible with a united government even among ourselves. The union has been prolonged thus far by miracles. I fear they cannot continue."[134]

That Christmas Marshall silently observed the first anniversary of his wife's passing. The same day, incidentally also less than one month after the Nullification Ordinance and Jackson's proclamation, Marshall again wrote to Story regarding the crisis and his concern that Virginia would follow suit. The Virginia legislature was preparing to vote on a series of resolutions regarding the nullification crisis. Though these resolutions noted that Virginia "regrets and deplores the course pursued by S. Carolina," it likewise disapproved of Jackson's Proclamation on Nullification, especially as it related to the "origin and character of the *confederacy*," specifically highlighting the committees' views on the nature of the federal union.[135] These proposed resolutions reiterated the state's commitment to the Virginia Resolutions of 1798 and 1799. Originally authored by Jefferson and Madison, these resolutions were designed to oppose the Federal Alien and Sedition Acts passed during the Adams administration. They characterized the Constitution as a compact among sovereign states; as such, a state could nullify unconstitutional federal laws within its borders. The committee also resolved that Virginia should participate in the constitutional convention of the states if Congress did not relent on its system of protective tariffs. Such proposals did not stiffen Marshall's resolve. Rather, after learning of the proposed resolutions, Marshall seemed to lose all fight:

> On Thursday these resolutions are to be taken up, and the debate will, I doubt not, be ardent, and tempestuous enough. I pretend not to anticipate the result. Should it countenance the obvious design of South Carolina to a form of a southern confederacy, it may conduce to a southern league—never to a southern government. Our theories are incompatible with a government for more than a single state. We can form no union which shall be closer

> than an alliance between sovereigns. In this event there is some reason to apprehend internal convulsion. The northern and western section of our State, should a union be maintained north of the Potowmac, will not readily connect itself with the south . . . Any effort on their part to separate from Southern Virginia, and unite with a northern confederacy, may probably be punished as treason. "We have fallen on evil times."[136]

For Marshall, these resolutions were evidence that the nullification heresy let loose again by South Carolina threatened the core of the Union. He did not see this as an isolated political event, or as a case where South Carolina had seemingly overplayed its hand and needed a way out. No other southern state—including Virginia—followed South Carolina down this path. Indeed, many passed resolutions that rebuked nullification.[137] Rather, Marshall wrote as someone who had witnessed decades of struggle over power in the new nation. He was pleased with Story's mention of Daniel Webster's forceful speech in Boston supporting Jackson's Proclamation on Nullification, and he noted that it was only the "well timed vigor of General Washington" that managed to tamp down the "western insurrection," a reference to the Whiskey Rebellion of 1794. In the twilight of his long career, this same problem came back, this time with a vigor that seemed different. Marshall laid the blame for this squarely with Jefferson, concluding that "we are now gathering the bitter fruits of the tree even before that time planted by Mr. Jefferson, and so industriously and perseveringly cultivated by Virginia."[138]

As the Supreme Court opened for its 1833 session a few weeks later, this concern did not subside. On February 8, 1833, the first day of oral arguments in the *Barron* case, Marshall wrote a brief note to his son-in-law, the Virginia state senator Jaquelin Harvie, to express his "Great doubts" regarding whether the compromise tariff bill or the Force Bill would pass.[139] Marshall's doubts were overblown. On March 1, 1833, Congress passed the compromise tariff as well as the Force Bill. Eleven days later, South Carolina repealed its Nullification Ordinance. While attempting to save face by nullifying the Force Bill—a purely symbolic act—South Carolina signaled that it accepted the resolution of the conflict.[140] Marshall's sense of foreboding over the state of the Union did not go away, however. On April 24, 1833, then back in Richmond, Marshall wrote again to Story to congratulate him on the publication of a one-volume edition of his *Commentaries on the Constitution*. Marshall felt that this abridged version would prove especially valuable for students. Again, however, Marshall took a pessimistic turn when he thought of Virginia and the other southern states, noting his fear that "south of the Potomack, where [Story's *Commentaries*] is most wanted, it will be least used. It is a Mahomedan rule, I understand, 'never to dispute with the ignorant,' and we of the true faith in the South abjure the contamination of infidel political works. It would give our orthodox Nullifyer a fever to read the heresies of your commentaries. A whole school might be infected by the atmosphere of a single copy should it be placed on one of the shelves of a book case."[141]

Shortly thereafter, Marshall wrote to Richard Peters, the court reporter for the Supreme Court. Marshall lamented the tendency of Virginians to value the nation while nonetheless being convinced that the rights of the states were in more jeopardy than the vigor of the Union. He also bemoaned Virginia's fear that their greatest threat came from "consolidation," that is, the notion that the federal government would gobble up the powers of the states.[142] Marshall followed up on this theme in a letter on May 7, 1833, to Humphrey Marshall on the occasion of the publication of the latter's treatise on federalism. Marshall agreed with his cousin that the states were never truly independent in the ways that nullifiers had portrayed. During the colonial era, the colonies were separate, but they were all united as part of the British Empire. The Declaration of Independence severed this relationship but was likewise made by a united government, again restating John Quincy Adams's concept. Marshall concluded his letter with an admonition that "the time is arrived when these truths must be more generally spoken or our union is at an end. The complete sovereignty in the states converts our government into a league, and if carried into practice, dissolves the union."[143]

Again on June 3, 1833, approximately four months after *Barron*, Marshall's correspondence to Story showed him continuing to agonize over the Southern crises. Marshall again congratulated Story on the use of his *Commentaries* in American universities, but he also used the occasion to air his concerns about how the younger generation in the South had failed to appreciate the importance of union. Marshall wrote Story, "The first impressions made on the youthful mind are of vast importance; and, most unfortunately, they are in the South all erroneous. Our young men, generally speaking, grow up in the firm belief that liberty depends on construing our constitution into a league instead of a government; that it has nothing to fear from breaking these United States into numerous petty republics. Nothing in their view is to be feared but that bugbear, consolidation; and every exercise of legitimate power is construed into a breach of the constitution."[144] A month later, Marshall followed up this correspondence to Story with another that lamented the political situation in Virginia, where any politician hoping to have success must pay absolute loyalty to the Virginia Resolutions of 1798 and 1799 and its creed of states' rights above all else.[145]

While Marshall would remain on the Court for two more terms before his passing in 1835, *Barron* was his final constitutional opinion. At the end of his career, Marshall tried to stare down Georgia and protect the federal government's exclusive jurisdiction over the native peoples with which it had treaties. He failed in a very public way. Immediately on the heels of this fiasco, Marshall sought to navigate the Court through the 1833 term while nullification raged directly above his courtroom. Looking at *Barron* as a product of these circumstances helps us understand it better. If we continue to try to explain all of Marshall's decisions in a way that creates a grand narrative, we will fail. If we explain *Marbury* simply as Marshall's pronouncement that the Supreme Court had arrived, we miss his mindset in 1803 of apprehension about the new Jefferson administration and his desire to tweak his cousin the president. If we look at *McCulloch* as an example of his extending his profederal jurisprudence, we miss the ways that the panic of 1819 helped inform his decision.

As the grand chief justice, Marshall occupies a revered space in the history of the United States. Marshall is rightly credited with establishing the Supreme Court as a truly coequal branch of government. Many of his eloquent and forceful decisions are celebrated as other founding documents; *Marbury v. Madison* is considered essential to the development of American democracy. However, we must not forget that Marshall is no different in some respects from any other Supreme Court jurist that has served since. As a fundamentally political body, the Supreme Court has never been insulated from the crises that swirled outside its chambers. Few legal commentators consider Chief Justice John Roberts's decision upholding the constitutionality of the Affordable Care Act in *Sebelius* solely within the confines of his other legal opinions without considering the external factors that helped the decision to turn out the way it did.[146] While scholars may disagree, few believe Justice Owen Roberts's switch in *West Coast Hotel v. Parrish* uninformed by President Roosevelt's court-packing plan.[147] When modern justices bemoan the political tenor of current Supreme Court decisions and pine for the days when "the disciplined legal reasoning of John Marshall and Joseph Story" held sway, they fall into the common mistake of considering past actors as somehow unconstrained by the concerns of their era.[148] John Marshall was an excellent jurist. However, he was able to establish and maintain the Court as a powerful institution for three decades not simply because of his legal acumen but also because he was also politically astute and aware. While he is considered by many as the personification of the Court, John Marshall is in this respect no different from any other justice before or since.

7 *Barron's* Reception

> You cannot estimate too highly my confidence in the medical gentlemen of Philadelphia. All that human skill can do, I should expect from them, but my old worn out frame cannot I believe be repaired. Could I find the mill which would grind old men, and restore youth, I might indulge the hope of recovering my former vigor and taste for the enjoyments of life. But as that is impossible, I must be content with patching myself up and dragging on as well as I can.
>
> John Marshall to Richard Peters, April 30, 1835

Consider this counterfactual: If *Barron* is best explained by Marshall's concern over the future of the Union, couldn't the Court have decided the case in a way that would not eviscerate the Bill of Rights? What if the Court had accepted jurisdiction? The appeal by Barron's attorneys plainly laid out the conflict between the state's acts and the Fifth Amendment as required by the 1789 Judiciary Act. Could not Marshall's court then have decided the case on nonconstitutional grounds? Could not the Court rule for or against Barron on common law principles and not comment on the Bill of Rights? In the era before *Swift v. Tyson* (1842), which allowed the federal courts to create a federal common law for commercial matters, or *Erie Railroad v. Tompkins* (1938), which then denied them this ability, the Court would routinely decide nonconstitutional cases on rules that it felt appropriate.[1] If Marshall was a master strategist, why did he feel the need to make such a forceful pronouncement that placed the Bill of Rights out of reach for the vast majority of Americans?

In the narrative that recounts the grand cases of the Marshall era, the Court consistently sought to expand its power; this ideology makes *Barron* seem out of place. Again, however, the timing of the case was critical. Nullification and the Cherokee cases showed Marshall that he needed to insulate the federal courts from battles that could inflict further damage. Recall that only a few years earlier, Justice Story had written to his wife to lament the attempt by Congress to repeal the Supreme Court's ability to review decisions of state courts and to limit the justices' terms to seven years. While he knew these measures would not gain enough votes to pass, Story rightly noted that they ominously reflected "the spirit of the times."[2] Thus, while Marshall's own jurisprudence shows that he consistently sought to protect the nationalist promise of the federal government, in *Barron* a different proposition was before the Court. Instead of a case that gave the Court the opportunity to expand its power or that of Congress, here the Court was asked to use its power on behalf of individuals to oppose the acts of a state. *Barron* is in line with the Marshall-court narrative as protecting the idea of a vigorous federal government and judiciary, only this time Marshall was protecting the federal courts instead of advancing their power. *Barron* helped shield the federal courts from individual-rights cases.[3]

Given the climate of the 1830s, Marshall was no doubt well aware of where this would lead. If the Court accepted jurisdiction and decided *Barron* on nonconstitutional grounds, it would not be long before other rights cases would appear in federal courts across the country. His acceptance of jurisdiction would at least implicitly signal that the Court was receptive. What cases would come before the Court next? Would a South Carolina Unionist stripped of his office bring a First Amendment claim? Would an abolitionist whose printing press was ransacked by a mob bring a First, Fourth, or Fifth Amendment claim? This possibility was very real in the 1830s, as many local communities began shutting down and destroying abolitionist publications. Far from a simple collection of ruffians who used nothing but brute force, anti-abolitionists relied primarily on two legal arguments to justify their actions in shutting down abolitionist newspapers: the common law doctrines of breach of the peace and public nuisance.[4] Although the idea of applying nuisance law to overshadow fundamental liberties such as freedom of the press is difficult today to appreciate, such an idea formed the basis for local governance in the nineteenth century, when larger constitutional rights such as freedom of the press were not considered as relevant to daily life and governance.[5]

Barron aided the federal courts by giving them a way to largely stay out of problematic questions, including those regarding slavery or abolition, the thorniest and most unresolvable legal issue of the era. For example, in 1859, a federal court in Virginia was presented with a criminal matter in which an enslaved woman was charged with stealing a letter. This case would normally have been disposed of by the state courts, but it wound up in federal court because the defendant ran afoul of an 1825 federal law. The enslaved woman's owner appealed the conviction under the grounds that the Fifth Amendment took his property without compensation. As a federal court case, the *Barron* rule would not apply. However, but for the federal law that made stealing mail a federal offense, this case would stay firmly with the states. Taney, while acting in his capacity as a circuit court judge, was forced to distinguish the Fifth Amendment claim by holding that it applied only to cases where the government was directly taking property and not to situations ancillary to criminal punishment.[6]

Thus, by taking the federal courts out of the equation when it came to individual-rights claims, the states were free to use their police power in more vigorous ways. In the American federal system outlined in the Constitution, the balance of power between the state and federal governments was based on the concept of divided sovereignty over the same geographic areas. The Tenth Amendment delineates the federal government as one that possesses delegated powers, that is, as a government that could exercise only those powers enumerated in the Constitution. Over the course of the early republic, there was a continual debate over the location of the boundaries where state power ended and federal power began. By removing the requirement that states observe the liberties recognized by the Bill of Rights, *Barron* helped cement the police power as a state function that was not answerable to federal interference, at least to the extent that states exercised their police power in ways that infringed on individual rights. If it wanted to, Maryland could now use its power to regulate drainage, abate nuisance, or even take property without compensation. The federal courts would not need to engage these debates.

In addition to the slavery issue, *Barron* kept the federal courts from dealing with other development cases similar to Barron and Craig's. In 1857, a California federal court heard a lawsuit from a wharf owner aggrieved by the plans of a neighboring property owner to construct a second wharf that would block access. As the offending construction proceeded by virtue of a grant of state coastlands, the original wharf owner claimed in part that the grant of land from the state was unconstitutional because it offended the takings clause of the Fifth Amendment. The court cited *Barron* and held that even if California took private property without payment, the court could not remedy this since this was an issue for the state authorities.[7] The court was skeptical of the attempts by counsel to argue that the new construction was a nuisance at common law. While this was the crux of Barron and Craig's claim from 1822 through 1833, the court in 1857 found the argument not only unpersuasive but worthy of ridicule:

> It is next urged, that the mischief complained of constitutes a nuisance within the meaning given by the definition annexed to that term by law. It may be admitted that the obstruction in this case may (although existing by an act of the legislature) be considered a nuisance, in view of the common-law definition of the term; yet it surely cannot be successfully contended, that it is within the power of this court to abate what the legislature has willed to exist, on the ground that it is a nuisance at common-law! Arguments and authorities adduced in relation to mere local nuisances, and as to the alleged injustice and inconsistency of these acts of the legislature of this state, are to be discarded by this court; and the question confined to the single inquiry, "Does either of these acts conflict with any provision of the constitution of the United States, or any act of congress passed under it?"[8]

Much in the same way that Justice Miller in the post–Civil War *Slaughterhouse Cases* (1873) interpreted the Fourteenth Amendment as protecting two types of rights—state and federal, each binding its respective government—rather than as protecting one set of universally applicable rights, *Barron* likewise gave the states the power to act in similar ways.[9]

In this way, *Barron* makes more sense if we think of it as a product of the last part of Marshall's tenure. According to many historians, the final decade of Marshall's term was either "a time of frustration, accommodation, and reluctant concession," or it was, to put it more charitably, a period of stasis following his first decades of grand success.[10] In the 1824 case of *Gibbons v. Ogden*, which has been described as Marshall's "last great opinion," the Court was faced with the constitutionality of a New York statute that granted a monopoly to Robert Livingston and Robert Fulton to operate steamships within the navigable waters of the state.[11] Livingston and Fulton later licensed this right to the partnership of Aaron Ogden and Thomas Gibbons. After an acrimonious dissolution of the partnership, Ogden retained the rights under the New York monopoly, but Gibbons obtained a federal license to operate the line.[12] After repeated enjoinment of the Gibbons line as a result of Ogden's exclusive rights to the monopoly by the New York State courts, the case came before the Supreme Court, which had to decide between the two permits, Ogden's exclusive state permit or Gibbons's federal license. This question of which license was superior gave Marshall a platform from which to enlarge federal powers through rendering an opinion based on an expansive reading of the commerce clause of Article I, Section 8. As could be expected, Marshall took aim, at least initially.

Marshall acknowledged that the Constitution created a federal government of enumerated powers, but with respect to the notion that Congress's enumerated powers ought to be strictly construed through the "necessary and proper" clause of Article I, Section 8, Marshall asked, "But why ought they to be so construed? Is there one sentence in the constitution which gives countenance to this rule?"[13] Marshall held that the power of Congress to regulate commerce governed the matter, but he also used this opinion to expound on the extent of the commerce clause by responding to those who believe that this power is to be strictly construed, famously writing that

> powerful and ingenious minds, taking, as postulates, that the powers expressly granted to the government of the Union, are to be contracted, by construction, into the narrowest possible compass, and that the original powers of the States are retained, if any possible construction will retain them, may, by a course of well-digested, but refined and metaphysical reasoning . . . explain away the constitution of our country, and leave it, a magnificent structure, indeed, to look at, but totally unfit for use.[14]

Although Marshall recognized the right of a state to use its police power to regulate its internal affairs, the validity of such law still depended on whether it interfered with "an act of Congress passed in pursuance of the constitution." Where such a conflict existed, the state law was invalid because "the constitution is the supreme law."[15] Although *Gibbons* appears in line with Marshall's profederal jurisprudence, William Wiecek noted that Marshall "waffled, uncharacteristically" when discussing federal superiority.[16] Instead of simply asserting that the federal government had exclusive power over interstate commerce, regardless of whether Congress had actually legislated in a particular area, "it seems reasonably clear that he [Marshall] recognized that, though commerce must be regulated by Congress, local interests pressed for and required recognition."[17] Wiecek surmises that Marshall was "mealy-mouthed" when failing to simply endorse federal supremacy over commerce in *Gibbons* because of a "hidden controversy" lurking under the surface of the opinion: slavery.[18] The year before, Justice William Johnson, while sitting as a U.S. circuit court judge, held that South Carolina's Negro Seamen Act violated the federal power to regulate commerce in *Elkison v. Deliesseline.*[19] Wiecek argues that, as a result of the extreme backlash against the strong federal position in *Elkison*, when *Gibbons* came before the Court one year later, the issue of slavery precluded what would normally have been a routine decision wherein Marshall would expand the federal commerce power to its fullest extent.[20] Similarly, five years later in *Willson v. Black Bird Creek Marsh Company* (1829), we can see that Marshall continued this line of thought.[21] In *Willson*, the owners of a sloop were sued to recover damages to a dam built across a Delaware river.[22] The defendants appealed the decision on the ground that the river was a public highway and that the state had violated the federal commerce clause by authorizing the dam that blocked public navigation. Much like his decision in *Gibbons*, Marshall held that Delaware could exercise this authority because the federal government had not passed any law regarding traffic or commerce on the river. Thus, the law that authorized the dam was constitutional since Delaware did not impede on the dormant federal commerce power.[23]

After *Gibbons*, Marshall not only continued to fail to press his federalist beliefs as he had so forcefully done in past cases, but in fact he began to chip away at his own precedent.[24] Three years later, as seen in *Ogden v. Saunders*, the Court showed "signs of the ending of the Marshall Court's activism, either through the aggressiveness of the Jacksonian administration as in the Cherokee cases or the breaking up of the old judicial consensus with Justice [Smith] Thompson [replacing Marshall-ally Henry Brockholst Livingston in 1824], were clear to see in the 1830's."[25] In *Ogden*, the Court, in a four-to-three opinion written by William Johnson, held a New York state bankruptcy law constitutional because it applied only prospectively and did not alter contracts retrospectively as did the New York bankruptcy law held unconstitutional in *Sturges v. Crowninshield*.[26] Finally, as we noted, Marshall had suffered indignity only a year earlier when he had forcefully and unequivocally ruled that Georgia could not usurp federal law in its convictions of the missionaries Worcester and Butler, only to have his decision ignored. The year 1833 saw the newspapers actively discuss his retirement and his possible successor.[27]

Barron granted the states the jurisprudential cover to allow them to use their police power without interference from the federal courts, as long as they did not interfere with private contracts or pass laws that would directly conflict with federal statutes that regulated matters of interstate commerce. In so doing, *Barron* not only fits with many of these later Marshall-court cases but is also in line with some of the cases in the early years of the Court under Roger Taney, Marshall's successor as chief justice. Consider *Miln v. New York* (1837). There, in August 1829, William Thompson, captain of the ship *Emily*, sailed into New York Harbor with a cargo of one hundred immigrants arriving for the first time to America.[28] While immigrants such as these embarked for a new life in America, officials of the city of New York were not always pleased at their arrival. In 1824, in an attempt to stem the flow of mostly indigent Irish immigrants, the city passed a statute that mandated that the master of every ship entering New York from a foreign port, within twenty-four hours, provide a written report of all persons disembarking.[29] This report was to include the name, place of birth, last legal settlement, age, and occupation of every passenger landing at the port of New York.[30] The statute also required the master of the ship to post a bond of up to $300 to cover expenses in the event any of these immigrants became an indigent charge on the city within two years of their arrival.[31] Failure to provide such a report would subject the master and commander, the owner, and any consignee or consignees to monetary penalties of $75.00 for each passenger not reported, or for every person whose biographical information was falsely reported.[32] In

Miln, the city assessed penalties of $15,000 for failing to submit the required report. Miln contested the assessment on the grounds that the law was an unconstitutional infringement on the federal commerce clause, which reserves to Congress the right to regulate foreign and interstate commerce.[33] When the case finally reached the Supreme Court, during Taney's first term, the Court upheld the New York law and held that it did not interfere with commerce and thus did not violate the commerce clause, ruling that it was a permissible function of state police power.[34]

What we see in a case like *Miln* is a conflict over the boundaries of power within the federal system, with the Taney court squarely behind the concept of balancing federal power by enunciating the role of the state police power at the federal level. Paul Finkelman argues that the Supreme Court specifically promoted the concept of state police power mostly in order to protect slavery. Finkelman tied the basis for the *Miln* opinion to growing sectional tensions over slavery, arguing that the Court was cognizant of the problems of laws such as the black seamen's laws, which South Carolina and many other states enacted to keep black sailors aboard their ships while docked in southern ports. Finkelman argues that the real message behind *Miln* was to announce to the southern states that they could regulate who could enter their jurisdictions, notwithstanding the commerce clause or the precedent set forth by the Marshall court's *Gibbons v. Ogden* opinion. As noted by Finkelman, *Miln* represented the first time the Supreme Court expressly used the notion of state police power to recognize the validity of a state law. Before this time, state laws challenged on the grounds of repugnancy to the commerce clause were routinely overturned.[35] The effect of the *Barron* decision allowed for a similar result. By viewing rights as granted by the U.S. Constitution and then holding them inapplicable, the Marshall court reaffirmed the dual sovereignty prescribed to the states in the federal system and rejected the view that the Constitution secured the liberties of a broadly defined "citizen" against encroachment by any American government, federal or state, as argued by Mayer.[36]

In pre-*Barron* cases, Marshall recognized the existence of the state police power but nonetheless found in favor of the federal government under its power to regulate commerce. Although *Barron* was not a commerce clause matter, Marshall was nonetheless certainly smart enough to know that a ruling explicitly exempting states from the Bill of Rights gave them ample room to use their police power in very similar ways by announcing to the states that they could violate individual rights in ways that the federal government could not. *Barron* had the effect of removing the federal courts from the business of sitting in judgment over state decisions, at least where individual rights were concerned.[37] In *Barron*, Marshall interpreted rights as granted by written constitutions. The federal constitution contained the rights operable against the federal government, while the state constitutions operated against their respective governments. *Barron* helped maintain the boundaries between the state and federal governments by allowing the states wide latitude to use their police power without interference. If rights were perceived of as having a natural inherent quality or universal application, these jurisdictional arguments would have easily collapsed.

TOWARD RIGHTS AS CREATURES OF POSITIVE LAW

We can think of Marshall's opinion as composed of two parts. The first is the explicit rule that the Bill of Rights did not apply to state action. The second part is implied by the first: rights, such as the entitlement to payment for the taking of private property put to public use, apply by virtue of their inclusion in written documents like the U.S. Constitution. As such, those rights are properly vindicated or denied by the predicate questions of jurisdiction that all courts address before determining matters of law. For example, if a creditor in Baltimore, Maryland, sues his debtor from Annapolis, Maryland, on a standard debt claim, the creditor would have to choose a court that possessed jurisdiction. Normally, this would require that suit take place in the debtor's residence of Annapolis, but it could also take place elsewhere if, for example, the breach of the contract occurred by failing to ship the goods to the agreed location of Baltimore. While a state court in Annapolis or Baltimore would have jurisdiction, a court in Pennsylvania would not. Likewise, if the creditor resided in Pennsylvania and sought to bring suit against the same Annapolis, Maryland, debtor, he could seek to remove the case to Maryland federal court under the diversity jurisdiction provision of Article III of the U.S. Constitution, which allows parties of different states to take matters to federal court under certain circumstances. The larger point is that all of these considerations are fundamentally the province of courts and lawyers who navigate these questions by looking to written rules of procedure and statutes. What Barron and Craig were arguing was fundamentally different. As we discussed in chapter 3, certain rights, such as the right of a property owner to receive compensation for a taking, were not thought of as created by positive law, or as a written command of a sovereign, like a statute, rule, or ordinance. This right was not something that existed based on satisfactory answers to standard legal questions like jurisdiction or venue. While this right was written down in the U.S. Constitution as well as many state constitutions, few agreed that these documents provided the basis for this right.

Barron aided in the evolution toward thinking about rights as effective only if contained in written documents such as constitutions, as opposed to the idea that written constitutions merely declared their existence. However, it is important to stress that this positive-law view of rights was not universally embraced overnight; in fact, *Barron* was mostly overlooked when it was released. Before, during, and after *Barron* came before the Court, Marshall was preoccupied with nullification, as was most of Washington. While *Barron* was being argued and decided, Daniel Webster was more concerned with the negotiations over resolving the underlying tariff issue and his rebuttal to Calhoun, who was likewise consumed by the controversy.[38] Henry Clay was preoccupied with shepherding his compromise tariff bill through the Senate and trying to reassure Nicholas Biddle that the Jackson administration would not remove federal deposits from his Bank of the United States.[39] Indeed, even the contemporaneous newspaper accounts largely overlooked both Mayer's argument and Marshall's ruling. Some of this may be due to the way the decision was reported in the papers. The D.C. *National Intelligencer* would note the business before the Court as part of its larger mission to cover the workings of the federal government. Otherwise, newspaper coverage of the Court was largely absent or simply derivative of the reports filed by the *Intelligencer.* The failure of national papers or magazines to have their own reporters working the Supreme Court meant that coverage of the Supreme Court in this era was not terribly accurate.[40]

The absence of any real commentary on *Barron* likely has much to do with this defect. Consider the way *Barron* was reported by the *Intelligencer.* The paper carried three mentions of the case: the first noted that Mayer's argument began for the plaintiff; the second mentioned that Mayer's argument continued "on the question of jurisdiction"; and the third stated that "Mr. Chief Justice Marshall delivered the opinion of this Court, dismissing the writ of error in this case for the want of jurisdiction."[41] In all three instances, *Barron* was mentioned along with a list of all the other cases heard that day. None contained any discussion of the substance of the case. The *Intelligencer* did not otherwise give any indication that a more significant issue was being litigated. No reader of these accounts would know that the Court just issued an opinion that granted the state governments the freedom to disregard the Bill of Rights. The exact descriptions of the case made by the *Intelligencer* were also reprinted verbatim in other newspapers, such as the *New-York Spectator*, the *Baltimore Gazette*, and the *United States' Telegraph* (D.C).[42]

This pattern was replicated in the courts as *Barron* was not fully accepted as persuasive authority for decades. *Barron* was not cited in a state supreme court case until 1839, six years after it was handed down, and it was cited at this court level only seven times in its first twenty years.[43] Further, two of those cases declined to follow Marshall's positive-law view of rights and held that the right to receive compensation for takings of or damage to property derived either from the common law or fundamental law.[44] A third case ignored Marshall's *Barron* opinion completely and instead relied on Judge Archer's trial court opinion, which was reprinted and widely circulated through the *American Jurist and Law Magazine*.[45] Indeed, Archer's trial opinion was almost as widely cited by courts as was Marshall's Supreme Court decision, and it was relied on by state courts from Maine to California throughout the remainder of the nineteenth century.[46] A review of the lower federal courts through 1853 also reveals a similar silence as *Barron* was cited only once in its first twenty years.[47] Finally, the Supreme Court mentioned the case only three times during this time.[48]

Rather, after *Barron* was issued, lawyers, litigants, and judges continued to express their claims to certain rights as secured by a variety of sources. While many found rights as emanating from written constitutions, *Barron* did not make this interpretation exclusive. Many still envisioned rights as secured by other sources, such as natural or fundamental law, or as arising from the common law. Some courts found *Barron* as binding on their decisions, some did not, and some ignored the case completely. Many courts even continued to apply the Bill of Rights to state action. Over time, the ruling in *Barron* came to be somewhat of an article of faith for judges. By the early twentieth century, most state and federal court citations of *Barron* appear almost apologetic in tone, as it was "elementary" that the Bill of Rights applied only to the federal government,[49] and anyone arguing that state courts must respect rights that were contained in these amendments made claims that were "palpably groundless."[50] By the 1920s the Ohio Supreme Court noted that "the question had been so clearly settled at such an early date, and so uniformly adhered to, and so repeatedly asserted as to leave no doubt in the minds of this court as to the proper conclusion to be reached."[51] However, the idea that *Barron* simply codified a universally accepted understanding about the role of the Bill of Rights in the American constitutional order is simply not accurate. The commonplace pre-*Barron* practice of locating rights in places other than written documents continued for decades. Although *Barron* fundamentally shaped the modern view of rights as applying only by virtue of their inclusion in written documents, few at the time could see it in this way. *Barron*'s rule ultimately became preeminent, but this evolution took time.

The question of where rights existed was a point of dispute not only in the *Barron* litigation but across the country. There are scholars, however, who minimize this rights debate precisely because of their view that *Barron* was correctly decided.[52] Akhil Amar argues that antislavery forces in the 1830s invented the idea that the Bill of Rights declared preexisting rights applicable to both state and federal government. He contends that abolitionists, in response to the censoring of their free speech and press by southern states attempting to maintain slavery, concocted an anti-*Barron* argument that the Bill of Rights amendments were inserted into the Constitution to declare the existence of preexisting fundamental rights.[53] However, courts across the country ignored *Barron*. The decision handed down in *Barron* did not present an obstacle that had to be addressed before gaining access to the Court, as a current Supreme Court decision would. While it is true that many abolitionists were forced to craft more expansive interpretations of the Bill of Rights given the legal reality many faced, many nonabolitionists expressed very similar views.

Consider the various rights claims that came before state supreme courts in the first decades after *Barron*. Across the country—in New Jersey, New York, Pennsylvania, Georgia, Arkansas, Maryland, Illinois, Louisiana, and Iowa—many courts maintained a view of rights as extraconstitutional in some fashion. In *Barron*, Marshall noted that if a citizen of a state wanted more protection against their state government, that person could not invoke the federal Bill of Rights but should demand that the state constitution provide more protection. In the early republic era, many states did just that, amending their constitutions to specifically provide more individual-rights protection. These states were not responding directly to Marshall's charge. Rather, they were amending their constitutions because they were also moving toward viewing rights as creatures of positive law. Nonetheless, many courts continued to decide rights cases through an interpretation of constitutions as merely declaring the existence of rights, whose true basis remained in the common law, fundamental law, or as a principle of natural right, regardless of the wording of their state constitution.

These jurists saw rights, such as prohibitions against taking private property without compensation or placing a defendant in double jeopardy, as fundamental principles that could not be given or taken away simply because of their inclusion or omission in a written constitution. For example, the Georgia Supreme Court routinely applied the Bill of Rights to the state. In 1846 in *Nunn v. State*, the court was asked to determine whether a Georgia law that prohibited concealed weapons was prohibited by the Second Amendment's guarantee of the right to bear arms.[54] Authored by Joseph Henry Lumpkin, the younger brother of the Georgia governor who presided over the state during the height of the Cherokee removal, the decision presents a good example that many continued to hold to the concept that rights were declared—but not granted—by written constitutions.[55] Lumpkin noted that courts in Kentucky, Alabama, and Indiana had addressed similar concealed-weapons laws and conceded that in all three cases, the courts rested on guarantees contained in their respective *state* constitutions; however, he noted that those "instruments confer no *new rights* on the people which did not belong to them before."[56] Second, Lumpkin recognized that the United States was created by the people and recognized also the dual role possessed by all citizens. Like Marshall in *Barron*, Lumpkin understood that the Bill of Rights was added to the Constitution at the insistence of the many states that wanted more restrictions on the new federal government. However, this act of textually including these rights in the federal or state constitutions was irrelevant; placing these guarantees into a constitution did not alter their universal availability. For example, Lumpkin argued that if the right to bear arms,

> "inestimable to freemen," has been guaranteed to British subjects, since the abdication and flight of the last of the Stuarts and the ascension of the Prince of Orange, did it not belong to our colonial ancestors in this western hemisphere? Has it been a part of the *English* Constitution ever since the bill of rights and act of settlement? And been forfeited here by the submission and adoption of our own Constitution? No notion can be more fallacious that this! On the contrary, this is one of the fundamental principles, upon which rests the great fabric of civil liberty, reared by the fathers of the Revolution and of the country. And the Constitution of the United States, in declaring that the right of the people to keep and bear arms, should not be infringed, only reiterated a truth announced a century before, in the act of 1689, "to extend and secure the rights and liberties of English subjects" —whether living 3,000 or 300 miles from the royal palace.[57]

Lumpkin approached the *Barron* issue under different assumptions than Marshall. Amending the Constitution to include the Bill of Rights, which prohibited the new federal government from violating certain individual rights, did not give the states license to violate those same rights as Marshall's court ruled in *Barron*. Without specifically naming *Barron*, Lumpkin asked whether, if the Bill of Rights was meant to restrict the powers of the new federal government, it necessarily followed that

> because the people refused to delegate to the general government the power to take from them the right to keep and bear arms, . . . they designed it to rest in the State governments? Is this a right reserved to the *States* or to *themselves*? Is it not an unalienable right, which lies at the bottom of every free government? We do not believe that, because the people withheld this arbitrary power of disenfranchisement from Congress, they ever intended to confer it on local legislatures. This right is too dear to be confided to a republican legislature.[58]

Lumpkin continued his line of thought in subsequent opinions. In *Flint River Steamboat Company v. Foster* (Ga. 1848), the court was presented with the legality of a state statute that allowed steamboat workers to file liens on vessels for unpaid wages.[59] After one steamboat company appealed the law on the basis that it violated the due process clause of the Fifth Amendment, the jury trial right of the Seventh Amendment, and the similar provisions of the Georgia constitution, Lumpkin again had the opportunity to set forth his view of the applicability of these rights to the states.[60] In discussing the right of the jury trial, Lumpkin explained:

> It would be out of place, on this occasion, to expatiate on the importance of trial by jury. In England, it has long been esteemed the great bulwark and safeguard, both of civil rights and of political freedom. It is incorporated prominently into *Magna Charta*. Our ancestors, when they removed to this country, brought this admirable system with them, as their *birth right* and inheritance. And for greater security, have had a guarantee for its preservation inserted, not only in the federal, but in all their State Constitutions.[61]

Georgia's 1789 constitution, though sparse, did in effect contain a jury trial provision. But this inclusion was immaterial for Lumpkin.[62] Similarly, in 1851 in *Allen v. Georgia*, Lumpkin held that the Eighth Amendment applied to state action, but one year later in *Campbell v. Georgia* he held that the Sixth Amendment right to confront witnesses also applied, though no similar provisions existed in the state constitution.[63] Indeed, in *Campbell*, Lumpkin argued that the entire Bill of Rights applied.

Lumpkin was not the only jurist in Georgia to make these types of arguments. Justice Hiram Warner of the Georgia Supreme Court also held in *Young v. McKenzie* that the takings clause of the Fifth Amendment applied.[64] Warner was not unmindful of *Barron* since counsel for the defendant cited it for the proposition that the Fifth Amendment did not apply.[65] Rather, for Warner, *Barron* simply did not apply. Warner explained:

> Does the amended Constitution of the United States, by declaring "Private property shall not be taken for public use without just compensation," introduce, or create, a *new principle of restriction*, which did not exist before? Did not the same principle of restriction exist, both as it regards the federal and State Government, before the adoption of the amendment in question? Does the amended constitution do anything more than declare a great common law principle, applicable to all governments, both State

> and federal, which has existed from the time of *Magna Charta*, to the present moment? The amended constitution of the Union asserts a great principle applicable, it is said, to the *National Government*. Why is not the same great principle equally applicable to the *State Government?*[66]

In *Parham v. Decatur County*, Justice Eugenius A. Nisbet of the Georgia Supreme Court heard an appeal that questioned the legality of a state law allowing local road commissioners to take unenclosed private property for road construction but required compensation only if the property was enclosed at the time.[67] Nisbet recognized that necessity sometimes warranted takings but held that this was not one of those occasions. Rather, the requirement that the sovereign provide compensation upon a taking was "founded in natural equity," was "of universal application," and could be found not only in the Bill of Rights but in the common law; Magna Carta; Blackstone's *Commentaries*; Kent's *Commentaries*; the writings of Continental theorists like Grotius, Vattel, and Pufendorf; the Napoleonic Code; the Civil Code of Louisiana; and even in the laws that governed exotic lands like Turkey.[68] Nisbet was also aware that the Bill of Rights had been held inapplicable to state action, but this did not change his opinion. This obligation to compensate an owner of private property for a taking was a right that the Fifth Amendment simply declared and recognized. Nisbet was incredulous that placing the right in the Fifth Amendment somehow meant that it no longer existed unless it was specifically spelled out in the state constitution. For Nisbet, the power to take private property without compensation did not belong to any government.[69] Under the Georgia constitution of 1789, which was in effect until 1865, the state did not constitutionally recognize a right to compensation upon a taking. For Lumpkin, Nisbet, and Warner, this did not matter.

Louisiana applied similar logic when it encountered rights claims. In two separate double jeopardy cases in 1844 and 1845, the Louisiana Supreme Court considered the double jeopardy prohibition of the Fifth Amendment applicable without reference to its applicability to state courts. The double jeopardy prohibition of the Fifth Amendment was simply a "re-affirmance of a *magna charta* maxim of the common law."[70] Although the state constitution in effect at the time did not contain any prohibition on double jeopardy prosecutions, this made little difference to the court.[71]

Decisions regarding the applicability of the Bill of Rights were not simply a southern phenomenon attributable to Lumpkin and a few like-minded judges. In 1863, the Maryland Court of Appeals heard an appeal of a murder conviction on the grounds that the defendant's second trial violated the double jeopardy clause of the Fifth Amendment.[72] As Maryland had no explicit prohibition on double jeopardy in the state constitution, the court could have simply cited *Barron* and rejected the Fifth Amendment claim.[73] Instead, it held that the double jeopardy rule applied to criminal trials as an indispensable part of the common law.[74] The court interpreted the prohibition on double jeopardy contained in the Fifth Amendment as declaratory of the common law.[75] Other state courts across the north also applied the Bill of Rights to state action and relied on similar constitutional assumptions. New Jersey, both before and after *Barron*, held the takings clause of the Fifth Amendment applicable in a trio of property cases. New Jersey also presents an interesting example of how courts addressed rights claims in which a state either did not have a constitution or had a constitution that contained few rights provisions. New Jersey's 1776 constitution announced its separation from Great Britain and provided a rudimentary frame of government, but it did not contain a separate declaration or bill of rights. Outside of a general provision for the applicability of the common law, the 1776 New Jersey constitution specifically listed only the rights of religious freedom, the right of a jury trial, and the right of assistance of counsel in criminal prosecutions, but little else.[76] While the subsequent constitution of 1844 corrected these omissions, New Jersey courts presented with rights claims before this time did not have the option of relying on written provisions in the state constitution in order to locate rights.

In *Scudder v. Trenton Delaware Falls Company*, the court heard an appeal by a property owner whose riverfront property was damaged by the construction of a nearby dam.[77] The property owner objected in part to the law allowing the construction of the dam since it took private property without a mechanism for providing compensation in an amount set by a local jury.[78] However, the court cited the applicability of the Fifth Amendment and held that private property could be taken for public use as long as compensation was made.[79] For the *Scudder* court, the lack of a takings clause in the New Jersey constitution did not mean the right of compensation did not exist as the Fifth Amendment enunciated the rule. While *Barron* was decided a year after *Scudder*, the New Jersey Supreme Court had the opportunity to revisit almost the same issue six years after *Barron* was decided. In *Sinnickson v. Johnson*, the court reviewed the legality of a state law that allowed a property owner to dam a canal on his property.[80] The question before the court was whether this law provided to the owner of the dam a defense from damages alleged by his upstream neighbors.[81] As in *Scudder*, the court regarded the absence of a state takings clause as immaterial. When counsel for the defendant argued that the state legislature had the ability to pass laws insulating the company since the state constitution did not contain a takings provision, the court balked.[82] The court held that *Barron* was irrelevant since the concept of taking property only upon providing a just compensation was "operative as a principle of universal law." Furthermore, the damages alleged by the neighboring property owners were proper.[83] For the court, the obligation to make payment for takings existed independently of any constitutional pronouncements and was recognized by natural law theorists like Pufendorf, Vattel, and Montesquieu; by Blackstone; and by American jurists like Kent, Story, and Supreme Court justice Henry Baldwin.[84] For the *Sinnickson* court, this principle operated as an innate part of universal law that served as an essential counterbalance to the sovereign's right to take property.

Finally, in 1841 the New Jersey Supreme Court heard a claim against a canal company by a property owner who alleged that their improvements caused a river to overflow and destroy his crops.[85] In *Ten Eyck v. The Delaware and Raritan Canal Co.*, the canal company defended the case with many of the same arguments made by the city of Baltimore in *Barron*, namely, that they had been chartered by a legislative act of the state to take these actions, that they did so in full compliance with the enabling law, and that the damages suffered were noncompensable public damages.[86] Like the *Barron* trial court, the New Jersey Supreme Court did not find these arguments persuasive. Although the right of eminent domain was an attribute of the state's sovereignty, that right was limited by "principles of natural justice and equity," which demand compensation to the affected property owner.[87] The court did not locate the right to compensation in the New Jersey constitution since such a right did not appear there, nor did it cite the Fifth Amendment. It simply held that the right of the sovereign to take property could be exercised only upon payment of compensation, as if such a rule were a given.

Across the river, New York courts also heard similar claims arising from takings of private property. While New Jersey courts found that the obligation to pay for takings of private property existed according to common law or as a matter of fundamental principle, the fact remains that the state constitution did not contain a specific takings clause until 1844, after these three cases. Nor did the Georgia or Maryland constitutions contain similar textual provisions in their decisions on the right to bear arms, on the prohibition of double jeopardy, or on the right to compensation upon takings of property. New York, however, presents a more compelling example given its richer state constitution. In 1843 in *Taylor v. Porter & Ford*, a property owner brought an action for trespass against the builders of a private road they laid across his land.[88] A 1772 state statute allowed road developers to apply to highway commissioners, who in turn would summon twelve local property owners to determine the necessity of the proposed road and set the proper compensation for the owner of the property.[89] The court held the statute unconstitutional since it allowed property to be taken for private use without the owner's consent.[90] For the majority of the court, this taking for private use violated the well-accepted principle that the security of property lied at the very heart of the social compact on which all free government rested. While the legislature was considered supreme, it could not violate this fundamental principle. To that end, the 1821 New York constitution included language similar to that contained in the Magna Carta and the Maryland constitution, and prohibited the deprivation of any of "the rights or privileges secured to any citizen thereof, unless by the law of the land, or judgment of his peers."[91] The court noted that the prohibition against the taking of private property without lawful process was codified in the New York constitution, as well as in the constitutions of several other states, such as North Carolina and Tennessee.[92] However, this codification was not the dispositive issue. Rather, Judge Bronson emphasized the importance of the phrase "law of the land," which was contained in the language of all of these prohibitions. He noted that this phrase required that only the common law could impose the manner through which private property could be taken, adding that the common law did not allow a taking for private use.[93] The court recognized that rights of private property against unauthorized takings were codified in many written constitutions, including New York's, but that the procedure to determine what constituted a lawful taking did not reside in those documents. Rather, the ultimate security of property was left to the restrictions handed down by the common law.

The dissenting judges in *Taylor*, however, took a narrower view of private property rights. They initially attempted to locate them solely within the written mandates of the applicable constitutions. The dissenting opinion noted that, unlike the current state constitution, the first constitution of 1777, which postdated the 1772 statute in question, did not contain a specific prohibition regarding this exact situation. Further, the dissent cited *Barron* as precedent that specifically excluded the Fifth Amendment from applicability.[94] Recognizing that a purely textual interpretation of the location of rights was not yet a completely accepted principle, the dissent noted that "whether the security of the citizen against such arbitrary legislation as the argument contemplates, depends upon this clause of the constitution, or rests upon the broader and more solid ground of natural right never delegated by the people to the law making power, it is unnecessary to enquire."[95] For the dissent, the law was constitutional as a valid exercise of the state's police power, broadly interpreting the power to conclude that in many instances a private road could still serve the public interest of community growth.[96] The majority and dissenting opinions in *Taylor* evidence an important interplay between ideas of the location of rights of property. For the majority, the constitutions of the several states emphasized the sanctity of private property, but the rights themselves did not come from those constitutions. Rather, the collective rulings contained in the common law provided the protection of those property rights from legislative encroachment. For the dissent, however, the constitutions themselves were the place where the right existed. Alternatively, even if the constitution did not provide the basis for the right, a broad view of the state's police power as paramount to individual rights made such a debate unnecessary.

In *People v. White*, New York took land for the construction of a canal in 1819. By 1842, when railroads had surpassed canals, the state abandoned the canal but maintained that it still owned the property.[97] Like the New Jersey courts, the *White* court held that the eminent domain power was an attribute of sovereignty that could be exercised only upon necessity and payment of just compensation. According to the court, who cited Grotius, Pufendorf, Blackstone, and Kent in support, this principle was recognized "throughout the civilized world."[98] Also similar to New Jersey, the *White* court was aware of the *Barron* ruling that held the Fifth Amendment inapplicable to state action.[99] Nonetheless, the court viewed the Fifth Amendment as "only declaratory of a previously existing and universal principle of law."[100] The court was aware that when the taking occurred in 1819, the New York constitution in effect at the time did not contain a similar takings prohibition.[101] New York had a similar constitutional experience as New Jersey. Until revision in 1821, the 1777 New York constitution provided little in the way of rights guarantees.[102] The *White* court deflected this problem and held that the obligation that takings be had only upon public necessity and just compensation was a principle recognized by the courts long before the provision was placed into the 1821 state constitution. In support, the court cited both Georgia supreme court justice Hiram Warner's decision in *Young v. McKenzie*, which held the takings clause of the Fifth Amendment as declaratory of a preexisting common law right, as well as the 1816 decision of Chancellor Kent of the New York Chancery Court in *Gardner v. Trustees of the Village of Newburgh*.[103] As we saw in chapter 3, Chancellor Kent held in *Gardner* that a property owner's right to the enjoyment of a stream that had been redirected was a right that could be found as far back as the Magna Carta. However, the obligation to make compensation for the redirection was a duty imposed on all governments as a matter of "natural equity."[104]

In *New York v. Westchester*, private property was taken by the county to improve a road. The 1845 statute required the road commissioners to reimburse a designated amount to any affected property owner, but a subsequent statute revoked the reimbursement.[105] After 1844, the New York constitution contained an explicit takings clause. However, this did not change the court's analysis of the concept that a government must provide compensation for takings of private property. The court held that the failure to reimburse the property owners not only violated this state takings clause, as well as the contract clause of the U.S. Constitution, but that as a larger matter the legislature fundamentally exceeded its powers by passing the statute, characterizing the liquidated damages award as a vested property interest.[106] To the court the legislature was not the supreme authority that could pass any law, regardless of whether the law was "against natural right and justice."[107] Rather, the purpose of all government was to protect life, liberty, and property.[108] In the court's estimation, the written constitutions of the various states did not provide this right, and the court similarly relied on Chancellor Kent's opinion in *Gardner v. Trustees of the Village of Newburgh*.[109] The court noted that while *Gardner* predated the inclusion of the takings provision into the 1821 New York constitution, Kent nonetheless held that the principle applied "independent of any positive constitutional provision" as a matter of universal law.[110] The court further noted that this principle of compensation for takings of property was well recognized by legal scholars like Chancellor Kent and Justice Story, as well as by decisions of many state courts.[111]

Finally, in *New York v. Toynbee v. Wynhammer*, the New York Court of Appeals was presented with an appeal from a conviction for violating an 1855 state prohibition law.[112] In holding the law unconstitutional, the court commented on its view of the role of the constitution in constraining the legislature. Many courts were beginning to hold the powers of the legislature supreme and limited only by the exact written prohibitions contained in the federal constitution or their own state constitution. In contrast, the *Wynhammer* court held that the legislature was limited not solely by the language of the constitution as written but also by "limitations implied from the nature and form of our government." The court recognized the tradition that held that "laws which, although not specifically prohibited by written constitutions, are repugnant to reason, and subvert clearly vested rights, are invalid, and must be so be declared by the judiciary."[113] For the court, the New York law deprived the charged person of his property and, just like any other deprivation of property, was improper unless done in accordance with the strictures of fundamental law.[114] The fundamental law cited by the court included the provisions in the New York constitution of 1846 against the deprivation of any rights or privileges except by the law of the land; the provision against the deprivation of life, liberty, or property without due process; and the provision outlawing takings of property without just compensation.[115] Importantly, the *Wynhammer* court held that the phrases "law of the land" and "due process of law" did not mean that the legislature could then take property as long as it properly passed legislation allowing the taking.[116] Rather, the court held that the common law determined whether the taking was done in accord with law. To hold otherwise would make the constitutional restraint on the legislature absurd since it would allow the legislature to circumvent its own prohibitions.[117]

In addition to New York courts, other state courts refused to embrace a positive-law view of rights, despite the availability of textual provisions in their state constitutions. In 1842, the Arkansas Supreme Court was presented with a challenge to a state law that outlawed the possession of concealed weapons as violating both the Arkansas constitution and the Second Amendment.[118] Although the court ultimately upheld the law as a valid exercise of the state's police power, it did not entertain any notion that the Bill of Rights protections were not applicable to state action.[119] The Arkansas Supreme Court maintained this view in 1855 when it was presented with an appeal of a criminal conviction on a double jeopardy claim.[120] The court again held that the prohibition against placing a defendant in jeopardy twice was prohibited by the Arkansas constitution, the Fifth Amendment, "and in, perhaps, all of the American bills of rights" as well as by the common law.[121] The court viewed the prohibition against double jeopardy as a right recognized by many sources: state constitutions, the federal constitution, and the common law. However, those sources did not provide the basis for the prohibition. The court felt no need to engage in jurisdictional questions over the applicability of the Fifth Amendment to state court proceedings. Prohibiting double jeopardy was a given. The Arkansas constitution in effect at the time also explicitly protected the right to bear arms as well as the right against double jeopardy.[122] This textual recognition of both rights by the state constitution was not relevant to the court's decision in either case about whether the actual right applied.

The Pennsylvania Supreme Court similarly addressed the issue of the applicability of the Fifth Amendment. In *Ervine's Appeal,* the court struck down an act of the state legislature that ordered the sale of a decedent's property in contravention of the terms of the will.[123] According to the court, the due process clause of the Fifth Amendment prohibited the unilateral passage of a law that ordered the sale against the wishes of potential beneficiaries.[124] Due process required notice and an opportunity to be heard.[125] The court held that the Fifth Amendment and the similar clause in the Pennsylvania constitution of 1838 (Article IX, Section 9) recognized this principle. The court did not address *Barron* or any argument holding the Fifth Amendment applicable only to the federal government. Rather, the court simply assumed the applicability of the due process clause as being "an affirmation of a great doctrine contained in Magna Charta."[126]

The due process clauses found in both the federal and state constitutions "address themselves to the common sense of the people, and ought not to be filed away by legal subtleties. They have their foundations in natural justice, and, without their pervading efficacy, other rights would be useless."[127]

The equation of fundamental principles with the common law was also shown in the 1844 case *Commonwealth v. Flanagan*, where the Pennsylvania Supreme Court was presented with a motion for a new trial after a trial court case for murder ended in a guilty verdict.[128] Among other grounds, the defendants argued that the intense excitement surrounding the charge of murder in the local community prejudiced them from having an impartial jury.[129] In denying the motion, the court addressed the portion of the Pennsylvania constitution that guaranteed a speedy trial by an impartial jury. The court stated that this provision was "declaratory of the common law." [130] Furthermore, the question of what constituted a fair trial was a question for the courts.[131]

In *Rhinehart v. Schuyler*, the Illinois Supreme Court in 1845 was presented with an appeal from a debtor whose property was sold to satisfy an outstanding tax bill.[132] The debtor argued that the law was unconstitutional because it violated the 1818 Illinois constitution.[133] Although the appellant made only a state constitutional argument, possibly informed by the *Barron* decision made a decade earlier, the court did not feel so constrained. The court equated the phrase "due process of law" contained in the Fifth Amendment with the phrase "law of the land" contained in the Illinois constitution. The court held that "in this respect" the U.S. Constitution is "obligatory on all the States of the Union."[134] The court ultimately held the law authorizing the sale constitutional, but nonetheless it did so by viewing the rights of due process as universal and not subject to jurisdictional limitations. For the court, the right that one's property can be taken only by following the dictates of law was a right "secured by his Anglo-Saxon forefathers by magna charta."[135]

In 1860 in *Henry v. Dubuque & Pacific Railroad*, the Iowa Supreme Court refused to adhere to a view of rights as existing in written constitutions.[136] In *Henry*, the Iowa Supreme Court was faced with a common fact pattern for the era: the state delegated its right of eminent domain to a railroad company for purposes of laying tracks across the state. The aggrieved property owner did not cite the Fifth Amendment as a basis, perhaps because of the *Barron* precedent or because the Iowa state constitution had a specific compensation requirement for all takings.[137] However, the existence of a takings clause in the state constitution was not dispositive since the obligation of the railroad to compensate the owner was not predicated on the state constitution. The court held that "the plaintiff needed no constitutional declaration to protect him in the use and enjoyment of his property against any claim or demand of the company. . . . To be thus protected and thus secure in the possession of his property is a right inalienable, a right which a written constitution may recognize or declare, but which existed independently of and before such recognition, and which no government can destroy."[138]

Finally, the Georgia legislature passed a similar law in 1872 to allow Western Union to place its telegraph lines on the right of way of the Southwestern Railroad Company, which ironically and presumably had its own law years earlier to gain this right of way. Nonetheless, while the 1868 Georgia constitution had as its very first section a statement holding that protection of property was a paramount duty of government, it did not contain a specific takings clause in the style of the Fifth Amendment. For the court, this was irrelevant. Because the compensation granted by the law was subject to arbitration, this decision could not be appealed to a court of law. Making the law was unconstitutional because "it is a fundamental principle of the law, as old as *Magna Charta*, that no person, either natural or artificial, shall be deprived of his property but by the judgment of his peers and according to the law of the land."[139]

Of course, while many judges subscribed to a view of rights as extraconstitutional, many other courts in this era decided rights cases with a view that they applied only if textually contained in written constitutions. Over time, many state courts began to recognize *Barron* and applied its view of the Bill of Rights accordingly. In the 1840s, courts in New Hampshire and Wisconsin applied *Barron*,[140] while in the 1850s this increased with Ohio, Alabama, Massachusetts, Vermont, Iowa, Tennessee, and Indiana courts also applying the rule.[141] Seven more states applied *Barron* in the 1860s,[142] six in the 1870s,[143] and ten in the 1880s.[144] The decisions that relied on extraconstitutional interpretations of rights receded bit by bit into the minority. Gradually, courts began to enunciate a vision of rights as part of the positive-law regime. Legislatures were supreme and could pass any law unless specifically limited by the explicit written prohibitions of the constitutions.

This was aided by the fundamental altering of the American constitutional order by the Civil War and the resulting amendments to the Constitution. In 1865, the Thirteenth Amendment was ratified, outlawing slavery and involuntary servitude throughout the United States. This prohibition applied everywhere and to every person, entity, and government. Despite the broad language of the Thirteenth, the former Confederate states interpreted its mandate as outlawing only actual physical bondage. As a result, many attempted to re-create the prewar system of labor and social control through the use of the Black Codes that stripped the freedmen of all political and civil rights. Furthermore, the codes used verbal sleight of hand to re-create the system of forced labor while still attempting to comply with the letter of the Thirteenth Amendment. The obstinacy expressed in the Black Codes, along with the open violence used to re-create the prewar order, ultimately resulted in military reoccupation of the former confederacy and the passage of the Fourteenth Amendment. The Fourteenth Amendment changed the constitutional order envisioned by *Barron* by specifically recognizing that citizens and persons in the United States had certain rights that every state was required to observe. Section 1 reads as follows:

> All persons born or naturalized in the United States, and subject to the jurisdiction thereof, are citizens of the United States and of the State wherein they reside. No State shall make or enforce any law which shall abridge the privileges or immunities of citizens of the United States; nor shall any State deprive any person of life, liberty, or property, without due process of law; nor deny to any person within its jurisdiction the equal protection of the laws.[145]

For the first time, the Constitution defined American citizenship as extending to anyone born within the U.S. With that predicate question definitively answered, the Fourteenth Amendment then turns to the specific prohibitions on the states as they relate to persons within their borders. The Fourteenth Amendment prohibits the states from passing laws that abridge the privileges and immunities of citizens; it mandates that any laws affecting the rights of life, liberty, or property of any person only be done in accord with due process; and it guarantees that all persons have the right to equal protection of the laws. In many ways, the Fourteenth Amendment was the constitutionalization of the universal view of rights that Mayer espoused before the Court in 1833.

Of course, laws are often aspirational statements that reflect the hopes of their drafters. After its ratification in 1868, the Fourteenth

Amendment was quickly stripped of its democratic and egalitarian promise in the late nineteenth century, with the Supreme Court in many ways recreating the prewar constitutional order by interpreting the Fourteenth Amendment narrowly. Instead of looking at the Fourteenth Amendment as confirming the idea that rights applied to all universally, without regard to jurisdiction, the Court held that the Fourteenth Amendment protected only a narrow sliver of federal rights. All others were state rights, and accordingly these rights had to be enforced, or disregarded, by state authorities.[146] Nonetheless, the rights debate occurred within the framework of the Fourteenth Amendment itself. By the twentieth century, courts addressed rights claims by determining which of the Bill of Rights were deemed critical enough to apply to the states by reading them as existing in the various clauses of the Fourteenth Amendment. Consider the right to a trial by a jury. While this right exists textually in the Sixth Amendment to the Constitution, in 1960s Louisiana, for example, it applied only to the extent a similar right was also found in the state constitution. For crimes that did not result in capital punishment or hard labor imprisonment, the right did not apply because the Louisiana constitution allowed for such an exemption. The right to trial by jury was a centerpiece of the English common law; it was even included in the Magna Carta, without the significant qualifications placed on it by the Louisiana constitution. By the 1960s, however, rights in the United States were considered as applicable only to the extent they were granted by the various state and the federal constitutions. As a result of *Barron,* the Sixth Amendment did not apply to Louisiana. By 1968, the U.S. Supreme Court finally ruled in *Duncan v. Louisiana* that the right to a jury trial in the Sixth Amendment was a fundamental right that would now universally apply as it was incorporated against the states through the due process clause of the Fourteenth Amendment.[147] *Duncan* is emblematic of the contemporary understanding of rights as grounded in written constitutions. Instead of holding that the Louisiana constitution violated fundamental liberties, such as the right to a jury trial, the Court had to locate the right in the U.S. Constitution and then seek to use the language of the Fourteenth Amendment to find that it now applied to the states.

Following the Civil War, more courts embraced this positive-law view of rights. Courts that envisioned rights in the way that many did in the prewar era were at this point very much in the minority, though there were a few holdouts. For example, in Arkansas, the state legislature delegated its takings power to a private railroad company to complete an interstate line to bisect the state from Missouri through Little Rock and on to Texas. In 1876 in *Cairo and Fulton R.R. Co. v. Turner*, the Arkansas Supreme Court heard an appeal from a property owner whose property was partially taken to construct the railroad, but for which he had not been compensated.[148] The court recognized the *Barron* ruling that held the Fifth Amendment inapplicable. The court also noted that the state constitution in effect at the time the railroad was granted this power did not contain a takings clause.[149] As with the Maryland constitution in effect during the *Barron* episode, the Arkansas constitution of 1836 contained a Magna Carta–inspired provision that stated "that no freeman shall be taken or imprisoned, or disseized of his freehold, liberties or privileges, or outlawed or exiled, or in any manner destroyed or deprived of his life, liberty or property, but by the judgment of his peers, or the law of the land."[150] Nonetheless, and despite the court's observation that most American states contained an explicit takings clause in their constitutions, the obligation to compensate for a taking was "founded in the fundamental principles of natural right and justice, and as lying at the basis of all wise and just government, independent of all written constitutions or positive law."[151] To support this claim, the court did not rely on Marshall's view of rights but instead reached back to the late 1820s and quoted Kent's *Commentaries* for the view that the American constitutional requirement of compensation is based on natural equity and universal law.[152] *Cairo Railroad* is a good example of the ways that the pre-*Barron* range of rights was maintained despite case law to the contrary. Note that the Arkansas court explicitly recognized *Barron* as authoritative law but only as far as in its main ruling. Certainly the rule that the Fifth Amendment did not apply was well known and difficult to openly challenge by 1876. However, *Barron*'s view of rights as emanating from written constitutions was still not exclusive. In many ways, the Arkansas court was mirroring an analysis that was more prevalent in the pre-*Barron* era. Here, there was no constitutional provision that applied—not the Fifth Amendment because of *Barron*, and not the state constitution because it was not included. Although the state constitution contained a Magna Carta provision on which the court could have based a view of these rights as coming from the "law of the land" or common law remedies, the court viewed the compensation requirement more broadly as located in principles of natural or universal law.

A few courts in the twentieth century continued this pattern. In 1905, a murder conviction was appealed in New Jersey on grounds that certain testimony given at trial should have been excluded because it compelled the defendant to serve as a witness against himself. In *State v. Miller*, the court noted that while this right existed in the Fifth Amendment, *Barron* held it inapplicable to the states. Regardless of the text of federal or state constitutions, the court still found itself obligated to recognize this right since it existed as a part of the common law that the court understood as governing its rules of procedure.[153] In 1936, the chief justice of the Montana Supreme Court recognized that the Seventh Amendment guarantee of a jury trial did not apply to state action, but since state law was allowing the Supreme Court to sit in judgment of both law and fact, the latter normally the province of the jury, the court was violating the right to jury trial. In dissent the chief justice did not locate the right in the Seventh Amendment or in a comparable provision in the state constitution. Rather, he argued that these constitutions recognized principles of rights that existed at the time of their framing. He argued that this right of a jury trial was the most important protections "reserved to the people" by the Magna Carta. As such, and likely in a moment of pique at the ascendancy of the New Deal, he nonetheless claimed it was more important than ever since "we in this age need protection from constantly increasing usurpation of authority of-not King John-but the courts of America."[154]

By 1936, the sentiments of the Montana chief justice made him an outlier on the question of rights. By the twentieth century, the macro issues of law and governance revolved around the legal accommodation of the administrative state; the role of Congress in reining in extralegal activities, especially in the area of labor disputes; and the so-called "civil rights revolution," where activists channeled the power of the Supreme Court and Congress toward providing a more robust framework for political, religious, and racial minorities to use the courts to vindicate individual rights.[155] An essential component of this rights revolution were the rulings of the Court that imposed the various provisions of the Bill of Rights against the states by expansive interpretations of the Fourteenth Amendment. *Barron* became shorthand for the correct interpretation of the pre-Fourteenth Amendment constitutional order. *Barron* is largely unexamined because many have presumed, like the judges of the later nineteenth and early twentieth century, that its ruling was so unobjectionable and correct that further inquiry was unnecessary. In many ways, *Barron* presaged the more positive-law turn that we see with the legal realist movement of the 1930s.[156] *Barron* reflects modern assumptions about the ways rights should operate. They apply if they exist in written documents such as constitutions, statutes, or treaties. As such, their applicability is determined by legislative bodies and courts and are subject to the same procedural hurdles that Marshall enunciated so long ago.

Epilogue

> I think what we've done is we've tried to lift up in a pluralistic culture what Jesus' story is about and that's the challenge, trying to figure out in a pluralistic culture how all of us come together and you know where it ends up coming together? It's the Constitution.
>
> Sister Simone Campbell, 2012

In March 1835, John Marshall suffered a painful and debilitating injury to his spine when his carriage flipped en route to Richmond after the close of the Court's term.[1] Subsequent visitors noted his emaciated frame and surmised that he would not live much longer.[2] Although he was able to attend the opening of his circuit court duties in May, by June Marshall traveled again to Philadelphia for medical treatment. Within weeks, Marshall's condition had deteriorated. An enlarged liver left him unable to eat, and by the end of the month he caught a severe cold. On July 6, 1835, John Marshall passed away in Philadelphia, a few months shy of his eightieth birthday.[3]

Charles Mayer continued his legal practice and by all accounts had a successful career spanning four decades. He represented clients in state and federal court until his death in 1864.[4] David Hoffman did not stay in Europe; after two years he returned to the United States, but not to Baltimore. Hoffman resided in Philadelphia and then New York, where he died from a stroke in 1854.[5] Roger Taney was controversially nominated to replace John Marshall as the chief justice of the Supreme Court. He served until his death in 1864 at eighty-seven, fundamentally at odds with the Lincoln administration during the Civil War. Though an able lawyer and jurist, Taney's *Dred Scott* decision continues to define his legacy.

Luke Tiernan lived a full and successful life, passing away in 1839 at the age of eighty-one.[6] While Tiernan spent years trying to recoup the monies he loaned to Craig, he likely harbored no particular ill will toward his former friend. As a successful businessman he loaned money to many people and routinely used the courts to collect.[7] Indeed, it is quite possible that Tiernan assisted Craig's son John get his start in life. The younger Craig was only twenty-one years old at the time of his father's passing in 1828.[8] Despite the loss of the wharf, Craig managed to acquire another wharf in Fell's Point as well as a nearby home and a significant amount of personal property.[9] Given his family circumstances, it is difficult to imagine this level of success without the intervention of some benefactor; Tiernan is the most obvious suspect. While it appears that the life of the younger John Craig was a story of redemption, it was also one of tragedy. In 1838, a woman named Mary Ann, described as a "consort" of John Craig, died at thirty years of age.[10] Craig himself was killed a year later in a carriage accident. While driving a carriage down a hill, some of the horses "ran off." While the other passengers in the carriage successfully jumped out, Craig was thrown from the carriage while trying to reestablish control. Craig's feet got caught in the wheels and he was fatally dragged down the bumpy stone street until the horse could be stopped. He was only thirty-two.[11] One year later, as if to add a final chapter to the tragedy, Craig's six-year-old son, also named John, wandered from the steps of his house where he was left unattended. The boy wandered out to the pier of his late father's wharf, fell in, and drowned.[12]

Craig and Barron's families never received reimbursement for the damages to the wharf. John Marshall's ruling made sure of that. Meanwhile, the city of Baltimore continued its evolution into a major American city. Fell's Point retained its gritty character, continuing to serve as a first home for immigrants. By the middle of the twentieth century, Fell's Point had fallen on hard times. In the 1960s, it managed to stave off destruction by successfully opposing the city's designation that it constituted a slum worthy of demolition for a proposed expressway.[13] Fell's Point today has rebounded, though it is no longer home to the maritime industry that was so important in its early years. Instead of large schooners seeking to tie up at wharves like Barron and Craig's, the primary watercraft in the district are largely water taxis shuttling tourists from the hotels of the inner harbor. John Craig's former home and grocery serves this new clientele as a bar and restaurant, while the wharf he owned with Barron is occupied by condominiums and a parking lot. Finally, the state of Maryland framed a new state constitution in 1851. Appreciating rights in much the same way as Marshall in *Barron*, the new constitution provided an explicit clause that prohibited the state from taking private property without just compensation.[14]

In 1989, the Voice of America commissioned a series of radio plays meant to dramatize the role of the Constitution in American history on the bicentennial of its ratification. Included in the stories about the lives of John Marshall and James Madison was episode nineteen, entitled "The Fifth Amendment Case That Lost." Hosted by actor Don Ameche, it told the story of *Barron v. Baltimore.* Before talking about Barron and Craig's Fifth Amendment right to compensation for the taking of their property, the radio play began with a recounting of the circumstances that led to the framing of the Constitution, a document it described as "that glorious testament to human freedom." It described how the founding fathers gathered in Philadelphia to begin their work on a new plan of government. In the light of the difficulties they faced, the play noted that "to create a union would require a miracle, and yet that is what happened." In many ways, the story of rights described in the radio play is one that reflects the view laid out by John Marshall in his final constitutional opinion, in particular that Barron and Craig's right to compensation depended on the interpretation of the specific words of the Constitution. Of course, the play did not mention the inconvenient problem that the Bill of Rights, on which Barron and Craig laid their claim, was not a part of the deliberations that summer but was inserted later at the insistence of many states jealous of guarding their power. Rather, it told the story of an inefficient and uncaring city government determined to run roughshod over Barron and Craig's rights, even though those rights should have been secured to them by the Constitution.[15]

While the play characterized *Barron* as a moment in which the Court inexplicitly allowed the city of Baltimore to violate the Fifth Amendment, it was fundamentally a case continued all the way to the Supreme Court by a creditor seeking to recover his losses. However, many cases outlast their original purposes, and *Barron* is no exception. On a micro level, this study hoped to illuminate the actual circumstances that gave rise to the case, from the lives of the people involved, to a snapshot of early Baltimore, to a view inside the courtrooms where Barron and Craig tried to remedy their misfortune. While an intimate history of the case itself is satisfying for constitutional history buffs, by digging deeper into the story we see that the case has an historical relevance that is easily overlooked if we treat *Barron* as simply a prelude to the Fourteenth Amendment. *Barron* matters on its own.

If we resituate Marshall's decision within its own era, it can help us better appreciate several critical legal and constitutional transformations that were taking place in the early republic. First, *Barron* is a good example of the role of popular constitutionalism in this era because it helps connect the activities of those outside of the courtrooms to the formal constitutional jurisprudence of the Supreme Court.[16] From nullifiers renouncing their attachment to the Union in the streets of Charleston and the Cherokees who came in from the fields to discover their homes taken over by their Georgia neighbors, to the state legislatures and conventions and ultimately the formal institutions of federal power in Washington, D.C., *Barron* serves as evidence that popular ideas regarding the correct functioning of the American constitutional order found their way into the Supreme Court much in the same way that popular agitation found its way into Congress. The *Barron* decision bears all the fingerprints of a decision that recognized the immediacy and danger presented by these conflicts. It is the product of the aging justice's sense that his lifelong work of trying to create a nation out of a collection of regional interests was ending in failure as many had come unmoored from their national attachments. Marshall's refusal to force the states to observe the Bill of Rights is less a product of legal reasoning and more a reaction to popular expressions of constitutionalism that were being expressed across the nation in forceful and frightening ways.

In a related sense, we can better place *Barron* within the larger jurisprudence of the Marshall court by recognizing that politics and outside pressure drove the Court to arrive at its particular decision. While *Barron* has puzzled scholars as an outlier to the rest of Marshall's jurisprudence, the decision makes more sense if we view the Court as a political body and Marshall as a political actor. From 1801 to 1835, Marshall led the Court through a period of incredible political and social upheaval for the young nation. The Court was able to survive, and indeed its reputation was strengthened because Marshall crafted his rulings by specifically recognizing the political opportunities and limitations presented in each era. Marshall's constitutional legacy came about not by resorting to a set of immutable legal principles; rather, it exists because he both reacted to political disputes brought to his Court and devised responses that recognized the political realities, possibilities, and limitations inherent in every case of constitutional import. This jurisprudential legacy emerged in response to the evolving political transformations of the country; in this way, the work of the Marshall court is important not merely as a body of law but as an essential part of the history of the early American republic itself. The intimate relationship between politics and Marshall's constitutional decisions forces us to understand cases like *Barron* as indisputably important events in the history of the early American republic.

Finally, *Barron* helps signal a sea change in terms of where Americans believed their rights existed. During the 1820s and 1830s, courts across the country became less inclined to view rights as granted by nature or God, nor did they understand rights as based in a fundamental principle of free governments. Courts were also less receptive to arguments that described rights as supplied by the malleable dictates of the common law. Instead, rights were being tied increasingly to written documents; as such, they were becoming interpreted in a manner similar to other positive law enactments, such as statutes or ordinances. *Barron* is an example of how the trend away from the eighteenth-century tradition of considering rights as outside the domain of courts and legislatures had reached the Supreme Court. Barron and Craig's right to receive payment for a taking of private property was not considered to exist in the common law or as a fundamental requirement of free government; rather, their right was disregarded because it did not overcome jurisdictional hurdles.

Barron's significance is often minimized because it is considered an accurate expression of the pre–Civil War U.S. constitutional order pertaining to rights. However, this flawed view of *Barron*'s accuracy fails to account for the very different ways that Americans in this era thought about the sources of their rights. Constitutions served as written evidence of the ways elites planned to manage conflict. The architecture of the U.S. Constitution informs us that the tension between the state and federal governments was envisioned as a prime method to ensure balance in national governance. The Constitution was designed as a political settlement to cure the ills of the 1780s and to provide a stable blueprint going forward. While it famously sanctioned slavery in order to secure the support of states like South Carolina, it contained many other political agreements designed to resolve other conflicts over power. For example, representation in Congress translated into influence in the federal government. As a result of political compromise, the Constitution ensured that small states got equal representation in the Senate, but revenue bills could originate only in the House, where proportional representation gave large states more control.[17]

Unlike these provisions that were included in the Constitution to resolve political disagreements, rights were not placed there under the same circumstances. Framing-era Americans did not consider their rights as a product of these same political agreements. Into the early republic era, rights retained this extraconstitutional identity. However, by deciding that the prohibition against taking private property was inapplicable because the Bill of Rights was not intended to apply to the states, *Barron* treated rights as similar to any of these other political compromises. By constitutionalizing this liberty, it became subject to the same rules of jurisdiction as any other law. In this way, *Barron* does not accurately represent the prewar constitutional order as it relates to questions of rights. Rather, it is better understood as a byproduct of the timing of its arrival on the Supreme Court docket in the early 1830s during a time of acute conflict between the states and the federal government.

Looking at *Barron* with a modern understanding of the source of rights gives the decision an undeserved sense of accuracy. Believing that rights are applicable only because the Constitution considers them applicable unhelpfully aggrandizes the Constitution. At the same time, it trivializes rights. Instead of an outline to structure government, allocate resources, provide security, or manage conflict, the Constitution has become the object of near worship in the inflating of its purpose to include the granting of rights. This view minimizes the people's role in maintaining the American constitutional order and leads to popular longing for the advice of unspecified founding fathers to tell us exactly how to solve all of our problems. The sense of omnipotence attached to the Constitution makes it difficult to debate policy, and the excessive veneration of the handiwork of the summer of 1787 often serves to limit good governance.

When Barron and Craig brought suit in the 1820s, they had a number of places from which they could locate their right to payment for the taking of their wharf. Whether from the common law, natural law, or general principles of all free governments, most viewed this right as existing extraconstitutionally. To the extent the right was in written constitutions, it was generally thought to simply remind everyone of its existence. Treating rights as effective only if included in these inherently legal documents supports the claim that these liberties can be vindicated only through formal law processes. An obvious reaction to the method of locating rights as emanating from written constitutions, statutes, conventions, or treaties is that it grants an enormous amount of power to the institutions of formal law since courts gain control over questions of applicability. However, this interpretation allows courts the power to ensure that the law reflects the economic, cultural, and technological realities present in an ever-changing nation. As such, it is important to recall the view of rights before *Barron*, but not out of a sense of outrage over the role of the judiciary claiming their role in determining the success of rights claims. *Diminishing the Bill of Rights* also does not long for a day when attorneys can again cast rights in terms of natural law. Indeed, claims that undergirded social hierarchy in the United States—the legal, political, and social subjugation of women or the enslavement of African Americans in the antebellum era, for example—were long predicated on arguments that cast these relations as natural or divinely ordained.

Rather, it is important to appreciate the pre-*Barron* pluralism of the sources of rights because excessive constitutionalization leads to gridlock. By envisioning the Constitution as the effective source of rights, it is only natural that parties will lobby the courts to endorse their various preferred liberties as constitutional. The right to own a firearm was considered variously as protected by the common law of self-defense, as the birthright of the English people, or as a principle recognized by all free governments. It was not considered an individual's constitutional right until recognized as such by the Court in 2008.[18] In so doing the Court first had to find that it was an individual right and then had to consider that the due process clause of the Fourteenth Amendment applied the right against the states.[19] Historians have noted that both sides in the Second Amendment debate were mistaken, primarily because of their sole emphasis on constitutional rights. On the one hand, pro-gun advocates were mistaken because the amendment was unquestionably designed to safeguard state control over the militia. At the same time, proponents of gun control failed to recognize that in the same era Americans also possessed an individual right to own a firearm. The difference was that the individual right was provided not by the Constitution but by the common law.[20]

In a similar manner, the right to privacy does not textually appear in the Constitution, though this right existed in some form in the common law as a tort for generations. However, to overcome the actions of a state that wanted to criminalize the sale of birth control, the Court in *Griswold v. Connecticut* (1965) faced a dilemma only by virtue of the era in which the case was decided.[21] The Court had to constitutionalize the right to privacy in order to make it effective against the state criminal law. The Court could no longer act as a tribunal that could weigh rights as existing across a spectrum of extra-constitutional places; rather, it had to locate the right somewhere in the U.S. Constitution. Thus, in *Griswold*, to apply a right of privacy the Court needed to constitutionalize it, leading to Justice Douglas's puzzling doctrine that the right of privacy existed within the interlocking shadows cast by many of the liberties in the Bill of Rights.[22]

A set of very specific historical circumstances informed the ruling in *Barron*. Nonetheless, the resulting constitutionalization of Barron and Craig's right to compensation both pervades modern legal thought and bears consequences. Casting rights as constitutional in effect creates hierarchies of rights, with constitutional rights at the apex. The more rights that attain premier status as constitutional, the more difficult it becomes to navigate the thorny questions that arise, for example, when the right to bear arms comes in conflict with rights to free speech, or when rights of privacy are in opposition to rights of religion. At that point, one of those penultimate rights must give way, either debasing the liberty or causing constitutional stalemate. Since *Barron* constitutes an essential step that led to this situation, we are wise to recall the unique circumstances that led to its outcome.

Notes

INTRODUCTION

1. 9 *Cong. Deb.* 1 (1833).

2. Daniel Walker Howe, *What Hath God Wrought: The Transformation of America, 1815–1848* (New York: Oxford University Press, 2007), 404; Ordinance of Nullification, November 24, 1832, in William W. Freehling, ed., *The Nullification Era: A Documentary Record* (New York: Harper, 1967), 150.

3. See, for example, the speeches by Senators Mangum (N.C.) and Bibb (Ky.) on December 24, 1832, 9 Cong. *Deb.* 22, 26 (1833).

4. Maxwell Bloomfield, "Supreme Court Buildings," in *The Oxford Guide to the Supreme Court*, ed. Kermit Hall et al. (New York: Oxford University Press, 2005), 119. Not until 1935 would the Supreme Court move into the magisterial building it presently occupies.

5. John C. Calhoun, "Speech on the Revenue Collection [Force] Bill," February 15–16, 1833, in John C. Calhoun, *Union and Liberty: The Political Philosophy of John C. Calhoun*, ed. Ross M. Lence (Indianapolis: Liberty Fund, 1992), 401.

6. *Niles' Weekly Register* (Baltimore, MD), February 23, 1833, 5.

7. *Marbury v. Madison*, 5 U.S. 137 (1803).

8. *Fletcher v. Peck*, 10 U.S. 87 (1810).

9. *McCulloch v. Maryland*, 17 U.S. 316 (1819).

10. Lindsay Robertson, *Conquest by Law* (New York: Oxford University Press, 2005), 135–36.

11. Some scholars have argued that the first eight amendments to the Constitution were not at the time considered a "Bill of Rights" in the same way as those lists of rights that appeared in the early state constitutions; rather, this designation came much later for purposes of aggrandizing federal power. Without

wading into this controversy, and given its common usage, this study chooses to use the term notwithstanding. See Gerald N. Magliocca, "How Did the Bill of Rights Become the Bill of Rights?" *Social Science Research Network* (June 12, 2015), http://papers.ssrn.com/sol3/papers.cfm?abstract_id=2617811.

12. *Barron v. Mayor of Baltimore*, 32 U.S. 243, Transcript of Record, File Date: July 1, 1831, 31 pp., Term Year: 1833, *U.S. Supreme Court Records and Briefs*, 1832–1978, Gale, Cengage Learning (hereinafter referred to as *Barron* Transcript), 17. *Barron v. Baltimore*, Case File #1695, Box 196, RG 267, Records of the United States Supreme Court, National Archives and Records Administration, Washington, D.C. (location in stacks: 17E3/01/16/05).

13. *Barron* Transcript, 4; *Black's Law Dictionary*, Revised 4th edition (St. Paul, MN: West, 1968), 1674–75.

14. See Francis Stites, *John Marshall: Defender of the Constitution* (New York: Longman, 1981); Mark Killenbeck, *M'Culloch v. Maryland: Securing a Nation* (Lawrence: University Press of Kansas, 2006); and Richard Ellis, *Aggressive Nationalism: McCulloch v. Maryland and the Foundation of Federal Authority in the Young Republic* (New York: Oxford University Press, 2007).

15. W. Allan Wilbur, "Review of *John Marshall: A Life in Law*," *American Journal of Legal History* (April 1976): 155, 157.

16. Peter Irons, *A People's History of the Supreme Court* (New York: Penguin Books, 1999), 136.

17. H. Jefferson Powell, "The Original Understanding of Original Intent," in *Interpreting the Constitution: The Debate over Original Intent*, ed. Jack N. Rakove (Boston: Northeastern University Press, 1990), 114, Note 325.

18. Scott Douglas Gerber, *To Secure These Rights: The Declaration of Independence and Constitutional Interpretation* (New York: New York University Press, 1995), 104.

19. Ibid., 117–23.

20. See, for example, Sister Simone Campbell, interview by Stephen Colbert, *The Colbert Report*, Comedy Central, December 13, 2012.

21. *Citizens United v. Federal Elections Commission*, 130 S.Ct. 876 (2010).

22. For a similar view, see John Phillip Reid, "The Authority of Rights at the American Founding," in *The Nature of Rights at the American Founding and Beyond*, ed. Barry Alan Shain (Charlottesville: University of Virginia Press, 2007), 69.

CHAPTER 1

Epigraph: Thomas Scharf, *The Chronicles of Baltimore* (Baltimore: Turnbull Brothers, 1874), 22–23.

1. Edward C. Papenfuse and Joseph M. Coale III, eds., *The Maryland State Archives Atlas of Historical Maps of Maryland, 1608–1908* (Baltimore: Johns Hopkins University Press, 2003), 167.

2. Sherry H. Olson, *Baltimore: The Building of an American City* (Baltimore: Johns Hopkins University Press, 1980), 57–58; and Richard J. Cox, "Trouble on the Chain Gang: City Surveying, Maps, and the Absence of Urban Planning in Baltimore 1730–1823," *Maryland Historical Magazine* 81, no. 1 (Spring 1986): 18.

3. Charles G. Steffen, *From Gentlemen to Townsmen: The Gentry of Baltimore County, Maryland, 1660–1776* (Lexington: University Press of Kentucky, 1993), 10–11.

4. Aubrey C. Land, *Colonial Maryland: A History* (New York: KTO Press, 1981), 4–9; Steffen, *Gentlemen*, 8.

5. Steffen, *Gentlemen*, 8.

6. Ibid., 8, 10–11.

7. Olson, *Baltimore*, 5; *Report of Isaac Trimble, the Engineer appointed by the Commissioners of the Mayor and City Council of Baltimore on the Subject of the Maryland Canal* (Baltimore: Lucas & Deaver, 1837), 4.

8. Charles G. Steffen, *The Mechanics of Baltimore: Workers and Politics in the Age of Revolution, 1763–1812* (Urbana: University of Illinois Press, 1984), 4.

9. Scharf, *Chronicles of Baltimore*, 20–21; Baltimore County was established in 1659–60. Steffen, *Gentlemen*, 11–12.

10. Scharf, *Chronicles of Baltimore*, 32–34.

11. Steffen, *Mechanics of Baltimore*, 4; Seth Rockman, *Scraping By: Wage Labor, Slavery, and Survival in Early Baltimore* (Baltimore: Johns Hopkins University Press, 2009), 79–80.

12. Rockman, *Scraping By*, 80; "Awful Calamity," *American & Commercial Daily Advertiser* (Baltimore, MD), August 11, 1817 (hereinafter "Baltimore *American*"); "Report on the Survey of Jones Falls," *Baltimore Patriot*, October 6, 1817, 4.

13. Steffen, *Mechanics of Baltimore*, 4; Rockman, *Scraping By*, 79.

14. Olson, *Baltimore*, 8.

15. Garrett Power, "Parceling Out Land in the Vicinity of Baltimore: 1632–1796, Part 2," *Maryland Historical Magazine* 88, no. 2 (Summer 1993): 160.

16. Lawrence A. Peskin, "Fells Point: Baltimore's Pre-industrial Suburb," *Maryland Historical Magazine* 97, no. 2 (Summer 2002): 153–56; Power, "Parceling Out Land," 157; Olson, *Baltimore*, 8.

17. This observation is taken from a 1752 drawing of Baltimore by resident John Moale. Moale's drawing has been the inspiration for a number of Baltimore historians, including Scharf, *Chronicles of Baltimore*, 47–48; Steffen, *Mechanics of Baltimore*, 4; and Power, "Parceling Out Land," 157.

18. Olson, *Baltimore*, 10; Scharf, *Chronicles of Baltimore*, 51.

19. Steffen, *Mechanics of Baltimore*, 6–7.

20. Stuart Weems Bruchey, *Robert Oliver, Merchant of Baltimore, 1783–1819* (Baltimore: Johns Hopkins University Press, 1956), 30–31.

21. Olson, *Baltimore*, 11; Steffen, *Mechanics of Baltimore*, 6; Scharf, *Chronicles of Baltimore*, 51.

22. Rockman, *Scraping By*, 28.

23. Steffen, *Mechanics of Baltimore*, 7; Jerome Garitee, *The Republic's Private Navy: The American Privateering Business as Practiced by Baltimore during the War of 1812* (Middletown, CT: Wesleyan University Press, 1977), 12.

24. Steffen, *Mechanics of Baltimore*, 8; Gary L. Browne, *Baltimore in the Nation, 1789–1861* (Chapel Hill: University of North Carolina Press, 1980), 25–26.

25. Browne, *Baltimore in the Nation*, 28.

26. Olson, *Baltimore*, 10; Cox, "Trouble on the Chain Gang," 8–9; Rockman, *Scraping By*, 3.

27. Sean Wilentz, *The Rise of American Democracy: Jefferson to Lincoln* (New York: W. W. Norton, 2005), 130–31.

28. Browne, *Baltimore in the Nation*, 52.

29. Ibid., 91.

30. *Deed from Mackubin to Craig and Barron*, December 8, 1815, Baltimore County Court (Land Records), Maryland State Archives (hereinafter "MSA"), CE 66-184, WG 134, p. 474.

31. See, generally, *Baltimore Directory and Register for 1814–15*, ed. James Lakin (Baltimore: J. C. O'Reilly, 1814).

32. U.S. Naturalization Records Indexes, National Archives and Records Administration (hereinafter "NARA") (Washington, D.C.), Indexes to Naturalization petitions to the U.S. Circuit and District Courts for Maryland, 1797–1951, Microform Serial M1168, Roll 1.

33. *Baltimore Directory for 1807*, ed. James M'Henry (Baltimore: Warner & Hanna, 1807), 16; *Baltimore Directory for 1817–18* (Baltimore: James Kennedy, 1817), 12; *Matchett's Baltimore Directory, for 1824* (Baltimore: Richard Matchett, 1824), 19; "New Rope Store," *Baltimore Patriot*, November 15, 1822.

34. *Baltimore Directory for 1807*, 16; *The Baltimore Directory for 1810*, ed. William Fry (Baltimore: G. Dobbin & Murphy, 1810), 29; *Fry's Baltimore Directory for 1812*, ed. William Fry (Baltimore: B. W. Sower & Co., 1812), 9; *Baltimore Directory for 1817–18*, 12; *Matchett's Baltimore Directory, 1822–23* (Baltimore: Richard Matchett, 1822), 20; *Matchett's Baltimore Directory, for 1824*, 19; and *Matchett's Baltimore Directory for 1827* (Baltimore: Richard Matchett, 1827), 25.

35. Power, "Parceling Out Land," 160–62; Peskin, "Fell's Point," 155.

36. Power, "Parceling Out Land," 162, 165; Olson, *Baltimore*, 23.

37. *Assignment from Bordley to Barron, Jr.*, July 18, 1807, Baltimore County Court (Land Records), MSA CE 66–145, WG 95, p. 108.

38. *Deed from Giles to Barron, Jr.*, June 18, 1808, Baltimore County Court (Land Records), MSA CE 66–149, WG 99, p. 299.

39. *Assignment from Barron, Jr. to Craig*, September 28, 1809, Baltimore County Court (Land Records), MSA CE-154, WG 104, p. 349.

40. *Maryland Marriages, 1801–1820*, compiled by Robert Barnes (Baltimore: Genealogical Publishing Co., 1993), 39.

41. Power, "Parceling Out Land," 162.

42. The southernmost parcel, at the corner of Ann and George, was deeded to Craig by John Lee on March 26, 1808 for $1,200. See MSA CE 66–147, WG 97, p. 151. The parcel directly north of this was assigned by David Fisher to Craig on October 5, 1808, but was not originally recorded until 1829, following the lawsuit by Tiernan to foreclose a mortgage given to him by Craig and secured by the property. See *Tiernan v. David and John Fisher, John Craig, and John H. Staples*, MSA S512–14–11311, Acc. No.: 17,898–11483, location: 1/39/3/.

43. *Baltimore Directory for 1807*, 34. Craig is also listed as a grocer or shopkeeper at this address in the directories for 1808, 1810, 1816, 1822–23, and 1824.

44. Baltimore City Archives (hereinafter "BCA"), RG 22 (War of 1812 Records), MSA SC5458–45–20–1042 and MSA SC5458–45–20–0140. Craig was noted as supplying "Junk." Presumably, this is more of a miscellaneous nature rather than a quality designation as Craig's contribution is listed with a value of $220.99. Craig's part ownership of the vessel is outlined in *Tiernan v. Rescaniere's Adm'rs*, 10 G. & J. 253 (Md. Ct. of App. 1838).

45. 1820 U.S. Census; Census Place: Baltimore Ward 1, Baltimore, Maryland; Page 4; NARA Roll: M33_42; Image: 12. While Craig owned at least one enslaved person in his life, there is no evidence that Barron did, though he was noted as having one free female of color as a dependent in 1820. See 1820 U.S. Census; Census Place: Baltimore Ward 1, Baltimore, Maryland; Page 3; NARA Roll: M33_42; Image 11.

46. Garitee, *Republic's Private Navy*, 47–49.

47. Ibid., 259.

48. Ibid., 67; J.P. Cranwell and W.B. Crane, *Men of Marque: A History of Private Armed Vessels out of Baltimore During the War of 1812* (New York: W.W. Norton, 1940), 381.

49. Cranwell and Crane, *Men of Marque*, 408.

50. David Head, "Baltimore Seafarers, Privateering, and the South American Revolutions, 1816–1820," *Maryland Historical Magazine* 103, no. 3 (Fall 2008): 271. For this proposition, Head is citing Garitee, *Republic's Private Navy*, 111–12.

51. Cranwell and Crane, *Men of Marque*, 376.

52. The *Sarah Ann* was captured on September 13, 1812; in Cranwell and Crane, *Men of Marque*, 393.

53. Ibid., 376.

54. Garitee, *Republic's Private Navy*, 273.

55. Cranwell and Crane, *Men of Marque*, 393–94.

56. *Tiernan v. Rescaniere's Adm'rs*, 10 G. & J. 217 (Md. 1838).

57. Robert J. Brugger, *Maryland: A Middle Temperament* (Baltimore: Johns Hopkins Press, 1988), 196.

58. Ibid., 196.

59. Head, "Baltimore Seafarers," 269–70.

60. Ibid., 273.

61. *Black's Law Dictionary*, 1635–36; Jesse Dukeminier and James Krier, *Property*, Third Edition (Boston: Little, Brown & Co., 1993), 325–26.

62. *Mackubin Deed*, MSA CE 66–184, WG 134, p. 474; *James Mackubin, Administrator of Frederick Mackubin v. John Craig and John Barron Jr.* (Baltimore County Court, 1818), MSA S512-4-3602, Acc. No. 17,898–3495–1/2, Location: 1/36/3/, December 14, 1815 Mortgage.

63. *Mackubin v. Craig and Barron* (September 16, 1818 Bill of Complaint).

64. *Mackubin v. Craig and Barron* (December 14, 1815 Mortgage).

65. *Baltimore Patriot*, November 28, 1815, 2; *Baltimore Patriot*, April 12, 1816, 3; and *Baltimore Patriot*, November 8, 1816, 3.

66. Papenfuse and Coale, *Atlas of Historical Maps*, 165.

67. *Baltimore Patriot*, April 6, 1816, 2.

68. *Baltimore Patriot*, September 18, 1817, 3.

69. *Mackubin v. Craig and Barron* (September 16, 1818 Bill of Complaint), 2.

70. *John Barron, Survivor of John Craig, for the use of Luke Tiernan, Executor of John Craig v. The Mayor and City Council of Baltimore*, 32 U.S. 243 (1833).

71. Olson, *Baltimore*, 11; Eugenia Calvert Holland and Louisa Macgill Gary, "Miniatures in the Collection of the Maryland Historical Society," *Maryland Historical Magazine* 51, no. 4 (1956): 343; Garitee, *Republic's Private Navy*, 67; Thomas Spalding, *The Premier See: A History of the Archdiocese of Baltimore, 1789–1989* (Baltimore: Johns Hopkins University Press, 1989), 29; Whitman H. Ridgway, *Community Leadership in Maryland, 1790–1840: A Comparative Analysis of Power in Society* (Chapel Hill: University of North Carolina Press, 1979), 232; Whitman H. Ridgway, "Community Leadership: Baltimore During the First and Second Party Systems," *Maryland Historical Magazine* 71, no. 3 (Fall 1976): 334, 346; C.B. Tiernan, "Luke Tiernan of Baltimore," *The American Catholic Historical Researches* 12 (Oct. 1895): 189, 191. Garitee places Tiernan's move to Baltimore in 1790, whereas Spalding, Ridgway, and C.B. Tiernan all contend it occurred in 1795.

72. *Baltimore Directory and Register for 1814–15*, 186.

73. *Fry's Baltimore Directory for 1812*, 19; Bernard F. Reilly, *American Political Prints, 1766–1876* (Boston: G.K. Hall & Co., 1991), 37.

74. Ridgway, *Community Leadership in Maryland*, 232.

75. Howe, *What Hath God Wrought*, 93–95.

76. Tiernan's affiliations followed national politics in many ways. He identified as a Republican during the first party system, then as a National Republican as the party frayed, and ultimately as a Whig. October 9, 1831, Letter from Luke Tiernan, et al. to Governor Allen Trimble, *The "Old Northwest" Genealogical Quarterly*, 1908, Vol. XI (Columbus, OH: Spahr and Glenn, 1908), 131–33; Spalding, *Premier See*, 58; Ridgway, *Community Leadership in Maryland*, 232; C.B. Tiernan, "Luke Tiernan of Baltimore," 191.

77. John Quincy Adams, *Memoirs of John Quincy Adams, Comprising Portions of his Diary from 1795 to 1848*, Vol. VII, ed. Charles Francis Adams (Philadelphia: J.P. Lippincott & Co., 1875), 329, 333–34.

78. C.B. Tiernan, "Luke Tiernan of Baltimore," 191; Seth Rockman, "Work, Wages, and Welfare at Baltimore's School of Industry," *Maryland Historical Magazine* 102, no. 1 (Spring 2007): 572, 593.

79. *Fry's Baltimore Directory for 1812*, 23–24; Frank Otto Gatell, "Secretary Taney and the Baltimore Pets: A Study in Banking and Politics," *Business History Review* 39, no. 2 (Summer, 1965): 205, 214; Taney was technically an interim appointment to Treasury and retained his Attorney General position. See Howe, *What Hath God Wrought*, 387–88.

80. *Fry's Baltimore Directory for 1812*, 31; Browne, *Baltimore in the Nation*, 55.

81. *Fry's Baltimore Directory for 1812*, 19, 23–24, 29–30, and 31; *Matchett's Baltimore Directory, for 1824*, 363, 365; "Maryland Colonization Society," Baltimore *American*, July 1, 1818.

82. Spalding, *Premiere See*, 86; William D. Hoyt, Jr., "Land for a Cathedral: Baltimore, 1806–1817," *Catholic Historical Review* 36, no. 4 (Jan. 1951): 441.

83. *Mackubin v. Craig and Barron* (January 7, 1817 Tiernan Mortgage).

84. *Mackubin v. Craig and Barron* (September 16, 1818 Bill of Complaint), 2.

85. Rockman, "Work, Wages, and Welfare," 575.

86. *James Colston v. John Craig* (Baltimore County Court, 1817), MSA S512–9-7151, Acc. No.: 17,898–7118–1/3, Location: 1/37/4/.

87. *Barron* Transcript, 14.

88. "City Ordinances," *Baltimore Patriot*, April 12, 1817. See also Chapters Two and Four.

89. *Baltimore Patriot*, June 5, 1818, 3; *Baltimore Patriot*, July 5, 1820, 3.

90. *Mackubin v. Craig and Barron* (September 16, 1818 Bill of Complaint).

91. *Deed from Barron to Schley*, September 18, 1818, MSA CE 66–200, WG 150, p. 236.

92. Though demurrers are outdated, in most states a motion to dismiss largely accomplishes the same purposes. See *Black's Law Dictionary*, 520–21.

93. *Mackubin v. Craig and Barron* (July 15, 1819 Demurrer).

94. *Mackubin v. Craig and Barron* (December 16, 1819 Order Denying Demurrer).

95. *Mackubin v. Craig and Barron* (February 7, 1820 Hoffman Answer).

96. Ibid.

97. Howe, *What Hath God Wrought*, 136–43.

98. Browne, *Baltimore in the Nation*, 74; Robert E. Shalhope, *The Baltimore Bank Riot: Political Upheaval in Antebellum Maryland* (Urbana: University of Illinois Press, 2009), 14.

99. Seth Rockman, "Work, Wages, and Welfare," 596–97; and Browne, *Baltimore in the Nation*, 76.

100. Browne, *Baltimore in the Nation*, 74.

101. Rockman, "Work, Wages and Welfare," 597.

102. *Mayor Johnson to City Council*, August 27, 1819, BCA BRG16–1-21, Location: BC/13/01/018, Document: 428.

103. *Mackubin v. Craig and Barron* (February 23, 1820 Decree).

104. 1819 Maryland Session Laws, Vol. 632, Chapter 162, Section 3 (Annapolis: Jonas Green, 1820), 101.

105. The bond was posted in the amount of $2,111.00, which Hoffman filed. As further evidence regarding who was driving the case, Hoffman also attested to the character and the large estate of Luke Tiernan. *Mackubin v. Craig and Barron* (April 25, 1820 Bond, filed May 2, 1820).

106. *Mackubin v. Craig and Barron* (January 7, 1817 Tiernan Mortgage), 1.

107. *Mackubin v. Craig and Barron* (February 1822 Ledger).

108. *Tiernan v. Margaret Craig, Margaret Staples, John Craig, and Robert Craig*, MSA S512–14–11237, Acc. No.: 17,898–11412–1/2, Location: 1/39/3; Mortgage from Craig to Tiernan, December 4, 1820, MSA CE 66–209, WG 159, p. 713. This is the southern parcel directly located at Ann and George, not the one to the north deeded to Craig by Fisher in 1805 and later assigned to Craig's son-in-law John Staples.

109. *Barron* Transcript, 26.

110. *Mackubin v. Craig and Barron* (December 12, 1821 Bond).

111. *Mackubin v. Craig and Barron* (January 3, 1822 Letter from Tiernan to Mackubin). With respect to the sunken vessels, Tiernan is apparently referring to the boats sunk in the harbor as a defensive maneuver to slow the British advance in the War of 1812. The lawsuit for reimbursement was eventually filed years later by Tiernan, as Craig's executor in *Tiernan v. Rescaniere's Adm'rs*, 10 G. & J. 253 (Md. Ct. of App. 1838).

112. *Mackubin v. Craig and Barron* (January 3, 1822 Letter from Tiernan to Mackubin).

113. *Mackubin v. Craig and Barron* (January 3, 1822 Letter from Hoffman to Mackubin).

114. *Mackubin v. Craig and Barron* (January 17, 1822 notation from R. Lemmon & Co., auctioneer).

115. *Mackubin v. Craig and Barron* (February 15, 1822 Petition by Tiernan, and March 20, 1822 Account and Auditor's Report).

CHAPTER 2

Epigraph: "Aristides," *Baltimore Patriot*, August 18, 1818.

1. Steffen, *Mechanics of Baltimore*, 4.

2. Laura Edwards, *The People and Their Peace: Legal Culture and the Transformation of Inequality in the Post-Revolutionary South* (Chapel Hill: University of North Carolina Press, 2009), 300n6.

3. Steffen, *Mechanics of Baltimore*, 122.

4. Ibid. In 1786, Baltimore residents were allowed to elect the offices of street commissioners and port wardens, while the 1776 Maryland constitution

gave Baltimore two representatives in the state legislature. On the whole, however, Baltimore was woefully underrepresented in the legislature, which exerted an enormous amount of control over the city itself until incorporation. See Steffen, *Mechanics of Baltimore,* 126.

5. Ibid., 122.

6. Browne, *Baltimore in the Nation,* 38; Steffen, *Mechanics of Baltimore,* 139–40.

7. Baltimore did receive permission to establish its own municipal criminal court in 1817. Two years later, the city was also allowed to appoint two justices of the peace, but otherwise its courts of law remained under the control of the county. Browne, *Baltimore in the Nation,* 37, 104–5; Olson, *Baltimore,* 135.

8. Baltimore *American,* September 26, 1818, 2.

9. "Mayor's Communication," *Baltimore Patriot,* February 19, 1817, 2.

10. "Lamentable and Awful Calamity!" *Baltimore Patriot,* August 11, 1817, 2.

11. "Mayor's Communication," *Baltimore Patriot,* February 16, 1818, 2.

12. Scharf, *Chronicles of Baltimore,* 381; Browne, *Baltimore in the Nation,* 105; Garitee, *Republic's Private Navy,* 48–49; *An Act to Enlarge the Bounds of Baltimore City,* 1816, Ch. 209, Code of the Public Local Laws of Maryland, 1930, 1330–33.

13. *Petition of the Eastern and Western Precincts,* BCA BRG16–1-17, Location: BC/13/01/014, Document: 235.

14. *Stevenson to Mayor Stiles,* June 15, 1817, BCA BRG 9–2-2, Location: BC/25/12/011, Document: 757.

15. *Resolution to petition legislature* (October, 1817), BCA BRG 16–1-19, Location: BC/13/01/016, Document: 583; *Baltimore Patriot,* February 28, 1818, 2.

16. *Memorial of the Mayor to the General Assembly,* BCA BRG 16–1-19, Location: BC/13/01/016, Document: 648.

17. *Resolution of the Mayor and City Council,* December 15, 1817, BCA BRG 16–1-19, Location: BC/13/01/016, Document: 632. It appears that whereas the letter was delivered to the Baltimore delegates, the offer was never formally presented because the general assembly had made clear their intention to stay in Annapolis by voting in favor of large expenditures to upgrade their current facilities. See *Baltimore Patriot,* February 28, 1818, 2.

18. Browne, *Baltimore in the Nation,* 105.

19. *Mayor's Communication,* November 24, 1817, BCA BRG 16–1-18, Location: BC/13/01/015, Document: 486.

20. Browne, *Baltimore in the Nation,* 105; *Baltimore Patriot,* February 28, 1818, 2.

21. *An Act relating to the City of Baltimore,* Chapter 148, § 4, passed February 9, 1818, 1817 Maryland Session Laws, Vol. 636 (Annapolis: Jonas Green, 1818), 158.

22. *An Ordinance to impose a tax on the real and personal property,* approved March 4, 1815, BCA BRG 16–1-16, Location: BC/13/01/013, Document: 403.

23. *An Act relating to the City of Baltimore*, Ch. 148, § 7, 159.

24. *An Act relating to the City of Baltimore*, Ch. 148, §§ 9, 16, 160–61.

25. *An Act relating to the City of Baltimore*, Ch. 148, §§ 12, 16, 18, 160–62.

26. *An Act relating to the City of Baltimore*, Ch. 148, § 10, 160.

27. *An Act to provide for the opening of Pratt Street, in the City of Baltimore*, Chapter 71, passed January 29, 1818, 1817 Maryland Session Laws, Vol. 636 (Annapolis: Jonas Green, 1818), 59.

28. Paul Finkelman, "The Root of the Problem: How the Proslavery Constitution Shaped American Race Relations," 4 *Barry Law Review* 1 (2003): 15.

29. Marcus Dirk Dubber, *The Police Power: Patriarchy and the Foundations of American Government* (New York: Columbia University Press, 2005), 3.

30. Harry N. Scheiber, "Private Rights and Public Power: American Law, Capitalism, and the Republican Polity in Nineteenth Century America," *Yale Law Journal* 107 (1997): 824n6; William Blackstone, *Commentaries on the Laws of England. A Facsimile of the First Edition of 1765–1769*. Vol. 4, *Of Public Wrongs*, with an introduction by Thomas A. Green (Chicago: University of Chicago Press, 1979), 162.

31. Blackstone, *Commentaries*, Vol. 4, 162.

32. Ibid., 162, 176.

33. Ibid., 163–75.

34. *An Ordinance directing the inspection of Ginseng*, 1817 Ordinances of the City of Baltimore (Baltimore: W. Warner, 1817), 14–16.

35. *A Further Supplement to the Ordinance entitled "An Ordinance Regulating the riding and driving of Horses and Carriages,"* 1817 Ordinances of the City of Baltimore, 18.

36. *A Supplement to an Ordinance entitled "An Ordinance to Regulate the weighing and measuring of grain, flour and meal,"* 1817 Ordinances of the City of Baltimore, 33.

37. *An Ordinance to prevent abuses in the sale of Candles*, 1818 Ordinances of the City of Baltimore (Baltimore: W. Warner, 1818), 20.

38. *An Ordinance for Erecting a bridge on Fayette Street*, 1818 Ordinances of the City of Baltimore, 37.

39. *An Ordinance for the admission and regulation of Brokers*, 1816 Ordinances of the City of Baltimore (Baltimore: W. Warner, 1816), 21.

40. *An Ordinance to regulate the sale of bread*, 1816 Ordinances of the City of Baltimore, 30.

41. *An Ordinance to more effectively diminish the number of dogs*, 1816 Ordinances of the City of Baltimore, 26.

42. Harry A. Ezratty, *Baltimore in the Civil War: The Pratt Street Riot and a City Occupied* (Charleston, SC: History Press, 2010), 21–23, 27–28.

43. See Olson, *Baltimore*, 57–58.

44. *An Act for the opening of Pratt Street*, Ch. 71, §11, 1817 Maryland Session Laws, 61–62.

45. *An Ordinance to appoint city commissioners*, 1807 Ordinances of the City of Baltimore (Baltimore: Warner & Hanna, 1807), 72–87.

46. *An Act for the opening of Pratt Street*, Ch. 71, §11, 1817 Maryland Session Laws, 59–62; Papenfuse and Coale, *Atlas of Historical Maps of Maryland*, 165.

47. See, for example, *An Act for Extending Green Street*, Ch. 39, passed December 4, 1812, 1812 Maryland Session Laws, Vol. 618 (Annapolis: J. Chandler, 1813), 27–29.

48. See *An Act relating to the City of Baltimore*, Ch. 148, §4, 158 and *An act for the opening and extending of Pratt-Street*, Ch. 8, passed June 13, 1812, 1812 Maryland Session Laws, Special Session (Annapolis: J. Chandler, 1812), 7.

49. *Baltimore Patriot*, December 5, 1815, 3.

50. *Report of the Committee on Ways and Means*, March 23, 1818, BCA BRG 16–1-19, Location: BC/13/01/016, Document: 554.

51. John Adams, *The Works of John Adams, Vol. 4, Novanglus, Thoughts on Government, Defence of the Constitution* (Boston: Charles Little, 1851); Carl J. Richard, *Greeks and Romans Bearing Gifts: How the Ancients Inspired the Founding Fathers* (Lanham, MD: Rowman & Littlefield, 2009), 124.

52. Baltimore *American*, August 28, 1818, 2; Baltimore *American*, September 22, 1818, 2.

53. Baltimore *American*, August 1, 1818, 2.

54. Baltimore *American*, August 19, 1818, 2.

55. *Baltimore Patriot*, August 17, 1818, 2.

56. Darcy Kern, "Parliament in Print: William Caxton and the History of Political Government in the Fifteenth Century," *Journal of Medieval History* 40, no. 2 (2014): 209; Baltimore *American*, August 24, 1818, 2; William Novak, *The Peoples' Welfare* (Chapel Hill: University of North Carolina Press, 1996), 9.

57. Baltimore *American*, August 24, 1818, 2.

58. Baltimore *American*, August 25, 1818, 2.

59. Baltimore *American*, August 28, 1818, 2.

60. Baltimore *American*, September 4, 1818, 2.

61. Novak, *Peoples' Welfare*, 17.

62. Baltimore *American*, August 8, 1818, 2.

63. Baltimore *American*, August 10, 1818, 2.

64. Baltimore *American*, August 10, 1818, 2; Baltimore *American*, August 11, 1818, 2.

65. Baltimore *American*, August 13, 1818.

66. Baltimore *American*, August 13, 1818, 2.

67. Baltimore *American*, August 14, 1818, 2.

68. Baltimore *American*, August 17, 1818, 2.

69. Baltimore *American*, August 18, 1818, 2.

70. Baltimore *American*, August 21, 1818, 2.

71. Ibid.

72. *Baltimore Patriot*, August 18, 1818, 2.

73. Ibid.

74. Steffen, *Mechanics of Baltimore*, 179. In 1816, the General Assembly of Maryland ordered the redrawing of ward districts as a part of Baltimore's forced annexation of the surrounding area. On June 12, 1818, the city approved the boundaries of the new wards, which raised the number of wards from eight to twelve. The new ward districts went into effect on September 30, 1818. *An Act to Enlarge the Bounds of Baltimore City*, 1816, Ch. 209, and *An Ordinance to provide for the division of the City of Baltimore into Twelve Wards*, Baltimore *American*, October 3, 1818, 3.

75. "Late First Ward," Baltimore *American*, August 6, 1818, 2.

76. Baltimore *American*, August 10, 1818, 2.

77. Baltimore *American*, August 17, 1818 and August 18, 1818, 2

78. "George Stiles," *Baltimore Patriot*, February 17, 1819 and "George Stiles," *Baltimore Patriot*, June 17, 1819.

79. "New Mayor," *Baltimore Patriot*, February 16, 1819.

80. *Report of the City Commissioners*, June 3, 1801, BCA BRG 9–2-2, Location: BC/25/12/001, Document: 349.

81. *Petition to the City Commissioners*, April 4, 1815, BCA BRG 3–1-19, Location: BC/11/01/019, Document: 53.

82. *Petition to the City Commissioners*, March 1, 1815, BCA BRG 3–1-19, Location: BC/11/01/019, Document: 60; *Paving Warrant, German Street*, BCA BRG 3–1-21, Location: BC/11/01/021, Document: 1; *Petition to Commissioners*, September 21, 1818, BCA BRG 3–1-23, Location: BC/11/01/023, Document: 138.

83. *Craig et al. v. Mayor and City Council*, MSA C2042–168, Baltimore County Court (Misc. Plats), 1826 (hereinafter *Barron* Trial Exhibit, also seen in figure 1 of chapter 4).

84. *Barron* Transcript, 14.

85. *Letter from the commissioners to the City Council*, July 19, 1815, BCA BRG 16–1-16, Location: BC/13/01/013, No Document Number.

86. *Proposal of Richard Lawrence*, June 28, 1815, BCA BRG 3–1-20, Location: BC/11/01/020, Document: 143.

87. *Deed from G. Hall to W. Dawson*, May 15, 1798, MSA CE 66–104, WG 54, p. 457; *Baltimore Patriot*, November 16, 1815, 1; *Baltimore Patriot*, January 5, 1830, 2.

88. *Assignment from A. Morgan to J. Curtis*, October 31, 1815, MSA CE 66–183, WG 133, p. 356.

89. *Barron* Trial Exhibit. See figure 1 in chapter 4 of this book.

90. *Price and Waters v. Montgomery, Owens, Boyd, and Stouffer*, Baltimore County Court (Chancery Papers), June 19, 1821, MSA C295–277, Location: 02/15/11/042, MdHR No.: 40,200–275–1/2.

91. *Petition of H. Waters and Others*, February 26, 1817, BCA BRG 16–1-17, Location: BC/13/01/014, Document: 246.

92. *An Ordinance providing for the appointment of Wardens of the Port of Baltimore,* 1813 Ordinances of the City of Baltimore, (Baltimore: William Warner, 1813), 12.

93. *An Ordinance providing for the appointment of Wardens of the Port of Baltimore,* 1813 Ordinances of the City of Baltimore, Sec. VIII, 17.

94. *Resolution authorizing the Mayor,* BCA BRG16–1-17, Location: BC/13/01/014, Document: 509; *Barron* Transcript, 15.

95. *Message from the second branch of the City Council,* March 17 and March 26, 1817, BCA BRG 16–1-18, Location: BC/13/01/015, Documents: 441, 442, and 443.

96. *Petition of H. Waters and others,* April 2, 1817, BCA BRG 16–1-18, Location: BC/13/01/015, Document: 356; Rockman, *Scraping By,* 81–83; Joseph Gary Norman, "Eighteenth-Century Wharf Construction in Baltimore, Maryland" (masters thesis, College of William & Mary, 1987), 93–95.

97. The ordinance was approved on April 10, 1817. "An Ordinance for paving Wilkes' street, Washington street, Castle alley and County street, within certain distances, and for other purposes, so as more effectually preserve the navigation," 1817 Ordinances of the City of Baltimore, 84.

98. *City Council Resolution,* April 4, 1817, BCA BRG 16–1-19, Location: BC/13/01/016, Document: 588.

99. *City Council Resolution,* April 5, 1817, BCA BRG 16–1-19, Location: BC/13/01/016, Document: 638.

100. *Report of the Mayor's Committee,* June 4, 1817, BCA BRG 16–1-18, Location: BC/13/01/015, Document: 437.

101. *Petition of H. Waters and others,* May 14, 1818, BCA BRG 16–1-19, Location: BC/13/01/016, Document: 396.

102. Specifically sending the water westward along Smith, German, Gough, and Wilkes Streets and into the cove through Harford Run or Caroline Street.

103. *Leave to bring resolution,* Undated, Approximately January or February 1819, BCA BRG 16–1-20, Location: BC/13/01/017, Document: 400.

104. *Report of the Committee,* February 26, 1819, BCA BRG 16–1-20, Location: BC/13/01/017, Document: 406.

105. Rockman, "Work, Wages, and Welfare," 597.

106. *Petition of H. Waters and others,* January 1821, BCA BRG 16–1-22, Location: BC/13/01/019, Document: 479.

107. *Report on Petition of H. Waters,* January 1821, BCA BRG 16–1-24, Location: BC/13/01/021, Document: 974.

108. *Resolutions of the Convention,* March 23, 1821, BCA BRG 16–1-24, Location: BC/13/01/021, Document: 844.

109. *A Further Supplement to the Ordinance entitled, "An Ordinance for Preserving the Health of the City,"* Chapter 108, approved December 3, 1821, 1822 Ordinances of the Corporation of the City of Baltimore, (Baltimore: William Warner, 1822), 12–14.

110. *Mackubin v. Craig and Barron* (January 17, 1822 notation from R. Lemmon & Co., auctioneer).

111. *A Supplement to an Ordinance entitled "A Further Supplement to the Ordinance entitled, "An Ordinance for Preserving the Health of the City,"* Ch. 36, approved March 18, 1822, 1822 Ordinances of the City of Baltimore, 49–50.

112. *Barron* Transcript, 4.

CHAPTER 3

Epigraph: John Quincy Adams, *Memoirs*, 336. The interaction occurred October 15, 1827. Quincy's quip illustrates the conceptual difference between a modern view of a constitution as a written document setting forth the framework of government and an older view of a constitution as a collection of documents, laws, and ideas that collectively constituted the structure of the state, making the welfare of a country akin to that of an individual. Daniel Hulsebosch elaborates on this point in *Constituting Empire: New York and the Transformation of Constitutionalism in the Atlantic World* (Chapel Hill: University of North Carolina Press, 2005).

1. Baltimore County Court, City Civil Docket, March Term 1828, (hereinafter City Civil Docket), MSA C301–14, Location: 02/15/06/031 and Edward C. Papenfuse, *Outline, Notes and Documents Concerning Barron v Baltimore, 32 U.S. 243*, http://mdhistory.net/msaref06/barron/index.html, Barron-0001 (hereinafter Papenfuse Outline). I would like to recognize Dr. Papenfuse for posting many of the documents held at the Maryland State Archives concerning the *Barron* case online. His efforts in this regard are very much appreciated.

2. Dukeminier and Krier, *Property*, 1228.

3. *Pennsylvania Coal Co. v. Mahon*, 43 S. Ct. 158, 160 (1922). Justice Scalia described Holmes's quote as an "oft-cited maxim" in *Lucas v. South Carolina Coastal Council*, 112 S. Ct. 2886, 2893 (1992). See also William Michael Treanor, "The Original Understanding of the Takings Clause and the Political Process," 95 *Columbia Law Review* 782 (1995): 798–801.

4. *Chicago, Burlington & Quincy Railroad Co. v. Chicago*, 166 U.S. 226 (1897). Later court decisions have also explicitly extended the right of a property owner to sue a municipality for uncompensated takings and overcame arguments that 42 U.S.C. §1983 actions negated the right to sue municipal corporations for Fourteenth Amendment violations. *Gordon v. City of Warren*, 579 F.2d 386 (6th Cir. 1978).

5. *Maryland Constitution* (1867), Article XI-B, Section 1 and Declaration of Rights, Article 24.

6. *Maryland Constitution*, Dec. of Rights, Article 24 (1867); Magna Carta, Article 39 (1215).

7. William Blackstone, *Commentaries on the Laws of England. A Facsimile of the First Edition of 1765–1769*, Vol. 1, *The Rights of Persons*, with an introduction by Stanley N. Katz (Chicago: University of Chicago Press, 1979), 134–35.

8. Sir Matthew Hale, *The History of the Common Law of England*, ed. Charles M. Gray (Chicago: University of Chicago Press, 1971), 36–38.

9. Arthur R. Hogue, *Origins of the Common Law* (Indianapolis: Liberty Fund, 1986), 5.

10. Hogue, *Origins*, 18–19.

11. Hale, *History*, 37–38; Hogue, *Origins*, 5.

12. See Hale, *History*, 18; Blackstone, *Commentaries*, Vol. 1, 76–78.

13. William Penn, "England's Present Interest Considered, with Honour to the Prince, and Safety to the People," in *The Founders' Constitution*, ed. Philip B. Kurland and Ralph Lerner (Indianapolis: Liberty Fund, 2001), Vol. I, Ch. 14, Doc. 3, 429.

14. Penn, "The Excellent Priviledge of Liberty and Property being the Birth-Right of the Free-Born Subjects of England," in Kurland and Lerner, *Founders' Constitution*, Vol. 1, Ch. 14, Doc. 5, 431–33.

15. General Assembly of Maryland, "An Act for the Liberties of the People (1639)," in Kurland and Lerner, *Founders' Constitution*, Volume 1, Chapter 14, Document 1, 428.

16. *Maryland Constitution*, Declaration of Rights, Art. III (1776).

17. G. Edward White, *History of the Supreme Court of the United States, Vols. III–IV: The Marshall Court and Cultural Change, 1815–1835* (New York: Macmillan, 1988), 128; Jeffrey K. Sawyer, "English Law and American Democracy in the Revolutionary Republic, Maryland 1776–1822," *Maryland Historical Magazine* (Fall 2013): 261–90.

18. Elizabeth Kelly Bauer, *Commentaries on the Constitution, 1790–1860* (New York: Russell & Russell, 1965), 18; M.H. Hoeflich, *Legal Publishing in Antebellum America* (New York: Cambridge University Press, 2010), 26.

19. See Hoeflich, *Legal Publishing*, 14; Lawrence Friedman, *A History of American Law*, 2nd ed. (New York: Simon & Schuster, 1985), 112.

20. Hoeflich, *Legal Publishing*, 25–27.

21. L. Friedman, *History*, 329, 331.

22. Bauer, *Commentaries*, 93, 144, 151.

23. Ibid., 158.

24. Ibid., 157–58; Novak, *The Peoples' Welfare*, 246.

25. 2010 Census, U.S. Census Bureau, "Population, Housing Units, Area Measurements, and Density: 1790 to 2010, Table 2" (September 2012).

26. Morton Horwitz, *The Transformation of American Law, 1780–1860* (Cambridge, MA: Harvard University Press, 1977), 4.

27. Charles Sellers, *The Market Revolution: Jacksonian America, 1816–1846* (New York: Oxford University Press, 1991), 47.

28. Novak, *Peoples' Welfare*, 9–17.

29. Sellers, *Market Revolution*, 46–47.

30. *Fletcher v. Peck*, 10 U.S. 87, 139 (1810).

31. *Trustees of Dartmouth College v. Woodward*, 17 U.S. 518 (1819).

32. *McCulloch v. Maryland*, 17 U.S. 316 (1819).

33. *Lindsay v. Commissioners*, 2 Bay 38 (S.C.Const.App. 1796).

34. *Lindsay*, 2 Bay at 38.

35. *Vanhorne's Lessee v. Dorrance*, 2 U.S. 304 (C.C.D.Penn. 1795).

36. *Middleton v. Bowman*, 1 Bay 252 (S.C.Com.Pl.Gen.Sess. 1792).

37. *Middleton*, 1 Bay at 253.

38. *Lindsay*, 2 Bay at 40.

39. *Lindsay*, 2 Bay at 42.

40. *Lindsay*, 2 Bay at 45.

41. *Lindsay*, 2 Bay at 45.

42. *Lindsay*, 2 Bay at 48.

43. *Lindsay*, 2 Bay at 49.

44. *Gardner v. Trustees of the Village of Newburgh*, 2 Johns. 162 (N.Y. 1816). While the opinion is simply written by "the Chancellor," Kent was the Chancellor of the New York Chancery Court at the time. Carl F. Stychin, "The Commentaries of Chancellor James Kent and the Development of an American Common Law," *American Journal of Legal History* 37, no. 4 (Oct. 1993): 440, 442.

45. *Gardner*, 2 Johns. at 163.

46. *Gardner*, 2 Johns. at 164.

47. *Gardner*, 2 Johns. at 164.

48. *Gardner*, 2 Johns. at 165.

49. *Shrunk v. Schuylkill Navigation Company*, 14 Serg. & Rawle 71 (Penn. 1826).

50. *Shrunk*, 14 Serg. & Rawle at 72; William Rawle, *A View of the Constitution of the United States of America*, 2nd ed. (Philadelphia: Philip Nicklin, 1829), 124–35.

51. *Shrunk*, 14 Serg. & Rawle at 72–74.

52. *Shrunk*, 14 Serg. & Rawle at 73.

53. *Shrunk*, 14 Serg. & Rawle at 78.

54. *Shrunk*, 14 Serg. & Rawle at 82.

55. Novak, *Peoples' Welfare*, 129.

56. Andrew M. Schocket, *Founding Corporate Power in Early National Philadelphia* (DeKalb: Northern Illinois University Press, 2007), 155.

57. *New York v. Goodwin*, 1 Wheeler C.C. 440 (N.Y. 1820).

58. *Goodwin*, 1 Wheeler C.C. at 477.

59. *Goodwin*, 1 Wheeler C.C. at 477.

60. Schocket, *Corporate Power*, 138–39.

61. S. Adam Seagrave, *The Foundations of Natural Morality: On the Compatibility of Natural Rights and Natural Law* (Chicago: University of Chicago Press, 2014), 2.

62. Reid cites Garry Wills, *Inventing America: Jefferson's Declaration of Independence* (New York: Doubleday, 1978) as a prime example. John Phillip Reid, "The Irrelevance of the Declaration," in *Law in the American Revolution and the Revolution in the Law*, ed. Hendrik Hartog (New York: New York University Press, 1981), 47.

63. Reid, "Irrelevance," 47–52.

64. Daniel Shute, "An Election Sermon," in *American Political Writing During the Founding Era, 1760–1805*, Vol. I, ed. Charles S. Hyneman and Donald S. Lutz (Indianapolis: Liberty Press, 1983), 111–12.

65. Shute, "Election Sermon," 109; see also Daniel Shute, *A Sermon Preached before his Excellency Francis Bernard* (Boston: Richard Draper, 1768), which lists the governor, lieutenant governor, the governor's council, and the Massachusetts House of Representatives among those in attendance for the sermon. Shute was the pastor of a church in Hingham, Massachusetts, while the sermon was apparently given in Boston.

66. See also Suzanna Sherry, "Natural Law in the States," 61 *University of Cincinnati Law Review* 171, 172 (1992–93).

67. Mark Graber, "Naked Land Transfers and American Constitutional Development," 53 *Vanderbilt Law Review* 73, 74 (2000).

68. Charles Grove Haines, *The Revival of Natural Law Concepts* (Cambridge, MA: Harvard University Press, 1930), 4–8; James H. Hutson, "The Emergence of the Modern Concept of a Right in America: The Contribution of Michel Villey," in *The Nature of Rights at the American Founding and Beyond*, ed. Barry Alan Shain (Charlottesville: University of Virginia Press, 2007), 28.

69. Hutson, "Emergence," 30; Arthur Stephen McGrade, "Ockham and the Birth of Individual Rights," in *Authority and Power*, ed. Brian Tierney and Peter Linehan (Cambridge: Cambridge University Press, 1980), 150.

70. Charles J. Reid, Jr., "The Medieval Origins of the Western Natural Rights Tradition: The Achievement of Brian Tierney," 83 *Cornell Law Review* 437 (1997–98): 440; Hutson, "Emergence," 33.

71. Hutson, "Emergence," 33; Fred D. Miller, Jr., "Aristotle and the Origins of Natural Rights," *Journal of Metaphysics* 49, no. 4 (Jun. 1996): 873–907.

72. Richard Tuck, *Natural Rights Theories: Their Origins and Development* (New York: Cambridge University Press, 1979), 5–6.

73. Haines, *Revival*, 17.

74. Ibid., 49.

75. Ibid., 18–19.

76. Ibid., 50–51.

77. Ibid., 22.

78. Samuel Pufendorf, *The Political Writings of Samuel Pufendorf*, ed. Craig L. Carr, trans. Michael J. Seider (New York: Oxford University Press, 1994), 6.

79. Jack N. Rakove, *Declaring Rights* (Boston: Bedford Books, 1998), 19.

80. Ibid., 19–20.

81. Ibid., 21–22.

82. Haines, *Revival*, 20–21.

83. Thomas Hobbes, *The Leviathan: Or the Matter, Forme and Power of a Commonwealth Ecclesiasticall and Civil*, ed. Ian Shapiro (New Haven: Yale University Press, 2010), Chapters 14 and 15, 79–98; Chapter 17, 102–5; Chapter 18, 105–12. See also Quentin Skinner, *Visions of Politics, Volume III: Hobbes and Civil Science* (Cambridge: Cambridge University Press, 2004), 220.

84. Hobbes, *Leviathan*, Chapter 26, 159–74; Haines, *Revival*, 21.

85. W.M. Spellman, *John Locke* (New York: St. Martin's Press, 1997), 20–21; Katherine M. Squadrito, *John Locke* (Boston: Twayne Publishers, 1979), 95.

86. Squadrito, *John Locke*, 102.

87. Ibid., 102; Hans Aarsleff, "The State of Nature and the Nature of Man in Locke," in *John Locke: Problems and Perspectives*, ed. John W. Yolton (Cambridge: Cambridge University Press, 1969), 100.

88. Hobbes, *Leviathan*, Chapter 26, 159–74; Haines, *Revival*, 21.

89. The Virginia Declaration of Rights (June 12, 1776), in Kurland and Lerner, *Founders' Constitution*, Vol. I, Ch. 1, Doc. 3, 6.

90. Declaration of Independence (July 4, 1776), in Kurland and Lerner, *Founders' Constitution*, Vol. I, Ch. 1, Doc. 5, 9–11.

91. "The Essex Result," in Kurland and Lerner, *Founders' Constitution*, Vol. I, Ch. 4, Doc. 8, 112–14; Donald S. Lutz, "The Articles of Confederation as the Background to the Federal Republic," *Publius* 20, no. 1 (Winter, 1990): 55, 63n12; Theophilus Parsons, Jr., review of *Memoirs of Theophilus Parsons, Chief Justice of the Supreme Judicial Court of Massachusetts, with Notices of Some of His Contemporaries*, by Theophilus Parsons, *North American Review* 89, no. 184 (July, 1859): 232, 234–35.

92. Lynn Hunt, *Inventing Human Rights: A History* (New York: W.W. Norton, 2007), 21.

93. "Return of Beverly, Massachusetts," in Kurland and Lerner, *Founders' Constitution*, Vol. I, Ch. 14, Doc. 17, 446. Beverly is located in Essex County, Massachusetts.

94. Massachusetts Constitution (1780), in Kurland and Lerner, *Founders' Constitution*, Vol. I, Ch. 1, Doc. 6, 11–14.

95. Suzanna Sherry, "The Founders' Unwritten Constitution," 54 *University of Chicago Law Review* 1127 (Fall 1987): 1131–32.

96. In 1776, Maryland, Pennsylvania, Delaware, New Hampshire, South Carolina, North Carolina, Virginia, and New Jersey all adopted written constitutions, while in 1777, Georgia and New York followed suit. G. Alan Tarr, *Understanding State Constitutions* (Princeton: Princeton University Press, 1998), 61.

97. 1776 Maryland Constitution, Declaration of Rights, Articles 38, 28, and 21.

98. 1776 Pennsylvania Constitution, Preamble, Declaration of Rights, Article I.

99. *Vanhorne's Lessee v. Dorrance*, 2 U.S. 304, 2 Dall. 304 (C.C. D. Penn., 1795).

100. Saul Cornell and Gerald Leonard, "The Consolidation of the Early Federal System, 1791–1812," in *The Cambridge History of Law in America*, Vol. 1, *Early America (1580–1815)*, ed. Michael Grossberg and Christopher Tomlins (New York: Cambridge University Press, 2008), 542.

101. *Vanhorne's Lessee*, 2 U.S. at 308.

102. *Vanhorne's Lessee*, 2 U.S. at 309.

103. Ibid.

104. Ibid.

105. *Elliot's Executor v. Lyell*, 3 Call 268 (Va. 1802).

106. *Elliot's Executor*, 3 Call at 276.

107. *Elliot's Executor*, 3 Call at 268.

108. *Elliot's Executor*, 3 Call at 276.

109. *Bradshaw v. Rogers and Magee*, 20 Johns. 103 (N.Y. Sup. Ct. 1822).

110. *Bradshaw*, 20 Johns. at 104.

111. *Bradshaw*, 20 Johns. at 105.

112. Ibid. The first New York constitution, ratified in 1777, did not contain a specific prohibition against uncompensated takings, whereas the second constitution of 1821 did. Spencer is apparently alluding to the fact that the 1821 constitution was not yet fully ratified as of the time of the case opinion. See N.Y. Constitution, Article VII, Section 7 (1821) and N.Y. Constitution (1777).

113. *Bradshaw*, 20 Johns. at 103.

114. *McArthur v. Kelly and Williams*, 5 Ohio 139 (Ohio 1831).

115. *McArthur*, 5 Ohio at 143.

116. Jack N. Rakove, *Original Meanings* (New York: Vintage Books, 1996), 295–96.

117. Bernard Bailyn, *The Ideological Origins of the American Revolution* (Cambridge, MA: Harvard University Press, 1967), 187.

118. *Proceedings of the First Branch of the City Council*, BCA M0345–0694, March 21, 1817, 191–93.

119. St. George Tucker, *View of the Constitution of the United States, With Selected Writings*, foreword by Clyde N. Wilson (Indianapolis: Liberty Fund, 1999), vii-viii, x.

120. Tucker, *View*, 91–92.

121. Ibid., 6.

122. Ibid., 91.

123. Mary Sarah Bilder, "Colonial Constitutionalism and Constitutional Law," in *Transformations in American Legal History: Essays in Honor of Morton J. Horwitz*, ed. Alfred L. Brophy and Daniel W. Hamilton (Cambridge, MA: Harvard University Press, 2009), 28–29; Hulsebosch, *Constituting Empire*, 6–7.

124. Bilder, "Colonial Constitutionalism," 31–32.

125. Hulsebosch, *Constituting Empire*, 7–8. Hulsebosch is arguing against the position taken by historians like Bernard Bailyn (*Ideological Origins of the American Revolution*) and Gordon Wood (*Creation of the American Republic*).

Hulsebosch traces this idea to Charles McIlwain and Oscar and Mary Handlin. Ibid., 310n24.

126. Tucker, *View,* 104.

127. Ibid., 104.

128. Ibid., 104.

129. Ibid., 246, Alexander Hamilton, Federalist No. 84, in John Jay, Alexander Hamilton, and James Madison, *The Federalist: A Commentary on the Constitution of the United States,* ed. Robert Scigliano (New York: Random House, 2000), 546, 550.

130. Tucker, *View,* 246.

131. *Barker v. New York,* 3 Cow. 686 (N.Y. 1824).

132. *Barker,* 3 Cow. at 686.

133. *Barker,* 3 Cow. at 689.

134. *Barker,* 3 Cow. at 689–90.

135. *Barker,* 3 Cow. at 693.

136. *Barker,* 3 Cow. at 693–95.

137. *Case of the plan of the Third Division of the District of Kensington,* 2 Rawle 445 (Penn. 1830).

138. *Kensington,* 2 Rawle at 447; Pennsylvania Constitution (1790), Art. IX, Section 10.

139. Stephen A. Conrad, "James Wilson," in Hall et al., *Oxford Guide,* 1091–92.

140. James Wilson, "On the Natural Rights of Individuals," in volume 2 of *The Collected Works of James Wilson,* ed. Kermit Hall and Mark David Hall (Indianapolis: Liberty Fund, 2007), 2:1053–54.

141. Wilson, "Natural Rights," 1054.

142. Ibid., 1062.

143. Ibid., 1057–58.

144. Ibid., 1058.

145. Ibid., 1068.

CHAPTER 4

Epigraph: "Baltimore as Seen by Moreau de Saint-Mery in 1794," translated by Fillmore Norfleet, *Maryland Historical Magazine* 35, no. 3 (September 1940): 221, 227.

1. Olson, *Baltimore,* 20; Scharf, *History of Baltimore City and County* (Philadelphia: Louis H. Evers, 1881), 727; Morris L. Radoff, *The County Courthouses and Records of Maryland, Part One: The Courthouses* (Annapolis: Hall of Records Commission, 1960), 27–29.

2. Scharf, *History of Baltimore,* 267–69.

3. Cox, "Trouble on the Chain Gang," 9; Rockman, *Scraping By,* 3.

4. Rockman, *Scraping By,* 224.

5. *Barron* Transcript, 4; Radoff, *Courthouses*, 27; and Fielding Lucas Jr., *Plan of the City of Baltimore, 1822*, in Papenfuse and Coale, *Atlas of Historical Maps*, 166.

6. *Barron* Transcript, 4.

7. *Black's Law Dictionary*, 1674–75.

8. While Scott was referred to as "Counsel for the City," the post would eventually be referred to as city counselor. Dan Friedman, "The History of the Baltimore City Solicitors," November 2003, Maryland State Archives, http://msa.maryland.gov/msa/speccol/sc2600/sc2685/text/solicitors.pdf (accessed May 10, 2016), 2.

9. *Barron* Transcript, 5.

10. Ibid., 5.

11. Ibid., 6.

12. Ibid., 7–8.

13. Ibid., 8.

14. U.S. Constitution, Fifth Amendment (emphasis added).

15. Maryland Constitution (1776), Ch. XXI.

16. Magna Carta, Section 39 (1215).

17. Browne, *Baltimore in the Nation*, 36.

18. *An Ordinance to provide for more effectually lighting the Streets, Squares, Lanes and Alleys of the City of Baltimore*, approved June 17, 1816, in 1817 Ordinances of the City of Baltimore (Baltimore: William Warner, 1817), 5–9.

19. *Baltimore v. Moore and Johnson*, 6 H. & J. 375 (Md. Ct. of App. 1825).

20. *Moore & Johnson*, 6 H. & J. at 375; *An Act to erect Baltimore Town, in Baltimore County, into a City, and to incorporate the inhabitants thereof* (1796), Section 9 and *A Supplement to the act, entitled an act to erect Baltimore town in Baltimore county, into a City, and to incorporate the inhabitants thereof* (1797), Section 2 both in Ordinances of the City of Baltimore, Passed February, 1797 and February, 1798 (Baltimore: John Cox, 1875), 1400–1401, 1404.

21. *Moore and Johnson*, 6 H. & J. at 375.

22. *Moore and Johnson*, 6 H. & J. at 377; *An Ordinance directing the paving of part of Dulaney street*, approved April 17, 1817, in 1817 Ordinances of the City of Baltimore, 32–33.

23. *Moore and Johnson*, 6 H. & J. at 377; *An Ordinance for paving Wilkes' street, Washington street, Castle alley and County street*, approved April 10, 1817, in 1817 Ordinances of the City of Baltimore, 34–35.

24. *Moore & Johnson*, 6 H. & J. at 377.

25. *Mayor and City Council of Baltimore v. Barron* (Baltimore County Court, 1818), MSA SC 5458–58–13989, Trial transcript.

26. *An Ordinance to appoint City Commissioners*, approved March 9, 1807, in Ordinances of the Corporation of the City of Baltimore, from 1803 to 1812, inclusive (Baltimore: John Cox, 1876), 119.

27. *An Ordinance to appoint City Commissioners* (1807), 123–24.

28. *Mayor and City Council of Baltimore v. Barron*, Trial transcript.

29. *Mayor and City Council of Baltimore v. Barron*, Bill of Exceptions.

30. *William Price, John Price, and Hezekiah Waters vs. John Montgomery, Joseph Owens, Samuel Boyd, and Henry Stouffer* (Baltimore County Court—Chancery, 1821), MSA C295–277 (Bill of Complaint). Specifically, they objected to the paving of Wolfe Street south from George Street to Pitt Street.

31. *Barron* Transcript, 8–9.

32. Ibid., 9.

33. *Baltimore Patriot*, March 10, 1824, 3.

34. Carl Brent Swisher, *Roger B. Taney* (New York: Macmillan, 1935), 107.

35. Swisher, *Roger B. Taney*, 114–15; Samuel Tyler, *Memoir of Roger Brooke Taney, L.L.D.* (Baltimore: John Murphy and Co., 1872), 67, 163–64; Rev. William Pinkney, D.D., *The Life of William Pinkney* (New York: D. Appleton and Co., 1853), 49.

36. Swisher, *Roger B. Taney*, 140–41.

37. *Nicholas v. Fearson*, 32 U.S. 99 (1833), *Lessee of Livingston v. Moore*, 32 U.S. 469 (1833), and *Scholefield v. Eichelberger*, 32 U.S. 586 (1833).

38. *Barron* Transcript, 9.

39. See "Sale of the Property of John Craig, Deceased," *Baltimore Patriot*, March 8, 1828, 3.

40. *Baltimore Patriot*, November 15, 1822; Baltimore *American*, November 15, 1822, 3.

41. *Baltimore Directory for 1817–18*, 12; *Matchett's Baltimore Directory, for 1824*, 19.

42. For example, the decree in the suit brought against Craig in 1817 for nonpayment for the boat he ordered from James, which was discussed in Chapter One, went in Colston's favor. On October 29, 1825, Chancellor Bland ordered Craig to pay Colston $3,664.45 with interest from the date of the decree. *Colston v. Craig* (Baltimore County Court, 1817) Accession No.: 17, 898-7118-1/3, MSA S512–9-7151, Location: 1/37/4/. To document Craig's continuing indebtedness to Tiernan, on February 21, 1826, Craig signed a note where he acknowledged that as of that date he owed Tiernan $8,846.76. *Tiernan v. Margaret, John, and Robert Craig, et al.* Accession No.: 17, 898-11412-1/2, MSA S512–14–11237, Location: 1/39/3/ (February 21, 1826, Note executed by Craig).

43. It should be noted, however, that these attorneys appeared at various times and at various points in the eleven years it took *Barron* to wind through the courts. They did not necessarily constitute a cohesive group or legal team as is often seen in modern high-profile litigation.

44. Eugene F. Cordell, *University of Maryland, 1807–1907* (New York: The Lewis Publishing Company, 1907), 337; Thomas L. Shaffer, "David Hoffman's Law School Lectures, 1822–1833," 32 *Journal of Legal Education* (1982): 127, 130–31.

45. Cordell, *University of Maryland*, 341; Bill Sleeman, "David Hoffman: A Biographical Sketch," in *David Hoffman: Life, Letters and Lectures at the University of Maryland, 1821–1837*, ed. Bill Sleeman (Clark, NJ: The Lawbook Exchange, Ltd., 2011), 17.

46. Kevin B. Sheets, "Saving History: The Maryland Historical Society and its Founders," *Maryland Historical Magazine* 89, no. 2 (Summer 1994): 133, 139.

47. Clement Dorsey, *The General Public Statutory Law and Public Local Law of the State of Maryland: From the Year 1692 to 1839*, V01.141 (Baltimore: John Toy, 1840), 44–45.

48. Dorsey, *The General Public Statutory Law*, 1032.

49. L. Friedman, *History*, 318.

50. Sleeman, "David Hoffman," 14–15.

51. Howard Schweber, "The Science of Legal Science: The Model Natural Sciences in Nineteenth-Century American Education," *Law and History Review* 17, no. 3 (Fall 1999): 438–39.

52. Shaffer, "Hoffman's Lectures," 127; Kermit Hall, William Wiecek, and Paul Finkelman, *American Legal History: Cases and Materials* (New York: Oxford University Press, 1991), 334.

53. David Hoffman, *A Course of Legal Study; Respectfully Addressed to the Students of Law in the United States* (Baltimore: Coale and Maxwell, 1817), xii; Sleeman, "David Hoffman," 18.

54. Sleeman, "David Hoffman," 40, and Maxwell Bloomfield, "David Hoffman and the Shaping of a Republican Legal Culture," *Maryland Law Review* 38, no. 4 (1979): 676.

55. Sleeman, "David Hoffman," 14.

56. Cruse was replaced after the initial filing of the lawsuit and appears to have little influence afterwards. Cruse ultimately spent less time in his legal practice and gained notoriety as a writer and journalist. He passed away in 1832, one year before the case reached the Supreme Court, from the effects of an epidemic of cholera that had broken out in Baltimore. Brantz Mayer, *Baltimore: Past and Present* (Baltimore: Richardson and Bennett, 1871), 295; *Appletons' Cyclopaedia of America Biography*, Vol. II, ed. James Grant Wilson and John Fiske (New York: D. Appleton and Company, 1888), 23; Francis F. Beirne, *The Amiable Baltimoreans*, 1st ed. (New York: Dutton, 1951), 357; Kevin J. Hayes, *Poe and the Printed Word* (New York: Cambridge University Press, 2000), 35–36; Charles H. Bohner, *John Pendleton Kennedy: Gentleman from Baltimore* (Baltimore: Johns Hopkins University Press, 1961), 36–37.

57. Evans served as city counselor from 1844 to 1846. See Scharf, *History of Baltimore*, 714, 716; D. Friedman, "History," 3.

58. Scharf, *History of Baltimore*, 714.

59. *Barron* Transcript, 9–10.

60. Ibid., 4.

61. Baltimore County Court, City Civil Docket, MSA Citation: C301-14, location: 02/15/06/031, MdHR No: 14284.

62. Kell served the state government through four terms as a state legislator in the state House of Delegates (1814, 1816–18). He also represented

Ward 4 of the First Branch of the Baltimore City Council for eight terms (1808–13), tied for the longest term on the council before the War of 1812. Kell was also Roger Taney's predecessor as Maryland attorney general (1824–27). Two of the Baltimore attorneys who recommended Kell to the governor for the position were Barron's attorneys David Hoffman and Upton S. Heath. See Archives of Maryland, Historical List, Baltimore City Council, First Branch, 1797–1923, http://msa.maryland.gov/msa/speccol/sc2600/sc2685/county/html/bc_council/firstbranch.html (accessed May 10, 2016); Steffen, *Mechanics of Baltimore,* 173; Archives of Maryland, Historical List, Attorneys General, 1777–present, Edward C. Papenfuse et al., *Archives of Maryland, Historical List,* new series, Vol. 1. (Annapolis, MD: Maryland State Archives, 1990), http://msa.maryland.gov/msa/speccol/sc2600/sc2685/html/attygen.html (accessed May 10, 2016); and *Recommendation Letter to Governor Samuel Stevens, Jr.,* Maryland State Archives, Special Collections, MSA SC 4645–3-4, http://msa.maryland.gov/megafile/msa/speccol/sc3500/sc3520/001400/001499/pdf/msa_sc4645–3-4.pdf (accessed May 10, 2016).

63. *Barron* Trial Exhibit; *Barron* Transcript, 11.

64. *Barron* Transcript, 11.

65. Ibid., 11–14.

66. Ibid.,14, 16.

67. Ibid.,14.

68. Pratt Street was formerly known as German Street. *Barron* Transcript, 14; *Barron* Trial Exhibit.

69. *Barron* Transcript, 15.

70. Ibid.,15.

71. Ibid.,15.

72. Ibid.,11–16; *Barron* Trial Exhibit.

73. *Barron* Transcript, 15.

74. Ibid.,15–16.

75. Ibid.,15.

76. Ibid.,15–16.

77. Cox, "Trouble on the Chain Gang," 15.

78. *Barron* Transcript, 16; Papenfuse and Coale, *Atlas of Historical Maps,* 166.

79. *Barron* Transcript, 16.

80. Ibid.

81. Ibid.,16–17.

82. Ibid.,17.

83. Ibid.,26.

84. Ibid.,17.

85. Ibid.

86. Ibid.

87. Rockman, *Scraping By,* 81–83; Norman, "Wharf Construction," 93–95.

88. *Barron* Transcript, 17.

89. Ibid.,17–18.

90. Ibid.

91. Ibid., 18.

92. Ibid.

93. Ibid.

94. Ibid.,19.

95. Ibid.,19–20.

96. Ibid.,25.

97. Michal Allen Wolf, *The Zoning of America:* Euclid v. Ambler (Lawrence: University Press of Kansas, 2008), 91.

98. *Barron* Transcript, 19–20.

99. Ibid., 21.

100. See for example *Petition to pave Strawberry alley*, BCA BRG3–1-20, Location: BC/11/01/020, Document: 77, and *Petition to pave Lexington road*, BCA BRG3–1-19, Location: BC/11/01/019, Document: 60.

101. See Paving Warrants, BCA BRG3–1-19, Location: BC/11/01/019 BCA, Documents: 1–8.

102. See for example BCA BRG3–1-20, Location: BC/11/01/020, Document: 5.

103. *Barron* Transcript, 21.

104. Ibid.

105. Ibid., 21–22.

106. Ibid., 21.

107. Ibid., 22.

108. Scharf, *History of Baltimore*, 172.

109. *An Act to erect Baltimore Town, in Baltimore County, into a City* (1796), reprinted in 1816 Ordinances of the City of Baltimore, Section VIII, 9–10.

110. *Barron* Transcript, 23.

111. Ibid., 23–24.

112. Ibid.

113. Ibid., 24.

114. Ibid.

115. Ibid., 25. Stevenson Archer, "Rights of Municipal Corporations," *American Jurist and Law Magazine* 2, no. 4 (Oct. 1829), 204.

116. *Barron* Transcript, 25.

117. Ibid., 26.

118. Ibid., 10–11, 25.

119. Baltimore County Court, City Civil Docket, MSA Citation: C301-14, location: 02/15/06/031, MdHR No: 14284.

120. Archer, "Rights," 205; Elmer E. Snead, "Sic Utere Tuo Ut Alienum Non Laedas: The Basis of the State Police Power," *Cornell Law Quarterly* 21 (1935–36): 276.

121. Archer, "Rights," 205–6.

122. Archer, "Rights," 206. Later in his opinion, Archer cited *Palmer v. Mulligan*, 3 Caines. 307 (N.Y. 1805) for the proposition that a cause of action against a municipality for acts of municipal improvement would not lie unless the damage from such acts rose to a serious and permanent level; otherwise, *damnum abseque injuria* will apply to bar such suits.

123. Archer, "Rights," 206.

124. Ibid., 207.

125. Ibid.

126. Ibid.

127. *Black's Law Dictionary*, 1767.

128. Archer, "Rights," 208.

129. Ibid., 206–7, 210–11.

130. Ibid., 211.

131. Ibid.

132. Ibid.; Rawle, 124–35.

133. Archer, "Rights," 214.

134. *Palmer v. Mulligan*, 3 Cai. R. 307 (N.Y. 1805).

135. Morton Horwitz argued that *Palmer* marked the beginning of a transformation of the idea of property ownership toward the appreciation that the most important function of property was as a commodity to be developed as a business asset. In contrast, William Novak framed *Palmer* not as one where the courts intentionally modified the common law to facilitate economic growth, as argued by Horwitz, but as an example of the state's assertion of its powers over an essential resource, namely, the Hudson River. For Novak, the court did not engage in a weighing of private interests to determine its result. Rather, it determined that the river was a public thoroughfare; accordingly, one private company could not assert superior rights over another with respect to this public channel. Horwitz, *Transformation*, 37; Novak, *Peoples' Welfare*, 133–34.

136. *Palmer*, 3 Cai. R. at 309.

137. *Black's Law Dictionary*, 1490.

138. *Palmer*, 3 Cai. R. at 311. Livingston was later named to the U.S. Supreme Court (1807–23) and later became a strong ally of John Marshall. Michael Dougan, "Henry Brockholst Livingston," in Hall et al., *Oxford Guide*, 587–88.

139. *Palmer*, 3 Cai. R. at 312. Smith Thompson was also later named to the U.S. Supreme Court, where he served from 1823 to 1843 and ruled in favor of the City of Baltimore in *Barron v. Baltimore* (1833). Donald Roper, "Smith Thompson," in Hall et al., *Oxford Guide*, 1018–19.

140. Archer, "Rights," 214.

141. *Palmer*, 3 Cai. R. at 312.

142. Ibid.

143. Archer, "Rights," 211.

144. *Barron* Transcript, 26; *Black's Law Dictionary*, 207.

145. Maryland Court of Appeals (Docket, Western Shore), MSA S414–11, Location: 01/66/14/029 and Papenfuse Outline, 0004, at http://mdhistory.net/msaref06/barron/html/barron-0004.html (hereinafter "Appellate Docket"); and *Statement of Pending City Cases*, BCA BRG 13–3-1, Location: BC/25/05/002, Document: 1167.

CHAPTER 5

Epigraph: Court of Appeals (Notes on Arguments, Western Shore) 6/1830–6/1831, Location: 01/67/06/016, MdHR No.: 492, MSA Citation: S427–14: 131–61 (hereinafter "Appellate Transcript"), 159.

1. Carol A. Dyer, *Tuberculosis* (Santa Barbara: Greenwood, 2010), 15–16, 40.

2. Barron died on June 11, 1828. *Baltimore Patriot*, June 12, 1828, 3.

3. 1820 U.S. Census; Census Place: Baltimore War 1, Baltimore, Maryland; Page 3; NARA Roll: M33_42; Image: 11.

4. Craig executed his will on June 18, 1827. Barron died on June 11, 1828, while Craig's estate was appraised on February 16, 1828, and his property was advertised for estate sale in March 1828, right before the trial. I am placing Craig's death as occurring sometime during January or early February 1828. See "Sale of the Property of John Craig, Deceased," *Baltimore Patriot*, March 8, 1828, 3; "Death Notice for John Barron," *Baltimore Patriot*, June 12, 1828, 3; and *John Craig Inventory* (February 16, 1828), MSA, CM155-37, Film Reel WK 1071-1072-2, Folio 25.37.63, Book 37.

5. Rockman, *Scraping By*, 163–65.

6. Ibid., 199.

7. *John Craig Inventory* (February 16, 1828), MSA, CM155-37, Film Reel WK 1071-1072-2, Folio 25.37.63, Book 37.

8. *Luke Tiernan v. Margaret, John, and Robert Craig, Margaret Staples and the Estate of John Craig* (Baltimore Chancery Court, 1829), Maryland State Archives, Accession No.: 17,898–11412–1/2, MSA S512–14–11237, Location: 1/39/3/, 14.

9. *John Craig Inventory* (February 16, 1828), MSA, CM155-37, Film Reel WK 1071-1072-2, Folio 25.37.63, Book 37.

10. *Mackubin v. Craig and Barron* (January 17, 1822 notation from R. Lemmon & Co., auctioneer).

11. *Tiernan v. Craig et al.*, 3–5.

12. C. B. Tiernan, *The Tiernan and Other Families* (Baltimore: W. J. Gallery & Co., 1901), 79.

13. *Tiernan v. Craig et al.*, 46–47.

14. *Tiernan v. David and John Fisher, John Craig and John H. Staples*, MSA S512–14–11311, Location: 1/39/3/ (Deed of Assignment) and Baltimore County Court (Land Records), MSA CE 66–235, WG 185, p. 655. On July 7, 1829,

the *Baltimore Patriot* reported on *Tiernan v. Fisher et al.* Apparently, in 1805 John Fisher had originally leased to John Craig the property at the corner of George and Ann Streets, but the lease was never recorded. Craig assigned the lease to son-in-law John Staples on May 4, 1827, who in turn assigned the lease to Luke Tiernan on June 16, 1829. "Luke Tiernan v. Elizabeth Fisher," *Baltimore Patriot*, July 7, 1829, 3; *Tiernan v. Fisher et al.*, Maryland State Archives, MSA S512–14–11311.

15. *John Craig v. Thomas Cowart* (Baltimore County Court—Chancery, 1826), MSA Location: 02/15/11/061, MdHR No.: 40,200–645, MSA Citation: MSA C295–647.

16. *Barron* Transcript, 30.

17. Carroll T. Bond, *The Court of Appeals of Maryland: A History* (Baltimore: Barton-Gillet, 1928), 129; "Court of Appeals," *Baltimore Patriot*, January 8, 1831, 2.

18. Bond, *Court of Appeals*, 126–27.

19. Ibid., 126–28.

20. Ibid., 113–14.

21. Ibid., 201 and Appellate Transcript, 131.

22. Bond, *Court of Appeals*, 96.

23. Appellate Transcript, 131.

24. The city also relied on cases like *Steele v. Western Inland Lock Navigation* 2 Johns. 283 (N.Y. 1807) and the English case of *Harman v. Tappenden*, 1 East. 555, 102 Eng. Rep. 214 (1801). These cases collectively stood for the proposition that agents of the state who engage in the making of improvements would not be held liable for their actions, absent some evidence of malice.

25. *British Glass Plate Manufacturers v. Meredith*, 100 Eng. Rep. 1306 (1792); *Sutton v. Clarke*, 128 Eng. Rep. 943 (1815).

26. L. Friedman, *History*, 191.

27. Archer, "Rights," 213.

28. Appellate Transcript, 137.

29. *Lansing v. Smith*, 8 Cow. 146 (N.Y. 1828).

30. *Lansing*, 8 Cow. at 146–47. The 1821 New York constitution contained a specific provision prohibiting the taking of private property without compensation. New York Constitution (1821), Article VII, Section 7.

31. *Lansing*, 8 Cow. at 151–52; Novak, *Peoples' Welfare*, 142. For example, Scott and Taney in their respective arguments also relied on *Butler v. Kent*, 19 Johns. 223 (N.Y. 1821).

32. *Lansing*, 8 Cow. at 149.

33. Maryland Constitution, Article XXI (1776).

34. Appellate Transcript, 141.

35. Appellate Transcript, 142, 145.

36. Appellate Transcript, 146; *Sutton v. Clarke*, 128 Eng. Rep. 948.

37. Appellate Transcript, 142–43. See also Dorsey, *The General Public Statutory Law*, Vol. II, 1396, 1399.

38. Appellate Transcript, 143, 147.

39. Ibid., 147.

40. *Vanhorne's Lessee*, 2 U.S. 304 (C.C. D. Penn. 1795).

41. Shaffer, "Hoffman's Lectures," 127, 130–31.

42. Appellate Transcript, 148.

43. Ibid., 151.

44. Ibid., 148.

45. Joseph K. Angell, *A Treatise on the Common Law in Relation to Water-Courses* (Boston: Wells and Lilly, 1824).

46. Appellate Transcript, 151–52; Angell, *Water-Courses*, 53–55. In support of this proposition, Angell cited *Gardner v. Trustees of the City of Newburgh*, 2 Johns. 162 (N.Y. 1816) discussed in more detail in chapter 3.

47. Horwitz, *Transformation*, 38.

48. Appellate Transcript, 150.

49. Ibid., 149.

50. Ibid.

51. Appellate Transcript, 152; *Sutton v. Clarke*, 6 Taunt. 30, 128 Eng. Rep. 943 (1815).

52. *Sutton*, 128 Eng. Rep. at 943.

53. *Sutton*, 128 Eng. Rep. at 949.

54. *Sutton*, 128 Eng. Rep. at 948.

55. Archer, "Rights," 213.

56. Ibid.

57. Appellate Transcript, 150.

58. Ibid.

59. *Black's Law Dictionary*, 859.

60. Appellate Transcript, 149.

61. Ibid., 151.

62. Ibid.

63. Hoffman cited Book 31, Chapter 13. See Livy, Books XXXI-XXXIV, Vol. IX, trans. Evan Sage (Cambridge, MA: Harvard University Press, 1935), 41–43.

64. A great description of Taney's handling of the Merryman affair is seen in Jonathan W. White, *Abraham Lincoln and Treason in the Civil War: The Trials of John Merryman* (Baton Rouge: Louisiana State University Press, 2011).

65. White, *History of the Supreme Court*, 581.

66. Appellate Transcript, 155.

67. David A. Thomas, "Finding More Pieces for the Takings Puzzle: How Clarifying History Can Clarify Doctrine," *University of Colorado Law Review* 75 (2004): 520–33.

68. Appellate Transcript, 156.

69. Ibid., 157.

70. Ibid., 158.

71. Maryland Constitution (1776), Article XXI.

72. Archer, "Rights," 207.

73. Appellate Transcript, 159.

74. Ibid.

75. Both Mayer and Hoffman cited *Vanhorne's Lessee v. Dorrance*, while only Mayer cited *Fletcher v. Peck.*

76. *Fletcher v. Peck*, 6 Cranch 87, 10 U.S. 87 (1810); Sandra F. VanBurkleo, "Fletcher v. Peck," in Hall et al., *Oxford Guide*, 352.

77. *Fletcher v. Peck*, 6 Cranch at 136.

78. *Fletcher v. Peck*, 6 Cranch at 139 (emphasis added).

79. *Fletcher v. Peck*, 6 Cranch at 135.

80. *Satterlee v. Matthewson*, 27 U.S. 380 (1829); Appellate Transcript, 159.

81. *Satterlee*, 27 U.S. at 413.

82. *Satterlee*, 27 U.S. at 413.

83. *Satterlee*, 27 U.S. at 413.

84. *Vanhorne's Lessee*, 2 U.S. 304, 308 (C.C. Dist. Penn., 1795)

85. *Vanhorne's Lessee*, 2 U.S. at 310.

86. *Satterlee*, 27 U.S. at 414.

87. *Satterlee*, 27 U.S. at 413. *Vanhorne's Lessee*, 2 U.S. 304 (C.C.Dist. Penn., 1795)

88. Appellate Transcript, 159; *Bradshaw v. Rogers and Magee*, 20 Johns. 103 (N.Y. 1822).

89. *Bradshaw*, 20 Johns. at 104–5.

90. *Bradshaw*, 20 Johns. at 106.

91. Robert I. Vexler, *Baltimore: A Chronological and Documentary History* (New York: Oceana, 1971), 30–31.

92. *Fletcher v. Peck*, 6 Cranch at 139.

93. *Green v. Biddle*, 21 U.S. 1 (1823); Robertson, 80.

94. *Green*, 21 U.S. at 89.

95. *Willson v. Black Bird Creek Marsh Company*, 27 U.S. 245, 2 Pet 245 (1829).

96. William Wiecek, "Willson v. Blackbird Creek Marsh Co." in Hall et al., *Oxford Guide*, 1091.

97. *Brown v. Maryland*, 25 U.S. 419, 443 (1827).

98. *Barron* Transcript, 30; "Court of Appeals," *Baltimore Patriot*, January 8, 1831.

99. *Baltimore Patriot*, January 8, 1831, 2.

100. At the time, Maryland had two courts of appeal, one for the western shore that sat in Annapolis and one for the eastern shore that met in Easton. In the 1851 constitution, Maryland reorganized the appellate court system and made the appeals court in Annapolis the sole one in Maryland. Maryland has not only

kept the court of appeals in Annapolis but still refers to it by that name, even though it operates much in the same way that a supreme court would operate in most other U.S. states. Bond, *Court of* Appeals, 109, 150–52.

101. *Barron* Transcript, 2, 30-31; *Barron v. Baltimore*, Records of the United States Supreme Court, National Archives and Records Administration, Washington, D.C., RG 267, Box 196, Case File #1695, location in stacks: 17E3/01/16/05.

102. Wiecek, *Liberty Under Law*, 44.

103. Seddig in Hall et al., *Oxford Guide*, 70–71, and Sandra VanBurkleo, "William Johnson," in Hall et al., *Oxford Guide*, 519.

104. *Bank of Columbia v. Okely*, 17 U.S. 235 (1819); Akhil Reed Amar, *The Bill of Rights: Creation and Reconstruction* (New Haven: Yale University Press, 1998), 145.

105. *Bank of Columbia*, 17 U.S. at 238–39.

106. *Bank of Columbia*, 17 U.S. at 244. The Court also held that Article 3 of the Declaration of Rights in the Maryland Constitution (1776), which also provided a right to a jury trial, was likewise inapplicable for the same reasons.

107. *Bank of Columbia*, 17 U.S. at 244.

108. *Bank of Columbia*, 17 U.S. at 242.

109. *Houston v. Moore*, 18 U.S. 1, 3 (1820).

110. *Houston*, 18 U.S. at 4.

111. *Houston*, 18 U.S. at 34. The decision was five to two with Justices Story and Washington holding the Pennsylvania law unconstitutional; Amar, *The Bill of Rights*, 145.

112. *Bonaparte v. Camden & A.R. Co.*, 3 F. Cas. 821 (C.C. Dist. N.J. 1830) and Patricia Tyson Stroud, *The Man Who Had Been King* (Philadelphia: University of Pennsylvania Press, 2005), 221.

113. *Bonaparte*, 3 F. Cas. at 821; Stroud, 222.

114. *Bonaparte*, 3 F. Cas. at 828. The editor preparing the casebook included a footnote that cited the recent *Barron* decision entered after the *Bonaparte* opinion was issued. *Bonaparte v. Camden & A.R. Co.*, 3 F. Cas. at 829.

115. *Bonaparte*, 3 F. Cas. At 831; *Bradshaw*, 20 Johns. 103 (N.Y. 1822)

116. *Bonaparte*, 3 F. Cas. at 828.

CHAPTER 6

Epigraph: Marshall to Joseph Story (August 2, 1832) in Marshall, *The Papers of John Marshall*, Vol. XII, ed. Charles Hobson (Chapel Hill: University of North Carolina Press, 2006), 226.

1. "Supreme Court United States," *Daily National Intelligencer* (Washington, D.C.) February 9, 1833, *19th Century U.S. Newspapers*, accessed May 6, 2015; "U. States' Supreme Court," *United States' Telegraph* (Washington, D.C.) February 13, 1833, *19th Century U.S. Newspapers*, accessed May 6, 2015; and

Anne Ashmore, "Dates of Supreme Court Decisions and Arguments," U.S. Reports Volumes 2 to 107 (1791–1882) (Aug. 2006), 33 at http://www.supremecourt.gov/opinions/datesofdecisions.pdf

2. William B. Bushong, *Glenn Brown's History of the United States Capitol* (Washington, D.C.: U.S. Government Printing Office, 1998), 195–96.

3. Bloomfield, "Supreme Court Buildings," in Hall et al., *Oxford Guide*, 118–19.

4. White, *History of the Supreme Court*, 203–4; "Things in Washington," *New-Bedford Mercury* (Mass.), March 1, 1833.

5. White, *History of the Supreme Court*, 254–89; "Things in Washington," *New-Bedford Mercury*, March 1, 1833.

6. There is no evidence that David Hoffman appeared before the Court; the notes of the argument written by the court clerk show that only Mayer presented argument. *Barron*, 32 U.S. at 246.

7. Cordell, *University of Maryland*, 338.

8. Irwin S. Rhodes, *The Papers of John Marshall: A Descriptive Calendar*, Vol. II (Norman: University of Oklahoma Press, 1969), 413.

9. Sleeman, "David Hoffman," 20; Cordell, *University of Maryland*, 344.

10. David Hoffman to James Madison, February 14, 1833, in the James Madison Papers, 1723–1836, Series 1 (General Correspondence, 1723–1859, microfilm reel 24), *Library of Congress*, at http://hdl.loc.gov/loc.mss/mjm.24_0014_0015, accessed May 6, 2015.

11. *Barron* Transcript, 30–31; *Barron*, 32 U.S. at 246–47.

12. Taney was appointed Attorney General for the United States in 1831. Swisher, *Roger B. Taney*, 140–41. Taney appeared before the Supreme Court as attorney general during the 1833 term in fourteen cases: *U.S. v. MacDaniel*, 32 U.S. 1 (1833); *U.S. v. Ripley*, 32 U.S. 18 (1833); *U.S. v. Fillebrown*, 32 U.S. 28 (1833); *U.S. v. Percheman*, 32 U.S. 51 (1833); *U.S. v. Turner*, 32 U.S. 132 (1833); *U.S. v. Mills*, 32 U.S. 138 (1833); *U.S. v. Wilson*, 32 U.S. 150 (1833); *U.S. v. Brewster*, 32 U.S. 164 (1833); *Sampeyreac v. U.S.*, 32 U.S. 222 (1833); *Barlow v. U.S.*, 32 U.S. 404 (1833); *Duncan's Heirs v. U.S.*, 32 U.S. 435 (1833); *U.S. v. 84 Boxes of Sugar*, 32 U.S. 453 (1833); *Ex Parte Watkins*, 32 U.S. 568 (1833); and *Heirs of Dubourge de St. Colombe v. U.S.*, 32 U.S. 625 (1833). Taney appears as private counsel in four others: *Nicholas v. Fearson*, 32 U.S. 99 (1833), *Lessee of Livingston v. Moore*, 32 U.S. 469 (1833), *Scholefield v. Eichelberger*, 32 U.S. 586 (1833), and *Barron*.

13. *Tiernan v. Jackson*, 30 U.S. 580 (1831); *Barron* Transcript, 2–3.

14. White, *History of the Supreme Court*, 158–59 and visit to the Supreme Court Chambers by the author (March 2015), photographs on file; "Things in Washington," *New-Bedford Mercury*, March 1, 1833. The decision announced by Marshall was unanimous. The following are the justices on the Supreme Court during the decision, along with the president who nominated them and their state: Marshall (John Adams—Virginia), William Johnson (Jefferson—South

Carolina), Joseph Story (Madison—Massachusetts), Gabriel Duval (Madison—Maryland), Smith Thompson (Monroe—New York), John McLean (Jackson—Ohio), and Henry Baldwin (Jackson—Pennsylvania). *The Supreme Court in American Life, Vol. II, The Marshall Court, 1801–1835*, ed. Adrienne Siegel (New York: Associated Faculty Press, Inc., 1987), 250; Hall et al., *Oxford Guide*, 1129–30.

15. *Barron*, 32 U.S. at 246.

16. 1 Stat. 73, Section 25 (1789).

17. "Supreme Court United States," *Daily National Intelligencer* (Washington, D.C.) February 9, 1833; "U. States' Supreme Court," *United States' Telegraph* (Washington, D.C.) February 13, 1833, and Ashmore, "Dates," 33.

18. See chapter 3.

19. *Barron*, 32 U.S. at 245; Appellate Transcript, 150; and *Black's Law Dictionary*, 859.

20. *Barron*, 32 U.S. at 245.

21. U.S. Constitution, Amendment XI (Ratified 1795)

22. *Chisholm v. Georgia*, 2 U.S. 419 (1793).

23. *Osborn v. The Bank of the United States*, 22 U.S. 738, 835–37 (1824).

24. *Barron*, 32 U.S. at 245–46.

25. *Barron*, 32 U.S. at 246.

26. 1 Stat. 73, Section 25 (1789).

27. *Barron*, 32 U.S. at 246.

28. *Barron*, 32 U.S. at 247

29. *Barron v. Baltimore*, Records of the United States Supreme Court, National Archives and Records Administration, Washington, D.C., RG 267, Box 196, Case File #1695, location in stacks: 17E3/01/16/05.

30. *Barron*, 32 U.S. at 247.

31. See James Madison, Federalist, No. 37 (January 11, 1788), Alexander Hamilton, Federalist, No. 84 (May 28, 1788), Patrick Henry, Speech in Virginia Ratifying Convention (June 4, 1788), and Brutus, No. 12 (February 7, 1788) in Kurland, *The Founders' Constitution*, Vol. II, 4–6, 9–10.

32. See "The Webster-Hayne Debate, 1830," in Freehling, *Nullficiation Era*, 62.

33. *McCulloch*, 17 U.S. at 402–5.

34. *Barron*, 32 U.S. at 247.

35. Strictly speaking, there are two other places in the Bill of Rights that have some designation as to applicability. The Seventh Amendment contains language that limits the ability of federal courts to reexamine issues of fact determined by juries, while the Tenth Amendment reaffirms the principle of federalism.

36. *Barron*, 32 U.S. at 249.

37. Ibid.

38. *Barron*, 32 U.S. at 250.

39. *Barron*, 32 U.S. at 250.

40. *Barron*, 32 U.S. at 251.

41. *Marbury*, 5 U.S. at 178.

42. *Marbury*, 5 U.S. at 176 (emphasis added).

43. *Marbury*, 5 U.S. at 177.

44. *Barron*, 32 U.S. at 249.

45. Stites, *John Marshall*, 40; J. Gordon Hylton, "Virginia and the Ratification of the Bill of Rights, 1789–1791," *University of Richmond Law Review* 25 (1990–91): 433, 437–38.

46. See, for example, W. Allan Wilbur, "Review of *John Marshall: A Life in Law*," *American Journal of Legal History* (April 1976): 155, 157; Irons, *People's History*, 136; Powell, "Original Intent," 114n325; Gerber, *Secure These Rights*, 123.

47. William Wiecek, *Liberty Under Law: The Supreme Court in American Life* (Baltimore: Johns Hopkins Press, 1988), 54. For these interpretations of *Barron*, see chapter 1.

48. Daniel Walker Howe is an exception. In his magisterial *What Hath God Wrought*, Howe not only aptly noted the unsettled question of whether the Bill of Rights applied to the states but also explained Marshall's decision in *Barron* as likely the result of the extreme agitation by many states that was certainly in the background during the Court's January 1833 session. Howe, *What Hath God Wrought*, 413–14.

49. Gregory A. Caldeira, "Process of Review," in Hall et al., *Oxford Guide*, 853.

50. White, *History of the Supreme Court*, 164–65.

51. Charles Hobson, ed., Introduction to Marshall, *The Papers of John Marshall*, Vol. 12, xxii.

52. Ibid.

53. Baldwin was appointed by Jackson in 1830 to replace Bushrod Washington. Richard Ellis, "Bushrod Washington," in Hall et al., *Oxford Guide*, 1072–73; Seddig, "Henry Baldwin," 70–71.

54. Seddig, "Henry Baldwin," 70–71; Hobson, Introduction, xxi.

55. White, *History of the Supreme Court*, 299; Joseph Story to Sarah Waldo Story (January 20, 1833), in Joseph Story, *Life and Letters of Joseph Story*, Vol. II, ed. William Story (Boston: Little & Brown, 1851), 116.

56. Hobson, Introduction, xxi–xxii.

57. William McLoughlin, *Cherokee Renascence in the New Republic* (Princeton: Princeton University Press, 1986), 277.

58. Francis Paul Prucha, *The Great Father: The United States Government and the American Indians*, abridged ed. (Lincoln: University of Nebraska Press, 1986), 48–51; Peter S. Onuf, *Jefferson's Empire: The Language of American Nationhood* (Charlottesville: University of Virginia Press, 2000), 48–52.

59. Prucha, *Great Father*, 64.

60. *Articles of Agreement and Cession* (The Georgia Compact) (1802), in *The Encyclopedia of American Indian Removal, Vol. 2*, ed. Daniel Littlefield and James Parins, (Santa Barbara: Greenwood, 2011), 1–4; Anthony F. C. Wallace,

The Long, Bitter Trail: Andrew Jackson and the Indians (New York: Hill and Wang, 1993), 63; Prucha, *Great Father*, 66.

61. Wallace, *Bitter Trail*, 59–60; Howe, *What Hath God Wrought*, 343–46.

62. *Constitution of the Cherokee Nation* (1827); Wallace, *Bitter Trail*, 62.

63. Acts of the General Assembly of the State of Georgia, Passed in Milledgeville at an Annual Session in November and December, 1827, December 19, 1827, Vol. 1, 249.

64. Robertson, *Conquest*, 124–25.

65. Wallace, *Bitter Trail*, 64; *An Act to add the Territory lying within the limits of this State, and occupied by the Cherokee Indians, to the counties of Carroll, DeKalb, Gwinnett, Hall and Habersham; and to extend the laws of this State over the same, and for other purposes* (1828), in Littlefield and Parins, *Encyclopedia*, 23–24.

66. Andrew Jackson, First Annual Message to Congress (December 8, 1829), at http://millercenter.org/president/jackson/speeches/speech-3632 (accessed April 14, 2015).

67. A. Jackson, First Annual Message to Congress; Prucha, *Great Father*, 75; *An act to provide for an exchange of lands with the Indians residing in any of the states or territories, and for their removal west of the Mississippi* (1830) in Littlefield and Parins, *Encyclopedia*, 27.

68. McLoughlin, *Cherokee Renascence*,437.

69. White, *History of the Supreme Court*, 262; Howe, *What Hath God Wrought*, 383–84.

70. Robertson, *Conquest*, 129–30; McLoughlin, *Cherokee Renascence*, 439. While Robertson refers to the defendant as George Tassells, McLoughlin refers to him as Corn Tassell, also known as George Tassel.

71. Robertson, *Conquest*, 130; *Cherokee Nation v. Georgia*, 30 U.S. 1, 3 (1831).

72. Ashmore, "Dates," 30.

73. U.S. Constitution, Art. III, Sec. 2.

74. *Cherokee Nation*, 30 U.S. at 16–17.

75. Grant Foreman, *Indian Removal: The Emigration of the Five Civilized Tribes of Indians* (Norman: University of Oklahoma Press, 1982), 235; Howe, *What Hath God Wrought*, 355.

76. Howe, *What Hath God Wrought*, 355–56; "At the recent session of the Supreme Court of Gwinnett County," *United States' Telegraph* (Washington, D.C.) October 7, 1831.

77. *Worcester v. Georgia*, 31 U.S. 515, 559, 561–63 (1832); Robertson, *Conquest*, 133–34.

78. Stephen G. Bragaw, "Thomas Jefferson and the American Indian Nations: Native American Sovereignty and the Marshall Court," *Journal of Supreme Court History* 31, no. 2 (2006): 156–57.

79. "Letter from Washington" (Report from the U.S. Gazette), *Scioto Gazette* (Chillicothe, Ohio), March 21, 1832.

80. *Macon Telegraph* (Macon, Georgia), March 31, 1832, 3.

81. Ashmore, "Dates," 32; Jill Norgren, "Lawyers and the Legal Business of the Cherokee Republic in the Courts of the United States, 1829–1835," *Law and History Review* 10, no. 2 (Autumn, 1992): 253, 293.

82. Bragaw, "Thomas Jefferson," 156–57.

83. Ibid.; Richard E. Ellis, *The Union at Risk: Jacksonian Democracy, States' Rights and the Nullification Crisis* (New York: Oxford University Press, 1987), 30–31.

84. Howe, *What Hath God Wrought*, 412.

85. Ellis, *Union at Risk*, 26.

86. Howe, *What Hath God Wrought*, 412; Norgren, "Lawyers," 296–97.

87. John C. Calhoun, February 4, 1817 speech, in Freehling, *Nullficiation Era*, 1.

88. Freehling, *Nullficiation Era*, x.

89. "An Act in alteration of the several acts imposing duties on imports," Chapter LV, Sess. I, Ch. 55 (Approved May 19, 1828).

90. William K. Bolt, "The Tariff in the Age of Jackson," (PhD diss., University of Tennessee, 2010), http://trace.tennessee.edu/utk_graddiss/679, 232; Howe, *What Hath God Wrought*, 274.

91. Lacy K. Ford, Jr., *Origins of Southern Radicalism: The South Carolina Upcountry, 1800–1860* (New York: Oxford University Press, 1988), 115–18.

92. John C. Calhoun, *John C. Calhoun: Selected Writings and Speeches*, ed. H. Lee Cheek, Jr. (Washington, D.C.: Regnery Publishing, 2003), 267, 295–96.

93. Howe, *What Hath God Wrought*, 398–99; Calhoun, *John C. Calhoun: Selected Writings*, 317.

94. Freehling, *Nullficiation Era*, xiv-xv; Howe, *What Hath God Wrought*, 402.

95. "The Ordinance of Nullification," November 24, 1832, in Freehling, *Nullficiation Era*, 150; Clyde Wilson in John C. Calhoun, *The Papers of John C. Calhoun*, Vol. XII, 1833–35, ed. Clyde N. Wilson (Columbia: University of South Carolina Press, 1979), 3.

96. *Andrew Jackson's Nullification Proclamation*, December 10, 1832, in Freehling, *Nullficiation Era*, 153.

97. Howe, *What Hath God Wrought*, 404.

98. C. Wilson in Calhoun, *The Papers of John C. Calhoun*, 3.

99. Calhoun to Bolling Hall (January 12, 1833) and Calhoun to Samuel D. Ingham (January 13, 1833), in *Papers of John C. Calhoun*, 7–8, 8–9.

100. The Court heard oral arguments in *Holmes v. Trout*, 32 U.S. 171 (1833) on January 15 and 16, 1833, the first arguments of the 1833 term; see Ashmore, "Dates," 33; see also "President Jackson's Message to the Senate and House Regarding South Carolina's Nullification Ordinance," at http://avalon.law.yale.edu/19th_century/ajack001.asp (accessed April 25, 2015).

101. Calhoun, "Remarks on the President's Message" (January 16, 1833), in *Papers of John C. Calhoun*, 11.

102. Calhoun, "Speech Introducing Resolutions Declaratory of the Nature and Power of the Federal Government," (January 22, 1833), in *Papers of John C. Calhoun*, 25–26.

103. Calhoun, "Remarks on the Postponement of his Resolutions," (January 28, 1833), in *Papers of John C. Calhoun*, 29–33.

104. Calhoun, "Substitute for Felix Grundy's Resolutions on the Powers of the General and State Governments (January 28, 1833), in *Papers of John C. Calhoun*, 33–35.

105. Calhoun, "Remarks during Debate on the Force Bill," (January 28–29, 1833), in *Papers of John C. Calhoun*, 35–36.

106. "The Missionaries," *New-York Spectator* (New York, New York) January 28, 1833.

107. "The President," *New-York Spectator* (New York, New York), Thursday, January 17, 1833.

108. Ashmore, "Dates," 33.

109. *Niles' Weekly Register* (Baltimore, MD), February 23, 1833; "Speech on the Revenue Collection [Force] Bill," February 15–16, 1833, John C. Calhoun, *Union and Liberty: The Political Philosophy of John C. Calhoun*, ed. Ross M. Lence (Indianapolis: Liberty Fund, 1992), 401. Lence considers this speech one of Calhoun's most important.

110. Calhoun, "Speech on the Force Bill," (February 15–16, 1833), in *Papers of John C. Calhoun*, 45, 63.

111. Ibid., 68–69.

112. Ibid., 75–76.

113. "Congress of the United States," *Daily National Intelligencer* (Washington, D.C.), February 18, 1833.

114. Robert V. Remini, *Daniel Webster: The Man and His Time* (New York: W. W. Norton, 1997), 381.

115. Daniel Webster, "The Constitution Is Not a Compact" (February 16, 1833), in Webster, *The Writings and Speeches of Daniel Webster*, Vol. Six (Boston: Little, Brown & Co., 1903), 197–98.

116. "Debate in the Senate," *Baltimore Gazette and Daily Advertiser*, February 18, 1833.

117. Clare Cushman, *Courtwatchers: Eyewitness Accounts in Supreme Court History* (New York: Rowman & Littlefield, 2011), 20.

118. Bauer, *Commentaries*, 21.

119. See Wiecek, *Liberty Under Law*, 32, 53–55.

120. *Johnson v. Tompkins*, 13 F. Cas. 840 (C.C.E.D. Penn., 1833).

121. *Johnson*, 13 F. Cas. at 852.

122. *Johnson*, 13 F. Cas. at 852.

123. Bauer, *Commentaries*, 21.

124. *Bank of Columbia v. Okely*, 17 U.S. 235 (1819); *Houston v. Moore*, 18 U.S. 1 (1820).

125. *Livingston v. Moore*, 32 U.S. 469 (1833) "Supreme Court United States," Daily National Intelligencer (Washington, D.C.), February 26, 1833.

126. *Livingston*, 32 U.S. at 482–83.

127. *Livingston*, 32 U.S. at 492.

128. *Livingston*, 32 U.S. at 548.

129. John Quincy Adams, *An Oration Addressed to the Citizens of the Town of Quincy on the fourth of July, 1831, the fifty-fifth anniversary of the independence of the United States of America* (Boston: Richardson, Lord & Holbrook, 1831).

130. J.Q. Adams, *An Oration*, 6–7.

131. Marshall to J. Q. Adams (August 9, 1831), in Marshall, *Papers of John Marshall*, 96.

132. See President Jackson's "Veto Message Regarding the Bank of the United States" (July 10, 1832) available at http://avalon.law.yale.edu/19th_century/ajveto01.asp (accessed May 19, 2016).

133. Marshall to J. Story (August 2, 1832), in Marshall, *Papers of John Marshall*, 226–27.

134. Marshall to J. Story (September 22, 1832), in Marshall, *Papers of John Marshall*, 237–38.

135. "The Committee of 21—and the Report," *Richmond Enquirer* (Richmond, Va.), December 20, 1832.

136. Marshall to J. Story (December 25, 1832), in Marshall, *Papers of John Marshall*, 248.

137. Howe, *What Hath God Wrought*, 406–7.

138. Marshall to J. Story (December 25, 1832), in Marshall, *Papers of John Marshall*, 249.

139. Marshall to Jaquelin B. Harvie (February 8, 1833), in Marshall, *Papers of John Marshall*, 259; Rhodes, *Papers of John Marshall*, 478; Louise Pecquet du Bellet, *Some Prominent Virginia Families*, Vol. IV (Lynchburg, Virginia: J.P. Bell Co., 1907), 68; *Thirteenth Annual Report of the Library Board of the Virginia State Library*, 1915–16 (Richmond, 1917), 385.

140. Howe, *What Hath God Wrought*, 408.

141. Marshall to J. Story (April 24, 1833), in Marshall, *Papers of John Marshall*, 273.

142. White, *History of the Supreme Court*, 302; Marshall to Richard Peters (May 4, 1833), in Marshall, *Papers of John Marshall*, 274.

143. Marshall to Humphrey Marshall (May 7, 1833), in Marshall, *Papers of John Marshall*, 276 and Ruth Wedgwood, "Cousin Humphrey," 14 *Constitutional Commentary* 247 (1997).

144. Marshall to J. Story (June 3, 1833), in Marshall, *Papers of John Marshall*, 281.

145. Marshall to J. Story (July 31, 1833), in Story, *Life and Letters of Joseph Story*, Vol. II, 135–36.

146. *NFIB v. Sebelius*, 132 S.Ct. 2566 (2012).

147. *West Coast Hotel v. Parrish*, 57 S.Ct. 578 (1937).
148. *Obergefell v. Hodges*, 135 S.Ct. 2584, 2629, n. 22 (2015).

CHAPTER 7

Epigraph: Marshall, *Papers of John Marshall*, 485–86.

1. White, *History of the Supreme Court*, 743–44; *Swift v. Tyson*, 41 U.S. 1 (1842); *Erie Railroad Co. v. Tompkins*, 304 U.S. 64 (1938).

2. Story to Mrs. Joseph Story (January 28, 1831), in Story, *Life and Letters of Joseph Story*, 43–45.

3. Jason Mazzone makes a related point, arguing that *Barron* was not decided in order to enact a blanket prohibition against holding the Bill of Rights applicable to the states. Rather, under the Judiciary Act of 1789, the Supreme Court could review state court decisions in which the state court had denied relief alleging a violation of the Constitution; however, the Court could not review the state court decision if that court had granted relief based on a violation of the Constitution. Mazzone's interpretation is compelling, especially with respect to his nuanced appreciation of how the federal system should free all levels of courts to expand individual rights instead of compartmentalizing them as a matter of jurisdiction. Jason Mazzone, "The Bill of Rights in the Early State Courts," *Minnesota Law Review* 92, no. 1 (2007): 3, 19, 73, 75–76.

4. Richard Kielbowicz, "The Law and Mob Law in Attacks on Antislavery Newspapers, 1833–1860," *Law and History Review* 24, no. 3 (Fall 2006): 559, 561, 574.

5. Kielbowicz, "Law and Mob Law," 575; Novak, *Peoples' Welfare*, 1–2, 9.

6. *U.S. v. Amy*, 24 F.Cas. 792 (C.C.D.VA., 1859).

7. *Griffing v. Gibb*, 11 F.Cas. 33, 36 (C.C.N.D.CA, 1857)

8. *Griffing*, 11 F.Cas. at 36.

9. *Slaughterhouse Cases*, 83 U.S. 36 (1873)

10. Wiecek, *Liberty Under Law*, 53; David P. Currie, "The Constitution in the Supreme Court: Contracts and Commerce, 1836–1864," *Duke Law Journal* 1983, no. 3 (June, 1983): 471, 473.

11. *Gibbons v. Ogden*, 22 U.S. 1 (1824); Wiecek, *Liberty Under Law*, 50.

12. Irons, *People's History*, 131; *An Act for Enrolling and Licensing Ships . . . in the Coasting Trade and Fisheries*, 1 Stat. 302, Ch. VIII, Feb. 18, 1793, cited in William F. Swindler, *The Constitution and Chief Justice Marshall* (New York: Dodd, Mead, 1978), 330.

13. *Gibbons*, 22 U.S. at 187.

14. *Gibbons*, 22 U.S. at 222.

15. *Gibbons*, 22 U.S. at 210–11.

16. Wiecek, *Liberty Under Law*, 52.

17. George L. Haskins, "Marshall and the Commerce Clause of the Constitution," in *Chief Justice John Marshall: A Reappraisal,* ed. W. Melville Jones (Ithaca: Cornell University Press, 1956), 155.

18. Wiecek, *Liberty Under Law,* 52.

19. The Negro Seamen Act required free black sailors arriving in South Carolina to remain on their ships; otherwise, the sailor would be detained if he came on land until such time as his ship departed. Further, the captain of the ship would also be required to pay all costs of the sailor's detention, and if refused, the sailor would be sold into slavery to recoup those costs. Wiecek, *Liberty Under Law,* 52; Michael Schoeppner, "Status Across Borders: Roger Taney, Black British Subjects, and a Diplomatic Antecedent to the Dred Scott Case," *Journal of American History* 100, no. 1 (June 2013): 46–67.

20. Wiecek, *Liberty Under Law,* 52–53. R. Kent Newmyer and Herbert Johnson both agree with Wiecek, in part, that *Gibbons* left some autonomy to the states as a result of Marshall's recognition of the growing power of the rising states' rights movement, but they are silent as to whether the slavery issue was a determinative factor. R. Kent Newmyer, *John Marshall and the Heroic Age of the Supreme Court* (Baton Rouge: Louisiana State University Press, 2001), 314–15; Herbert A. Johnson, "Federal Union, Property, and the Contract Clause: John Marshall's Thought in Light of *Sturges v. Crowninshield* and *Ogden v. Saunders,*" in *John Marshall's Achievement: Law, Politics, and Constitutional Interpretations,* ed. Thomas C. Shevory (Westport, CT: Greenwood Press, 1989), 48.

21. *Willson v. Black-Bird Creek Marsh Company,* 27 U.S. 245, 2 Pet 245 (1829).

22. *Willson,* 27 U.S. at 246.

23. *Willson,* 27 U.S. at 251–52.

24. Wiecek, *Liberty Under Law,* 54.

25. Swindler, *Constitution and Chief Justice Marshall,* 21.

26. *Ogden v. Saunders,* 25 U.S. 213 (1827); *Sturges v. Crowninshield,* 17 U.S. 122 (1819).

27. "The Chief Justice," *Alabama Intelligencer and State Rights Expositor* (Tuscaloosa, Ala.), March 2, 1833.

28. *New York v. Miln,* 36 U.S. 102 (1837).

29. Finkelman, "Root of the Problem," 15.

30. *Miln,* 36 U.S. at 104.

31. *Miln,* 36 U.S. at 105.

32. *Miln,* 36 U.S. at 104–5; Finkelman, "Root of the Problem," 15.

33. U.S. Const., Article I, Section 8, Clause 3.

34. *Miln,* 36 U.S. at 152.

35. Finkelman, "Root of the Problem," 15–16.

36. *Barron,* 243 U.S. at 246.

37. See Brendan J. Doherty, "Interpreting the Bill of Rights and the Nature of Federalism: *Barron v. City of Baltimore,*" *Journal of Supreme Court History* 32, no. 3 (November 2007): 223.

38. See, for example, Webster to Joseph Hopkinson (February 9, 1833), Joseph Hopkinson (February 15, 1833), and Nathan Appleton (February 17, 1833), in *The Papers of Daniel Webster*, Correspondence, Vol. 3, ed. Charles Wiltse and David Allen (Hanover, NH: University Press of New England, 1977), 213–17.

39. Henry Clay, "Draft Compromise Tariff Bill," (February 11, 1833), Clay to Francis T. Brooke (February 14, 1833), Nicholas Biddle (February 16, 1833); Peter Porter (February 16, 1833), and John Clayton (February 20, 1833) in Henry Clay, *The Papers of Henry Clay*, Vol. 8, ed. Robert Seager and Melba Hay (Lexington: University Press of Kentucky, 1984), 619–25.

40. White, *History of the Supreme Court*, 928–29.

41. "Supreme Court United States," *Daily National Intelligencer* (Washington, D.C.), February 9, 1833, February 13, 1833 and February 18, 1833.

42. "United States Supreme Court," *New-York Spectator* (New York, New York), February 18, 1833, February 28, 1833; "Supreme Court United States," *Baltimore Gazette and Daily Advertiser*, February 18, 1833; and "U. States' Supreme Court," *United States' Telegraph* (Washington, D.C.), February 13, 19, 1833.

43. *Sinnickson v. Johnson*, 17 N.J.L. 129 (N.J. 1839); *Taylor v. Porter & Ford*, 4 Hill 140 (N.Y. 1843); *Concord R.R. v. Greely*, 17 N.H. 47 (N.H. 1845); *Newcomb v. Smith*, 2 Pin. 131 (Wisc. 1849); *Boring v. Williams*, 17 Ala. 510 (Ala. 1850); *Woodfolk v. Nashville* R.R., 32 Tenn. 422 (Tenn. 1852); and *Bank of Toledo v. City of Toledo*, 1 Ohio St. 622 (Oh. 1853).

44. *Sinnickson v. Johnson*, 17 N.J.L. 129 (N.J. 1839) and *Taylor v. Porter & Ford*, 4 Hill 140 (NY 1843).

45. *Hatch v. Vermont Central R.R. Co.*, 25 Vt. 49 (VT 1852).

46. See *Hatch v. Vermont Central* (VT 1852), *Baltimore v. Marriott*, 9 Md. 160 (Md. 1856); *Stone v. Augusta*, 46 Me. 127 (Me. 1858); *Harvard v. Stearns*, 81 Mass. 1 (Mass. 1860); *Nevins v. Peoria*, 41 Ill. 502 (Ill. 1866); *Houck v. Wachter*, 34 Md. 265 (Md. 1871); *Eaton v. Aiken*, 51 N.H. 504 (N.H. 1872); *Williams Bros. v. Tripp*, 11 R.I. 447 (R.I. 1877); *Cumberland v. Willison*, 50 Md. 138 (Md. 1878); *Providence Steam Engine v. Providence Steamship*, 12 R.I. 348 (R.I. 1879); *Carson v. Hartford*, 48 Conn. 68 (Conn. 1880); *Coniff v. San Francisco*, 67 Cal. 45 (Cal. 1885); *Peck v. Michigan City*, 149 Ind. 670 (Ind. 1898).

47. *Clark v. Sohier*, 5 F.Cas. 925 (C.C.D.ME 1846).

48. *Poole v. Fleeger*, 36 U.S. 185 (1837); *Holmes v. Jennison*, 39 U.S. 540 (1840); and *Fox v. Ohio*, 46 U.S. 410 (1847).

49. *Smith v. Tate*, 227 S.W. 1026, 1028 (Tenn. 1921).

50. *Palmer v. Ohio*, 248 U.S. 32, 34 (1918).

51. *Burke v. State*, 104 Ohio St. 220, 225–26 (Ohio 1922).

52. Doherty, "Interpreting," 211, 223.

53. Akhil Reed Amar, "Creation, Reconstruction, and Interpretation of the Bill of Rights," in *The Nature of Rights at the American Founding and Beyond*, ed. Barry Alan Shain (Charlottesville: University of Virginia Press, 2007), 165. See also Amar, *The Bill of Rights*, 140–62.

54. *Nunn v. State*, 1 Kelly 243 (Ga. 1846).

55. For a biographical sketch of Lumpkin, see Bond Almand, "History of the Supreme Court of Georgia, The First Hundred Years," in *A History of the Supreme Court of Georgia*, ed. John Harris (Macon: J.W. Burke Co., 1948), 24.

56. *Nunn*, 1 Kelly at 251.

57. Ibid.

58. *Nunn*, 1 Kelly at 252. Michael Kent Curtis has also used and addressed the same two above-cited excerpts from Justice Lumpkin's opinion in *Nunn* in his book, *No State Shall Abridge: The Fourteenth Amendment and the Bill of Rights* (Durham, NC: Duke University Press, 1986). Curtis argues that slavery was the real issue lurking behind Marshall's decision in *Barron*. Curtis, *No State*, 22–25.

59. *Flint River Steamboat Company v. Foster*, 5 Ga. 194 (Ga. 1848).

60. *Flint River*, 5 Ga. at 197.

61. *Flint River*, 5 Ga. at 204.

62. Georgia Constitution, Article IV, Section 3 (1789).

63. *Allen v. Georgia*, 10 Ga. 85, 90 (Ga. 1851); *Campbell v. Georgia*, 11 Ga. 353 (Ga. 1852).

64. *Young v. McKenzie*, 3 Ga. 31 (Ga. 1847); Almand, 24–25.

65. *Young*, 3 Ga. at 35.

66. *Young*, 3 Ga. at 38.

67. *Parham v. Decatur County*, 9 Ga. 341, 345 (Ga. 1851); Almand, 25–26.

68. *Parham*, 9 Ga. at 346–47.

69. *Parham*, 9 Ga. at 347.

70. Citing *State v. Brown*, 8 Rob. 566 (La. 1844); See also *State v. Hornsby*, 8 Rob. 583 (La. 1845).

71. Louisiana Constitution (1812).

72. *Hoffman v. State*, 20 Md. 425 (Md. 1863).

73. Maryland Constitution (1851).

74. *Hoffman*, 20 Md. at 434.

75. *Hoffman*, 20 Md. at 432.

76. New Jersey Constitution (1776), Articles 16, 18, 19, and 23. See also Wood, *The Creation of the American Republic*, 271, n. 21.

77. *Scudder v. Trenton Delaware Falls Company*, 1 N.J. Eq. 694 (N.J. 1832).

78. *Scudder*, 1 N.J. Eq. at 710.

79. *Scudder*, 1 N.J. Eq. at 721.

80. *Sinnickson v. Johnson*, 17 N.J.L. 129 (N.J. 1839).

81. *Sinnickson*, 17 N.J.L. at 145.

82. Ibid.

83. *Sinnickson*, 17 N.J.L. at 146.

84. *Sinnickson*, 17 N.J.L. at 145. The court cited Henry Baldwin's circuit opinion in *Bonaparte v. Camden & A.R. Co.*, 3 F Cas. 821 (C.C. Dist. N.J. 1830) in support.

85. *Ten Eyck v. The Delaware and Raritan Canal Co.*, 18 N.J.L. 200 (N.J. 1841).

86. *Ten Eyck*, 18 N.J.L. at 201.

87. *Ten Eyck*, 18 N.J.L. at 203.

88. *Taylor v. Porter & Ford*, 4 Hill 140 (N.Y. Sup. Ct. 1843).

89. *Taylor*, 4 Hill at 141–42.

90. *Taylor*, 4 Hill at 148.

91. *Taylor*, 4 Hill at 147; 1821 New York Constitution, Article VII, Section 1; 1776 Maryland Constitution, Section XXI; Magna Carta (1215), Section 39.

92. *Taylor*, 4 Hill at 146.

93. Ibid.

94. *Taylor*, 4 Hill at 149.

95. Ibid.

96. *Taylor*, 4 Hill at 149–50.

97. *People v. White*, 11 Barb. 26 (N.Y. 1851).

98. *White*, 11 Barb. at 30.

99. Ibid.

100. Ibid.

101. Ibid. The New York constitution of 1821 incorporated a takings clause (Article VII, Section 7), as did the New York constitution of 1846 (Article I, Section 6).

102. The 1777 New York constitution provided for the right to a jury trial (Art. XLI) and religious freedom (Art. XXXVIII). New York Constitution (1777).

103. *White*, 11 Barb. at 30; *Gardner v. Trustees of the Village of Newburgh*, 2 Johns .Ch. 162 (N.Y. 1816).

104. *Gardner*, 2 Johns. at 167.

105. *New York v. The Board of Supervisors of the County of Westchester*, 4 Barb. 64, 65 (N.Y. Sup. Ct., N.Y. County, 1848).

106. *Westchester*, 4 Barb. at 75–80.

107. *Westchester*, 4 Barb. at 71.

108. Ibid.

109. *Westchester*, 4 Barb. at 72.

110. Ibid.; *Gardner*, 2 Johns. 162 (N.Y. 1816).

111. *Westchester*, 4 Barb. at 72–74. In addition to *Gardner* and Story's *Commentaries* on the Constitution, the court also cited *Bowman v. Middleton*, 1 Bay (S.C. 1792), discussed in more detail in chapter 3.

112. *New York v. Toynbee v. Wynhammer*, 13 N.Y. 378, 2 Parker Crim. Rep. 490 (N.Y. 1856).

113. *Wynhammer*, 13 N.Y. at 390.

114. *Wynhammer*, 13 N.Y. at 384–87.

115. *Wynhammer*, 13 N.Y. at 392; New York Constitution (1846), Article I, Sections 1 and 6.

116. *Wynhammer*, 13 N.Y. at 392–93.

117. *Wynhammer*, 13 N.Y. at 445–47.

118. *State v. Buzzard*, 4 Ark. 18 (Ark. 1842).

119. *Buzzard*, 4 Ark. at 28.

120. *Atkins v. State*, 16 Ark. 568 (Ark. 1855).

121. *Atkins*, 16 Ark. at 575.

122. Arkansas Constitution, Article 2, Sections 12 and 21 (1836)

123. *Ervine's Appeal*, 16 Pa. 256 (Pa. 1851).

124. *Ervine's Appeal*, 16 Pa. at 263–64.

125. *Ervine's Appeal*, 16 Pa. at 263.

126. Ibid.

127. Ibid.

128. *Commonwealth v. Flanagan*, 7 Watts & Serg. 415, 1844 WL 5033 (Penn. 1844).

129. *Flanagan*, 7 Watts & Serg. at 418.

130. *Flanagan*, 7 Watts & Serg. at 421–22.

131. *Flanagan*, 7 Watts & Serg. at 421.

132. *Rhinehart v. Schuyler*, 7 Ill. 473 (Ill. 1845).

133. Specifically, the appellant argued that the sale violated three provisions of the Illinois constitution (1818). First, it violated Article VIII, Section 11, which contained a provision similar to the takings clause of the Fifth Amendment. Second, he argued that it violated Article VIII, Section 8, which contained language similar to Section 39 of the Magna Carta, namely, "That no freeman shall be imprisoned or disseized of his freehold, liberties, or privileges, or outlawed or exiled, or in any manner deprived of his life, liberty, or property, but by the judgment of his peers or the law of the land." Third, the appellant argued that it violated Article VIII, Section 20, which provided that property taxes be determined by land value. The appellant argued this too was violated since his property was either exempt or the law in question allowed for an arbitrary method of valuation. *Rhinehart*, 7 Ill. at 473–74.

134. *Rhinehart*, 7 Ill. at 522.

135. Ibid.

136. *Henry v. Dubuque & Pacific Railroad*, 10 Iowa 540 (Iowa 1860).

137. Iowa Constitution, Art. I, Section 18 (1857).

138. *Henry v. Dubuque*, 10 Iowa at 543–44.

139. *Southwestern Railroad Company v. Southern and Atlantic Telegraph Company*, 46 Ga. 43, 53 (Ga. 1872).

140. *Concord R.R. v. Greely* (NH 1848), *Newcomb v. Smith* (Wisc. 1848).

141. *Boring v. Williams*, 17 Ala. 510 (Ala. 1850), *Bank of Toledo v. City of Toledo*, 1 Ohio St. 622 (Ohio 1853), *Noles v. State*, 24 Ala. 672 (Ala. 1854), *Commonwealth v. Hitchings*, 5 Gray 482 (Mass. 1855), *Jones v. Robbins*, 74 Mass. 329 (Mass. 1857), *Lincoln v. Smith*, 27 Vt. 328 (Vt. 1855), *Cavender v. Smith*, 5 Clarke 157 (Iowa 1857), *State v. Paul*, 5 R.I. 185 (R.I. 1858), *Woodfolk v. Nashville* R.R., 32 Tenn. 422 (Tenn. 1852), *Lake Erie, Wabash, and St. Louis R.R. v. Heath*, 9 Ind. 558 (Ind. 1855); *Herman v. State*, 8 Ind. 545 (Ind. 1855); and *Ableman v. Booth*, 11 Wisc. 498 (Wis. 1859).

142. *State v. Schricker*, 29 Mo. 265 (Mo. 1860), *Baker v. Wise*, 16 Gratt. 139 (VA 1861), *Griffin v. Wilcox*, 21 Ind. 370 (Ind. 1863), *In re: Bryan*, 60 N.C. 1 (N.C. 1863), *Burnes v. Atkinson*, 2 Kan. 454 (Kan. 1864), *Kansas v. Barnett*, 3 Kan. 350 (Kan. 1865), *State v. Jackson*, 21 La.Ann. 574 (La. 1869), and *State v. Shumpert*, 1 S.C. 85 (S.C. 1869).

143. *Andrews v. State*, 50 Tenn. 165 (Tenn. 1871), *Burt v. Merchants*, 106 Mass. 356 (Mass. 1871), *Commonwealth v. Byrne*, 20 Gratt. 165 (Va. 1871), *Trombley v. Humphrey*, 23 Mich. 471 (Mich. 1871), *Frierson v. Pres. Church*, 54 Tenn. 683 (Tenn. 1872), and *N. Mo. R.R. v. Maguire*, 49 Mo. 490 (Mo. 1872).

144. *Cox v. State*, 8 Tex.App. 254 (Tex.Ct.App. 1880), *St. Louis v. Richeson*, 76 Mo. 470 (Mo. 1882), *Peerce v. Kitzmiller*, 19 W.Va. 564 (W.Va. 1882), *Butler v. State*, 97 Ind. 378 (Ind. 1884), *Bohannon v. State*, 18 Neb. 57 (Neb. 1885), *Missouri v. Kaub*, 19 Mo.App. 149 (Mo.App. 1885), *State v. Parker*, 66 Iowa 586 (Iowa 1885), *State v. Flynn*, 16 R.I. 10 (R.I. 1887), *Ex Parte Snyder*, 29 Mo.App. 256 (Mo.App. 1888), and *Kemmler v. Durston*, 7 N.Y.S. 813 (N.Y. 1889).

145. U.S. Constitution, Fourteenth Amendment (1868).

146. See *Slaughterhouse Cases*, 83 U.S. 36 (1873); *U.S. v. Cruikshank*, 92 U.S. 542 (1875); *Civil Rights Cases*, 109 U.S. 3 (1883).

147. *Duncan v. Louisiana*, 391 U.S. 145 (1968); Charles H. Sheldon, "Duncan v. Louisiana" in Hall, *Oxford Guide*, 277; Article I, Section 9, Louisiana Constitution (1921).

148. *Cairo and Fulton R.R. Co. v. Turner*, 31 Ark. 494 (Ark. 1876).

149. *Cairo and Fulton R.R.*, 31 Ark. at 499.

150. Arkansas Constitution, Article II, Section 10 (1836).

151. *Cairo and Fulton R.R.*, 31 Ark. at 500.

152. Ibid.

153. *State v. Miller*, 60 A. 202, 203–4 (N.J. Ct. of App. 1905).

154. *Boepple v. Mohalt*, 54 P.2d 857, 864 (Mont. 1936)

155. See, for example, Elizabeth Dale, *Criminal Justice in the United States, 1789–1939* (New York: Cambridge University Press, 2011), and Bruce Ackerman, *We the People: The Civil Rights Revolution* (Cambridge, MA: Harvard University Press, 2014).

156. See Brian Leiter, "Legal Realism and Legal Positivism Reconsidered," *Ethics* 111, no. 2 (January 2001): 278–301.

EPILOGUE

Epigraph: Sister Simone Campbell, interview by Stephen Colbert, *The Colbert Report*, Comedy Central, December 13, 2012.

1. Marshall, *Papers*, 489.

2. Interview with James Kent, May 16, 1835, in Marshall, *Papers*, 486.

3. *Daily National Intelligencer (Washington, D.C.)*, July 9, 1835; Marshall, *Papers*, 489–90.

4. Scharf, *History of Baltimore*, 714.

5. Ibid.

6. "A Public Deprivation," *Baltimore Sun* (November 11, 1839), 2.

7. See for example *Tiernan v. Poor*, 1 G. & J. 216 (Md. Ct. of App., 1829).

8. "Fatal Accident," *Baltimore Sun*, Volume IV, Issue 146 (May 7, 1839), 2.

9. According to the notice of the auction following his death, Craig owned a home in Fell's Point on Thames Street, between Bond and Market Streets. May 20, 1839 *Baltimore Sun*, Volume V, Issue 3, Page 3.

10. "Died," February 16, 1838 *Baltimore Sun*, Volume II, Issue 28, p. 2.

11. "Fatal Accident," May 7, 1839 *Baltimore Sun*, Volume IV, Issue 146, p. 2.

12. "Drowned," June 9, 1840 *Baltimore Sun*, Volume VII, Issue 20, p. 2.

13. Jacqueline Greff, *Fell's Point* (Charleston, SC: Arcadia Publishing, 2005), 51–52.

14. Maryland Constitution, Art. III, Sec. 46 (1851).

15. "The Fifth Amendment Case that Lost," National Archives (Audio Recording), Record Group 306, National Archives Identifier: 565711, Local Identifier: 306-SO-18.

16. Larry Kramer, *The People Themselves: Popular Constitutionalism and Judicial Review* (New York: Oxford University Press, 2005).

17. Rakove, *Original Meanings*, 70.

18. Saul Cornell, *A Well-Regulated Militia* (New York: Oxford University Press, 2006), 91–92; *Nunn v. State*, 1 Kelly 243 (Ga. 1846); *District of Columbia et al. v. Heller*, 554 U.S. 570 (2008)

19. *McDonald v. City of Chicago, Ill.*, 130 S.Ct 3020, 3030–3031 (2010)

20. Cornell, *Militia*, 4–5.

21. John Johnson, *Griswold v. Connecticut* (Lawrence: University Press of Kansas, 2005), 56–57.

22. *Griswold v. Connecticut*, 381 U.S. 479 (1965).

Bibliography

ARCHIVES CONSULTED

Baltimore City Archives, Baltimore, Maryland
Maryland State Archives, Annapolis, Maryland
Maryland Historical Society, Baltimore, Maryland
National Archives, Washington, D.C., and College Park, Maryland
Library of Congress, Washington, D.C.

COURT CASES

U.S. Supreme Court

Chisholm v. Georgia, 2 U.S. 419 (1793)
Marbury v. Madison, 5 U.S. 137 (1803)
Fletcher v. Peck, 10 U.S. 87, 139 (1810)
Bank of Columbia v. Okely, 17 U.S. 235 (1819)
McCulloch v. Maryland, 17 U.S. 316 (1819)
Sturges v. Crowninshield, 17 U.S. 122 (1819)
Trustees of Dartmouth College v. Woodward, 17 U.S. 518 (1819)
Houston v. Moore, 18 U.S. 1 (1820)
Goszler v. Corporation of Georgetown, 19 U.S. 593 (1821)
Green v. Biddle, 21 U.S. 1 (1823)
Gibbons v. Ogden, 22 U.S. 1 (1824)
Osborn v. The Bank of the United States, 22 U.S. 738 (1824)
Ogden v. Saunders, 25 U.S. 213 (1827)
Brown v. Maryland, 25 U.S. 419 (1827)

Satterlee v. Matthewson, 27 U.S. 380 (1829)

Willson v. Black-Bird Creek Marsh Company, 27 U.S. 245 (1829)

Cherokee Nation v. Georgia, 30 U.S. 1 (1831)

Tiernan v. Jackson, 30 U.S. 580 (1831)

Worcester v. Georgia, 31 U.S. 515 (1832)

John Barron, survivor of John Craig, for the use of Luke Tiernan, Executor of John Craig v. the Mayor and City Council of Baltimore, 32 U.S. 243 (1833)

Holmes v. Trout, 32 U.S. 171 (1833)

Nicholas v. Fearson, 32 U.S. 99 (1833)

Lessee of Livingston v. Moore, 32 U.S. 469 (1833)

Scholefield v. Eichelberger, 32 U.S. 586 (1833)

U.S. v. MacDaniel, 32 U.S. 1 (1833)

U.S. v. Ripley, 32 U.S. 18 (1833)

U.S. v. Fillebrown, 32 U.S. 28 (1833)

U.S. v. Percheman, 32 U.S. 51 (1833)

U.S. v. Turner, 32 U.S. 132 (1833)

U.S. v. Mills, 32 U.S. 138 (1833)

U.S. v. Wilson, 32 U.S. 150 (1833)

U.S. v. Brewster, 32 U.S. 164 (1833)

Sampeyreac v. U.S., 32 U.S. 222 (1833)

Barlow v. U.S., 32 U.S. 404 (1833)

Duncan's Heirs v. U.S., 32 U.S. 435 (1833)

U.S. v. 84 Boxes of Sugar, 32 U.S. 453 (1833)

Ex Parte Watkins, 32 U.S. 568 (1833)

Heirs of Dubourge de St. Colombe v. U.S., 32 U.S. 625 (1833)

New York v. Miln, 36 U.S. 102, 131 (1837)

Poole v. Fleeger, 36 U.S. 185 (1837)

Holmes v. Jennison, 39 U.S. 540 (1840)

Swift v. Tyson, 41 U.S. 1 (1842)

Fox v. Ohio, 46 U.S. 410 (1847)

Slaughterhouse Cases, 83 U.S. 36 (1873)

U.S. v. Cruikshank, 92 U.S. 542 (1876)

Civil Rights Cases, 109 U.S. 3 (1883)

Chicago, Burlington & Quincy Railroad Co. v. Chicago, 166 U.S. 226 (1897)

Palmer v. Ohio, 248 U.S. 32, 34 (1918)

Pennsylvania Coal Co. v. Mahon, 43 S. Ct. 158, 160 (1922)

West Coast Hotel v. Parrish, 57 S.Ct. 578 (1937)

Erie Railroad Co. v. Tompkins, 304 U.S. 64 (1938)

Brown v. Board of Education, 347 U.S. 483 (1954)

Heart of Atlanta Motel v. U.S., 379 U.S. 21 (1964)

Griswold v. Connecticut, 381 U.S. 479 (1965)

Duncan v. Louisiana, 391 U.S. 145 (1968)

District of Columbia et al. v. Heller, 554 U.S. 570 (2008)

McDonald v. City of Chicago, Ill., 130 S.Ct. 3020 (2010)
Citizens United v. Federal Elections Commission, 130 S.Ct. 876 (2010)
NFIB v. Sebelius, 132 S.Ct. 2566 (2012)
Obergefell v. Hodges, 135 S.Ct. 2584 (2015)

Lower Federal Courts

Vanhorne's Lessee v. Dorrance, 2 U.S. 304 (C.C. Penn. 1795)
Elkison v. Deliesseline, 8 F. Cas. 493 (C.D. S.C. 1823)
Bonaparte v. Camden & A.R. Co., 3 F Cas. 821 (C.C. Dist. N.J. 1830)
Johnson v. Tompkins, 13 F. Cas. 840 (C.C. E. Dist. Pa. 1833)
U.S. v. Amy, 24 F.Cas. 792 (C.C.D.Va., 1859)
Griffing v. Gibb, 11 F.Cas. 33, 36 (C.C.N.D.Ca., 1857)
Gordon v. City of Warren, 579 F.2d 386 (6th Cir. 1978)

State Courts

Middleton v. Bowman, 1 Bay 252 (S.C.Com.Pl.Gen.Sess. 1792)
Lindsay v. Commissioners, 2 Bay 38 (S.C.Const.App. 1796)
Elliot's Executor v. Lyell, 3 Call 268 (Va. 1802)
Palmer v. Mulligan, 3 Cai. R. 307 (N.Y. 1805)
Steele v. Western Inland Lock Navigation, 2 Johns. 283 (N.Y. 1807)
Stevens v. Proprietors of Middlesex Canal, 12 Mass. 466 (Mass. 1815)
Gardner v. Trustees of the Village of Newburgh, 2 Johns. Ch. 162 (N.Y. 1816)
James Colston v. John Craig (Baltimore County Court, 1817), MSA S512-9-7151
James Mackubin, Administrator of Frederick Mackubin v. John Craig and John Barron Jr. (Baltimore County Court, 1818), MSA S512-4-3602
Mayor and City Council of Baltimore v. Barron (Baltimore County Court, 1818), MSA SC 5458-58-13989
New York v. Goodwin, 18 Johns. 187 (N.Y. 1820)
William Price, John Price, and Hezekiah Waters vs. John Montgomery, Joseph Owens, Samuel Boyd, and Henry Stouffer (Baltimore County Court—Chancery, 1821), MSA C295-277
Browne v. Kennedy, 5 H. & J. 195 (Md. 1821)
Bradshaw v. Rogers and Magee, 20 Johns. 103 (N.Y. 1822)
Barker v. New York, 3 Cow. 686 (N.Y. 1824)
Crittenden v. Wilson, 5 Cow. 165 (N.Y. 1825)
Mayor and City Council of Baltimore v. Moore & Johnson, 6 H. & J. 375 (Md. Ct. App. 1825)
John Craig v. Thomas Cowart (Baltimore County Court—Chancery, 1826), MSA C295-647
Shrunk v. Schuylkill Navigation Company, 14 Serg. & Rawle 71 (Penn. 1826)
Lowry v. Tiernan & Williamson, 2 H. & G. 34 (Md. 1827)
Peter Rescaniere v. John Hanna, Charles Malloy, Richard Williams, John Craig, and Luke Tiernan (Baltimore County Court—Chancery, 1827), MSA S512-13-10519

Lansing v. Smith, 8 Cow. 146 (N.Y. 1828)

Barron & Craig v. The Mayor and City Council of Baltimore (Baltimore County Court, March Term 1828) reprinted in *The American Jurist and Law Magazine* 2, no. 4 (October 1829): 203

Luke Tiernan v. Margaret, John, and Robert Craig, Margaret Staples and the Estate of John Craig (Baltimore County Court—Chancery, 1829), MSA S512-14-11237

Tiernan v. David and John Fisher, John Craig and John H. Staples (Baltimore County Court–Chancery, 1829), MSA S512-14-11311

Tiernan v. Poor, 1 G. & J. 216 (Md. Ct. of App., 1829)

Case of the plan of the Third Division of the District of Kensington, 2 Rawle 445 (Penn. 1830)

McArthur v. Kelly and Williams, 5 Ohio 139 (Ohio 1831)

Scudder v. Trenton Delaware Falls Company, 1 N.J. Eq. 694 (N.J. 1832)

Tiernan v. Rescaniere's Adm'rs, 10 G. & J. 253 (Md. Ct. of App. 1838)

Sinnickson v. Johnson, 17 N.J.L. 129 (N.J. 1839)

Ten Eyck v. The Delaware and Raritan Canal Co., 18 N.J.L. 200 (N.J. 1841)

State v. Buzzard, 4 Ark. 18 (Ark. 1842)

Taylor v. Porter & Ford, 4 Hill 140 (N.Y. Sup. Ct. 1843)

Commonwealth v. Flanagan, 7 Watts & Serg. 415, 1844 WL 5033 (Penn. 1844)

State v. Brown, 8 Rob. 566 (La. 1844)

State v. Hornsby, 8 Rob. 583 (La. 1845)

Rhinehart v. Schuyler, 7 Ill. 473 (Ill. 1845)

Concord R.R. v. Greely, 17 N.H. 47 (N.H. 1845)

Nunn v. Georgia, 1 Ga. 243, 250 (Ga. 1846)

Clark v. Sohier, 5 F.Cas. 925 (C.C.D.Me. 1846)

Young v. Mckenzie, 3 Ga. 31 (Ga. 1847)

Flint River Steamboat Co. v. Foster, 5 Ga. 194 (Ga. 1848)

New York v. The Board of Supervisors of the County of Westchester, 4 Barb. 64 (N.Y. Sup Ct., N.Y. County, 1848)

Newcomb v. Smith, 2 Pin. 131 (Wis. 1849)

Boring v. Williams, 17 Ala. 510 (Ala. 1850)

Bank of Toledo v. City of Toledo, 1 Ohio St. 622 (Oh. 1853)

Noles v. State, 24 Ala. 672 (Ala. 1854)

Commonwealth v. Hitchings, 5 Gray 482 (Mass. 1855)

Jones v. Robbins, 74 Mass. 329 (Mass. 1857)

Lincoln v. Smith, 27 Vt. 328 (Vt. 1855)

Cavender v. Smith, 5 Clarke 157 (Iowa 1857)

State v. Paul, 5 R.I. 185 (R.I. 1858)

Ableman v. Booth, 11 Wisc. 498 (Wis. 1859)

Allen v. Georgia, 10 Ga. 85 (Ga. 1851)

Parham v. Decatur County, 9 Ga. 341 (Ga. 1851)

People v. White, 11 Barb. 26 (N.Y. 1851)

Ervine's Appeal, 16 Pa. 256 (Pa. 1851)
Campbell v. Georgia, 11 Ga. 353 (Ga. 1852)
Hatch v. Vermont Central R.R. Co., 25 Vt. 49 (Vt. 1852)
Atkins v. State, 16 Ark. 568 (Ark. 1855)
Baltimore v. Marriott, 9 Md. 160 (Md. 1856)
New York v. Toynbee v. Wynhammer, 13 N.Y. 378, 2 Parker Crim. Rep. 490 (N.Y. 1856)
Stone v. Augusta, 46 Me. 127 (Me. 1858)
Henry v. Dubuque & Pacific Railroad Company, 10 Iowa 540, 541 (Iowa 1860)
State v. Schricker, 29 Mo. 265 (Mo. 1860)
Harvard v. Stearns, 81 Mass. 1 (Mass. 1860)
Baker v. Wise, 16 Gratt. 139 (Va. 1861)
Griffin v. Wilcox, 21 Ind. 370 (Ind. 1863)
In re: Bryan, 60 N.C. 1 (N.C. 1863)
Burnes v. Atkinson, 2 Kan. 454 (Kan. 1864)
Kansas v. Barnett, 3 Kan. 350 (Kan. 1865)
Nevins v. Peoria, 41 Ill. 502 (Ill. 1866)
State v. Jackson, 21 La.Ann. 574 (La. 1869)
State v. Shumpert, 1 S.C. 85 (S.C. 1869)
Hoffman v. State, 20 Md. 425 (Md. 1863)
Andrews v. State, 50 Tenn. 165 (Tenn. 1871)
Burt v. Merchants, 106 Mass. 356 (Mass. 1871)
Commonwealth v. Byrne, 20 Gratt. 165 (Va. 1871)
Trombley v. Humphrey, 23 Mich. 471 (Mich. 1871)
Houck v. Wachter, 34 Md. 265 (Md. 1871)
Frierson v. Pres. Church, 54 Tenn. 683 (Tenn. 1872)
N. Mo. R.R. v. Maguire, 49 Mo. 490 (Mo. 1872)
Southwestern Railroad Co. v. Southern and Atlantic Telegraph Co., 46 Ga. 43 (Ga. 1872)
Eaton v. Aiken, 51 N.H. 504 (N.H. 1872)
Cairo and Fulton R.R. Co. v. Turner, 31 Ark. 494 (Ark. 1876)
Williams Bros. v. Tripp, 11 R.I. 447 (R.I. 1877)
Cumberland v. Willison, 50 Md. 138 (Md. 1878)
Providence Steam Engine v. Providence Steamship, 12 R.I. 348 (R.I. 1879)
Cox v. State, 8 Tex.App. 254 (Tex.Ct.App. 1880)
Carson v. Hartford, 48 Conn. 68 (Conn. 1880)
St. Louis v. Richeson, 76 Mo. 470 (Mo. 1882)
Peerce v. Kitzmiller, 19 W.Va. 564 (W.Va. 1882)
Butler v. State, 97 Ind. 378 (Ind. 1884)
Bohannon v. State, 18 Neb. 57 (Neb. 1885)
Missouri v. Kaub, 19 Mo.App. 149 (Mo.App. 1885)
State v. Parker, 66 Iowa 586 (Iowa 1885)
Coniff v. San Francisco, 67 Cal. 45 (Cal. 1885)

State v. Flynn, 16 R.I. 10 (R.I. 1887)
Ex Parte Snyder, 29 Mo.App. 256 (Mo.App. 1888)
Kemmler v. Durston, 7 N.Y.S. 813 (N.Y. 1889)
Peck v. Michigan City, 149 Ind. 670 (Ind. 1898)
State v. Miller, 60 A. 202, 203–4 (N.J. Ct. of App. 1905)
Smith v. Tate, 227 S.W. 1026, 1028 (Tenn. 1921)
Burke v. State, 104 Ohio St. 220 (Ohio 1922)
Boepple v. Mohalt, 54 P.2d 854, 864 (MT. 1936)

English Cases

British Glass Plate Manufacturers v. Meredith, 100 Eng. Rep. 1306 (1792)
Harman v. Tappenden, 1 East. 555 (1801)
Sutton v. Clarke, 128 Eng. Rep. 943 (1815)

NEWSPAPERS

Alabama Intelligencer and State Rights Expositor (Tuscaloosa)
American & Commercial Daily Advertiser (Baltimore, Md.)
Baltimore Gazette and Daily Advertiser (Baltimore, Md.)
Baltimore Patriot & Evening Advertiser, after 1817 known as the *Baltimore Patriot & Mercantile Advertiser* (Baltimore, Md.)
Daily National Intelligencer (Washington, D.C.)
Macon Telegraph (Macon, Ga.)
New-Bedford Mercury (New Bedford, Mass.)
New-York Spectator (New York, N.Y.)
Niles' Weekly Register (Baltimore, Md.)
Richmond Enquirer (Richmond, Va.)
Scioto Gazette (Chillicothe, Oh.)
United States' Telegraph (Washington, D.C.)

DIRECTORIES

Baltimore Directory for 1807, ed. James M'Henry (Baltimore: Warner & Hanna, 1807)
The Baltimore Directory for 1810, William Fry (Baltimore: G. Dobbin & Murphy, 1810)
Fry's Baltimore Directory for 1812, ed. William Fry (Baltimore: B.W. Sower & Co., 1812)
Baltimore Directory and Register for 1814–15, ed. James Lakin (Baltimore: J.C. O'Reilly, 1814)
Baltimore Directory for 1817–18 (Baltimore: James Kennedy, 1817)

Matchett's Baltimore Directory, for 1824 (Baltimore: Richard Matchett, 1824)
Matchett's Baltimore Directory, 1822–23 (Baltimore: Richard Matchett, 1822)
Matchett's Baltimore Directory for 1827 (Baltimore: Richard Matchett, 1827)

RADIO AND TELEVISION PROGRAMS

"The Fifth Amendment Case That Lost." National Archives (Audio Recording), Record Group 306, National Archives Identifier: 565711, Local Identifier: 306-SO-18.

Sister Simone Campbell, interview by Stephen Colbert. *The Colbert Report*, Comedy Central, December 13, 2012.

BOOKS AND ARTICLES

Aarsleff, Hans. "The State of Nature and the Nature of Man in Locke." In *John Locke: Problems and Perspectives.* Edited by John W. Yolton. Cambridge: Cambridge University Press, 1969.

Ackerman, Bruce. *We the People: The Civil Rights Revolution*. Cambridge, MA: Harvard University Press, 2014.

Adams, John. *The Works of John Adams*. Edited by Charles Francis Adams. Vol. 4, *Novanglus, Thoughts on Government, Defence of the Constitution.* Edited by Charles Francis Adams. Boston: Little and Brown, 1851.

Adams, John Quincy. *Memoirs of John Quincy Adams, Comprising Portions of his Diary from 1795 to 1848*. Edited by Charles Francis Adams. Vol. 7. Philadelphia: J. P. Lippincott & Co., 1875.

———. *An Oration Addressed to the Citizens of the Town of Quincy on the Fourth of July, 1831, the Fifty-Fifth Anniversary of the Independence of the United States of America*. Boston: Richardson, Lord & Holbrook, 1831.

Almand, Bond. "History of the Supreme Court of Georgia, The First Hundred Years." In *A History of the Supreme Court of Georgia*. Edited by John Harris. Macon, GA: J. W. Burke Co., 1948.

Amar, Akhil Reed. *The Bill of Rights: Creation and Reconstruction*. New Haven: Yale University Press, 1998.

———. "The Creation, Reconstruction, and Interpretation of the Bill of Rights." In *The Nature of Rights and the American Founding and Beyond*. Edited by Barry Alan Shain. Charlottesville: University of Virginia Press, 2007.

Angell, Joseph K. *A Treatise on the Common Law in Relation to Water-Courses*. Boston: Wells and Lilly, 1824.

Archer, Stevenson. "Rights of Municipal Corporations." *American Jurist and Law Magazine* 4 (Oct. 1829): 203–14.

Bailyn, Bernard. *The Ideological Origins of the American Revolution*. Cambridge, MA: Harvard University Press, 1967.

Bauer, Elizabeth Kelly. *Commentaries on the Constitution, 1790–1860*. New York: Russell & Russell, 1965.

Beirne, Francis F. *The Amiable Baltimoreans*. New York: Dutton, 1951.

Bilder, Mary Sarah. "Colonial Constitutionalism and Constitutional Law." In *Transformations in American Legal History: Essays in Honor of Morton J. Horwitz*. Edited by Alfred L. Brophy and Daniel W. Hamilton. Cambridge, MA: Harvard University Press, 2009.

Blackstone, William. *Commentaries on the Laws of England. A Facsimile of the First Edition of 1765–1769*. Vol. 1, *The Rights of Persons*, with an introduction by Stanley N. Katz. Chicago: University of Chicago Press, 1979.

———. *Commentaries on the Laws of England. A Facsimile of the First Edition of 1765–1769*. Vol. 4, *Of Public Wrongs*, with an introduction by Thomas A. Green. Chicago: University of Chicago Press, 1979.

Bloomfield, Maxwell. "David Hoffman and the Shaping of a Republican Legal Culture." *Maryland Law Review* 38, no. 4 (1979): 673–88.

Bohner, Charles H. *John Pendleton Kennedy: Gentleman from Baltimore*. Baltimore: Johns Hopkins Press, 1961.

Bolt, William K. "The Tariff in the Age of Jackson." PhD diss., University of Tennessee, 2010.

Bond, Carroll T. *The Court of Appeals of Maryland, A History*. Baltimore: Barton-Gillet, 1928.

Bragaw, Stephen G. "Thomas Jefferson and the American Indian Nations: Native American Sovereignty and the Marshall Court." *Journal of Supreme Court History* 31, no. 2 (2006): 155–80.

Browne, Gary L. *Baltimore in the Nation, 1789–1861*. Chapel Hill: University of North Carolina Press, 1980.

Bruchey, Stuart Weems. *Robert Oliver, Merchant of Baltimore, 1783–1819*. Baltimore: Johns Hopkins University Press, 1956.

Brugger, Robert J. *Maryland: A Middle Temperament*. Baltimore: Johns Hopkins Press, 1988.

Bushong, William B. *Glenn Brown's History of the United States Capitol*. Washington, D.C.: U.S. Government Printing Office, 1998.

Calhoun, John C. *Union and Liberty: The Political Philosophy of John C. Calhoun*. Edited by Ross M. Lence. Indianapolis: Liberty Fund, 1992.

———. *John C. Calhoun: Selected Writings and Speeches*. Edited by H. Lee Cheek, Jr. Washington, D.C.: Regnery, 2003.

———. *The Papers of John C. Calhoun: Vol. XII, 1833–1835*. Edited by Clyde N. Wilson. Columbia: University of South Carolina Press, 1979.

Clay, Henry. *The Papers of Henry Clay, Vol. 8: Candidate, Compromiser, Whig, March 5, 1829–December 31, 1836*. Edited by Robert Seager and Melba Hay. Lexington: University Press of Kentucky, 1984.

Cordell, Eugene F. *University of Maryland, 1807–1907*. New York: Lewis Publishing Company, 1907.

Cornell, Saul and Gerald Leonard. "The Consolidation of the Early Federal System, 1791–1812." In *Early America (1580–1815)*. Vol. 1 of *The Cambridge History of Law in America*. Edited by Michael Grossberg and Christopher Tomlins. New York: Cambridge University Press, 2008.

Cox, Richard J. "Trouble on the Chain Gang: City Surveying, Maps, and the Absence of Urban Planning in Baltimore, 1730–1823." *Maryland Historical Magazine* 81, no. 1 (Spring 1986): 8–49.

Cranwell, J. P., and W. B. Crane. *Men of Marque: A History of Private Armed Vessels out of Baltimore During the War of 1812*. New York: W. W. Norton, 1940.

Currie, David P. "The Constitution in the Supreme Court: Contracts and Commerce, 1836–1864." *Duke Law Journal* 1983, no. 3 (1983): 471–513.

Curtis, Michael Kent. *No State Shall Abridge: The Fourteenth Amendment and the Bill of Rights*. Durham: Duke University Press, 1986.

Cushman, Clare. *Courtwatchers: Eyewitness Accounts in Supreme Court History* (New York: Rowman & Littlefield, 2011).

Dale, Elizabeth. *Criminal Justice in the United States, 1789–1939*. New York: Cambridge University Press, 2011.

Doherty, Brendan J. "Interpreting the Bill of Rights and the Nature of Federalism: *Barron v. City of Baltimore*." *Journal of Supreme Court History* 32, no. 3 (November 2007): 211–28.

Dubber, Marcus Dirk. *The Police Power: Patriarchy and the Foundations of American Government*. New York: Columbia University Press, 2005.

Du Bellet, Louise Pecquet. *Some Prominent Virginia Families: Vol. IV*. Lynchburg, VA: J. P. Bell Co., 1907.

Dukeminier, Jesse, and James Krier. *Property*. 3rd ed. Boston: Little, Brown & Co., 1993.

Dyer, Carol A. *Tuberculosis*. Santa Barbara, CA: Greenwood, 2010.

Edwards, Laura F. *The People and Their Peace: Legal Culture and the Transformation of Inequality in the Post-Revolutionary South*. Chapel Hill: University of North Carolina Press, 2009.

Ellis, Richard. *Aggressive Nationalism: McCulloch v. Maryland and the Foundation of Federal Authority in the Young Republic*. New York: Oxford University Press, 2007.

———. *The Union at Risk: Jacksonian Democracy, States' Rights and the Nullification Crisis*. New York: Oxford University Press, 1987.

Ezratty, Harry A. *Baltimore in the Civil War: The Pratt Street Riot and a City Occupied*. Charleston, SC: History Press, 2010.

Finkelman, Paul. "The Root of the Problem: How the Proslavery Constitution Shaped American Race Relations." *Barry Law Review* 4 (2003): 1–19.

Ford, Jr., Lacy K. *Origins of Southern Radicalism: The South Carolina Upcountry, 1800–1860*. New York: Oxford University Press, 1988.

Foreman, Grant. *Indian Removal: The Emigration of the Five Civilized Tribes of Indians.* Norman: University of Oklahoma Press, 1982.

Freehling, William W. *The Nullification Era: A Documentary Record*. New York: Harper, 1967.

Friedman, Dan. "The History of the Baltimore City Solicitors." Maryland State Archives, November 2003. http://msa.maryland.gov/msa/speccol/sc2600/sc2685/text/solicitors.pdf (accessed May 20, 2016).

Friedman, Lawrence M. *A History of American Law*. 2nd ed. New York: Simon & Schuster, 1985.

Garitee, Jerome. *The Republic's Private Navy: The American Privateering Business as Practiced by Baltimore During the War of 1812*. Middletown, CT: Wesleyan University Press, 1977.

Garry, Patrick M. *Liberalism and American Identity*. Kent: Kent State University Press, 1992.

Gatell, Frank Otto. "Secretary Taney and the Baltimore Pets: A Study in Banking and Politics." *Business History Review* 39, no. 2 (Summer 1965): 205–27.

Gerber, Scott Douglas. *To Secure These Rights: The Declaration of Independence and Constitutional Interpretation*. New York: New York University Press, 1995.

Graber, Mark. "Naked Land Transfers and American Constitutional Development." *Vanderbilt Law Review* 53 (2000): 71–121.

Greff, Jacqueline. *Fell's Point*. Charleston, SC: Arcadia Publishing, 2005.

Haines, Charles Grove. *The Revival of Natural Law Concepts*. Cambridge, MA: Harvard University Press, 1930.

Hale, Sir Matthew. *The History of the Common Law of England*. Edited by Charles M. Gray. Chicago: University of Chicago Press, 1971.

Hall, Kermit, James Ely, and Joel Grossman, eds. *The Oxford Guide to the Supreme Court of the United States*. New York: Oxford University Press, 2005.

Hall, Kermit, with William Wiecek and Paul Finkelman. *American Legal History: Cases and Materials*. New York: Oxford University Press, 1991.

Haskins, George L. "Marshall and the Commerce Clause of the Constitution." In *Chief Justice John Marshall: A Reappraisal*. Edited by W. Melville Jones. Ithaca, NY: Cornell University Press, 1956.

Hayes, Kevin J. *Poe and the Printed Word*. New York: Cambridge University Press, 2000.

Head, David. "Baltimore Seafarers, Privateering, and the South American Revolutions, 1816–1820." *Maryland Historical Magazine* 103, no. 3 (Fall 2008): 269–93.

Hobbes, Thomas. *The Leviathan: Or the Matter, Forme and Power of a Commonwealth Ecclesiasticall and Civil*. Edited by Ian Shapiro. New Haven: Yale University Press, 2010.

Hoeflich, M. H. *Legal Publishing in Antebellum America*. New York: Cambridge University Press, 2010.

Hoffman, David. *A Course of Legal Study; Respectfully Addressed to the Students of Law in the United States*. Baltimore: Coale and Maxwell, 1817.

Hogue, Arthur R. *Origins of the Common Law*. Indianapolis: Liberty Fund, 1986.

Holland, Eugenia Calvert and Louisa Macgill Gary. "Miniatures in the Collection of the Maryland Historical Society." *Maryland Historical Magazine* 51, no. 4 (1956): 341–54.

Horwitz, Morton J. *The Transformation of American Law, 1780–1860*. Cambridge, MA: Harvard University Press, 1977.

Howe, Daniel Walker. *What Hath God Wrought: The Transformation of America, 1815–1848*. New York: Oxford University Press, 2007.

Hoyt, Jr., William D. "Land for a Cathedral: Baltimore, 1806–1817." *Catholic Historical Review* 36, no. 4 (Jan. 1951), 441–45.

Hulsebosch, Daniel. *Constituting Empire: New York and the Transformation of Constitutionalism in the Atlantic World*. Chapel Hill: University of North Carolina Press, 2005.

Hunt, Lynn. *Inventing Human Rights: A History*. New York: W. W. Norton, 2007.

Hutson, James H. "The Emergence of the Modern Concept of a Right in America: The Contribution of Michel Villey." In *The Nature of Rights at the American Founding and Beyond*. Edited by Barry Alan Shain. Charlottesville: University of Virginia Press, 2007.

Hylton, J. Gordon. "Virginia and the Ratification of the Bill of Rights, 1789–1791." *University of Richmond Law Review* 25 (1990–91): 433–74.

Irons, Peter. A *People's History of the Supreme Court*. New York: Penguin Books, 1999.

Jay, John, Alexander Hamilton, and James Madison. *The Federalist: A Commentary on the Constitution of the United States*. Edited by Robert Scigliano. New York: Random House, 2000.

Johnson, Herbert A. "Federal Union, Property, and the Contract Clause: John Marshall's Thought in Light of *Sturges v. Crowninshield* and *Ogden v. Saunders*." In *John Marshall's Achievement: Law, Politics, and Constitutional Interpretations*. Edited by Thomas C. Shevory. Westport, CT: Greenwood Press, 1989.

———. *The Chief Justiceship of John Marshall, 1801–1835*. Columbia: University of South Carolina Press, 1997.

Johnson, John. *Griswold v. Connecticut*. Lawrence: University Press of Kansas, 2005,

Kern, Darcy. "Parliament in Print: William Caxton and the History of Political Government in the Fifteenth Century." *Journal of Medieval History* 40, no. 2 (2014): 209–24.

Kielbowicz, Richard. "The Law and Mob Law in Attacks on Antislavery Newspapers, 1833–1860." *Law and History Review* 24, no. 3 (Fall 2006): 559–600.

Killenbeck, Mark. *M'Culloch v. Maryland: Securing a Nation*. Lawrence: University Press of Kansas, 2006.

Kramer, Larry. *The People Themselves: Popular Constitutionalism and Judicial Review*. New York: Oxford University Press, 2005.

Kurland, Philip B., and Ralph Lerner, eds. *The Founders' Constitution*. Vols. I and II. Indianapolis: Liberty Fund, 2001.

Land, Aubrey C. *Colonial Maryland: A History*. New York: KTO Press, 1981.

Law, David and Mila Versteeg. "The Declining Influence of the United States Constitution." *New York University Law Review* 87 (June 2012): 762–858.

Leiter, Brian. "Legal Realism and Legal Positivism Reconsidered." *Ethics* 111, no. 2 (January 2001): 278–301.

Littlefield, Daniel and James Parins, eds. *The Encyclopedia of American Indian Removal: Volume 2*. Santa Barbara, CA: Greenwood, 2011.

Livy. *History of Rome, Volume IX: Books 31–34*. Translated by Evan T. Sage. Cambridge, MA: Harvard University Press, 1935.

Lutz, Donald S. "The Articles of Confederation as the Background to the Federal Republic." *Publius* 20, no. 1 (Winter, 1990): 55–70.

Magliocca, Gerard N. "The Bill of Rights as a Term of Art." *Notre Dame Law Review* (forthcoming). Available at http://ssrn.com/abstract=2617811.

Marshall, John. *The Papers of John Marshall*. Edited by Charles Hobson. Vol. XII, *Correspondence, Papers, and Selected Judicial Opinions, January 1831–July 1835, with Addendum, June 1783–January 1829*. Edited by Charles Hobson. Chapel Hill: University of North Carolina Press, 2006.

Mayer, Brantz. *Baltimore: Past and Present*. Baltimore: Richardson and Bennett, 1871.

Mazzone, Jason. "The Bill of Rights in the Early State Courts." *Minnesota Law Review* 92, no. 1 (2007): 7–82.

McGrade, Arthur Stephen. "Ockham and the Birth of Individual Rights." In *Authority and Power*. Edited by Brian Tierney and Peter Linehan. Cambridge: Cambridge University Press, 1980.

McLoughlin, William. *Cherokee Renascence in the New Republic*. Princeton: Princeton University Press, 1986.

Miller, Jr., Fred D. "Aristotle and the Origins of Natural Rights." *Journal of Metaphysics*, 49, no. 4 (1996): 873–907.

Newmyer, R. Kent. *John Marshall and the Heroic Age of the Supreme Court*. Baton Rouge: Louisiana State University Press, 2001.

Norgren, Jill. "Lawyers and the Legal Business of the Cherokee Republic in the Courts of the United States, 1829–1835." *Law and History Review* 10, no. 2 (Autumn, 1992): 253–314.

Norman, Joseph Gary. "Eighteenth-Century Wharf Construction in Baltimore, Maryland." Master's thesis, College of William & Mary, 1987.

Novak, William. *The Peoples' Welfare: Law & Regulation in Nineteenth Century America*. Chapel Hill: University of North Carolina Press, 1996.

Olson, Sherry. *Baltimore: The Building of an American City*. Baltimore: Johns Hopkins University Press, 1980.

Onuf, Peter S. *Jefferson's Empire: The Language of American Nationhood*. Charlottesville: University of Virginia Press, 2000.

Papenfuse, Edward C. *Outline, Notes and Documents Concerning Barron v Baltimore, 32 U.S. 243*, http://mdhistory.net/msaref06/barron/index.html.

Papenfuse, Edward C., and Joseph M. Coale III, eds. *The Maryland State Archives Atlas of Historical Maps of Maryland, 1608–1908*. Baltimore: Johns Hopkins University Press, 2003.

Parsons, Jr., Theophilus. "Review of *Memoirs of Theophilus Parsons, Chief Justice of the Supreme Judicial Court of Massachusetts, with Notices of Some of His Contemporaries*, by Theophilus Parsons." *North American Review* 89, no. 184 (1859): 232–44.

Peskin, Lawrence A. "Fells Point: Baltimore's Pre-Industrial Suburb." *Maryland Historical Magazine* 97, no. 2 (Summer 2002): 153–73.

Pinkney, Rev. William. *The Life of William Pinkney*. New York: D. Appleton and Co., 1853.

Powell, H. Jefferson. "The Original Understanding of Original Intent." In *Interpreting the Constitution: The Debate over Original Intent*. Edited by Jack N. Rakove. Boston: Northeastern University Press, 1990.

Power, Garrett. "Parceling Out Land in the Vicinity of Baltimore, 1632–1796, Part 2." *Maryland Historical Magazine* 88, no. 2 (Summer 1993): 151–80.

Prucha, Francis Paul. *The Great Father: The United States Government and the American Indians*. Abridged ed. Lincoln: University of Nebraska Press, 1986.

Pufendorf, Samuel. *The Political Writings of Samuel Pufendorf*. Edited by Craig L. Carr. Translated by Michael J. Seider. New York: Oxford University Press, 1994.

Radoff, Morris L. *The County Courthouses and Records of Maryland, Part One: The Courthouses*. Annapolis: The Hall of Records Commission, 1960.

Rakove, Jack N. *Original Meanings: Politics and Ideas in the Making of the Constitution*. New York: Vintage Books, 1996.

———. *Declaring Rights*. Boston: Bedford Books, 1998.

Rawle, William. *A View of the Constitution of the United States of America*. 2nd ed. Philadelphia: Philip Nicklin, 1829.

Reid, Jr., Charles J. "The Medieval Origins of the Western Natural Rights Tradition: The Achievement of Brian Tierney." *Cornell Law Review* 83 (1997–98): 437–63.

Reid, John Phillip. *Constitutional History of the American Revolution: The Authority of Rights*. Madison: University of Wisconsin Press, 1986.

———. "The Irrelevance of the Declaration." In *Law in the American Revolution and the Revolution in the Law*. Edited by Hendrik Hartog. New York: New York University Press, 1981.

———. "The Authority of Rights at the American Founding." In *The Nature of Rights at the American Founding and Beyond*. Edited by Barry Alan Shain. Charlottesville: University of Virginia Press, 2007.

Reilly, Bernard F. *American Political Prints, 1766–1876*. Boston: G. K. Hall, 1991.

Remini, Robert. *Daniel Webster: The Man and His Time*. New York: W. W. Norton, 1997.

Rhodes, Irwin S. *The Papers of John Marshall: A Descriptive Calendar.* Vol. 2. Norman: University of Oklahoma Press, 1969.

Richard, Carl J. *Greeks and Romans Bearing Gifts: How the Ancients Inspired the Founding Fathers*. Lanham, MD: Rowman & Littlefield, 2009.

Ridgway, Whitman H. *Community Leadership in Maryland, 1790–1840: A Comparative Analysis of Power in Society*. Chapel Hill: University of North Carolina Press, 1979.

———. "Community Leadership: Baltimore During the First and Second Party Systems." *Maryland Historical Magazine* 71, no. 3 (Fall 1976): 334–48.

Robertson, Lindsay. *Conquest by Law: How the Discovery of America Dispossessed Indigenous Peoples of Their Lands*. New York: Oxford University Press, 2005.

Rockman, Seth. *Scraping By: Wage Labor, Slavery, and Survival in Early Baltimore*. Baltimore: Johns Hopkins University Press, 2009.

———. "Work, Wages, and Welfare at Baltimore's School of Industry." *Maryland Historical Magazine* 102, no. 1 (Spring 2007): 572–607.

Saint-Mery, Moreau de. "Baltimore as Seen by Moreau de Saint-Mery in 1794." Translated and edited by Fillmore Norfleet. *Maryland Historical Magazine* 35, no. 3 (September 1940): 221.

Sawyer, Jeffrey K. "English Law and American Democracy in the Revolutionary Republic, Maryland 1776–1822." *Maryland Historical Magazine* 108, no. 3 (Fall 2013): 261–90.

Scharf, J. Thomas. *The Chronicles of Baltimore.* Baltimore: Turnbull Brothers, 1874.

———. *History of Baltimore City and County.* Philadelphia: Louis H. Evers, 1881.

———, with Thompson Westcott. *History of Philadelphia, 1609–1884*. Philadelphia: L. H. Everts and Co., 1884.

Scheiber, Harry. "Private Rights and Public Power: American Law, Capitalism, and the Republican Polity in Nineteenth Century America." *Yale Law Journal* 107 (1997–98): 823–61.

Schocket, Andrew M. *Founding Corporate Power in Early National Philadelphia*. DeKalb, Illinois: Northern Illinois University Press, 2007.

Schoeppner, Michael. "Status Across Borders: Roger Taney, Black British Subjects, and a Diplomatic Antecedent to the Dred Scott Case." *Journal of American History* 100, no. 1 (June 2013): 46–67.

Schweber, Howard. "The Science of Legal Science: The Model Natural Sciences in Nineteenth-Century American Education." *Law and History Review* 17, no. 3 (Fall 1999): 421–66.

Seagrave, S. Adam. *The Foundations of Natural Morality: On the Compatibility of Natural Rights and Natural Law*. Chicago: University of Chicago Press, 2014.

Seddig, Robert. "Henry Baldwin." In *The Oxford Guide to the Supreme Court*. Edited by Kermit Hall, James Ely, and Joel Grossman. New York: Oxford University Press, 2005.

Sellers, Charles. *The Market Revolution: Jacksonian America, 1816–1846*. New York: Oxford University Press, 1991.

Shaffer, Thomas L. "David Hoffman's Law School Lectures, 1822–1833." *Journal of Legal Education* 32, nos. 1–5 (1982): 127–38.

Shalhope, Robert E. *The Baltimore Bank Riot: Political Upheaval in Antebellum Maryland*. Urbana: University of Illinois Press, 2009.

Sheets, Kevin B. "Saving History: The Maryland Historical Society and its Founders." *Maryland Historical Magazine* 89, no. 2 (Summer 1994): 133–55.

Sheldon, Charles H. "Duncan v. Louisiana." In *The Oxford Guide to the Supreme Court*. Edited by Kermit Hall, James Ely, and Joel Grossman. New York: Oxford University Press, 2005.

Sherry, Suzanna. "The Founders' Unwritten Constitution." *University of Chicago Law Review* 54, no. 4 (1987): 1127–77.

_____. "Natural Law in the States." *University of Cincinnati Law Review* 61 (1992–93): 171–222.

Shute, Daniel. "An Election Sermon." In *American Political Writing During the Founding Era, 1760–1805*. Vol. I. Edited by Charles S. Hyneman and Donald S. Lutz. Indianapolis: Liberty Press, 1983.

———. *A Sermon Preached before his Excellency Francis Bernard*. Boston: Richard Draper, 1768.

Skinner, Quentin. *Visions of Politics*. Vol. 3, *Hobbes and Civil Science*. Cambridge: Cambridge University Press: 2004.

Sleeman, Bill. "David Hoffman: A Biographical Sketch." In *David Hoffman: Life, Letters and Lectures at the University of Maryland, 1821–1837*. Edited by Bill Sleeman. Clark, NJ: Lawbook Exchange, 2011.

Snead, Elmer E. "Sic Utere Tuo Ut Alienum Non Laedas: The Basis of the State Police Power." *Cornell Law Quarterly* 21, no. 2 (1935–36): 276–92.

Spalding, Thomas W. *The Premier See: A History of the Archdiocese of Baltimore, 1789–1989*. Baltimore: Johns Hopkins University Press, 1989.

Spellman, W. M. *John Locke*. New York: St. Martin's Press, 1997.

Squadrito, Katherine M. *John Locke*. Boston: Twayne Publishers, 1979.

Steffen, Charles G. *From Gentlemen to Townsmen: The Gentry of Baltimore County, Maryland, 1660–1776*. Lexington: University Press of Kentucky, 1993.

———. *The Mechanics of Baltimore: Workers and Politics in the Age of Revolution 1763–1812*. Urbana: University of Illinois Press, 1984.

Stites, Francis N. *John Marshall: Defender of the Constitution*. New York: Longman, 1981.

Story, Joseph. *Life and Letters of Joseph Story*. Edited by William Story. Vol. 2. Boston: Little & Brown, 1851.

Stroud, Patricia Tyson. *The Man Who Had Been King*. Philadelphia: University of Pennsylvania Press, 2005.

Stychin, Carl F. "The Commentaries of Chancellor James Kent and the Development of an American Common Law." *American Journal of Legal History* 37, no. 4 (October 1993): 440–63.

Swindler, William F. *The Constitution and Chief Justice Marshall*. New York: Dodd, Mead and Company, 1978.

Swisher, Carl Brent. *Roger B. Taney*. New York: Macmillan, 1935.

Thomas, David. "Finding More Pieces for the Takings Puzzle: How Clarifying History Can Clarify Doctrine." *University of Colorado Law Review* 75 (2004): 497–547.

Tiernan, C. B. "Luke Tiernan of Baltimore." *American Catholic Historical Researcher* 12, no. 4 (October 1895): 189–92.

Treanor, William Michael. "The Original Understanding of the Takings Clause and the Political Process." *Columbia Law Review* 95 (1995): 782–887.

Tuck, Richard. *Natural Rights Theories: Their Origins and Development*. New York: Cambridge University Press, 1979.

Tucker, St. George. *View of the Constitution of the United States, With Selected Writings*. Foreword by Clyde N. Wilson. Indianapolis: Liberty Fund, 1999.

Tyler, Samuel. *Memoir of Roger Brooke Taney, L.L.D.* Baltimore: John Murphy and Co., 1872.

Vexler, Robert I. *Baltimore: A Chronological and Documentary History*. New York: Oceana, 1971.

Webster, Daniel. *The Writings and Speeches of Daniel Webster.* Edited by Edward Everett. Vol. 6, *Speeches in Congress*. Boston: Little, Brown & Co., 1903.

White, G. Edward. *History of the Supreme Court of the United States, Vol. III-IV: The Marshall Court and Cultural Change, 1815–1835*. New York: Macmillan Publishing Co., 1988.

White, Jonathan W. *Abraham Lincoln and Treason in the Civil War: The Trials of John Merryman*. Baton Rouge: Louisiana State University Press, 2011.

Wiecek, William M. *Liberty Under Law: The Supreme Court in American Life*. Baltimore: Johns Hopkins Press, 1988.

Wilbur, W. Allan. "Review of *John Marshall: A Life in Law*." *American Journal of Legal History* 20, no. 2 (April 1976): 155–58.

Wilentz, Sean. *The Rise of American Democracy: Jefferson to Lincoln*. New York: W. W. Norton, 2005.

Wills, Gary. *Inventing America: Jefferson's Declaration of Independence*. New York: Doubleday, 1978.

Wilson, James. "On the Natural Rights of Individuals." In *The Collected Works of James Wilson, Vol. 2*. Edited by Kermit Hall and Mark David Hall. Indianapolis: Liberty Fund, 2007.

Wiltse, Charles, and David Allen, eds. *The Papers of Daniel Webster, Correspondence, Vol. 3*. Hanover: University Press of New England, 1977.

Wolf, Michal Allen. *The Zoning of America:* Euclid v. Ambler. Lawrence: University Press of Kansas, 2008.

Index

References to illustrations appear in italics.